THE

Colonial Agents

OF THE

Southern Colonies

THE
Colonial Agents
OF THE
SOUTHERN COLONIES

BY

Ella Lonn
PROFESSOR OF HISTORY
GOUCHER COLLEGE

Chapel Hill

THE UNIVERSITY OF NORTH CAROLINA PRESS

1945

PREFACE

PROBABLY the author owes the reader an explanation for a departure from her chosen field of research, the Civil War and Reconstruction Period in American history, to a field so remote as the Colonial Period. Years ago, while she was wavering in her choice of fields, she began a study of the Colonial Agent of the American Colonies and had gathered a vast mass of notes from American archives and from the Public Record Office in London. Before she was able to put them into written form, the great bulk of the notes was destroyed in a fire. One small packet escaped the flames. For years she could neither bring herself to begin the study afresh nor to consign the small remaining fragment of her work to the flames.

A few years ago a sabbatical leave, which afforded opportunity for research in England, revived thoughts of this subject. To her great surprise and delight the writer found that this subject was still virgin ground and so the little batch of notes was lovingly dug out of the dust-covered box in which it had lain buried.

A somewhat hasty return to America precluded consultation of some manuscripts in one of the provincial ports of England as the author had planned. Since then the war has intervened so that it seems advisable not to delay longer the publication, especially as it is highly unlikely that she would have found any important data to change conclusions or to throw significant light on the work of any official who functioned in London.

Since the second edition of notes was collected in England, although her subject had been duly announced, the scope of the work has been whittled away until practically only the southern agents are left. Even so, a certain unity manifests itself in the history of this group of agents.

It is with pleasure that the writer acknowledges the kindness of many librarians and of the custodians of various archives. To Mr. A. S. Salley acknowledgment is made not only for making available the manuscripts under his care at Columbia, South Carolina, but also for checking some references. To Mr. Morris L. Radoff and the members of his staff of the Maryland State Archives appreciation is expressed. Miss Florence Kennedy of the Maryland Historical Society has been unfailing in courtesy and helpfulness. I am indebted to the members of the staff of Peabody Library, of the Enoch Pratt Library, and of the Bar Library—all of Baltimore; to members of the Library of Congress; to the librarian of the Virginia State Library; to the custodians of the manuscripts at the Public Record Office and of the British Museum in London; and of the Bodleian Library in Oxford for courtesies and privileges in the use of their resources.

Finally, I wish to express gratitude to Professor Anna Irene Miller, who has read the entire manuscript, and to Professor Ola Elizabeth Winslow for helpful suggestions.

September, 1942   E. L.

Table of Contents

THE

Colonial Agents

OF THE

Southern Colonies

CHAPTER I.

GENESIS OF THE COLONIAL AGENT

THE PERPLEXITIES connected with the subject of the colonial agent, which are many and at times baffling, begin with the very word "agent." This work will follow the traditional usage and regard the word "agent" as designating the colonial representative who resided in London and officially looked after the interests of a particular colony, although it must be acknowledged that the word was applied to a number of officials. There were agents not infrequently sent over or employed in London by the colonial governors to guard their special interests;[1] there were agents for individuals, as Lord Fairfax, or for companies, as the Ohio Land Company; there were Indian agents; occasionally a city or a group of counties sent over an agent, as was the case with Boston on the eve of the Revolution, and with the Six Northern Counties of North Carolina in 1748, which sent over an agent when threatened with loss of their larger representation in the assembly as compared with the other counties of the colony;[2] there was even to be found an agent for the Moravian Brethren of New York.[3] Most confusing of all, however, were the so-called crown agents to be found in East and West Florida and in Georgia,[4] especially in the last-named colony, because they

[1] To cite but a single instance out of many, one might note the presence at the session of the Board of Trade on February 2, 1702/3, of a Mr. Thrale and a Captain Matthews for Lord Cornbury and of Mr. Champante for the Earl of Bellomont during the discussion of the accounts of the four companies of British soldiers in New York.—C. O. 391/15, pp. 405-6.   [2] See Chapter II.

[3] The Moravian Brethren of New York sent Monsieur de Gersdorff and two of their pastors to London to appear against an Act for Securing His Majesty's Government of New York: the Moravians felt themselves oppressed by the act, especially since they were named in it. See a letter by the Board of Trade to Governor Clinton, dated June 28, 1745.—C. O. 5/1326, p. 285. References to obscure persons will not be explained unless they have relevance to this story.

[4] The crown agents were, of course, appointed by the crown, disbursed the salaries to the civil officers in these colonies, paid the expense of the public defenses, were concerned when complaints were made against the governor of one of these crown colonies, and seem to have themselves been paid by parliamentary grants.

discharged for a few years in part the duties of a regular provincial agent.[5] The researcher feels inclined to throw up his hands when he encounters one Richard Harrison as agent for Virginia at the islands of Martinique and St. Eustatius at the beginning of the American Revolution, though he was more properly an official accredited by the revolting colony to a French and to a Dutch colony primarily to secure supplies.[6] Many instances of dual agents from the same colony or of plural agency-holding by one agent complicate the picture. The reader must, therefore, be forewarned against the loose use of the word in source material.

Representatives quite properly termed colonial agents in the customary use of the word were sent over within a few years of the first planting of the colonies. They continued to be sent throughout the seventeenth century, but they can hardly be considered as belonging to the period of the officially recognized and accredited agency. This earlier period, when the office was characterized by a lack of continuity, might perhaps be logically termed that of the genesis of the regular agency, which became established at various dates, it is true, in the various colonies, but roughly through the closing years of the seventeenth and the early years of the eighteenth century.

In the earlier period special representatives were sent irregularly to England to accomplish certain specific objectives, and special agents for special missions continued until well into the eighteenth century. The agent arose simply as the answer to the problem of dealing with the home government. Gradually and quite naturally arose the idea of the creation of an agent with a more permanent and general status than was accorded the agents who preceded him. The only charter provision for an agent seems to have been in the Pennsylvania Charter of 1681. By the close of the seventeenth century England had come to recognize the agency as an established institution.

The colony first planted not unnaturally produced the first agent. Virginia sent back to England her first representative of this type

---

[5] This fact will be brought out in connection with the agency of Benjamin Martyn for Georgia in Chapter II.

[6] See "Virginia Legislative Papers," *Virginia Magazine of History and Biography*, XVII, 258; "Miscellaneous Colonial Documents," *ibid.*, XVIII, 63.

at an almost unbelievably early date. It will be recalled that a royal commission was sent to Virginia in 1624 in the midst of the royal controversy against the London Company by the Privy Council to investigate conditions in the colony, or, in bald language, to gather evidence against the Company which would justify annulment of the charter. Two of the five commissioners, Captain John Harvey and John Pory, who arrived in Jamestown on March 4, 1624, went quickly before the Virginia assembly to read the orders of the Privy Council, orders which called for resumption of control by the king without the slightest hint of continuance of the assembly. These orders seemed to the agitated colonials a blow at the entire structure of colonial self-government, especially since the commissioners had asked the council and burgesses to subscribe to a declaration of approval of the change. Quietly ignoring the commissioners, the assembly promptly decided to send their written remonstrance to the king and to the Privy Council and to pray them not to destroy the liberal institutions of Virginia. Apparently distrusting the impartiality of the commission, the assembly elected to dispatch the papers to England by one of their own number, though Commissioner Pory did succeed in obtaining a copy of the documents by bribing the acting secretary of the colony, Edward Sharpless. For his offense the council later sentenced Sharpless to the pillory and to the loss of part of one ear.[7]

The messenger who enjoys the distinction of being the first agent sent from mainland America was one John Pountis, whose name was variously spelled,[8] sent "to solicite the generall cause of the countrey to the King and the Counciel" (being "willing by our entreaty to accept of that emploiment").[9] Pountis, who was described in the

---

[7] Accounts of this portion of Virginia history may be found in Andrews, *Virginia, the Old Dominion*, p. 109; Brown, *English Politics in Early Virginia History*, p. 52; Brown, *The First Republic in America, passim*; Bruce, *Institutional History of Virginia in the Seventeenth Century*, II, 519; Chalmers, *Political Annals of the present United Colonies from their Settlement to the Peace of 1763*, Book I, p. 65; Wertenbaker, *Virginia under the Stuarts*, p. 61. The other three commissioners were Abraham Peirsey, Samuel Mathews, and John Jefferson, whose identity is doubtful.—*Acts of the Privy Council, Colonial Series*, I, sec. 113. John Jefferson did not act, according to Brown (*English Politics*, p. 52, note). Robert Cushman, sometimes listed for Plymouth, was hardly a true agent.

[8] In official records, printed and manuscript, the author has found the name spelled Pountus, Pountis, Powntis, Pontis, Puntis, Poyntz, Pountys, Pounts, Pontice, Pountess.

[9] "Documents of Sir Francis Wyatt," *William and Mary College Quarterly Historical Magazine*, ser. 2, VII, 128 (referred to hereafter as *William and Mary Quarterly*).

petition as "a worthy member of our bodye," being a member of the council,[10] was clearly an outstanding person in the infant colony. A London cloth worker, he was sufficiently interested in the new world to own £127 of stock in a Virginia fishing company. As he was preparing in December, 1618, to sail in his ship for Virginia, he was given three shares admitting him to membership in the London Company. He seems to have left England in January, 1619, but not to have arrived in Virginia until July 5. He brought with him fifty emigrants, corn, and cattle.[11] In little over a year, June 28, 1620, the council of state of Virginia added him to its membership, while about a year and a half later, on November 14, 1621, the Michaelmas quarter court confirmed his commission as vice-admiral of Virginia for three years.[12] The wording of a motion at the quarter session court of the London Company held on July 10, 1621, is indicative of the esteem in which he was held in England. "A moc̃on was made y^t m^r John Pontice as well in respect of his owne worth and sufficiencie as allso in reward of his paynes and endeav^rs in the Companies service that some place of Comaund might be bestowed uppon him, and for somuch as ther was so great use of a Vice Admirall in Virginia to take care of the Companies Ships that cam thither and of other matters thereunto appetayninge. . . ."[13] He was accordingly appointed vice-admiral provisionally for one year.

[10] The name of Mr. John Pountis appears in the list of the council in the Ordinance and Constitutions for Council and Assembly in Virginia announced by the London Company on July 24, 1621.—*The Records of the Virginia Company of London*, III, 482-83. The petition is printed in *Journals of the House of Burgesses of Virginia*, 1619-1658/9, pp. 25-26.

[11] He made his will on January 8, 1619, "being in haste about his journey for Virginia."—*New England Historical and Genealogical Register*, 1895, p. 510. The *Triall*, which brought the emigrants, corn, and cattle, is thought to have belonged to Pountis. Pountis seems to have continued his interest in fishing, for in a letter to Sir Edwin Sandys, dated January, 1619/20, John Rolfe records: "The Sturgeon Shippe and the Triall departed hence togeth about the five of July. Mr. Pountys hath taken greate pains in fishing and toward Michellms (the weather being somewhat temperate) made some good sturgeon. He hoped by the spring to be better fitted, wth Cellars and houses, and to do some good therein."—*Records of the Virginia Company of London*, III, 243.

[12] Brown, *First Republic in America*, p. 430. Brown is in error as to the date. See *Records of the Virginia Company of London*, I, 379, 383. It is interesting that the Court felt it so desirable to have a vice-admiral in Virginia on November 21, 1621, that it allotted 300 acres of land for a residence and for the use of the incumbent of the office and assigned twelve tenants to cultivate the soil.—*Ibid.*, I, 549, 558. I find no evidence that Pountis was serving as councillor earlier than November 30, 1621, when his name is signed to a notice by the governor and council.—*Ibid.*, III, 528.

[13] *Ibid.*, I, 506, 546.

In late April[14] and early in May the *Furtherance* and two other ships set sail for England. On the *Furtherance* went John Pountis, armed with a number of documents: a general letter from the governor and council to the London Company and copies of seven documents prepared by the assembly from March 1 to 15, including a letter to the Privy Council and the petition to the king, in which the Virginians beg that his Majesty would not credit the late declarations presented to him "concerneinge the happie, but indeed miferable estate of the Collony," neither "the malicious imputations, wch have been layde on the latter," but be pleased to behold its true estate presented in the relation delivered by their agent. One paper answered in a spirited and able manner the plea for the king to take over Virginia, "holding it a finne against God, and ou^r owne fufferings," to permit the world to be abused with false reports, and to give to vice the reward of virtue.[15] There were three sets of these papers: one sent to the London Company by the hands of Pountis, one retained for the colony, and one sent to the Privy Council by Pory, who sailed a week later than Pountis with the report of the royal commission.[16] In addition to the official documents the governor and five of the council joined in an appeal to the Earl of Southampton and the Company for their advice and aid to Pountis in furthering their cause.[17]

Unfortunately, this first venture at an agency from the daughter to the mother country ended disastrously, for in June, on this voyage, Pountis died just off the coast of England. On June 24 Chancellor Weston wrote Pountis' cousin, Sir Thomas Merrie, clerk of the Green Cloth, who proved to be executor of Pountis' will,

[14] Pountis might have sailed before April 17, for on that date a letter states that the assembly had sent over John Pountis.—"Virginia Colonial Records (Miscellaneous Records, 1621-1623)," *Virginia Magazine of History and Biography*, XV, 38. But that letter may have accompanied him at a later date.

[15] *Journals of the House of Burgesses, 1619-1658/9*, pp. 21, 25-26; Howe, *Historical Collections of Virginia*, p. 49. It is interesting that one paper, marked G, was signed by Wyatt and by Pountis himself, as a member of the council, along with the governor, six other councillors, and by the burgesses. Hening, *The Statutes at Large*, I, 128 (referred to hereafter as Hening, *Statutes*).

[16] John Harvey wrote to Sir Nathaniel Rich, April 24, 1624, alluding to the copies, "whereof wee have attained unto," and hoped they would arrive before the originals by Mr. Pountis.—*Records of the Virginia Company of London*, IV, 476. The report of the commission was, of course, for annulment of the charter.

[17] This letter, dated Apr. 17, 1624, is published in the *Records of the Virginia Company of London*, IV, 474-75.

asking him in the name of the king to keep carefully official letters and papers "against such time as use may be made of them," and likewise to see that any other papers which might be in the custody of others were preserved. And thus it came about that the seven original documents and other papers though widely scattered have been preserved.

Pory's arrival soon after Pountis' death, about June 13, added the reports of the royal commissioners together with the attested copies of the papers drawn up by the assembly. This first mission must be recorded as a failure, for the fact that the Virginia charter was overthrown is a matter of history. Indeed, it is not certain that the various papers ever reached the royal hands.

When the death of Pountis became known in Virginia, Governor Francis Wyatt, the council, and the burgesses assembled under the impression that their petition for their charter rights had not found its way to the king and decided to make a fresh appeal. In June, 1625, they sent their second petition by the hands of Sir George Yeardley. Yeardley had remained in Virginia as a member of the council since 1621, after he had asked to be relieved of the gubernatorial office and had been succeeded in office by Wyatt. The effort to save the existence of the assembly after the overthrow of company rule was largely owing to Wyatt and Yeardley, for they wrote again and again for its reëstablishment. The first assembly held in Virginia under royal rule had met May 10, 1625, and had done nothing beyond drawing up a petition to the king expressing the desire of the people to be allowed a representative assembly, and objecting to the king's making a monopoly of the tobacco trade. Sir George Yeardley arrived with the petition about October 12. He pleaded with Charles, who had succeeded to the throne the preceding April, to avoid the oppression of governors in the colonies, to confirm and continue the liberty of general assemblies, and to grant the people a voice in the election of officers as in other corporations.[18] The petition declared that in their extreme discouragement great numbers of the planters had resolved to go to England expressly to petition for redress, but, lest the clamors of so many might prove

[18] Fiske, *Old Virginia and her Neighbors*, I, 241; *Journals of the House of Burgesses 1619-1658/9*, p. xxx. Fiske was in error in thinking that the colony already knew of the death of James.

troublesome, with unanimous consent, they had selected Sir George Yeardley, "the importance of the caufe requireinge no leffe then one, whoe haveinge formerly comanded heere, in cheife and by imeadiate Com̃iffion from yor Matie hath againe been nominated to suceffion in the Government" to show how unfit their rulers in England were to manage the affairs of the colony.[19] When Yeardley upon arrival learned that a new king sat upon the throne, he altered the petition and presented it. What he was really seeking was the restoration of many of the original charter rights and in addition their confirmation by parliament. The rights he so ardently sought were not restored.

Meanwhile there was dispatched officially a third petition to the king and Privy Council by Sir Francis Wyatt some time later, in May, 1626. He was a natural choice, for as governor he had maintained the original popular form of government as far as possible since 1625. He presented a letter from the governor and council to the Privy Council[20] covering the situation in Virginia.

Finally in the autumn of 1627, Charles I yielded to the wishes of the people and graciously permitted Virginia to retain her assembly and other political rights. Accordingly, a royal order restoring the precious right of assembly arrived at Jamestown on March 4, 1628. The assembly had been saved by the unselfish conduct of Wyatt and Yeardley and their councils. One scene in the strange see-saw of fortune between these two men was the removal of Sir Francis and the designation of Yeardley to return to Virginia once again as governor, but he was destined not to see the restoration of the House of Burgesses, for he died in November of 1627.[21]

Shortly afterwards in 1628 Sir Francis Wyatt was again representing Virginia as a member of a triple agency with Edward Bennett and Michael Marshart. When Edward Bennett came over to Virginia soon after 1626, after the death of his brother Richard,[22]

---

[19] *Ibid.*, p. 43. The petition sought to appeal to the king by representing his officers as having "erred and proceeded foe contrary, even in the fundamentall points of Government, to yor highnes gratious charters and inftructions."

[20] This letter may be found in "Documents of Sir Francis Wyatt," *William and Mary Quarterly*, ser. 2, VIII, 163-67. It is dated James City, May 17, 1626, and signed by Wyatt with five of his council.

[21] Brown, *English Politics in Early Virginia History*, pp. 93-94; Brown, *First Republic in America*, pp. 646-47; Wertenbaker, *op. cit.*, pp. 63-64.

[22] Not to be confused with Richard Bennett, who settled in Nansemond, Virginia, around

who had been managing his plantation, we catch a glimpse through the action of the Virginia House of Burgesses in March, 1628, as to how King James's tobacco monopoly was being received by the planters. Bennett was evidently sitting in the House as deputy for his plantation, Warrosquoake, for he appears on the records as a member in the spring of 1628.[23]   No minutes of the action of the assembly have been preserved, but there is extant, dated March 29, 1628, the commission to Bennett and Marshart, also a member of the lower house, directing them to join Sir Francis Wyatt then in England to represent Virginia and to care for the interests of the Virginia planters in the matter of the royal monopoly of the trade in tobacco.[24]   Unofficial in the sense that it is directed to no minister in England, it is still primary evidence.   Bennett and Marshart were given explicit directions as to their procedure.   On arrival in England they were to repair to the home of Sir Francis Wyatt in order to have his counsel and advice.   They were directed to work, if possible, with the agent of Bermuda and St. Christopher in order to reduce the expense of the contracts for handling the tobacco.   They were charged with delivery of letters to the Lords (probably of the Privy Council), with a petition to the king, and with the duty of informing the treasurer, attorney general, and chancellor of the exchequer of their business.   They were empowered to agree to settle the customs on tobacco at six pence a pound; if the king would not allow the price of tobacco at 3/6 per pound, or 4/ delivered in England, as desired by the colony, they might agree to 3/ a pound or 3/6 delivered in England.   They were to inform the Lords that importation of all the Virginia tobacco into England and prohibition of entry to Spanish tobacco would increase the customs, and London would soon supplant Spain as the center for tobacco.   They were to send back a barque of about fifty tons loaded with meal, twelve field carriages for demiculverins, twenty barrels of powder, two or three tons of great shot, with ladles and sponges, two hundredweight of match; it was also to carry twenty men—as many as possible to be carpenters, gunsmiths, and other smiths—together with necessary pro-

---

1622, and is identified with the Virginia Puritans.   Richard was a nephew of this Edward Bennett.—*William and Mary Quarterly*, ser. 2, XIII, 126.

[23] See *Journals of the House of Burgesses*, 1619-1658/9, p. viii.

[24] The manuscript is preserved in the Library of Congress.

visions of food and clothing for a year. Of course, they were to keep the assembly informed of the progress of events.[25] Failure to secure a modification of the royal monopoly of tobacco was their portion.

The next instance of the sending of agents to England, the dispatch of Captain Francis West and William Claiborne, came the very next year, 1629. This mission was, like the preceding, partly concerned with the tobacco monopoly and partly with the proposed planting of a new settlement within the limits of Virginia. Upon the death of Governor Yeardley, despite royal provisions for the succession, the council of Virginia assumed the privilege of electing Captain Francis West governor on November 24, 1627; he continued in this post until March 5, 1629, when he was selected as agent to go to England. Under West the assembly had been called together to receive the royal commands concerning the tobacco monopoly. The assembly declared its refusal to accept these proposals, even though the refusal was cloaked under expressions of loyalty. West was chosen to represent the interests of the assembly in England. As a younger brother of the late Lord De La Warr, he was acquainted in England and well qualified for the work. During his stay in England he also resisted the proposal to plant Lord Baltimore's colony within the bounds originally assigned to Virginia. He returned to Virginia some time prior to December, 1631.[26]

It seems almost impossible at this distance of time to disentangle the relations of William Claiborne to the Virginia agency. Whether he was named with West and whether they coöperated in opposing the Baltimore claim does not clearly appear. Lord Baltimore had come to the Old Dominion in 1629 from his venture in Newfoundland to find the Virginians loath to receive a Catholic or to concede him a portion of the land which they held under royal charter.

[25] The instructions were signed by Edward Bennett and Marshart as members of the House of Burgesses.—*Journals of the House of Burgesses,* 1619-1658/9, pp. 50-51; reprinted in part in the *William and Mary Quarterly,* ser. 2, XIII, 120-21. There is also an allusion in the council records for January 31, 1628, to Marshart's bringing back sixteen field carriages according to a commission of the last assembly.—*Minutes of the Council and General Court of Colonial Virginia,* I, 185.

[26] Election of West as governor was not an act of defiance, for Sir John Harvey, who was under royal order to have succeeded Yeardley, was in the service of Buckingham. The council, therefore, passed to the next in succession in the order.—Andrews, *Virginia, the Old Dominion,* p. 114. For a note on Francis West, see Withington and Waters, "Virginia Gleanings in England," *Virginia Magazine of History and Biography,* XI, 360. The last mention of his name in the records is February, 1633.

Hence, they shrewdly proffered him the oath of supremacy, which they knew he could not as a good Catholic take, and so put themselves in the safe position of loyal subjects requesting him to depart. But, cognizant of his intention to apply for a tract of land within their borders, they promptly sent Secretary William Claiborne to London to watch his actions and to thwart his designs. Despite the combined efforts of Claiborne and Captain West, Lord Baltimore secured a patent to a province north of the Potomac.[27] Claiborne did not return to American until 1631.

The next set of agents was dispatched from Virginia in 1635 to protest against Governor Harvey. Apparently by his contrivance large defalcations from Virginia occurred, and not only the land itself, quitrents and all, but jurisdictions belonging to that province were given away. Irregular in this matter, Harvey was regarded as unjust and arbitrary in his other methods of government. He exacted rigorously the fines and penalties which the unwary assemblies had voted chiefly to his office and was so haughty to the councillors and leading men that they felt his attitude to be insupportable. But the main causes for the hostility towards him were, according to Samuel Mathews, his favoring the settlement of Maryland by Lord Baltimore, so bitterly opposed by the Virginians; his refusing to transmit the assembly's protest against the king's monopolizing the tobacco trade; and his usurpation of additional powers regardless of the disapproval of the council. The immediate occasion of his expulsion from office was his arrest of several men of the council. It is highly probable also that his conduct in giving up Claiborne instead of protecting him in his controversy with Maryland over Kent Island was an important factor in incensing the colonists against their governor, for they firmly regarded the Maryland charter as an infringement of their rights. The truth is that the charges which history has laid against Governor Harvey seem to have been exaggerated.[28] Finally,

[27] Wertenbaker, op. cit., pp. 69-70. The story of Claiborne's personal controversy with Lord Baltimore over trading rights and the armed conflict between the forces of Governor Calvert and a pinnace commanded by one of Claiborne's men at Kent Island in the Chesapeake Bay is no part of this story. See Knott, A History of Maryland, p. 7. In the absence of references in the council records or in the Journals of the House of Burgesses, Claiborne cannot be declared an official agent. He went to England on his own affairs and probably consented to look after the affairs of Virginia against Lord Baltimore. See also Claiborne, William Claiborne of Virginia, p. 62. The fact that he was secretary of the colony at the time gave a certain official aspect to his actions.

[28] For an account of the reasons for objecting to Harvey, see Bruce, op. cit., II, 355-56

in May, 1635, the council deposed him and elected a successor, John West, whose choice the burgesses ratified with enthusiasm. The assembly then drew up a paper enumerating Governor Harvey's misdeeds, which they directed to the Lords Commissioners of Foreign Plantations, the body in England then in charge of colonial affairs. It happened that on the same ship which conveyed the deposed governor to England as a prisoner sailed also Thomas Harwood and Captain Francis Pott as agents for the colony. One could hardly suppose that the three proved congenial fellow-passengers particularly within the narrow confines of a sailing vessel of the early seventeenth century. No sooner had the boat touched dock at Plymouth, July 14, than Harvey was off to the mayor of the city and prevailed on that official to have the papers taken from Harwood and delivered to himself. He thus neatly nipped in the bud the plan of the agents to "make good their case" against him by hastening to London ahead of them. Instead, leaving Pott a prisoner for being a principal actor in the rebellion against him, the governor went on his way rejoicing to complain to the British authorities of the indignities against him.[29]

King Charles, astounded at his subjects' temerity in dismissing a governor, flatly refused to receive the two commissioners or to hear a word from them. The matter came before the Privy Council in December, 1635. The outcome was foreordained, for the Virginians, fearing to mention their real grievances for fear of arousing the court against them, since to condemn Governor Harvey was to condemn the Stuarts, fell back on weak grounds, such as the governor's personal unfitness, his unpopularity, his lack of diplomacy, and his contentiousness. The king insisted that Harvey must again be the chief executive, even if for only a day; he was accordingly

---

Beverley, *The History of Virginia*, pp. 47-48; Fiske, *op. cit.*, I, 295-99. Howe feels that the charges against him are without evidence and that historians filled in the gap as to the reasons for his deposition.—Howe, *op. cit.*, p. 56.

[29] The testimony of John Martyn, mayor of Plymouth, to the Privy Council, stating that Harwood had sealed divers letters in a trunk, was printed in "Virginia in 1635," *Virginia Magazine of History and Biography*, VIII, 400. For the petition of Pott from Fleet Prison see *ibid.*, p. 406; for the "Declaration of Sir John Harvey," see *ibid.*, I, 425-30; for Harvey's petition see *Calendar of State Papers, Colonial*, 1574-1660, pp. 212-13. A letter from Mayor John Martyn to the Privy Council, dated July 14, Plymouth, asks what is to be done with Francis Pott.—*Calendar of State Papers, Colonial, America and West Indies*, 1574-1660, p. 212. For testimony taken at Exeter from Ant. Browne, see *ibid.*, p. 214.

acquitted and reinstated. More than that, four Virginia councillors in addition to Deputy Governor West were ordered to appear before the Star Chamber on charge of treason. However, through influential friends they were able to get their complaints to the ears of Privy Council members so that ultimately Harvey was declared guilty of misconduct and replaced by Sir Francis Wyatt.[30] Meanwhile both agents were imprisoned, Pott being still detained in Fleet Prison as late as May 20, 1636.[31]

Scarcely more than three years elapsed before the assembly of Virginia felt moved to name another agent. In 1639,[32] eager for a renewal of the rights granted to the colonists by the old company, the assembly sent to be delivered to the king a petition embodying their wishes. The bearer was a brother of Sir Edwin Sandys, George Sandys, who had probably returned to England not later than 1632. The burgesses thus appointed a man who had been treasurer of Virginia before the abrogation of the charter of the London Company to watch over their interests in England under the new royal régime. The petition probably reached England in the fall of 1640, after both Edwin Sandys and Sir John Danvers had retired from the king's personal service in his privy chamber. In opposition to colonial desires, as declared later, George Sandys interpreted the petition as advocating the restoration of the London Corporation, except that the crown should reserve the right to appoint the governor, thus reviving the project which had been pressed ten years earlier. Presented not to the king, but to a parliament, which was known to be favorably inclined to the popular party,[33] a resolution authorizing revival of the patent rights of the London Company, was actually passed. But this action was more than Charles I was willing to countenance, and so he replaced Wyatt by William Berkeley as governor. Two years later, yielding to Berkeley's strong influence, the new assembly declared its opposition to renewal of the old charter.

[30] Andrews, *Virginia, the Old Dominion*, p. 126; Squires, *Through Centuries Three*, pp. 132-33; Wertenbaker, *op. cit.*, pp. 77-79. For the order, see *Calendar of State Papers, Colonial*, 1574-1660, p. 217. The four councillors were Samuel Mathews, George Menifie, Will Peirce, and John Utie.

[31] Stanard, *The Story of Virginia's First Century*, p. 200.

[32] The date presents difficulties: it may have been at the October session, 1639, the date given in a paper drawn up by the 1641/2 assembly. But it may have been 1639/40. See *Journals of the House of Burgesses*, 1619-1658/9, pp. xxxvii, 66.

[33] Randolph MSS, III, 241. Note that Sandys presented these petitions not to the king, but to the House of Commons at the beginning of the Long Parliament.

It sent to the king a declaration in the form of an act, stating that the agent had mistaken his instructions. This paper, entitled "A Declaration against the Company," said that it never was the meaning of the assembly or the inhabitants to reintroduce the company; signed by the governor, the council, and nearly all the burgesses, it protested vigorously against revival of the company and against the great distance which the company would interpose between the king and his subjects in Virginia. The colony declared that company rule would be "intollerable" and drew a melancholy picture of their sufferings before the revocation of the charter. Unfortunately, the instructions to Sandys have not survived; hence it is impossible to know whether he did really misinterpret the wishes of Virginia or whether the assembly, having suffered a change of heart, disclaimed their agent in order to escape a difficult situation. Not unnaturally, the new petition was highly acceptable to Charles, who sent a gracious answer from his court at York on July 5, 1642, promising never to restore the company. He probably had had no idea of doing so, but it was agreeable to be thus confirmed in his determination.[34]

It cannot be determined whether the "Declaration against the Company" was sent over by special agents in 1642 or not. The last paragraph of the "Remonstrance of the Grand Assembly," drawn up to explain why the assembly remained so long in session, seems to indicate that a large outlay of money had to be made. This may have been to pay the expenses of the representatives of the colony who took the Declaration to the king, and conceivably to furnish money with which to buy the king's favor or that of his ministers. If so, the name of any agent or agents has been lost.[35] At the hands of the Puritan parliament, which, as is well known, was favor-

---

[34] For this episode see Brown, *English Politics in Early Virginia History*, pp. 102-3; Bruce, *op. cit.*, II, 261-62; Chandler and Thames, *Colonial Virginia*, p. 212; Colonial Entry Book, 1606-1662, p. 237; Force, *Tracts and other Papers*, II, No. 6, pp. 3-4; Neill, *Virginia Carolorum*, pp. 158-59; Wertenbaker, *op. cit.*, pp. 87-88. For the text of the "Declaration against the Company to be entered as the twenty-first act," see Hening, *Statutes*, I, 230-35.

[35] ". . . and we apprehended no time could be mifspent or labour mifplaced in gaining a firm peace to ourfelves and pofterity and a future immunity and eafe from taxes and impofitions which we expect to be the fruits of our endeavours and to which end we have thought it feafonable for us liberally and freely to open our purfes not doubting but all well affected perfons will with all zeal and good affection embrace the purchafe and pray to Almighty God for the fuccefs." Dated 1st of July, 1642.—*Journals of the House of Burgesses*, 1619-1658/9, pp. xxxix, 70.

ably disposed to the colonies, Virginia enjoyed her old rights until 1660.

To the list of these early agents must now be added the names of Colonel Samuel Mathews, Richard Bennett, and Edward Digges, who functioned in England during some of the years of the Protectorate. After the adjournment of the Virginia assembly of April, 1652, Colonel Samuel Mathews was dispatched to obtain a ratification of the articles of agreement with the commissioners of parliament sent over to receive the submission of the colonies.[36] It was especially hoped that he might also accomplish two other objects: win the annexation of Maryland and secure some relief from the navigation laws. By May 28 of the next year we find evidence that he was in addition trying to look out for his colony's interests in general, because a petition of some merchants and others trading to Virginia and the West Indies, asking prohibition of tobacco planting in England, was signed by Samuel Mathews, "Agent for the Inhabitants of Virginia." At the very close of the year, December 29, he secured an order from the Council of State for a letter to the governor and assembly of Virginia establishing the governor who was then in office until further notice.

That the Navigation Act of 1651 seriously hurt the tobacco trade the colonial planters expressed in the phrase, "the British shaved them up one side and down the other." At last they decided that Richard Bennett must join Samuel Mathews in England. Surely, the obnoxious laws would be repealed if Oliver Cromwell, parliament, and the people could be made to understand how unjust and onerous was this burden placed on them by "special privilege," especially if their cause was presented by a Virginia Puritan.[37] But it proved a futile hope, for the English merchants and shipmasters had millions invested on which they expected a reasonable return, and it was British attorneys, not Puritan divines, who decided what constituted a reasonable return. Bennett had reached London before September 13, 1655, as a petition referred on that date to the

[36] Neill, *op. cit.*, p. 227.
[37] *Calendar of State Papers, Colonial*, 1574-1660, p. 403. They pray that an act passed in April, 1652, prohibiting tobacco planting in England, may receive some encouragement. Apparently Bennett was something of a religious fanatic, for Cromwell ordered Claiborne and him "not to busy themselves about religion."—Bozman, *History of Maryland*, I, 540, note.

Committee for Foreign Affairs bears the names of both Mathews and Bennett.[38]

In view of the fact that Cromwell reserved the question of the boundaries between Virginia and Maryland to himself and the Council of State in his order of September 26, 1655, the Virginia assembly must have concluded that their two original agents were not powerful enough to support their sinking cause with the Protector, for they decided on October 15, 1656,[39] to dispatch still a third agent to England. They selected for the task their governor, Edward Digges, another Puritan, who had been living in Virginia since 1650, "whose occafions were calling him into England." As a part of his instructions, he was directed to assure the Lord Protector that, according to his Lordship's directions, the colonists had not interested themselves in the business betwixt Maryland (and the Puritans settled there?) and have been "unconcerned in their quarrel from the beginning until this time and so fhall continue. . . ." He was instructed to unite with Mathews and Bennett and to treat with the leading merchants in the Virginia trade, and to inform them how much the provincial assembly had endeavored to diminsh the quantity and improve the quality of tobacco with a view to securing a better price from the merchants.[40] Digges, departing for England in the spring of 1656/7, would seem to have coöperated for a short period with both the other agents.[41]

A rather extraordinary situation thus existed in Virginia. Colonel Mathews remained in England for at least five years, from 1652 to 1657;[42] ex-Governor Bennett went over in 1655; and then Gover-

[38] Squires, op. cit., pp. 161-62; Calendar of State Papers, Colonial, 1574-1660, pp. 428-29.

[39] Burk, (History of Virginia, II, 116) gives the date as December 15, 1656, but October is probably correct, as the letter to Secretary Thurloe (published in Hazard, Historical Collections, I, 632) gives October 15. One distrusts Burk, as he is full of blunders, and the instructions, probably, drawn later, are dated December 15.

[40] Bozman, op. cit., I, 540; Journals of the House of Burgesses, 1619-1658/9, p. 105. The blank seems to have appeared in the record; the insertion made above seems logical.

[41] Campbell, History of the Colony and Ancient Dominion of Virginia, pp. 234-35, 236. Digges was directed to "assist" the other commissioners: "Join yourself to our friends, colonel Mathews and mr. Bennett."—Squires, op. cit., p. 164. He was to deliver letters to Colonel Mathews, to Cromwell, and to Secretary of State John Thurloe, these letters bearing date of December 15, 1656.—Hening, Statutes, I, 425, 426; Journals of the House of Burgesses, I, 101, 104, 105.

[42] A moot point exists as to whether Colonel Mathews returned to Virginia to serve his colony as governor. Miss Cook argues very plausibly that he did not and that it

nor Digges was dispatched early in 1657, thus leaving the direction of local affairs almost entirely to the council. The approach to the Protector was to be made through Secretary Thurloe, whom the Virginians in a properly humble frame of mind addressed: "Though we are persons soe remote from you, yet wee have heard so honourable a Character of your worth, that we cannot make a second choice without Erring, of one soe fitt and propper as your felfe by whome to make our Addrefses to his Highnefs the Lord Protectour." They besought his aid in gaining access to Cromwell, and held out a hint of largess, "so wee are confident he [Digges] will undertake for us, that wee are a people not altogether ungratefull; But will shortly find a nearer way than by saying soe, to Exprefse Realie how much wee esteem the honour of your Patronage."[43] The letter to the Protector stated that Digges as their representative was authorized to say that Virginia would interfere in no way with the affairs of Maryland.[44]

What the agents were able to achieve is told in detail in a letter to the governor and council from Secretary Thomas Povey of the newly-created Committee for America. Induced by the representations of the three agents, he writes, "We have from time to time endeavoured to obtain from his Highnefs and the Counselle a Comifsion and Directions whereby the Govern^r and Counselle may more warrantably and effectually proceed in their Duty. . . . Nevertheless his Highnefs hath been pleafed to declare himself that he will forthwith reeftablish the Governm^t by his Comifsion Wee have also endeavoured as much as in us lyes to represent the hard condition of Virginia as to the great Customs and other Duties now continuing upon it and we shall take all oportunities wee may toward the gaining some redrefs therein. But we have more especially not without great trouble, charge and travail bin busyed in the preventing a most considerable mischiefe, wch was well nigh ripened, and had certainly proved to yor disadvantage, if it had not in a most seasonable instant, bin happily prevented," by which he refers to the proposed destruc-

---

was his son who was elected in 1657 to succeed Digges. If Mathews signed an agreement as agent in London, November 30, 1657, he could not have issued a land patent in Virginia on November 28, 1657. The author is inclined to accept her contention. See Cook, "Governor Samuel Mathews, Junior," *William and Mary Quarterly*, ser. 2, XIV, 107.

[43] Rawlinson MSS, A 45, folio 174, Bodleian Library.
[44] *Journals of the House of Burgesses*, 1619-1658/9, p. 105.

tion of the greatest crop of English tobacco yet planted. This prevention had been effected only by "continuall Sollicitations, by collection of Severall Sums of money, and by the hazard of some of our persons, employed in the execution of the Laws and Acts of State."[45]

A second matter with which these agents were deeply concerned was the dispute with Lord Baltimore over the boundaries of his province, which had not yet been settled. An order was issued in September, 1655, to confirm Cromwell's former order forbidding Virginia or Maryland to resort to force to settle their dispute.[46] Since Bennett attended personally at Whitehall, it is possible that the order may have been delivered to him. During the remainder of 1655 and through 1656 a petition of Lord Cecilius Baltimore followed the slow routine of reference by the Protector to the Council of State, reference to Commissioners Whitelock and Widdrington for report, while the petition of the two Virginia agents, Bennett and Mathews, dragged through a similar devious course from the Council of State to the Committee for Foreign Affairs and to a special committee of five. Finally the whole matter was referred by the Council of State to the Committee for Foreign Plantations for consultation with the parties concerned and for report.[47] At last in disgust the Virginia assembly decreed in December, 1656, that letters be sent the two agents asking that, since the difference with Lord Baltimore was as far from settlement as at first, the agents desist until further order from this country.[48] The Lord Protector had no time for the petty concerns of a distant colony.

After the arrival of Digges, however, an agreement was negotiated by his friendly endeavors with Lord Baltimore. The proprietor agreed to waive his right of jurisdiction so as to leave settlement of past differences to the disposal of his council and himself;

[45] Povey's Letter Book, Add. MSS, II, 411, folio 19. The committees dealing with the plantations during the Commonwealth are very confusing.

[46] Bozman, op. cit., p. 533.

[47] The petition of the Virginia agents was referred by the Council of State to the Committee for Foreign Affairs on September 13, 1655.—Calendar of State Papers, Colonial, 1574-1660, pp. 428-29; on July 13, 1656, to a "special named committee."—Ibid., p. 445; on December 17, 1656, the whole matter, including the report on Lord Baltimore's petition was referred to the Committee of the Council for Foreign Plantations.—"Virginia in 1656-1658," Virginia Magazine of History and Biography, XVIII, 152. The statements drawn up by Mathews and Bennett were printed in Thurloe, State Papers, V, 482.

[48] Hening, Statutes, I, 425.

to allow the land claims of the people opposed to his jurisdiction without exacting an oath of fidelity from them, contenting himself with an engagement to support him; and lastly never to allow repeal of the law for freedom of conscience.[49] This adjustment was reached on November 30, 1657, probably after many interviews.

In 1661 the old London Company was reported to be once again making an effort for the restoration of its charter, so that the assembly feared possible loss of their liberties at the hands of the Plantation Commission. Even more serious was the concern over the Navigation Law, the evil effects of which were clearly manifesting themselves. Unwilling to believe that their newly restored sovereign intended to strangle the colonies, the assembly commissioned Governor Sir William Berkeley, on his intended visit to England, to attend especially to their interests and to endeavor to procure more friendly legislation. Embarking in May, 1661, with a personal gift for the king and a gift from the people, the latter of Virginia silk, he arrived in London in the summer of 1661 while England was still in a delirium of joy over the return of Charles II and in the high tide of reaction against Puritanism.

Much was expected of Governor Berkeley, as he was himself *persona grata* to the king, and his brother a royal favorite and high in power.[50] But his accomplishments during a long absence—from about the first of April, 1661, until November, 1662—must have been disappointing to the Virginians. He feasted his eyes on royalty, secured the king's acceptance of the gifts,[51] obtained some privileges for himself, but secured not one concession for the colony. It is interesting as a harbinger of the duties of a regular agent, that the assembly sent over a copy of the laws of the session of 1661-1662 to Berkeley with the request that he procure their confirmation.[52]

---

[49] Squires, *op. cit.*, p. 166.

[50] A hint of what was hoped for can be seen in the phraseology of the law which commissioned him: "Whereas the necessity of the country being in danger of the oppression . . . for want of such an agent in England as is able to oppose the invaders of our freedomes and truly to represent our condition to his sacred majestie enforceth the employing a person of quality to present our grievances to his majesty's gracious consideration and endeavour the redresse which the right honorable Sir William Berkeley his majestyes governor hath been pleased to undertake. . . ." Dated Mar. 23, 1660/1.—Hening, *Statutes*, II, 17.

[51] Berkeley states that fact in a letter to Lord Arlington soon after his arrival.—Stanard, *Virginia's First Century*, p. 242.

[52] Hening, *Statutes*, II, 147-48.

His departure from England was hardly glorious. He petitioned the king for the customs from a ship of tobacco to enable him to "wait on" the king's royal person for one half year. From Whitehall came a cold, sarcastic answer. Sir William Berkeley should have a ship of tobacco of 300 tons, customs free, when he sent over a ship laden with silk, hemp, flax, pitch, and potash produced in Virginia. With abruptness he was ordered to return to his government speedily. But the Council of Foreign Plantations showed him some favor, for after a debate on his petition, it ordered his salary of £1,000 continued as well as his grant of the two shillings per hogshead on tobacco.[53]

A single scant reference to a religious mission in this early period, March, 1661, may not be omitted. A certain Phillip Mallory, who was described in an act of the Virginia legislature as "eminently faithfull in the ministry and very dilligent in endeavouring the advancement of all those meenes that might conduce to the advancement of religion in this country," was desired to undertake the soliciting of the colony's church affairs in England, for which service he was to be paid. Specifically, he was sent over to arrange for a greater number of English clergymen to be sent out to the colony. This was merely following up the pressing appeal of the assembly of the preceding session to the king to use his personal influence with the two universities to lead them to furnish Virginia with all the ministers needed for the vacant parishes.[54] Our curiosity as to the nature and success of his services is left unsatisfied, except that he seems to have returned empty-handed.

The next instance of an agent smacks so strongly of the establishment of a regular agency, except for the absence of a fixed salary and of any continuity in office, that one is tempted to close the genesis in Virginia here. The governor evidently had stated to the lower house early in 1663 his conviction of the necessity of an agent to manage the country's affairs in England, "if an honourable perſon would be found fit to be intruſted." The house accordingly appointed a committee of seven to ask the governor to suggest some proper persons.[55] The governor recommended Colonel Morrison—

[53] Stanard, *op. cit.*, p. 242.

[54] Hening, *Statutes*, II, 31, 34. The amount he was to be paid will be discussed in Chapter IX. See also Bruce, *op. cit.*, I, 123.

[55] *Journals of the House of Burgesses*, 1659/60-1693, p. 39.

clearly Colonel Francis Moryson, who had been Governor Berkeley's substitute in the colony during his London absence, and who was about to return to England for a three-year visit on his own affairs— whereupon the House requested and instructed his honor to choose an agent for the ensuing year, such agent to proceed under the governor's instructions.[56] From these requests of the House it is obvious that at this period which begins to see the crystalization of the agency the governor both chose and instructed the agent. The records prove that this Francis Moryson was serving before the Privy Council on December 4, 1663,[57] and was appearing at intervals before the Committee of the Council for Plantation Affairs up until June, 1670. His most significant appearance was possibly January 4, 1667, when he presented his view of the necessity of sending guns and ammunition for the defense of Virginia. He also petitioned for a frigate for the defense of the ships plying to Chesapeake Bay. The writer finds no final disposition of the request for arms after it had been referred to the Commissioners of Ordnance for report, but the Privy Council on January 11 authorized the high admiral to order a frigate to Chesapeake Bay by the date mentioned. He was, however, functioning much as a regular agent and even applied for a regular salary of £200 for life from the two-shilling tax per hogshead on tobacco.[58]

The rôle of Sir Henry Chicheley as agent in July, 1673, represents, it is believed, an isolated appointment for a specific mission. Sometime prior to July 16, 1673, the governor and assembly chose him to present a petition to the king, which, after setting forth the helplessness of the country against possible invasion, by virtue of their inability to arm more than one in ten of the twenty regiments of foot and horse, asked for a supply of arms and ammunition. They also suggested duties on ships sufficient to raise the necessary funds, as the soldiers "will not serve for tobacco."[59] Again nothing further is revealed.

[56] *Ibid.*, p. 43.

[57] A bare reference to the appearance of Colonel Moryson before the Privy Council on December 4, 1663, proves his presence in London at that time.—*Acts of the Privy Council, Colonial*, I, sec. 611.

[58] *Ibid.*, sec. 695. See also *Calendar of State Papers, Colonial*, 1661-1668, secs. 428, 855, 975, 1037, 1194, 1618; *ibid.*, 1669-1674, secs. 71, 195. For the request for salary, see *ibid.*, 1661-1668, sec. 973.

[59] *Ibid.*, 1669-1674, p. 508. The above appears from a letter by Henry Chicheley to Sir Thomas Chicheley, dated July 16, 1673.

To thwart, if possible, the Culpeper grant was the object of the last mission which contributed to the development of the Virginia agency during the period of genesis. King Charles II, to gratify some noblemen about him, had bestowed several grants carved out of Virginia in what is known as the Northern Neck. Rendering the action more offensive, these grants were made not out of the uncultivated woodland only but also out of plantations which for many years had been improved under charters legally granted by the king's ancestors to founders of that colony. These patentees were to receive fees, remainders, reversions, and escheats and were given power to grant patents for all land that had not been taken up. The grants had lain dormant some years, but in 1673 they seemed about to be put into execution. The colony sent an agent to England to persuade the king to annul the grants, but then came the astounding news that Charles had granted the whole of Virginia for thirty-one years to his old friends, the Earl of Arlington and Lord Culpeper, bestowing on them feudal powers which would have rendered the government at Jamestown almost a nullity. As soon as the colony realized that the grants were actually to be made effective, remonstrances began with greater fervor. The assembly drew up a humble petition to the king, complaining that the grants were contrary to the previous charters given to the colony. But in so serious a situation they did not rest there. By action of September, 1674, the burgesses named as agents to England Colonel Francis Moryson, Major General Robert Smith, who was already in England, and Thomas Ludwell, secretary of state, to beg the king to vacate those grants; they were also "to negotiate in England all other publique affaires of this country," which really meant, in addition to revocation of the grant, to secure for Virginia a new charter which had been pushed by Ludwell and Parke. In the quoted phrase one sees again a forerunner of the regular agency.[60]

[60] Hening, *Statutes*, II, 311-14; Beverley, *History of Virginia*, pp. 61-62; Burk, *op. cit.*, II, 142-43, 151, 152. The records make it clear that Moryson was sent over from Virginia; hence he must have returned to his colony after June, 1670, and have stayed there until late in 1674. For the last entry of 1670 see *Calendar of State Papers, Colonial, 1669-1674*, sec. 195. The writer believes it is an error to regard Colonel Daniel Parke as a regularly accredited agent with the other three. It is true that he was in England for a great portion of the time of this agency and appeared before the Board of Trade several times, but one entry makes it clear that he was not regarded as an agent by the Board: the three agents of Virginia, Thomas Ludwell, Francis Moryson, and General Robert Smith, "as also Colonel Parke," attended on June 15, 1676.—*Ibid.*, 1675-1676, sec. 949.

These men were not sent at the same time. As early as September 20, 1671, a grand assembly at James City, recognizing the emergency arising from the "Dammages like to be fuftained by the inhabitants of the Northern parts," had sent Major General Smith with a petition to negotiate the public affairs in England according to instructions.[61] It is impossible to fix the date of his departure; records only prove that he was functioning by July 2, 1673, for on that date the governor and council ordered him as "agent *in England*" to purchase all or as many shares as he could of the northern patent of land from the Rappahannock to the Potomac Rivers.[62] The three men had been formally named on September 21, 1674, to secure revocation of the grant of February 25, 1673, to Arlington and Culpeper. Ludwell was apparently about to depart soon after November 19, 1674, for on that date he appointed Lieutenant Colonel Philip Ludwell as his deputy during his absence.[63]

The agents labored earnestly and long with the patentees, Lords Arlington and Culpeper, holding many conferences with them or with their commissioners. They secured from the grantees a renunciation of the grant, with the exception of the quitrents and escheats. But then the government interposed delays. Their patience at length well nigh exhausted after twelve months of efforts, the agents petitioned the Lord Privy Seal for the passing of the grant at once or for a copy of the objections in order that they might put in their answer so that there might be a conclusion of this business, "whose delay have been ruinous to us already here, and may we fear be prejuditial hereafter to his majesties service, in that country."[64]

In propounding the basis of a new charter in 1675, the agents declared that the Virginians had no objection to the king's veto on legislation provided he signified disapproval within two years.[65] The report of the king's attorney and solicitor general was entirely favorable to the agents and was adopted by the king in council; and

[61] *Journals of the House of Burgesses*, 1659-1693, p. 57.

[62] *Minutes of the Council*, pp. 347, 518.

[63] *Journals of the House of Burgesses*, 1659-1693, p. 63. A minute of the Court session records the action as owing to the fact of Thomas "being bound for England uppon the Countries Service."—*Minutes of the Council*, p. 396.

[64] Hening, *Statutes*, II, 538. This paper was signed only by Ludwell and Moryson, but the exact date does not appear.

[65] Bruce, *op. cit.*, II, 504. This rule in regard to the constitutional period to register a veto remained in force till the close of the century.

a charter was twice ordered to be passed under the great seal. New objections by the officers of the crown were repelled with great firmness by the agents. But the news of Bacon's rebellion[66] furnished an excuse to the crown to recede, and so after two years of unwearied efforts the agents gained nothing but a miserable skeleton of a charter with little more than a declaration of Virginia's dependence on the crown. Probably no other three citizens of Virginia at that time were so competent by long experience and observation to represent their people or understood better the spirit toward the throne than Moryson, Ludwell, and Smith. Though they failed to attain the type of charter desired, their efforts doubtless contributed to the final disposition of the Culpeper grant. Lord Arlington on September 10, 1681, conveyed all his interest under the patent to Culpeper, who later assigned his entire estate to the king.[67] The agents came so near success that even the present-day reader could sigh with disappointment for them. The crown lawyers reported favorably for them; the Privy Council approved the report; the Committee of Plantations confirmed the report with a few amendments;[68] Charles II gave his royal assent and ordered letters patent prepared precisely in conformity with their petition, providing against the grievances of which they complained. But despite the insistence of the agents, the measure was so long delayed in going through the official forms, aided possibly by hints of sedition in Virginia, that completion of the transaction was prevented for some months. Then came Bacon's Rebellion and the chancellor was suddenly ordered not to affix the seal to the patent. Thus were dashed the hopes and success of the agents. The Culpeper issue lived on.

Virginia does not thus present a striking series of successes for the agents during the period of development. Wyatt may be

[66] Ludwell attended the Committee of Trade and Plantations on June 8, 1676, to show a letter concerning the disturbance in Virginia.—C. O. 391/1, p. 133.

[67] For negotiations in regard to the charter, see Hening, *Statutes*, II, 523-33; Bruce, *op. cit.*, II, 281, 532, note; Brown, *English Politics in Early Virginia History*, p. 121. Most of the papers on this subject are given in the appendix to Burk, *History of Virginia*, Vol. II. Culpeper surrendered his rights to the king in 1684.—Hening, *Statutes*, II, 521-22.

[68] The attorney general recommended that no tax should be laid but by common consent of the governor, council, and burgesses, which "had been heretofore used."—Bruce, *op. cit.*, II, 523, note 1. The amendments were added in the presence of the agents and read somewhat like a prophecy of 1765: ". . . this fhall be no bar to any imposition which may be laid here by the king in parliament."—Chalmers, *Political Annals*, I, 331.

regarded as having won the only striking success in securing the restoration of the assembly. The failure of Bennett and Marshart to win withdrawal of the royal monopoly of tobacco was followed by the failure of Captain Francis West and William Claiborne to prevent a patent to Lord Baltimore for Virginia soil; the failure of Potts and Harwood against Governor Harvey was foreordained; the mission of Sandys, whether owing to his misunderstanding or to the fumbling of the assembly, cannot be termed a success; Governor Berkeley, despite high station and influence, failed to gain alteration of the laws of trade; and Ludwell, Smith, and Moryson, after apparently achieving success, lost the fruits of their efforts by an untoward event in the colony—Bacon's Rebellion.

Maryland, like her sister to the south, saw the agency evolve through a genesis period. Her first agent appeared much earlier than those in the Carolinas but later than that in Virginia, and arose first in Britain's troubled Commonwealth period. After the republic was firmly established in England under Cromwell as Lord Protector, Richard Bennett and William Claiborne were named by parliament as two of the four commissioners to secure the submission of Maryland, the other two being lost at sea. On March 29, 1652, the commissioners removed Governor Stone and named a council of six men to conserve peace and administer justice in Maryland. Lord Baltimore appears to have felt that on the dissolution of parliament the authority of the commissioners appointed by it ceased and that since Cromwell took no action against the charter he was automatically reinstated in power. Accordingly he instructed Governor Stone to assert his old authority.[69] Then reappeared upon the scene Bennett and Claiborne who issued a commission to ten men, all Puritans, among whom were Leonard Strong and Captain William Fuller, to administer the government of Maryland. There followed the battle on the Severn on March 25, 1655, between the Puritans under Captain William Fuller and the forces loyal to Lord Baltimore under Governor Stone; the Puritans were triumphant.[70]

[69] Hall, *Narratives of Early Maryland*, pp. 236-37. This is the same Richard Bennett whom we have already encountered in Virginia. Providence later became Annapolis. Captains Dennis and Steg were the other two commissioners, according to Langford.—*Ibid.*, p. 256.

[70] For fuller accounts see Andrews, *History of Maryland*, pp. 114-29; *Founding of Maryland*, pp. 231-43; McSherry, *History of Maryland*, pp. 53-60.

Probably Commissioner Richard Bennett abdicated the office of governor of Virginia about March, 1655, and embarked for England in the dual capacity of Virginia agent and commissioner to report to Cromwell on the revolt in Virginia and Maryland. He evidently carried over his and Claiborne's joint report, dated June 29, 1655. In England he secured an audience with Cromwell, to whom he doubtless gave an account of the battle in Maryland in terms as favorable as possible to the Puritan side. If one may judge from the Protector's subsequent neglect of Maryland's contests, he does not seem to have produced much effect upon the Protector. Though the matter did come before the Council of State, the Protector never made a decision on the subject. Indeed, he had no leisure for the petty affairs of distant colonies and furthermore seemed rather well disposed than otherwise to Baltimore. The medley of agents for Virginia and Maryland at this point is highly confusing, for Bennett and Mathews seem to have been serving as agents for the Puritans of Maryland as well as of Virginia in the fall of 1655.[71]

Immediately after the battle, Captain Fuller and the Puritan group at Providence (now Annapolis) dispatched their messenger to England to forestall the accounts of their opponents, while in order to predispose the minds of the British government in their favor, Governor Stone and the other prisoners were set at liberty. Leonard Strong in all probability was this agent. He departed, it is thought, on the *Golden Lion*, as its captain sympathized with the Puritans.[72] In London he published a pamphlet, *Babylon's Fall in Maryland: A Fair Warning to Lord Baltamore; or a Relation of an Assault made by divers Papists and Popish Officers of the Lord Baltamore's against the Protestants in Maryland*, in which is given an account of the Protestant revolt in Maryland.[73] Though Strong alluded to Governor Stone and Thomas Hatton, his secretary, as

[71] The evidence on which this statement is based is that Bennett wrote Governor Fuller of Maryland at once of the agreement with Lord Baltimore, when it was reached about November 30, 1657.—Bozman, *History of Maryland*, pp. 555-56.

[72] See Steiner, *Maryland under the Commonwealth*, p. 100.

[73] While it cannot be proved that Strong went to London, since there is nothing in the laws of 1654, 1657, 1658, 1661, or 1662, or in the *Proceedings of Maryland* on this point, the other evidence seems to sum up to that conclusion. The author of the pamphlet is described on the title page as "Agent for the people of Providence in Maryland. Printed for the author, 1655"; Strong is accepted as the author; the pamphlet was printed in London; the assumption is strong that he was in London at the time of its printing. This is found in Hall, *Narrative of Early Maryland*, pp. 235-46.

"Popish councellors," obviously in order to prejudice the people of
England against Lord Baltimore's government, the words were false,
for Stone and a majority of his council were Protestants though not
Puritans. The agent complained to Lord Baltimore of the rigorous
oath of fealty which he exacted. When Baltimore refused to remove
this oath and other inconveniences, Strong presented a petition at the
office of the Council of State, where it lay nearly four years without
a hearing. Long before these years were up, indeed shortly after
his arrival, Strong died in England.

The man chosen to answer Strong was John Langford, employed
by Lord Baltimore in connection with Maryland affairs for more
than twenty years, who described himself on the title page of his
pamphlet, *Refutation of Babylon's Fall*, as "Gentleman, servant to
the Lord Baltemore." Another pamphlet, *Leah and Rachel*, was
published in 1656 by one John Hammond who had lived twenty-
one years in the American plantations and had escaped sentence of
death for supporting Governor Stone. In this pamphlet he charged
that though Cromwell had sent orders not to disturb Baltimore's officers in Maryland, yet the rebels still held the province. The author
seems to have drawn a certain comfort from the fact that the agent
of the Protestants "hath long since given up his account to the great
avenger of all injuries."[74] Maryland was ultimately surrendered
peaceably to Baltimore in 1658 by agreement between him and
Richard Bennett, an agreement which by implication seems to have
settled the religious issue as well. When Baltimore sent Josias
Fendall as lieutenant governor, the turmoil aroused by the change
of government in England seemed over.

No further occasion to send agents home from Maryland arose
until 1689. The Revolution of 1688 brought its counterpart in
Maryland as in the other colonies. On the report that James II
had been deposed and replaced by the Protestant sovereigns, William
and Mary, a revolt sprang up under John Coode in July, 1689.[75]
The two contending factions ceased their open warfare, and both
carried their cases on appeal, so to speak, to London. A hearing was

[74] Both of these pamphlets are printed in Hall, *op. cit.*, pp. 254-74 and 281-307. He
designates Virginia as Leah and Maryland as Rachel. See pp. 284, 300, 305.
[75] See *Archives of Maryland*, VIII, 123. For an account of the revolt see Andrews,
History of Maryland, pp. 178-81.

set for December 23, 1690. John Coode, leader of the revolt,[76] and Kenelm Cheseldyne, speaker of the lower house, were dispatched to London to present the case of the revolutionists, taking their departure probably in the very early fall of that year. The counts in the indictment against the Calverts followed the usual pattern: nepotism, partiality to the Catholics, invoking of illegal laws, and failure to protect the settlers from the Indians. Though Coode was not an heroic figure from any standpoint[77]—rather the reverse— and Cheseldyne only important by virtue of his office, they were well received at the British court by the Lords of Trade and Plantations before whom they received their first hearing on December 5. Both the agents and Lord Baltimore were present with their counsel and presented their respective sides. Both sides were heard again on December 22, when the whole matter was referred to the new governor to be sent out to Maryland.[78] They appeared before the Lords of Trade and Plantations again, for a third time, February 23, 1691/2, a date which helps to mark the length of their presence in England. The issue on that occasion seemed to be revenues. It was decided that the sums raised by the duty of fourteen pence per ton and half of the sum raised by the two-shilling duty per hogshead on tobacco should be collected and allowed Lord Baltimore; the other half from the two-shilling duty and one "moity" of the fourteen-pence duty were to be applied to the support of the

[76] Coode left Nehemiah Blakiston as his successor during his absence in England. The record is dated September 17, 1690.—*Ibid.*, p. 206. The date of departure of the agents is fairly well fixed as Governor Nicholson had heard from Coode shortly before October 27.— *Calendar of State Papers, Colonial*, 1689-1692, sec. 1061. He was in London by November 20.—*Ibid.*, p. 1195.

[77] Captain Coode seems to have been later regarded as a trouble maker. He seems to have deteriorated greatly in the years after his return to Maryland from his agency. After Governor Nicholson demanded his dismissal from the assembly on the ground that he was a priest and stripped him of all his military offices, he fled to Virginia. Although convicted of treason on his return, punishment was remitted through the council, where he had friends. William Browne referred to him as "this unsavory person."—*Maryland: The History of a Palatinate*, p. 187. See Bibbins, *The Beginnings of Maryland in England and America*, pp. 97-100.

[78] It would seem that a case involving rebellion might more properly have gone before the Privy Council, but charges against the proprietor came regularly before the Lords of Trade, and so the episode was apparently classified as under its jurisdiction. The change in date for the initial hearing was probably owing to the impatience of the agents who wished the hearing held, once they were on the scene. For the complaint to the Lords see Journals of the Lords of Trade, C. O. 391/6, p. 361; *Calendar of State Papers, Colonial*, 1689-1692, secs. 1206, 1228, 1263.

government under the treasury board.[79]   Coode and Cheseldyne received the thanks of the provincial assembly for their services in England on May 13, 1692, but a final echo of the agency is still heard on June 1, when the assembly finally arranged for the pay for Cheseldyne.[80]

Almost immediately after the return of Coode and Cheseldyne came the appointment of Peter Pagan as agent, an appointment which so closely resembles that of the later regular agency that the scholar hesitates long over his classification.   Indeed, only the absence of a regular term and salary precludes his classification with the regular agents.   Despite the satisfaction which the assembly expressed with the new royal government, it thought that it was necessary to have an agent in London "to defend and Promote all things for the good of this Province and also Maintain all Matters that may come in debate or otherwise relate to the good" of Maryland, and accordingly the post was filled by action of both houses on June 8, 1692. Their unanimous choice was Captain Peter Pagan, a merchant trading to Maryland.   That he had, however, already been rendering services of that character is proved by the fact that the house voted on June 7 to give him twenty pounds sterling for his kindness.[81] Apparently the issue which had induced the assembly to feel the need of an agent was the difficulty over Sir Thomas Lawrence, who had been made royal secretary of the province in September, 1691. On his arrival early in 1692, he immediately became involved in conflicts over the fees and perquisites belonging to his office, and aroused dissatisfaction among the people.   Scarcely was Pagan notified of his appointment before the clerk of the council was instructed to send him "under a flying seal" a letter from the governor and

[79] C. O. 391/7, pp. 1-2; Calendar of State Papers, Colonial, 1689-1692, sec. 1330. We have here again an example of the early agent taking on other duties than the specific one for which he was sent and thus foreshadowing a regular agent.—Ibid., sec. 1333.

[80] Though the original manuscript record is badly mutilated, enough is left to make the purport clear: "Motion made by a   yett that any thankes   Capt Cood (Agents for the   in England for this Countery and the house does unanimously   harty   to Mr Speaker and Capt Cood for their   and dilige   Used about the Managem^t of the Publick (business) of this Province . . . half of the Countery in England, . . ."— Archives of Maryland, May 10-June 9, 1692, XIII, 364. The question of pay is dealt with in a later chapter.

[81] Archives of Maryland, May 10-June 9, 1692, XIII, 342, 467. The bill was signed by the governor the same day. There is no evidence that the council concurred in this vote of pay.—Ibid., p. 416.

council, complaining of the irregular proceedings of Sir Thomas, against whom he was to appear, if necessary, before the Committee of Trade and Plantations.[82]   Late in December the council informed Pagan of the account which they were sending to the Lords of the Treasury of the fees formerly allowed the secretary of the province for ordinary licenses and for other perquisites, such as fees for entering and clearing ships, gratuity from county clerks known as secretary's fees; they also complained that the power to collect these fees had been altered and vested in the governor, who employed proper officers for those purposes.[83]

Another person who caused great annoyance was Edward Randolph, surveyor of customs. The people felt that he was oppressing and abusing them under color of his office by impressing their servants, boats, and horses without pay. It did not increase his popularity that he was suspected of disloyalty to the crown because of associating with papists and malcontents, who drank "to the man who should have his mare again before May day next," by which obscure expression was signified the return of James II. So tense grew the situation that Lawrence was summoned to appear before the council to answer charges of high crimes and misdemeanors, was arrested and suspended from the council and even from his office of public notary.[84]   Randolph was also arrested for seditious speeches and reports tending to alienate the subjects of Maryland. The Lords of the Committee of Trade and Plantations declared on September 15, 1693, that they had no grounds on which to dismiss Lawrence, who was to return his answers to the charges and await Their Majesties' pleasure.   Meanwhile he must be freed and

[82] This letter was dated Oct. 22, 1692.—*Archives of Maryland*, VIII, 420-21. His is another name variously spelled: Paggin, Pagin, Pannant. Lawrence had understood that he was to have all the funds enjoyed by the secretary of Lord Baltimore under the old Proprietary régime. The assembly had diverted part of these funds to the governor for governmental costs, which left little for the secretary. That official thereupon made up the deficiency by dismissing a number of the old clerks, substituting his minor son and others of his adherents, allowing assistants to do the work, and by offering to other clerks reappointment on condition of dividing their salaries with him.—Andrews, *Founding of Maryland*, pp. 332-33.

[83] The ordinary in colonial usage meant an inn for the conduct of which a license was required. For the letter of Dec. 21, 1692, about the account sent to the Lords of the Treasury, see *Archives of Maryland*, 1687/8-1693, VIII, 435.

[84] *Ibid.*, pp. 482-83. In all, the council brought thirteen charges against the secretary, which Pagan was directed to take to the Committee on Trade and Plantations.—*Ibid.*, pp. 500, 510-11.

restored to office.[85]   Pagan's commission as agent was repealed in 1694; he seems to have been given a formal commission as purchasing agent in 1697. On April 30, 1697, when he was summoned to appear before the Board of Trade, he declared that he was not authorized to act as agent for Maryland, but did give certain information desired by the Board.[86]   Only by July 21, 1698, does the council in Maryland seem aware that Pagan had given up the agency for purchase of arms.   On that day it authorized a letter acknowledging his letter (date not given) to the governor, in which he stated that his business was so pressing that he had committed the affairs of Maryland, i.e., the purchasing of arms, to a Mr. Isaac Milner, a London merchant.   They expressed their pleasure that he had chosen a person "so worthy and discreet."   The general tenor of this letter shows clearly that the commission must have been largely concerned with the purchase of arms and payment of bills from money placed in his hands, and that it is thereby further distinguished from the regular agency.   The records show Mr. Milner functioning as purchasing agent, especially for arms, at least as late as January, 1698/9.[87]

Possibly the strangest instance of a person discharging some of the duties of an agent and thus serving as one of the group to lay the groundwork for the later agency was Sir Thomas Lawrence—the same Secretary Lawrence who had been hated by the lower house and removed from office.   Yet his offer of services during a later visit to England was accepted by all branches of the legislature, for the record of the Journal of the Lords of Trade of July 4, 1695, cannot be denied: "That the said Sr Thomas Lawrence is at

---

[85] *Ibid.*, pp. 564-65.

[86] *Laws of Maryland at Large*, 1694, Chapter XVII; *Archives of Maryland*, XXXVIII, 5-6; C. O. 391/10, p. 92.   He stated that none of the Maryland acts had been approved since 1692; and that there was no duty upon the importation of any European commodity into Maryland.

[87] *Archives of Maryland*, XXIII, 462.   There is a problem concerned with the name of Pagan's successor; in the letter just cited, he is referred to first as Mr. Isaac and later as Mr. Milner.   As subsequent references are to Mr. Isaac Milner, the variation is to be attributed to carelessness of a clerk.   The usual variations in spelling occur: Millner, Miller, etc.

For evidence that Milner was acting in January, 1699, see *Calendar of State Papers, Colonial*, 1699, sec. 597.   In the year 1695 some members of the lower house thought that *if an agent were appointed* to make known the danger threatening Maryland, she would not be asked to aid in the defense of New York.   See Journals of the House of Assembly, May 15, 17, Oct. 10, 1695, *Archives of Maryland*, XIX, 182, 247.

present authorized by the Govern^r Councill and Afsembly of that Province to solicite the Publick affairs of that Province here in England." He was not long in arriving in England, despite having been captured by the French on the voyage over: sailing some time after October 18, 1694, he was in London before February 13, 1694/5, as by that date the attorney general had examined him about land grants in Maryland. On April 27, 1695, he presented to the Lords of Trade such proceedings of the assembly as he had managed to save from the enemy. Entries of July 25, October 30, November 25, show him presenting memorials and appearing before that same board to solicit their approval of several laws. At least twice he reported to the governor much in the manner of later agents.[88] Again in 1698, obliged to return to England because of his health, he was approved on May 9 as the colony's agent. A few days later one Captain Richard Hill, who had offered to wait on the Board, was ordered to attend the Board of Trade in case of Sir Thomas Lawrence's illness.[89]

Governor Nicholson reveals clearly that the colony had not yet reached the point of creating a real agency, for he writes to the Lords Commissioners of Trade and Plantations on May 28, 1698: "With the Council's advice I laid before the Delegates some paragraphs of your letter of 17 November, but they have very undutifully not answered your directions concerning an Agent. Still we thought it our duty as far as in us lay to comply with your commands, and have desired Sir Thomas Lawrence, the Secretary, to represent to the King the full state, both ecclesiastical and civil, of the Province." As in Virginia, the agent at this early period was more particularly the representative of the governor and council; this particular agent was appointed, to judge by a long letter from the Maryland council to the Lords Commissioners of Trade and Plantations, to look after

---

[88] See *Calendar of State Papers, Colonial,* 1693-1696, secs. 1789, 1415, 1676, 1937 (in text as in C. O. 391/8, p. 13), 1977, 2108, 2156. On October 30 he was trying to get the one penny per pound on the side trade of tobacco of Pennsylvania to be granted for maintenance of Protestant divines for that colony. See secs. 2117, 2151; *Archives of Maryland,* XIX, 90, 99.

[89] There is no evidence that Hill ever appeared for Lawrence. Also there is no proof that William Frisby, who was appointed on May 15, 1695, to join Lawrence in soliciting for Maryland ever did so. For the appointment see *Archives of Maryland,* XIX, 182. He was a member of the lower house of assembly. For appearances of the agent before the Board of Trade, see *Calendar of State Papers, Colonial,* 1697-1698, secs. 435, 517, 518.

the interests of the Protestants. Lawrence served at least until the close of that year.[90]

The genesis period in Maryland produced, as has been shown, five agents—Leonard Strong, John Coode and Kenelm Chesledyne, sent over together, Peter Pagan, and Sir Thomas Lawrence. The first died on his mission without having accomplished anything. Since Lord Baltimore did not receive back his proprietorship at the hands of William and Mary, Coode and Chesledyne would seem to have justified the Revolution, and so their mission may be counted a success; on the other hand, Pagan's services were probably not to be recognized as any marked success, as Secretary Lawrence, whose activities had probably been the special incentive for the appointment, was freed and restored to office by the Lords of the Committee of Trade and Plantations; and Sir Thomas served acceptably along the lines of the regular agent.

North Carolina is the only one of the other Southern colonies which furnished an important chapter to the story of the genesis of the agency. Agents were dispatched from the northern section of Carolina, by 1676-1677. Even then there was ill-feeling among the people over taxes and trade restrictions. Some fifteen years after the first settlement, when a considerable number of planters had opened lands on the Albemarle and the crop of tobacco had become important, the crown officers tried to collect duties on tobacco shipped from Albemarle to New England, a fact which aroused great opposition in the colony. The settlers demanded freedom from taxes on tobacco and expressed their loathing of the navigation laws. Rebellion was in the very air. In this tense situation the assembly removed from office and arrested Acting Governor Jenkins even though the council supported him. Agents from both factions were soon on their way to London to appeal to the proprietors.

Details, rather sordid, are needed for grasping the situation which led to the sending of these first agents from North Carolina. Apparently bad blood existed between Jenkins, acting governor and president of the council, and a certain Thomas Miller who was an apothecary of some standing, though a heavy drinker. Possibly con-

[90] *Ibid.*, 1697-1698, secs. 435, 453, 517; for the long letter of the Maryland council see sec. 518, iv; he was apparently before the Board for the first time July 20, 1698.— *Ibid.*, sec. 680; *Archives of Maryland*, XXIII, 488.

spiring with John Culpeper, former surveyor general of North Carolina, the acting governor in 1676 charged Miller with uttering treason against the king and the monarchy and with the help of the council had him arrested, put in irons, and imprisoned. Then by applying directly or by using his influence, he had Governor Berkeley issue a mandate for removing Miller to Virginia for trial. Any such action the assembly at Albemarle refused to countenance and proceeded to hear evidence. Jenkins himself was charged with misdemeanor partly because of his treatment of Miller and partly because of his complacency toward custom duties on tobacco. The assembly removed him from office and imprisoned him, even though he was sustained by a majority of the council. Meanwhile Miller, carried to Virginia, was acquitted by Governor Berkeley, whereupon he brought action for damages against Culpeper and in May sailed for London to put his case before the Privy Council. He was bearer from the assembly to the proprietors of a remonstrance which had been adopted the preceding November and likewise of an address adopted in March concerning the deposition of Jenkins, on which issue the legislators sought instructions.[91]

About the same time Thomas Eastchurch, speaker of the assembly, also sailed for London to carry an appeal of his own from the courts to the proprietors. The writer cannot be positive whether he also acted as agent for the colony[92] to lay the remonstrances of the people before the proprietors, though it is likely. He had had a case in one of the courts, over which Captain John Willoughby presided, in which the decision went against him. When he proposed to appeal to the proprietors, Willoughby denied the appeal, declaring his court to be "the court of courts."[93]

[91] Ashe, *History of North Carolina*, I, 115, 118-19, 120; *Colonial Records of North Carolina*, I, 269, 314. The dates of the two addresses were Nov. 17 and Mar. 28.—*Ibid.*, p. 228.

[92] Hawks, *History of North Carolina*, II, 468; Moore, *History of North Carolina*, I, 22; Williamson, *History of North Carolina*, I, 126. All these writers definitely say that he had gone over as the agent of the colony, but I find no evidence in the *Colonial Records*, while there is a clear statement that Miller delivered documents from the assembly (I, 228). However, it is probably true that Eastchurch acted as spokesman for a faction and certainly as speaker was listened to by the proprietors.

[93] Willoughby was said to have been a great tyrant. For his oppression he was cited before the Palatine's court, but he beat the officer of that court, and refused to attend; then he was held in contempt and outlawed, and a price put on his head by the succeeding assembly. He thereupon fled to Virginia where he remained until the government of Albemarle became unsettled.—Ashe, *op. cit.*, I, 119.

The proprietors at once took the whole matter into consideration. Fearing to lose their colony by their muddling in governing it, they assured the assembly of the northern portion that they would never part with their county of Albemarle and would preserve for the settlers their British rights. After talking with Speaker East-church and Thomas Miller, who had brought the letters from the assembly, they were satisfied that the fault lay not in the assembly but in those persons to whom the proprietors had committed the government. They thus formally approved the action of the assembly in removing Jenkins. Finding that Mr. Eastchurch was not merely a gentleman of very good family but related to Treasurer Clifford, serving as one of the Lords of Trade, that he was speaker of the assembly and deeply interested in the prosperity of the colony, the proprietors commissioned him on November 21, 1676, governor of the Albemarle colony.[94] They flattered themselves with the hope that in him they had found a man on whom they could rely to carry out their instructions and wishes. Miller was named secretary of the colony and made a councillor as deputy of one of the proprietors. He was also made first collector of the customs. The colony was thus inadvertently thrown into his hands to be used for revenge on his enemies.[95]

The newly appointed officials, sailing at the beginning of the next year, stopped at the West Indies where Eastchurch tarried to woo the lady of his choice but prudently sped Miller on his way to act as deputy governor until his arrival. Miller's landing in July seems to have started the tiny colony of fourteen hundred on a two-year period of civil turmoil, so that a faction refused to receive East-church as governor when he arrived a year later.[96]

The rebels carried on two years of successful revolt with Miller, Timothy Biggs, deputy collector of customs, and several other deputies confined in log-houses, ten feet square. Then the citizens, in

[94] The above is based on a letter from the proprietors to the government and assembly of Albemarle, dated October 21, 1676.—*Calendar of State Papers, Colonial, 1675-1676*, pp. 472-73. They refer Miller's complaints to the council and assembly and desire to see justice done.

[95] Hawks, *op. cit.*, II, 468. Miller was made deputy of Lord Shaftesbury, and the eight deputies made up the colonial council.—Chalmers, *Political Annals*, p. 533. Durant warned the proprietors against their appointments, and declared that there was trouble ahead.—Arnett, *The Story of North Carolina*, p. 87.

[96] Chalmers, *op. cit.*, p. 533; Williamson, *op. cit.*, I, 127-32; *Colonial Records of North Carolina*, I, 278, 296.

order to forestall punishment, determined to convene the assembly
for the purpose of sending commissioners to England to seek restoration of the government to the proprietors; but in order to convince
them that the colonists had been holding it from zeal for the true
owners and not for their own benefit, the agents were instructed to
enlarge on Miller's tyranny and to seek his punishment. These
agents may have been John Culpeper and George Durant, one of
the most influential men in the colony. At least they seem to have
been together shortly afterward in London.[97] It was said that one
of the commissioners went over promptly, as a revolutionary furnished the funds,[98] and that the other, George Durant, was to sail
in the *Carolina*. Meanwhile, more than a year later, Timothy Biggs,
one of the prisoners, and Miller later managed to escape from Albemarle and hastened to England.[99] The Miller faction told their tale
in vain. The proprietors, refusing the proposals of the warlike Biggs,
sought to coöperate with the agents of the people, accepting their
assurance that they had no intention of opposing legitimate authority.
On this basis they strove to establish law and order at Albemarle on a
surer footing. It was believed that the presence of a proprietor
would give the government dignity and perhaps allay the internal
factional dissensions. Accordingly, they proposed to send over Seth
Sothel, who had purchased the share of the deceased Lord Clarendon
and stood well with the other proprietors. Durant and his associates,
perhaps regarding this as an easy solution of the problem, promised
for the people the utmost submission to Sothel as governor.[100] It is
obvious that all these were agents of factions.

The third agency in North Carolina, while not properly engaged

[97] Chalmers gives these agents as Culpeper and Holden (*op. cit.*, Book I, p. 536),
but Ashe correctly points out that Holden, when he stopped in Boston on his return to
Virginia, wrote to the commissioners of customs, mentioning that he had never seen Culpeper.—Ashe, *op. cit.*, I, 128. The reason which actuates the author to think it may
have been Culpeper is that at a session of the Commissioners of Plantations, of December,
1679, his name is tentatively entered for further examination.—*Calendar of State Papers,
Colonial,* 1677-1680, sec. 1246. Williamson says Culpeper was sent.—*Op. cit.*, I, 133.

[98] Williamson, *op. cit.*, I, 129-33; *Colonial Records of North Carolina,* I, 283.

[99] There seems to be confusion on this point among the historians of North Carolina.
Williamson and Chalmers speak as if Miller escaped at this time to England; Ashe shows
that he escaped from a fresh arrest in 1679.—*Op. cit.*, I, 132. A deposition of Miller
taken in England on January 31, 1679/80 is definite proof that he was in England.—
Colonial Records of North Carolina, I, 278-83.

[100] Ashe, *op. cit.*, I, 131. Culpeper was tried for treason but was acquitted.—Williamson, *op. cit.*, I, 133.

on a religious mission, was concerned with the question of religion. In South Carolina, adherence to the Anglican church had been required for membership in the lower house of assembly partly through the efforts of Lord Granville, palatine of Carolina. In the north province, however, the Quakers were settled in large numbers. The British law of 1704, enacted not long after Queen Anne's accession as administered by Deputy Governor Daniel, requiring oath of allegiance to the sovereign from all members of the provincial legislature, the council, and judges, did not mark the beginning of religious friction in the Carolinas. Though an effort to establish the Church of England in the Albemarle section of Carolina would be the signal for combined opposition from the great part of the people, Daniel by his skilful political manipulation, secured passage of a law to that effect. The southern colony resolved to send an agent to England to complain against the trickery by which the Anglican church had been established there; with this group the people of the Albemarle settlement made common cause and dispatched a fellow agent to add the story of their grievances to that of the southern colony. That agent was Edmund Porter, who was not unnaturally a Quaker. He turned for aid to the proprietor, John Archdale, a co-religionist, lodging his complaint against the man whom Sir Nathaniel Johnson had sent as his deputy to Albemarle. He won an order from the proprietors to Johnson to appoint another governor over the northern colony.

Unfortunately this order did not immediately bring religious freedom. Thomas Cary, sent to Albemarle in 1705, was deputy governor during the latter part of Edmund Porter's agency in England. Cary proceeded the next year to enforce the existing law strictly, refusing to allow the Quakers to "affirm" as had been formerly allowed. By thus excluding Quakers he secured a majority which would sustain his measures in the assembly. He then succeeded in having passed an act imposing a fine on any person who should assume office before taking the oath and another declaring void election of any one who promoted his own candidacy. These acts bound the legislature hand and foot.[101] The situation so in-

[101] Ashe (*op. cit.*, I, 160-61) fails to mention Edmund Porter. One of the few books which speak of Edmund Porter is Hawks, *op. cit.*, II, 508. For the British Statute of 1704 see *Statutes of the Realm*, I Anne, chapter 16. Cf. *Biographical History of North Carolina*, II, 371.

flamed the dissenters, especially the Quakers, who would take no oath whatsoever, that they sent John Porter, father of the previous agent, to England in 1706 with fresh grievances and complaints against Sir Nathaniel Johnson and his deputy, Governor Cary. Arriving at the opportune moment, when attention was focused on Carolina affairs by the agitation of John Ash and Joseph Boone, he could hardly fail. By his clever management, and with the help of John Archdale, ex-governor and Quaker proprietor, Porter secured suspension of the laws imposing oaths, suspension of Sir Nathaniel Johnson's power in that province, removal of Deputy Governor Cary, and the superseding of several deputies appointed by the proprietors by new ones with power to choose a president from among themselves. It should be recalled that the deputies of the proprietors constituted the council. Perhaps the cleverest move was having himself and some other Quakers made deputies. With these significant gains, he arrived home in Carolina in October, 1707. In the interests of historical accuracy it must be added that Cary's removal was probably owing to the fact that he had created a disturbance in enforcing the oath. The proprietors were not especially displeased with Cary, but he was rigid and had offended the dissenters—Presbyterians as well as Quakers.[102]

The fifth instance of the use of an agent in this colony concerns the mission of Arthur Goffe, Edmund Porter, and Nathaniel Duckenfield, who were chosen about November 12, 1725. This action must have had a connection with some dispute between Governor George Burrington and some officials supported by the proprietors. In a letter of April 12, 1726, from the assembly to Governor Burrington after he had been removed, the members alluded to a rumor, "tho' Notoriously false," that Burrington's alleged intent of causing a revolution had led the proprietors to supersede him in so much haste. Accordingly, the assembly selected the three men just mentioned as the agents to reveal to the proprietors the underhand practices which underlay that situation and to give a just account of Burrington's faithful discharge of duty. To strengthen his cause they spoke of his zeal in promoting the welfare of the province, especially

---

[102] Raper, *North Carolina*, p. 11; Hawks, *op. cit.*, II, 509; Ashe, *op. cit.*, pp. 163-64; *Colonial Records of North Carolina*, I, 709-10. The remainder of this story is more properly told in the section which deals with South Carolina.

of that "Cape Fair portion, which is like to become a strong Barrier & Security from any Attempts hereafter on our Southern Settlements."[103]   Likewise on November 12, 1725, the lower house protested to the proprietors their happiness under proprietary rule despite the sudden change and arbitrary proceedings of some of the officers and their intention to preserve peace until the state of the province is laid before the proprietors by their three agents.   There seems, however, to have been a faction in the house unfavorable to Governor Burrington which brought about a prorogation about November 12, "unwarrantable" in the eyes of the majority of the chamber.[104]   The new governor, who seemed to nurse a certain spite against Arthur Goffe, vulnerable by virtue of his office of receiver general, suggested to the council that, since Goffe had departed for Great Britain without leave from the executive and the council, the office be declared vacant.   He nominated, accordingly, a William Little for the post, a suggestion approved by the council.   A delicious bit of irony was the addition that if approved by the proprietors, the new incumbent might "allow Goffe the same amount as his Deptys should have done."[105]

The earliest of the North Carolina agents may be said to have scored a success in 1677.   Certainly the treatment accorded by the proprietors to Thomas Miller, emissary of the assembly, in making him secretary of the colony and in addition a member of the colonial council by naming him deputy of one of the proprietors, and also the treatment by the government in constituting him first collector of the customs for this region would argue not only personal success, but success also for the cause which he was sent to represent. Durant's mission was followed by appointment of a proprietor for governor—whether or not a direct consequence is not clear; Edmund Porter in 1704 secured an order suspending Governor Daniel; and John Porter in 1707 secured the order to remove Governor Cary as well as the vesting of the government in the president of the council and the appointment of new deputies for some of the proprietors —actions which proclaim these agencies successful.   Due credit must be granted John Porter, for he was a skilful negotiator and sought

[103] *Colonial Records of North Carolina*, II, 577-78, 619.   It was revealed at a later date that Governor Burrington proposed Porter and Goffe himself for the agency, but seemed to dislike Duckenfield.—*Ibid.*, III, 508.

[104] *Ibid.*, II, 578.   [105] *Ibid.*, pp. 603-4.

and secured powerful aid in Archdale. When it is recalled that the deputies constituted the council in the colony, and when it is recorded that John Porter and several other Quakers were among these new appointees, and that Porter himself carried the instrument which ordered Cary home to give an account of his conduct, Porter's success seems complete. The commission borne by Porter for settling the government suspended the laws imposing oaths, the very issue which had brought about the agency, and vested the power of Governor Cary in the president of the council to be chosen by that body, of which Porter was one.

In what is now South Carolina the first agent appears in 1703. John Ash was sent to England, from the southern portion of the Carolinas to protest against the tyrannical proprietary government but especially against Governor Nathaniel Johnson's bill to proscribe dissenters by requiring every member of the assembly to take a prescribed oath and to conform to the Church of England. The fact that Deputy Governor Moore, interregnum executive, was an Anglican had been quite sufficient to arouse the jealousy of the dissenters, who had hoped that their party would be continued in power by the selection of one Morton. It should be recalled that by mere chance dissenters had been in control of the government in the southern section ever since 1692. This conformity law, therefore, constituted the first real test of strength between Anglicans and dissenters, and when the latter lost, they refused to yield without a struggle. As these nonconformists, constituting a large and powerful body—said to be about two-thirds of the population—were being subjected to greater hardships than Englishmen in England, they raised a great outcry against injustice, some threatening to abandon the colony. Even conformists were discontented with the law. The inhabitants of Colleton County, which was settled mostly by dissenters,[106] met in 1703 and drew up a state of their "grievous circumstances," praying the proprietors for redress. If necessary, their grievances were to be laid before the royal government. Associated with them were two landgraves and deputies of proprietors, Colonel Joseph Moreton and Edmund Bellinger, all the representatives in the lower house from Colleton County, and several men of

[106] Hewatt, *An Historical Account of the Rise and Progress of the Colonies of South Carolina and Georgia*, I, 147-48.

the highest reputation in Berkeley County—over 150 in all.[107] The petition, dated June 26, 1703, was addressed to Palatine John Granville and the other proprietors. John Ash, one of the most zealous dissenters and a member of the lower house for Colleton County, was prevailed on to embark for England as agent.[108] Fearing that the opposing faction would do its utmost to prevent his obtaining a passage in any ship belonging to Carolina, he hurried to another port. Only with the greatest difficulty did he get away from Carolina to Virginia, passing through Albemarle on his way, where he induced Edmund Porter, as already stated, to accompany him on a similar mission for the northern province. While in Virginia, powers and instructions were conveyed to him before he set sail for England shortly after July 25, 1703.[109] It is notable that no allusion to actual religious oppression appears in the statement of grievances.

After his arrival Ash waited on Lord Granville to acquaint him with the purpose of his mission but was received coldly. That nobleman was too interested in supporting the church establishment in the Carolinas to lend a favorable ear to dissenters on any mission. Ash gave the proprietors all the information in his possession relating to public affairs but gained nothing but Lord Granville's promise that he would have his secretary write to the governor an account of the grievances complained of and require an answer. Despairing of success, he drew up a representation of the case and had printed two

[107] In the riot in the streets of Charleston brought about by opposition to the bill for regulating elections in the Commons House, John Ash and Joseph Boone were fearfully beaten. It might also be noted that the family of Boone lived in Colleton County.—Rivers, *A Sketch of the History of South Carolina*, pp. 202-3, 206. See also Moore, *op. cit.*, I, 29; Oldmixon, *The History of Carolina*, in Carroll, *Collections*, II, 430-31.

[108] Opinions of Ash differ so that it seems wise not to attempt an appraisal. Hawks calls him "an influential and highly respected gentleman" (*op. cit.*, II, 508), while Salley says that he had heretofore "played no conspicuous part in the province" (*Narratives of Early South Carolina*, p. 268). The comment of Archdale can hardly be regarded as unprejudiced: ". . . their first agent seem'd not a Person suitably qualified to Represent their State here, not that he wanted Wit but Temper, which is a necessary Qualification in Persons in that Employ."—*A New Description of that Fertile and Pleasant Province of Carolina*, in Carroll, *Collections*, II, 112. For the petition presented by Ash to the proprietors, June 26, 1703, see Rivers, *op. cit.*, App., pp. 453-60.

[109] Landgrave Smith wrote Ash while still in Virginia on June 30, 1703, and again on July 25 reflecting sharply on the conduct of the lower house of assembly. These letters fell into the hands of Governor Johnson on the death of Ash. On the reconvening of the South Carolina assembly on October 5, 1703, he laid them before the lower house in order to abuse Smith and others who appeared to be opposing the governor.—Oldmixon, *History of Carolina*, in Carroll, *Collections*, II, 431; McCrady, *South Carolina under the Proprietary Government, 1670-1719*, p. 413.

sheets but died before he was able to complete it. By improper means his papers fell into the hands of his enemies.[110] He was not privileged to see his purpose effected in the resolution of the peers and in the action of the queen, as it was some three years later.

Joseph Boone enjoyed not only the distinction of being the second agent to be sent from South Carolina but also the greater distinction of being sent several times. His first mission, like that of Ash, was to secure greater religious freedom. Spurred to fresh efforts by passage of the religious law in November, 1704, the South Carolina dissenters[111] proposed to send an application to the House of Lords praying their intercession with Her Majesty for their relief. A petition to this effect was drawn up and carried over in 1705 by Joseph Boone, a merchant engaged in the trade with England, who had apparently been living in South Carolina since about 1694. A rigid dissenter, Boone found on his arrival in England about May, 1705, that he had not left behind him in Carolina the passions and excitement evoked by a religious controversy but on the contrary had but come to its source, where it was raging with even greater violence. Contemporaneously with the enactment of the Church Act in Carolina, of which he was complaining, the British House of Commons, strongly Tory, had been making a renewed effort to pass the occasional conformity bill.[112] In the midst of the heat engendered between the two houses of parliament this first parliament of Anne expired by limitation. It was in the midst of the elections for the new House of Commons that Boone arrived in London in the spring of 1705.

As the palatine, Lord Granville, was a violent partisan of the colonial statute, Boone failed, of course, to get relief from the proprietors. He solicited the palatine seven weeks before he could even prevail on him to have a meeting of the board of proprietors called. It was no easy matter to get a meeting of that body in quiet times to transact the ordinary business of the colony. Naturally, it

[110] He entitled his paper *The Present State of Affairs in Carolina*. It is published in Salley, *op. cit.*, pp. 269-76. This is the only original document of the affair, naturally a partisan account. In addition, see Hawks, *op. cit.*, II, 508.

[111] It is interesting that the dissenters considered transporting their families to Pennsylvania to settle under Penn's indulgent government.—Hewatt, *op. cit.*, p. 151.

[112] This bill had passed its second reading, and the Commons, knowing that it would be rejected by the House of Lords, tacked it on to a tax bill. The Lords then rejected this bill as well as its tack, the occasional conformity bill.—McCrady, *op. cit.*, p. 426.

was much more difficult at a time of political turmoil, especially when the avowed purpose was to present a protest against a measure warmly aproved, if not indeed suggested, by the palatine himself. Indeed when Archdale, one of the proprietors, opposed ratifying the bill against dissenters, the palatine was very short with him. When Boone prayed to be heard by counsel, he received a very brusque reply: "What business has council here? It is a prudential act in me; and I will do as I see fit. I see no harm at all in this bill, and I am resolved to pass it."[113]

Boone turned then to the House of Lords, still the stronghold of the Whigs. Several London merchants, convinced of illegality in the passage of the Carolina laws and of their pernicious effect on trade, joined Boone's petition to the Lords. To it were subscribed some of the most distinguished names in England, among others those of the poet Prior and of such leading merchants as Micajah Perry, Joseph Paice, and Christopher Fowler.[114] The petition recounted events in the colony, representing them as in contravention of the toleration provided in the charter and in the *Fundamental Constitutions*. With great adroitness Boone laid special stress upon the interference with the jurisdiction of the Bishop of London. He pointed out that the dissenters had petitioned the proprietors but without success. The reader can hardly help feeling that this was a curious document to have presented to parliament by a Puritan and Roundhead in behalf of those who had left England because of the Stuarts and the reëstablishment of the church there. After the petition was read in the House of Lords and the lord palatine heard by his counsel a week later, the Whig House of Lords on March 12, 1706, declared after "having fully and maturely weighed the nature of the two acts" of South Carolina, they found the act to set up a lay board illegal and the act requiring the oath of the members of the lower house and conformity to the rites of the Church of England repugnant to the laws of England and to the charter. They went so far as to declare the latter act an encouragement to atheism and irreligion, destructive to trade, and as tending "to the depopulation and ruin of the province."[115] They voted an address to the

[113] Carroll, *Collections*, II, 436.
[114] The petition is printed in Rivers, *op. cit.*, App., pp. 461-63. A fairly full paraphrase of the memorial is to be found in McCrady, *op. cit.*, 431-42.
[115] Carroll, *Collections*, I, 154-55.

queen praying for the abolition of the lay board and annulment of the act excluding dissenters from the assembly.

The Board of Trade, to which the address was referred by one of the secretaries of state, eagerly listened to Boone as opening a way to annulment of the proprietors' charter and promptly commissioned the attorney general and solicitor general to consider the acts in question. These officials declared the acts not warranted by the charter; held that the power granted the proprietors had been abused and merited forfeiture. The queen ordered the law officers to inform themselves as to the procedure by *quo warranto* against the charter. On June 13 an order in council directed the proprietors to declare the acts null and void. The Board of Trade also was eager to have the charter annulled. A final difficulty arose when it was revealed that only four of the proprietors had consented to the acts. The two law officials presenting the case reported to a Privy Council on June 26 the lack of sufficient evidence to carry on the prosecution to the end; suggested, in fact, that these proceedings might be derogatory to the privileges of the peers, as nearly all the proprietors were of the peerage. Hence, no action against the charter was taken, but the queen on June 10, 1706, declared the two acts of the South Carolina assembly void.[116]

Boone took advantage of the death of Lord Granville, who had been a staunch supporter of the governor, to press charges before the proprietors just before leaving England against Sir Nathaniel Johnson, charging him with being responsible for the chaos in both the civil and the religious interests of the province, and for the threatened danger of loss of the province to the French and Spanish by his unwise treatment of the Indians. Boone was assisted in this issue by Archdale, the Quakers, and the former governor, the Quakers having sent complaints to England by a special agent from North Carolina. Johnson turned to the assembly for vindication, begging them to summon Mr. Boone before them and to demand proof of the charges he had made at such a distance from the colony that there had been no opportunity for prompt refutation.[117] Boone, however, refused to heed the summons, claiming exemption by virtue

[116] McCrady, *op. cit.*, pp. 434-37; Rivers, *op. cit.*, pp. 223-25; *Acts of the Privy Council, Colonial*, II, 506-7.
[117] Snowden, *History of South Carolina*, I, 148.

of his appointment by Madame Blake as deputy for the infant proprietor Blake. When the other deputies refused to recognize him, he left town to evade the messenger of the house sent to marshal him before that body. The assembly rallied strongly to the governor's defense, stigmatizing in a long complimentary address Boone's accusations as "false and scurrilous" and charging him with contempt.[118]

Finally the South Carolina assembly passed an act on November 30, 1706, to repeal all laws in regard to the church and enacted a new law for the establishment of religion according to the Anglican church, with no reference to a lay commission or to a religious test for office-holders. Thus the church controversy was settled, and a few years of quiet ensued for the province.[119]

In South Carolina, as in Virginia, we see the trend to dispatch men to England to settle problems in the daughter colony. Boone scored a genuine success, for he had secured the coöperation of the British merchants dealing with the provinces, as has been recounted earlier; it was in all likelihood their petition to the House of Lords that led that body to address the queen, pointing out the illegality of the proceedings at Charleston and leading the Privy Council to declare the church legislation of Governor Johnson null and void. It was a tribute to the liberality of the churchmen of the time, but may also have been a tribute to Boone's adroitness that the church dignitaries expressed strong disapproval of the measures by which the Anglican church party in South Carolina had tried to carry through their political purposes. Boone's appointment as a deputy for an infant proprietor by the child's mother was a purely personal triumph, for the other deputies denied him recognition.

Last to be created of these Southern colonies, Georgia was naturally the last to return an agent of any sort to the mother country. Thomas Stephens Jr. emerges about 1742 as the first representative of an agent for Georgia. It appears that as early as 1740 and 1741 Stephens, son of the president of the governing board in Georgia, was acting as solicitor before parliament in behalf of a

---

[118] *Ibid.*, p. 247. The Commons drafted questions with which to confront Boone, such as (1) Did he own to the petition? (2) When he was in England, how came he to know that this province was in great danger of falling into the hands of the French and Spanish by the ill administration of the Governor?—McCrady, *op. cit.*, p. 467.

[119] Smith, *South Carolina as a Royal Province, 1719-1776*, p. 11; *Statutes at Large of South Carolina*, II, 281-84.

group of men discontented with the conduct of affairs in that colony in order to secure parliamentary inquiry into the bad state of affairs in Georgia. The complete misunderstanding between father and son and the poignancy of the grief of the father over what was to him disloyalty to the government on the part of his son touches the reader as keenly as if the entries in his diary had been made yesterday. The son returned suddenly from England, arriving in Savannah late in September, 1741, to the father's great surprise. The younger man had embraced the view that the colony was lost unless the restrictions on slaves and on the holding of land were removed. The poor old father complained of his son's associates and had begged the latter not to keep company with them; and the son had promised not to see them. The father could not, of course, with his inflexibility of mind understand how the son could consort with his father's open opponents. As early as June 28, 1740, the father knew that a paper was secretly circulating in "Charles Town" full of complaints against the rulers and inferior magistrates. Perhaps nothing in the *Journal* is more pathetic than the father's entry of September 28, 1741, that he could not allow his son to sleep under the same roof. He was so far led astray, "as to have a Conceit that he was labouring to uphold the Colony," but the father knew that "the Trustees needed no Assistance from such as he advised with."[120] Just prior to October 14, 1741, Stephens junior had the "honour," as his father sarcastically records, to be chosen agent in a formal election of a group of some twenty-eight persons, who also selected five men to correspond with him, thus creating Georgia's first Committee of Correspondence. The new agent was authorized to act "discretionally, to conduce to those several Grievances being redress'd," and to give "an Account from Time to Time of his Proceedings to his elect Correspondents here." The faction collected a sum of money to defray his expenses, which the father sadly records, "to his utter Shame he took," but the amount of which the father could not learn, though no contribution under half a crown was accepted, "which very few among them could well spare," three or four only of the leaders being able to give on the scale of

[120] *Colonial Records of the State of Georgia*, IV, 576-77, 606; Supplement, pp. 251, 252, 260. On October 6 he charged his son with aiding the design at Charles Town to put Georgia and South Carolina under the same rule.—*Ibid.*, p. 256.

pounds.[121]   Upon meeting "this hopeful Agent" unexpectedly on October 14, the father begged him with tears in his eyes to flee in order to avoid arrest as disturber of the colony and as agent of the enemy.   On October 28 the son came for a farewell visit and to read to his father the paper he was carrying over in order to prove to him its inoffensiveness, but the father declined to hear it. They parted coldly but with wet eyes.[122]

The Earl of Egmont records for us accommodatingly the date of Stephens' arrival in England as just before February 9, 1742.[123] By March 26 he had gone to the office of the Privy Council to let the clerk know that he was preparing a petition to the king against the Trustees.[124]   By April his activities were sufficiently disquieting to the Board of Trustees so that a meeting had to be called for April 27 to consider the authority under which he "pretends" to act as agent for the people of Georgia.   The Board on April 27 and 30 agreed to an answer to Stephens' petition to the Privy Council. It was arranged that Mr. Digby, one of the Trustees who was also a member of parliament, should rise and complain to the House of Commons of a virulent libel against the Trustees printed by Stephens, handed by him to various members, and signed by him under the character of agent.   Mr. Digby, however, seems to have discharged his duty so "calmly and indifferently" that no one paid the least attention.   Then a Mr. Cary, taking his cue, presented a petition in Mr. Stephens' name and moved its reference to a private committee.   The son of the Earl of Egmont opposed this disposition of the petition on the ground that only prejudiced members would attend and so bring in a partial report; he held that inquiry into the state of affairs in Georgia was a serious matter, meriting the attention of the entire house.[125]   In a fortnight the matter accord-

---

[121] *Ibid.*, p. 268.   Two of the group had voted for some one else for agent.   The *Journal* even meticulously records the names of Georgia's first Committee of Correspondence: John Lyndell, Thomas Ormston, William Woodroffe, William Ewen, and Peter Morrell.— *Ibid.*, pp. 263-64, 268, 274-75.

[122] *Ibid.*, pp. 264, 274-75.

[123] "This day Mr Verelts acquainted me. . . . That Tho. Stephens arrived in the same ship."—*Colonial Records of Georgia*, V, 594, 9th February, 1741/2.   Egmont was the first president of the Board of Trustees, one of the most earnest and active supporters of the Georgia movement.   He was a scholar, a patriot, and a philanthropist, as deeply sympathetic with the unfortunate debtors who crowded the jails of England as Oglethorpe himself.—Prefatory Note, *ibid.*, V.

[124] *Ibid.*, p. 611.   [125] *Ibid.*, pp. 614, 615-16.

ingly came before the Commons. Mr. Stephens' evidence made so great an impression that there was a disposition to take the colony out of the hands of the Trustees, but not to drop the matter without action. Members also thought that the magistrates had acted tyrannically, and that the Trustees had not received correct information. The evidence, in the opinion of the Earl of Egmont's son, bespattered Governor Oglethorpe and tended to show a decline of the population of the colony from 4,000 to 500 or at most 1,000.[126] Meanwhile on April 1, Stephens' petition to the king in council had been referred to the Committee for Plantation Affairs and a copy of the petition sent to the Georgia Trustees for their answer to the charges, which they sent in on May 3. The Trustees were heard by counsel on June 15 and evidently made good their defense, for on June 30 Thomas Stephens, Jr., was brought to the bar. On his knees he was obliged to receive the severe reprimand of the speaker before being discharged upon payment of his fee.[127]

Second in Georgia's list of embryo agents stands Edmund Gray. The year before the Trustees gave up their charter, they decided to test out the Georgians with a little more self-government. Conscious that the king would acquire Georgia in 1753, and that if they surrendered it without the slightest vestiges of self-government, they might be seeming to give their approval to an autocratic type of government, they called an assembly at Savannah in 1751, in which all towns and groups of families numbering ten members were to be represented. It was given no authority to pass laws, but only to make reports on conditions in the various parts of the colony, to offer suggestions to the Trustees, and to debate. This assembly expressed itself on several matters, two of considerable importance: the need for a renewal of their charter in order to prevent South Carolina from annexing the colony, and the desire of the people for the right to make their own laws. Though the Trustees did not accept all the recommendations, they allowed the assembly to meet again in 1752.[128]

[126] *Ibid.*, p. 619. We owe this account of this session of parliament to the son of the Earl of Egmont who reported it to the Earl.

[127] *Ibid.*, pp. 632, 641; Coulter, *A Short History of Georgia*, p. 64. It might have been some small comfort to Stephens, if he could have known it, that the charges for defending themselves against his complaints cost the Georgia Trustees £177/13s/6d.— *Colonial Records of Georgia*, V, 625.

[128] Coulter, *op. cit.*, pp. 72-73.

But the answer of the Trustees to the recommendation of this first assembly that the people be given the right to make by-laws gave great offense and uneasiness as to the future government and is thought to have been the cause of a determination to send an agent to England. The president and council wrote to the secretary of the Trustees that this measure was effected against their best efforts by the artifice of two or three men of the assembly and contrary to the wishes of most of the inhabitants. This agent selected proved to be Mr. Edmund Gray of Augusta, who was speaker of the assembly and had been living in the colony about eighteen months. The council professed surprise at this choice, for little was known of him beyond the fact that he had been born in Virginia and that he had practiced law there.[129]

Gray, nevertheless, took passage in the *Defiance*, scheduled to sail April 21, 1752, but not actually lifting anchor until April 29. By July 21 he had reached England and laid a memorial before the Commissioners of Trade and Plantations. Oddly enough, his first petition was not concerned with the civil establishment but was directed against the incorporation of Georgia with South Carolina. He pointed out that the assembly of the latter acknowledged the usefulness of a buffer state and had instructed their agent to oppose the union of the two as serving no useful purpose for either, but on the contrary as affording an opportunity for the French and Spanish to stir up the Indians against any alterations of boundaries.[130] When, however, he was summoned to appear before the Board of Trade on December 19, 1752, the subject under consideration was the plan of government for what was soon to be a royal colony. He was assured that though the board objected to several of the regulations proposed by him, there was no objection to the plan in general. He was also assured that a government for Georgia would soon be established on a plan granting as generous civil liberties and "privileges" to the people as in any of the colonies under the king's immediate government. The following day the Board of Trade sent a representation to the king that his subjects in Georgia

[129] The council, while sympathetic to the Trustees, regretted that the latter had not granted the Georgia assembly the right to make bylaws unless disallowed by the Trustees, as it would have given general satisfaction, whereas now all actions by the Trustees were called in question.—C. O. 5/373.

[130] *Colonial Records of Georgia*, XXVI, 353-54.

were uneasy because they had not yet received a plan of government and that lack of a permanent establishment deterred many people from settling in the colony and thus discouraged its development.[131]

With Benjamin Martyn we encounter the first person for Georgia who for ten years under royal rule discharged some of the duties of a regular provincial agent. The Georgia Trustees, recognizing the necessity of having an agent to take care of and transact matters concerning the colony in England and to carry on the correspondence with the government of Georgia, turned naturally to the man who had served the Trustees ably and faithfully since the day their charter was granted and was better acquainted with the affairs of the colony than any other person in England. They, therefore, on December 14, 1751, recommended him to the Lords of the Treasury; on January 8, 1753, to the Privy Council, and on February 11, to the Board of Trade.[132] The Board of Trade, accordingly, "reposing especial confidence in his integrity and capacity," because of his long experience as secretary of the Board of Trustees appointed him agent for Georgia on February 14, 1753. Yet in the very instrument appointing him to the agency occur phrases which show that it is a hybrid office, part provincial but part crown. He should also "receive the Monies that shall from time to time be judged proper to be issued to such Agent for this Service"; and the commission was issued "By the King's command."[133] Furthermore, his instructions emanated from the king and smacked strongly of a crown office: "You are therefore diligently and carefully to discharge your Duty as such by taking care of the said affairs, well husbanding the Expenses you shall be intrusted with, and rendering regular accounts thereof, and by keeping proper Correspondence and making Representations from time to time to the Commissioners of the Treasury or Our Commissioners for Trade and Plantations of your Proceedings herein and of all such Matters as you shall judge necefsary toward rendering effectual Our

[131] C. O. 5/672, pp. 6-7.

[132] *Colonial Records of Georgia*, I, 570; C. O. 5/373. In the recommendation to the Board of Trade occurs a phrase which shows clearly that they were thinking of him also as a provincial agent. They recommend him as agent for the colony "during their Inability to maintain one, especially as they know it will be highly satisfactory and encouraging to the colony, to have that Person continual, for whom They have often exprefsed a particular regard."—Journals of the Board of Trade, C. O. 5/375.

[133] This commission was found among the Board of Trade papers, C. O. 324/60, pp. 301-2.

Royal Intentions and Purposes."[134]   Finally, his salary was paid by the British government, the amount evidently being fixed by the Lords of the Treasury.[135]   That the appointment was in general acceptable to the colony may be inferred from the satisfaction expressed by Ottolenghe, the director of the silk culture, in September, 1753.[136]

With the appointment on December 12, 1761, of William Knox, member of the Georgia council and provost marshal, to assist Benjamin Martyn, and with the creation of a Committee of Correspondence to direct him, the period of genesis in Georgia was drawing to a close.   The record for the early agents of Georgia presents a complete failure for Thomas Stephens in the severe rebuke administered him by the House of Commons and success for Edmund Gray, though the determination of the government to give Georgia equal rights with other crown colonies was perfectly natural.   He may have expedited the civil government for that colony.

[134] The instructions bear the same date as the commission.—C. O. 324/60, p. 302.

[135] In the recommendation of the Board of Trade to the Treasury, Dec. 20, 1752, they say, "with such allowance as your Lordships shall think adequate to the nature and Businefs of that office."—C. O. 5/672, p. 13.

[136] Sept. 11, 1753: "I esteem it a Happiness to Georgia in General, & to me in Particular, yt ye Affairs of this Colony are to pass thro' ye Hands of her undoubted and sincere Friend, and real good Wisher to her Prosperity."—Colonial Records of Georgia, XXVI, 422.

CHAPTER 2.

THE DEVELOPMENT OF THE REGULAR AGENCY

T HE ATTITUDE of the home government toward the regular colonial agent was a matter not only of interest but of the first importance to the success of the agencies.

The initiative for appointment of such an official as a part of the governmental machinery came not from the colonies but from the British government and at an almost incredibly early date. Sometime between 1655 and 1660,[1] during the Commonwealth period it will be noted, Thomas Povey, secretary and later member of the Committee for America appointed in 1757, entered in a letter to the governor and council of Virginia the following: "Soe that seeing the good and advantage of yor Collonies from time to time so many wais concern'd by what maybee done or omitted here in England, we cannot but mind you that yor Interest leads you to putt yor Affaires, which relate hither into such a posture and method that you may have the more comfortable account of them hereafter, wch wee conceive cannot bee done with any advantage to yo^{rs} unless you doe recomend them to the care, kindnefs, and consultacon of some select Persons heere; of good reputation, who may from time to time meete, and advise, and act therein as occasion shall require. And because such as are Merchants, or Planters are not proper of themselves to prosecute and solicit such businefs, as not being versed in the waies and addrefses thereunto and not sufficiently at Leisure to give this attendance wch we find necefsary to matters of that nature. We doe conceive it to be absolutely requisite that some person of known trust, Interest, and abilitie may be intrufteed, and impowered, and owned by you as yor Counselle and publick Agent, with whom you are continually to correspond at large, and who re-

[1] The exact date of the entry does not appear, but the Letter Book covers the years 1655-1660.

ports Such Results, as shall arise from your Counsells or the advice of yor ffriends here, may move in your behalfe, for the preventing of such evils as may at anytime arise in yor Concernments, or the removing, or easing such as are upon you, or answering for you when by Suggestions or misreports . . . anything shall bee stirr'd against you in this Court, or for the obtaining any priviledges, afsistance or advantage wch may be necefsary to yor preservation, or improvement."[2]   And then followed intimation that in the opinion of the members of the Committee Thomas Povey might be such a suitable person.

Since most of the colonies did not take to heart the hint given Virginia so early, the Commissioners of Trade and Plantations, as the body created in 1696 was called, recurred to the subject on October 5, 1697, in a general direction: "Upon occafion of this want of Agents authorized by the respective Colonies, with whom to Consult about Virginia, Maryland, and New Yorke; Ordered that in the next Letters to be writ by the Board to the Governours of thefe respective Colonies, it be intimated to them that Barbadoes[3] and other places have Agents constituted there by Acts of thofe general Afsemblies, and that their want of having fuch Agents is an inconvenience in this present occafion, and may happen in some Occafions to prove prejudicial to them, by delays in their publick Affaires, and lofs of Opportunities for their respective advantages."[4]

Only a few months later the Board sought to impress the necessity for an agent on Governor Bellomont and through him on New York. "There is one thing very ufefull practifed by some of his Majesty's Plantations; which is to have some persons constantly refiding here as Agents, whom we may call upon for further information, as may be requisite upon occasion. The want thereof has occafioned Delays in publick affaires. . . ."[5]

As late as 1768 Lord Hillsborough, Secretary of State for the

[2] Povey's Letter Book, B. M. 11, 411, pp. 19-20. For an account of Povey see Andrews, *British Committees, Commissions, and Councils of Trade and Plantations*, pp. 51-53.

[3] Barbados and the sugar islands had agents very early. See Penson, *The Colonial Agents of the British West Indies*, Chapter III.

[4] Journal of the Board of Trade, C. O. 391/10, pp. 310-11. That this admonition had some effect on Maryland is apparent, for the council sent down a copy of the paragraph to the lower house on March 24, 1702.

[5] C. O. 5/1079, no. 11. This letter was dated Feb. 23, 1697/8.

Colonies, recommended to North Carolina appointment of an agent as "the Affairs of N° Carolina must, in some degree, necessarily suffer delay and disappointment for want of a regular Agent here duly authorized to act in every case in which the interests of the Colony may be concerned."[6]

But the reaction of the Board of Trade was distinctly unfavorable to the creation in 1702 by the lower house of assembly of an agent of their own; the governor appeared the proper avenue for transmission of communications from the colony. Sustaining this view, the council declared on May 21, 1702, "That we humbly conceive it would prove of very ill consequence in the government of Yo^r Ma:^{tys} Plantations, if Countenance should be given to this Manner of Applycacon And that the Councills and Afsemblys, should thereby be encouraged to make representations to Yo^r Ma:^{ty} by particular Agents of their own Appointment, without the Governor's Consent; Except only when those Representations containe matter of Complaint againft the Governor for Mal-Administration, or that he refuse to represent what they Desire."[7] In all except the charter colonies, dissension arose between the governor and council on the one side and the lower house on the other over the appointment of agents. Because this resulted for some of the colonies in long deadlocks, the offices in England became increasingly irritated until they even challenged the desirability of the agency system. The Board of Trade on November 29, 1765, wrote very sharply to Governor Tryon of North Carolina, but the shaft was probably directed at most of the colonies. "The Irregularity in the mode of appointing Agents in all the Colonies has been long a Subject of complaint and difficulty in the Administration of the Affairs of the Colonies in this Kingdom; and if the Assembly should in their next Session not admit a proper Number of the Council to be the Committee of Correspondence, . . . We shall consider what step it may be proper for His Majesty to take."[8]

Indeed, to the end of the colonial period the home government consistently objected to the payment of an agent unless he had been

[6] This was written at a time of serious dissension in the state over appointment of an agent.—*Colonial Records of North Carolina*, VII, 868. He specifically stipulated that the agent be appointed by a "Law of Governor, Council, and Assembly."

[7] C. O. 5/1312, pt. 2, f. 496.

[8] *Colonial Records of North Carolina*, VII, 132-33.

appointed by all branches of the legislature and forbade governors to assent to the pay of an agent not so appointed. But it was on the very eve of the Revolution and to that prince of agents, Benjamin Franklin, that the British government's complete annoyance with the agency system manifested itself. In an official report to the Georgia Commons House of Assembly, Franklin stated that he had waited on Secretary Hillsborough to deliver its address to the king only to find that the answer had already been transmitted to the governor of that colony, as he was the channel of communication chosen by Lord Hillsborough, "who seems to think Agents unnecessary (perhaps troublesome) and says all applications from the Colonies to Government here ought to be thro' the hands of the Respective Governors, and thro' the same hands The Assemblies should receive the Answers." And then he added, "But I apprehend America, will in many Cases find this new Mode inconvenient and perhaps not readily come into it."[9] We learn that the answer had indeed been so returned through Governor Wright, who reported back that the king disapproved transmission through any other channel than the governorship as irregular and disrespectful and furthermore disapproved the address itself as challenging the authority of parliament. Another governor, Horatio Sharpe, also gave Maryland to understand that the assembly should send petitions to the king through the proprietor or his deputy, as other modes of transmission were held "disrespectful to the crown."[10]

To trace the story of the regular provincial agency through each of the colonies will probably prove tedious, recording in most of them much the same tiresome quarrels between governor and assembly or between council and lower house. But a correct understanding of the problems of the agency, since they differed greatly in details,

[9] *Colonial Records of Georgia*, XV, 26-27.

[10] *Ibid.*, p. 34; Flippin, "The Royal Government in Georgia, 1752-1776," *Georgia Historical Quarterly*, VIII, 119-20. For Maryland see C. O. 5/1301, pp. 3-4.

On one occasion, possibly because it touched a matter in which Hillsborough was interested, he was disposed to be more friendly toward agents. On June 6, 1772, he wrote to Governor Dunmore in Virginia: "I am very happy to find that the House of Burgesses concur in the Ideas concerning a Copper Coinage contained in my letter No. 4, and as I should be glad to see a Measure of so much Advantage to the Colony carried into Execution as speedily as may be, I hope they have not failed to appoint some proper person to solicit this Business in the different offices through which it must pass; for my part I will give every facility that depends upon me in order to the acceleration of it."—C. O. 5/1375, p. 172.

seems to require this procedure, as did the account of the genesis of the agency. Maryland, despite the prolonged struggle from 1725 to 1774, never had what might be considered a fully recognized colonial agent, while Georgia had only two fully accredited agents. Yet in every one of the five Southern colonies there was staged a serious conflict over the agency question.

The date of the regular agency in Virginia is usually placed in 1680.[11] In all the Southern colonies considerable latitude has to be allowed in fixing the date which marks the beginning of the regular agency as distinguished from earlier missions. In general, the criteria which might fairly be applied are (1) selection for a fixed term, (2) a fixed salary, (3) continuity in office. The author may perhaps be charged with arbitrariness in selection of her dates, for she has occasionally disregarded the element of continuity and at times even the element of a fixed term. Where an agent is chosen formally by one of the legislative bodies for a given term at a set salary, the formal agency has in her opinion been created, even though it may afterwards have been allowed to lapse for a considerable period.

At a council meeting held in Virginia on July 8, 1680, it was held absolutely necessary for the colony that an "able and discreet person" be chosen to reside near the court, to report speedily to the governor, and to solicit and take care of all things necessary in England. The council therefore unanimously decided that the governor should choose some person for the post, at a salary of one hundred pounds a year.[12] The name of the agent so chosen and those of his successors for a decade do not appear in the records. It would seem that from 1680 for some years an agent must have been regularly appointed by the governor[13] and that until 1759, except for special

[11] The author is accepting this date as the beginning of the regular agency, not because it is conventional to do so, for there are decided gaps after that date when there was no recorded agent, but because agents and officials writing at an early period declare that there had been agents regularly after that date. Most important of all, however, is the fact that an agency was formally created at that date with a regular annual salary, though not, it will be noted, with a fixed term.

[12] *Executive Journals of the Council*, I, 8.

[13] In 1703 and 1704 in connection with complaints against the governor, Colonel Nicholson, the issue of where the appointment of the agent lay was raised. The current agent, Thrale, asserted that since 1674 or 1675 (he probably meant 1680) the council had never tried to nominate the agent, but left that prerogative to the governor "without the consent of the Council, or any other body of men in this Country, though he goes under the character of the Agent for Virginia." Colonel Ludwell in due course on May 17, 1704, replied heatedly that no "Councill could for ever give away the right of naming the agent,

agents to be discussed in the next chapter, the person known as the Virginia agent really represented mainly the governor and council. Until that date a single agent sufficed, but beginning with that year, because of the jealousy between them each of the two legislative branches employed an agent. The first regular agent whom the writer has been able to identify is Jeffrey Jeffreys, an Englishman, who was selected in 1691 to present the congratulatory address of Virginia to the new sovereigns, William and Mary. Chosen as a special agent, he still was charged with general duties which partook of the nature of a regular agent: with presenting a petition for confirmation and enlargement of the charter which should include the Northern Neck, with making efforts for improving the defenses of the country, and with conducting negotiations regarding the three pence a pound duty on tobacco.[14] On May 22, 1691, when the assembly thanked him for his good offices in procuring a favorable answer to their petition to the Commons about the tobacco duty, it asked him to be the solicitor or agent for "all the colony's business in England which might arise from time to time." Members of the assembly tried to encourage him in continuing in office by declaring their confidence that any inhabitants of Virginia resident in England would help him, and bespoke his aid for the Reverend Mr. James Blair in procuring a grant for a college. If he foresaw any difficulty, he was to secure counsel of a competent lawyer, and the assistance of men of note and quality influential at Whitehall.[15] The writer finds no evidence that Jeffreys was serving after January 7, 1693.[16]

It is clear that the agency had been allowed to lapse by 1698, for

whatever they might do upon a particular occasion." The six of the council, for whom Ludwell spoke, hoped that the Board of Trade would inquire into the matter so that the agent should be "the Countrey's Agent, and not ye Govs[rs], as Mr. Thrale now is, and that the Country may have the assistance of their Agent against the Govern[r] himself when ever there shall be occasion to complain of him."—C. O. 5/1314, Bundle 5, p. 2, Bundle 16, Bundle 17.

[14] *Journals of the House of Burgesses*, 1659-1693, p. 372. The first hint we have of a task with regard to the tobacco duty laid on the agents is on May 22, 1691.—*Calendar of State Papers, Colonial*, 1689-1692, sec. 1516.

[15] *Ibid.* The agency of the Reverend Mr. Blair is discussed with the other special agencies in Chapter III.

For his instructions of May 22, 1691, see Bruce, *Institutional History of Virginia*, II, 520-21; *Calendar of State Papers, Colonial*, 1689-1692, sec. 1516.

[16] A petition of "Jeoffreys" was considered on that date by the Board of Trade.—C. O. 5/1358, p. 216; *Calendar of State Papers, Colonial*, 1693-1696, sec. 7.

on February 23 of that year, Lord Shrewsbury of the home government was urging the need of such an office. His communication, forwarded by the governor of Virginia to the council on June 1, was referred to the next council; though the issue was raised repeatedly by the governor, it was as repeatedly deferred.[17] A reminder by the governor on October 24, 1698, brought action by the council in the appointment of William Byrd II, who served presumably for a year and a quarter.[18]

John Povey, a secretary of the Privy Council, followed immediately on the heels of Byrd, according to the warrants for his salary, entering upon his services the day Byrd ceased to function, June 24, 1699, and continuing for almost four years, until April 24, 1703.[19] But on October 27 preceding, a letter had arrived from Povey, recommending for his place Mr. John Thrale, who was accordingly appointed by the governor since there were no objections to him.[20] Already by January 27, 1702/3, the Board of Trade had received information of the new appointment. Thrale's agency ended with his death, which occurred sometime before December 16, 1704, for on that date Governor Nicholson informed the council of Virginia of the vacancy, and offered himself for the post. The council could not have regarded this proposition favorably, as the governor reported to the Board of Trade on January 2, 1705/6, that he had not appointed any one after Thrale's death.[21]

[17] Shrewsbury's letter was first presented to the council on June 1, 1698, and referred to the next council; on August 18 it was referred to the next assembly; on September 29 the council declined action; on October 5 it was referred to the next day, and on October 7 referred to the next council.—*Executive Journals of the Council*, I, 384-85, 387, 388, 389, 390.

[18] *Ibid.*, p. 394. The statement in the text as to the length of his agency is based on a record of payment of salary for that period on June 24, 1699, to the "solicitor of Virginia" £125 sterling—solicitor obviously referring to Byrd.—*Ibid.*, p. 461. The other agencies of Byrd must be regarded as special missions and must, therefore, be dealt with in the chapter devoted to that subject.

[19] The warrants for payment of the salary of the solicitor of Virginia affairs appear regularly from December 24, 1699, each six months to April 24, 1703.—*Ibid.*, II, 34, 138, 208, 276, 317.

John Povey is not to be confused with Thomas Povey, prominent merchant and secretary of the Committee for America about 1657, and pioneer in colonial administration.—Jacobsen, *William Blathwayt, passim.*

[20] *Executive Journals of the Council*, II, 278. It is spelled Thrails here.

[21] Nicholson declared that for his own part he had no occasion for an agent, but if the Queen or the Board of Trade found one necessary, he desired the nomination, "wch he takes to be best for her Matys interest & Service."—*Ibid.*, p. 419. Nicholson appeared before the Board on January 2, 1705/6, apparently negotiating the Virginia affairs informally

Hence there was another gap in the agency until the arrival of Governor Nott, who proposed Colonel Nathaniel Blakiston on August 16, 1705. A man who had served acceptably as governor of Maryland and still more recently as agent for Maryland, could hardly fail of unanimous acceptance by the council.[22] This marked the beginning of one of the longer agencies in Virginia history, for the incumbent served continuously from December 4, 1705, when he first appeared before the Board of Trade to signify his appointment to act for Virginia, until after May 6, 1721.[23]

When the death of Blakiston after sixteen years' service in July, 1721, left the post vacant, the session of the legislature of May, 1722, was faced with the question of a successor. An added impetus for the selection of an agent at that time was the fact that South Carolina had appointed an agent to solicit approval of a recent act regulating the Indian trade. Two candidates were proposed on June 23, both natives of Virginia and both then residents of England—the almost ubiquitous William Byrd II and John Carter. Governor Spotswood professed indifference as to the choice, and the majority of the council voted for Carter, a barrister of the Middle Temple, whose agency accordingly dates from June 23, 1722.[24]

But almost immediately the council had to choose a successor to Carter, for he had by September 27, 1722, obtained the appointment of secretary of Virginia and soon returned to his native land.

after his return to England. He stated that he had been informed that Mr. Wilcocks had acted as solicitor, but since the writer finds no official confirmation, he does not appear in her list of Virginia agents.—*Journal of the Board of Trade*, Apr. 1704-Feb. 1708/9, p. 201.

[22] Governor Nicholson in his controversy with Virginia had sent Dionysius Wright and Secretary Jennings to England to report on affairs to the Board of Trade. The latter took various public papers with him, copies of the laws, journals, etc. The governor advanced £100 from the public fund toward Jennings' expenses, and £60 to Wright, which he hoped the Board of Trade would allow. But they are clearly personal agents for the governor.—C. O. 5/1313, pp. 219-21; C. O. 5/1314, No. 42; C. O. 5/1361, p. 117, Entry Book. For Blakiston's appointment see *Executive Journals of the Council*, III, 27; also the governor's letter of notification to the Board of Trade, C. O. 5/1314, Bundle 66. Some modern authorities have accepted "Jenings" as the approved spelling of this name. Most of his contemporaries seem to spell it "Jennings." Even when it appears as a signature the form varies. See *Executive Journals of the Council*, I, 452, where both spellings occur on the same page.

[23] His semi-annual payments may be traced through the entire period in the *Executive Journals of the Council*.

[24] *Ibid.*, IV, 19. In a letter to the Board of Trade Governor Spotswood reveals a rather curious circumstance. Upon consulting every member of the council, he found the general trend was for Byrd, but the vote proved to be for Carter.—C. O. 5/1319, p. 78.

The governor therefore on April 1, 1723, read applications in behalf of the three persons, William Byrd, a Mr. Langley, and Peter Leheup, who had long acted as agent for New York. The last-named, despite the fact that Langley had been recommended by Lord Orkney upon the death of Blakiston, was selected by the council, possibly because he had already been employed in case of Carter's absence to solicit for Virginia in the matter of the quitrents of the newly erected counties in the western part of the colony. This employment constituted in the opinion of the councillors an obligation to continue him.[25]

Continuity in office now prevailed at last, but by March, 1754, the long agency of Leheup came to an end, as he had so provoked the frowns of the ministry as to render himself of no further service to the colony. James Abercromby became his successor. The governor on June 24, 1754, read a letter from Abercromby, advising the council of Leheup's resignation, and requesting appointment to the post. The council promptly complied, satisfied that he was a gentleman of integrity and ability.[26]

In order to preclude confusion it must be added that Abercromby had already been employed as agent on a special mission by both houses on April 20, 1752, to present an address of condolence to the king for both council and burgesses and that a special lump sum had been voted him for that particular piece of solicitation. He had, therefore, at that time served as a special agent, but of the type which might properly be designated provincial agent. He then became agent for the council alone, but still the only agent for Virginia for five years.[27]

Then began the period when the House of Burgesses, annoyed over the failure of the agent of the council properly to support certain contentions of the burgesses, insisted on having an agent of their own. Their dissatisfaction with the existing situation had been brewing for some years, especially after the dispute with Governor Dinwiddie over the pistole fee to be later explained. The burgesses

[25] *Ibid.*, p. 30. On December 12, 1722, the council had sent orders, as soon as it knew of Carter's impending return, to turn over their instructions to Micajah Perry, to be delivered, in case Mr. Carter had departed without turning over the business to some one, to Peter Leheup with the request that he would solicit the Virginia affairs.—*Ibid.*, p. 28.

[26] C. O. 5/1329, p. 353.

[27] *Ibid.*, p. 1093; *Journals of the House of Burgesses*, 1752-1758, p. 103.

lamented the lack of an agent to represent them in matters of this sort, supposing naturally that Abercromby, who was paid by the governor and council, would solicit no action against the governor, and so sent home a special agent, as explained later,[28] at great expense. It may be that the strenuous exertions to make good the drain in both men and money occasioned by the war then in progress with the French and Indians was a factor in the desire for an agent, though it found no specific expression. Above all, the burgesses wanted an official to represent the grievances of the *people* and to justify their conduct to the king and parliament. From that time they were intent on sending an agent who should represent Virginia as a whole, but could not obtain one while Dinwiddie was governor. In 1755 a bill was introduced providing for the appointment of an agent, but evidently the measure was thought inopportune by the house itself for it defeated the measure.[29] In the session of 1756 the house did pass a bill providing for the appointment of an agent in the naming of whom they should have a part and over whom they should have control; but Governor Dinwiddie thought affairs properly cared for under Abercromby and assured the council, a majority of whom were with him, that he would refuse his assent.[30] Two more futile gestures were made in the spring and fall sessions of 1758 by sending up such a bill to the council, but the council objected on the ground that the measure was introducing a power unknown to the constitution, was striking at the prerogative of the crown, and would take exclusive power from the governor, the king's representative. It thus forced the dropping of the bill. The assembly even tried to tack the provision to a money bill in 1758, but the new governor, Fauquier, declared he would certainly refuse them an agent under such conditions.[31]

[28] This entire issue is discussed in Chapter III.

[29] *Ibid.*, p. 314. The governor's comment is natural for the time: "They [the assembly] behav'd with much Insolence, endeavour'g to form a secret Committee and to choose an Agent at Home; y't on the whole I tho't it for H. M'j's Service and the Peace of y's Colony to dissolve them and take my Chance of a new Election; w'ch I hope will be better than the former; and come with Spirit to serve their Co'try."—Dinwiddie, *Official Records*, in Virginia Historical Society *Collections*, II, 277.

[30] It would appear in a letter of Governor Dinwiddie to Abercromby of May 24, 1756, that the person whom the house had in mind was Edmund Jennings, former secretary of state of Maryland.—*Ibid.*, pp. 419, 437.

[31] *Journals of the House of Burgesses*, 1752-1758, p. 501; *ibid.*, 1758-1761, pp. 34, 288-89; *Legislative Journals of the Council*, III, 1196. For a statement of the attitude

But the time was approaching when the insistence of the burgesses would brook no further denial; on March 27, 1759, the assembly passed a bill by "Governor, Council, and Burgesses," providing for an agent "to solicit and properly represent the affairs of
this colony" in Great Britain and appointed Edward Montague such
agent after vesting in the majority of the Committee of Correspondence, created by the same act and composed of members from both
houses, the power to remove and replace the agent.[32] Governor
Fauquier rather shrewdly tried to secure selection of Abercromby,
who would then be representing both branches of the legislature,
but so strong was the feeling of the burgesses because the agent
had opposed them in the matter of the pistole fee that they would
have "anyone but him."[33] Fauquier at first refused his assent to
the act but was persuaded by Peter Randolph and other leaders to
yield. He finally expressed himself as unable to see any ill consequence from letting them have an agent, since they raised the money
"on themselves" to pay him. Of course, Abercromby still continued
as agent for the governor and council.[34]

It was feared by the house that the act might be vetoed by the
crown; accordingly the agent was directed not to show the act until
it had been transmitted in the usual way by the governor to the
Board of Trade. The agent was then to use every effort to prevent
the rejection of the act. When the act came before the Privy Council
in 1760,[35] that body ordered the governor to inform the assembly

of the council see letter of Richard Corbin to Abercromby, of Oct. 21, 1758.—C. O. 5/1329,
p. 367.

[32] *Legislative Journals of the Council*, III, 1210, 1220; Hening, *Statutes*, VII, 276-77.

[33] Fauquier had evidently had Blair, president of the council, sound out the members of
the lower house on Abercromby. See letter of Blair to Abercromby, dated May 30, 1759.—
C. O. 5/1329, p. 373. His argument that Abercromby would serve the house as effectually
as the council, fell on deaf ears.

[34] Osgood, *The American Colonies in the Eighteenth Century*, p. 236; Governor
Fauquier to the Board of Trade, Sept. 1, 1760, *Journals of the House of Burgesses*, 1758-
1761, App. pp. 288-89.

[35] The opinion of the attorney general of the crown is found in the Treasury Board
papers, I/389, No. 30. The opinion of Lamb, attorney for the Board of Trade, seems
liberal at a time when the lower houses of assembly were proving distinctly annoying in
many of the colonies. He said: "But as the Legislature have thought fit by this Act to
appoint an Agent for the Province, I have no objection thereto in that Respect, as they
have the same Right so to do, as the other Provinces have, and which they have usually
done, provided the same was consistent with, and did preserve the Powers that belong
to the different Branches of the Legislature." But he did think that the act should not
be confirmed because of the manner and power of removal of the agent.—C. O. 5/1329,

that it could not be approved unless amended, as it held the law loosely drawn and the powers of the Committee of Correspondence too great. Rather than lose their agent, the burgesses agreed to an alteration, not, indeed, providing for any change during the term of Montague, but requiring approval of his successor by the governor and providing that the agent could act only until the next session of the general assembly.[36] The act was to be in force seven years.

In justification for the action of the lower house it must be added that their desire was entirely natural and well sustained. It is rather odd that Virginia should for so long have been content with an agent representing the governor and small upper house, and the burgesses had a point in their claim that an agent speaking for the entire colony must carry more weight than one representing only a part—and that the smaller part. The interests of the two branches of the legislature might well differ and call forth different instructions, and in the case of an agent for the council only leave the body of the people "without the shadow of a representative."[37] Control of the pay of the agent meant here, as elsewhere, control of the actions of the agent.

Some adjustment of the relations between the two agents now became necessary. Abercromby, disappointed and resentful that the House of Burgesses had not seen fit to make him its agent,[38] was also sincerely disturbed as to the distribution of duties between the two. In June he was disturbed because the act did not recognize in any way his agency for the council, and he wondered undoubtedly whether he would be allowed to complete the several matters with which he was then concerned, which had already cost him "much

---

pp. 407-9. The Board of Trade recommended a new bill omitting the clause vesting power of removal and appointment in the Committee of Correspondence.—C. O. 5/1367, p. 409.

[36] In a letter to Montague of November 5, 1760, the Committee of Correspondence declared that it was never the intent of the act to deprive any branch of the legislature of a concurrent power in the appointment of an agent.—"Proceedings of the Virginia Committee of Correspondence," *Virginia Magazine of History and Biography*, XI, 13. The Board thought that "General Assembly" should be used rather than "Assembly."

[37] See the reasons for the desire for a separate agent as voiced by a subcommittee of the Committee of Correspondence, *ibid.*, X, 342; also the statement of the Committee of Correspondence to Montague, *ibid.*, pp. 244-45.

[38] Abercromby sent a long paper to Councillor Corbin under date of June 24, 1759, arguing against the legality of the act giving the lower assembly control of the agent, which he held the governor had done by giving his assent to the bill.—Abercromby Letter Book, p. 152. In similar strain he wrote the Board of Trade on November 21, 1759. —C. O. 5/1329, pp. 344, 346.

trouble and more expense."[39] During the period of adjustment Abercromby tried to take no other steps than those absolutely neces- sary, but he justified them by pointing out the strange dilemma in which Virginia would have found herself if he had not "adhered to conduct of affairs." If he had not acted, "Ministerial Measures for national Purposes and for the Good of the whole, must have stood still for Want of some Body to appear for Virginia."[40]

Since the agency for the lower house had been created in the midst of the efforts to secure reimbursement to the colonies for their expenses in the colonial wars, naturally that issue loomed large in the adjustment of duties between the two agents. November 5, 1760, the Committee of Correspondence notified Montague that he was to consider himself the agent of Virginia and to allow no interference in the work of his office; it would appear that Abercromby had ap- proached Montague to sign a paper recognizing the former as pro- vincial agent. When the latter refused, the Committee upheld his action, although he was allowed to join Abercromby in efforts to win approval of Virginia measures. Suspicion that Abercromby had over- charged for his collection of the reimbursement for the wars led the Committee to direct Montague to learn the rate of commission of the other agents. Abercromby was to cease acting as collecting agent and to turn over the sum he had obtained to Montague.[41]

Montague, receiving his credentials sometime between January 19 and March 9, 1761, began to function. The two men conferred at the invitation of Abercromby as to the division of duties. Aber- cromby wisely declined to attend the Board of Trade with Montague for fear of hindering rather than promoting success. In general they agreed as follows: Abercromby was to continue to handle the

[39] Abercromby Letter Book, p. 157.

[40] Ibid. He adds naively, "I leave it then to the Govr and Council to judge, how much they are indebted to me on their own account and that of the Publick for my Conduct in their Service. I hope I shall meet with a suitable Return."—Ibid. He could not refrain from some aspersions on the man who was appointed as agent for the Assembly. He told the governor that he and the council had been blamed by the administration for throwing affairs into so precarious a channel as that depending on the agency law, which was attended with so many apparent objections, and rendered more precarious from the un- certainty of "a Gentleman in Mr Montague's Situation in Life, taking upon him the Charge and Business. . . ."—Ibid., p. 203. But he later alludes to him as a "Man of Honour and business."—Ibid., May 10, 1769.

[41] "Proceedings of the Virginia Committee of Correspondence," loc. cit., XI, 14, 22, 24, 132, 354.

business respecting royal revenues and all matters of the colony "cognizable" by the governor and council and to coöperate with Montague in legislative matters; he would negotiate matters pertaining to large land grants, military supplies, import and export duties, and appointment of officials; would forward to the governor commissions and all other papers passed on by the Board of Trade. Montague, on the other hand, was to concern himself with matters over which the lower house had control or in which it was especially interested, such as presenting the addresses of the house to the king, negotiating matters of trade and finance, gaining royal assent to the acts of assembly, and attending to the interests of the people in general in their relationship to the policies of the home government.[42] Montague served the house until about February, 1772, when an agency act was rejected, and Abercromby at least until September 1, 1774.[43]

The history of the South Carolina agency follows a devious channel with many turns and obstacles. A clear, connected story is impossible. The first formal act for appointing an agent in Great Britain passed on December 12, 1712. Landgrave Kettleby was appointed the first regular agent to represent the interests of the province before parliament and the proprietors. The author so classifies this agency despite the fact that two of her canons are violated: no term of service was mentioned and no fixed salary provided. Two years later a second act fixed an annual salary but provided not for a fixed term but only for his continuance in office until removal by a vote of the South Carolina Commons House of Assembly. In addition, a committee to instruct and correspond with him was created after the usual type. For simplicity, therefore, the agency will be regarded as beginning with Kettleby's first appointment.[44]

[42] Abercromby Letter Book, entries for May 10, 1760, Mar. 9, 1761; Flippin, *The Royal Government in Virginia, 1624-1775*, pp. 183-84. As late as May 10, 1769, there was a question of jurisdiction.—Abercromby Letter Book, p. 347.

[43] An entry in the *Journals of the House of Burgesses, 1770-1772*, for Feb. 21, 1772, alludes to Montague as the "late" agent for this colony (p. 181). The last entry for payment of salary for Abercromby which the author has been able to find is on Feb. 13, 1774/5.

[44] *Statutes at Large of South Carolina*, II, 159, 621-22. Even in the second law of 1714 there is no fixed term, but continuity is clearly in mind, for the act reads that the Commons House of Assembly shall have power "to appoint and depose the aforesaid agent and his *successors* according to their discretion *forever*." The wording of the law of 1714

Though the instrument creating the office was couched in general terms, the purposes underlying its creation were special and clearly avowed. The Board of Trade in Britain was pressing ever more strongly the enforcement of the navigation laws in the colonies, particularly in the Carolinas, and was alert to any infringement of them as a cause for a forfeiture of the proprietary charter. The principal exports of the colony were rice and naval stores, and these were among the enumerated articles forbidden for export except to England. Bounties, on the other hand, were offered for importation into England of pitch, tar, turpentine, and other naval stores. It was felt a matter of great importance, naturally, to send an agent to England to watch over the colonial interests. Specifically, Kettleby was charged to secure removal of the pressures on trade by application to parliament, to the proprietors of the province, or to any other persons in Great Britain with power to redress the grievance; permission to export rice and naval stores to Spain, Portugal, and all other places in America and Africa; and to secure continuation of the bounty money on pitch, tar, turpentine, and other naval stores exported to Britain from Carolina. So earnest was the assembly for this last concession that the agent was charged not to allow his solicitation for free export of rice to interfere with the bounty on naval stores.[45] Thus by the act of 1712 the policy which prevailed in most of the American colonies of maintaining an agent in London to guard the interests of the province was adopted also in Carolina. The agency thus established became of great consequence in the subsequent history of the province, especially as a precedent during the impending revolution against the proprietors, and indeed also during the entire period of royal rule.

The assembly evidently became doubtful of Kettleby's ability to represent adequately the interests of the inhabitants of Carolina in their contest with the proprietors; it accordingly appointed th same Joseph Boone—who had served as agent for the dissenters

---

indicates the regular character of the post: "Whereas, it is necessary . . . to appoint and establish a fit person residing in Great Britain, in the quality of an Agent, to solicit and transact the publick affairs of this Province. . . ."—*Ibid.*, p. 621. The writer thus agrees with Rivers (*A Sketch of the History of South Carolina*, p. 255) and differs from Snowden (*History of South Carolina*, I, 206-7), who does not regard the agency as existing until after the royal government.

[45] *Statutes of South Carolina*, II, 600-2.

against Governor Johnson in 1706—with Richard Beresford in February, 1715, to deal first with the proprietors, and, in case of failure with them, to appeal to the crown. An anomalous situation now existed in the relations of the colony to the proprietors, to the royal government, and even to their own agents. The formal channel of communication for the proprietors was still the governor and council, but behind this regular medium their lordships were conducting a private correspondence with Chief Justice Trott, who was at odds with the people of Carolina. In equally devious fashion, the governor, council, and assembly had selected Landgrave Kettleby as their regular agent in London to look after the affairs of the colony generally, but they also sent over two special agents to appeal directly to the royal government, in which Deputy Governor Daniel joined, an act which scarcely seemed loyal to the proprietors. Such an anomalous state of affairs was terminated by the dismissal of Kettleby on November 30, 1716, after four years of office, though his salary was to continue to the sixteenth of the ensuing month.[46]

The condition of the province at this time was thoroughly deplorable. In 1715, the war against the Yemasee Indians had just broken out, a war in which the young colony lost four hundred men and incurred a heavy debt for the garrisons. The proprietors must furnish assistance in generous measure if they hoped to retain their charter. With good cause the assembly was doubtful whether the proprietors would be inclined to involve their English estates in debt in order to support property of dubious value they had never seen.[47] While there was dissatisfaction in general with the proprietary rule and a desire for the surrender of the charter to the crown, there was also profound discontent over the powers with which Chief Justice Nicholas Trott had been vested. During his visit to England in 1714 he had been made one of the council without whose presence there could be no quorum. The proprietors were to consult him upon every measure proposed; he had the appointment at will of provost-marshal of courts; his emoluments as chief justice were increased; in a word, Trott was the most important man in the

[46] *Collections of South Carolina Historical Society*, I, 229; Journal of the Commons House of Assembly of South Carolina, V, 187. The assembly seemed fearful of any further obligation to the lawyer Kettleby, as on November 30, 1716, they charged their other agents sent over from America "to consult with him no farther."—C. O. 5/387, f. 34 or p. 12.
[47] Carroll, *Collections*, I, 200; Force, *Tracts*, II, 7.

colony.[48] When Trott arrived in South Carolina so armed with authority, Joseph Boone and Richard Beresford, a member of the Church of England, were sent to England to protest against this extraordinary grant of powers and to obtain from the proprietors some abatement of the objectionable measures, invoking the aid of the crown if necessary. The instructions of the assembly to their agents concluded with a sentence which was prophetic of future developments: "And in case the proprietors do not redress our grievances after all necessary measures have been taken with them, we direct you to apply yourselves to a superior power in order that the same may be redressed."[49]

The Carolina merchants entered heartily into the measure for making application to the Whig upper house of parliament considering it the most effectual expedient for retrieving their fallen credit in England, lost by the dangers of war and by the pirates that infested the coast.

About the middle of the year 1715 the agents waited on the proprietors with a plea for relief. Not satisfied with the answer which they received, they petitioned the House of Commons. The Commons in turn addressed the king for his interposition and immediate aid to the colony. From the king the matter passed to the Commissioners of Trade and Plantations, who raised objections to giving royal aid to a proprietary province. If the crown were to bear the expense of defending it, the government should be vested in the crown. One of the proprietors admitted that the crown would be justified in taking over the colony if the advances of money were not repaid. Hence the agents soon sent back an account that they found a disposition in the king to lend relief, but encountered an indisposition to aid in the defense of a proprietary colony.[50]

Boone, elated by his success with the Board of Trade and the

[48] McCrady, *South Carolina under the Proprietary Government*, pp. 528-29. For a sketch of Chief Justice Trott, see *ibid.*, pp. 368-69.

[49] *Ibid.*, pp. 530-31; Rivers, *op. cit.*, p. 258.

[50] Lord Carteret had written the Board of Trade that the proprietors were unable to give the proper assistance so that, unless the king intervened, the colony would be destroyed. It was in response to a direct query from the Board of Trade whether the government ought not devolve on the crown if the government assumed the burden of defense, that Lord Carteret gave the above reply.—Carroll, *Collections*, I, 201. See the account by Agent Yonge, "A Narrative of the Proceedings, of the People of South Carolina," Force, *Tracts*, II, 7; Rivers, *op. cit.*, pp. 270-74.

House of Lords, presented another petition to the Lords Proprietors, charging the governor with crimes against the political and religious interests of the province. He attacked Chief Justice Trott for corrupting justice, for plural office-holding, for assuming to exercise ecclesiastical authority, and even countenancing riots.[51] The agents presented a petition, dated March, 1717, asking that the palatinate be made a royal colony, a fact which indicates their continued presence in England though Berresford seems to have returned about August, 1717.

In 1719 came the rebellion. The people of South Carolina deposed their lawful governor, Robert Johnson, and his council and proclaimed Colonel James Moore as their governor in order to overthrow the charter and bring the province under the immediate government of the king. Unquestionably they rejoiced at breaking the rule of Speaker Rhett and his brother-in-law, Judge Trott, who they felt had constantly misrepresented them to the home government.

With the overthrow of proprietary rule and establishment of royal rule came another set of agents. Associated with Joseph Boone, whose name seems inevitably to have presented itself when choice was to be made for an important mission, stood Colonel John Barnwell. Joseph Boone was probably still present in London as agent in 1720,[52] but Colonel John Barnwell, who had commanded the first expedition against the Tuscarora Indians of North Carolina

[51] McCrady, op. cit., pp. 550-54. For the petition of 1717 see Rivers, op. cit., appendix, pp. 464-65.

[52] The question whether Boone returned to Carolina between 1716 and 1720 eludes the writer's researches, but a record from the Board of Trade shows that the lower house sent directions to Boone on May 6, 1720.—C. O. 5/358, f. 4.

An entry of Feb. 12, 1720, in the Journal of the Commons House of Assembly is very confusing. The assembly orders a letter or other authentic writing sent to *William* Boone, "one of the agents appointed to transact their affairs," impowering him to act separately without *Rowland Tryon, the other agent* appointed for that purpose, "if Tryon should act disagreeable to the sentiments of the said Mr Boone."—Journal, V, 433-34. Tryon seems to have been a resident of Montserrat in London in July, 1719.—*Journal of the Board of Trade*, 1718-1722, p. 87. Earlier, Aug. 26, 1718, he is recorded as agent for the Leeward Isles (*ibid.*, 1714/15-1718, p. 428) though Penson records no such agent. The only explanation the author can offer is that Tryon, already in England and presumably familiar with the Western world from conversance with the West Indies, was offered the agency and refused it. The only plausible explanation which the author can further suggest is that after Tryon declined the appointment Barnwell was chosen. The entries of the appearance of Boone and Barnwell before the Board of Trade leaves no doubt as to who were actually serving as agents at this time. The statement of *William* Boone was probably the error of a careless clerk.

in 1711, was later dispatched as an additional agent to lay the case of the colonists before the crown. Sixteen months elapsed before the royal decision was known in South Carolina from the letters from the agents, a period of confusion with dual governments in power.[53]

Leaving Carolina in March, 1720, Barnwell arrived in London in time to attend a session of the Board of Trade with his fellow-agent on August 16, 1720. But the Board contented itself with merely asking a few questions about the condition, government, and military strength of both North and South Carolina.[54] A simple comment, slipped in only incidentally, may seem to indicate the outcome of this mission, for the Board of Trade on September 15, 1720, held that "the Government of Carolina being provisionally assumed to the crown, no government derived from the proprietors could interfere," and by January 19, 1720/1 several men of the colony were felicitating Boone on the news of the expected arrival of their new governor, obviously a royal appointee, that month. Still distrustful of the influence of the proprietors, they begged him to follow their every step closely. The selection of regular agents in 1721 makes it logical to assume that this agency ended early in the year.[55]

With the selection of Francis Yonge and John Lloyd as regular agents to solicit the affairs of the province in England with the full panoply of a Committee of Correspondence, we encounter men, especially Francis Yonge, with whom we must long reckon in this account. Indeed, until 1736—when he decided not to return to South Carolina—he steps in and out of the agency story in a bewildering way. The assembly, taking action on September 19, 1721, made the first agency under the royal government a dual agency by selecting Yonge to speak for the council and Lloyd for the lower house. Lloyd departed almost at once, but Yonge was detained by family affairs from sailing until March, 1721/2. Lloyd seems to have returned to South Carolina in the winter of 1722-1723; but with one or two short intermissions, during which the province had

[53] Joseph W. Barnwell, "Dual Governments in South Carolina," *Collections of the South Carolina Historical Society*, V, p. x.

[54] *Journal of the Board of Trade*, Nov., 1718-Dec., 1722, p. 197.

[55] *Ibid.*, p. 209; C. O. 5/387, p. 33. Barnwell returned with Governor Nicholson, May 22, 1721. Strictly speaking, the Boone-Barnwell agency should be entered with the special missions, but it finds its place here in order not to break the continuity of this record and to give clarity to the account.

no agent, Yonge was regularly reëlected till 1727.[56] Elaborate instructions were prepared by the council for Yonge before his first departure.   Upon their arrival in England the two were to attend Lord Carteret, the most amenable of the proprietors, and if the title to the province had not already passed to the crown, they were to represent the problem of settling the frontiers until it had done so.   But, as events were to prove, this problem was not soon solved. The provisional government, which Sir Francis Nicholson was even then inaugurating, was to last seven years, while negotiations between the royal government and the proprietors dragged on so interminably that not even after seven years had the proprietors made a complete surrender, for Lord Carteret refused to join in the surrender.[57]

By 1724 the lower house no longer saw the need of an agent. On June 13, 1724, a committee of the house met one of the council; the house group felt that there was no compulsion for an agent at that time, while the council group felt otherwise. But as the house sustained its committee and maintained its position, despite urging by the governor and the council, the agency lapsed.[58]

By March, 1724/5, the house had returned to the conviction that an agent was necessary and had selected Francis Yonge again. Obviously he had been functioning as unofficial agent during the lapse of the post, for papers had been transmitted to him so that the assembly conscientiously decided to pay him £100 for services in England since he was last paid, the council concurring the same day to that arrangement.[59]   However, by December 1 of that year

[56] *Statutes of South Carolina*, III, 183, 251-52, 267-68.   See also Nicholson's letters to the Board of Trade of October 6, 1721, and of January 6, 1721/2, February 17, 1721/2.—C. O. 5/397, f. 37; C. O. 5/358, f. 109.

[57] McCrady, *South Carolina under the Royal Government, 1719-1776*, pp. 38, 39. It is to be noted that Governor Nicholson addressed the proprietor, Lord Carteret, as well as the Duke of Newcastle.   See his letters of May 23, 1723, July 15, 1723, Aug. 8, 1724, Aug. 25, 1724, to Newcastle, C. O. 5/387, ff. 109, 111, 133, 190.

[58] Journals of the Commons House of Assembly of South Carolina, VII, 55-56, 57, 58; for comments of the governor, see C. O. 5/359, p. 202; C. O. 6/406, f. 10.   It is interesting and puzzling that only a few months earlier, on March 27, a joint committee of both houses reported an agent as absolutely necessary to solicit the "weighty affairs of the Province" and voted to make Colonel John Barnwell agent for one year. (The reason for turning from Yonge does not appear.)   The governor professed himself as pleased that they "pitched on so good a man in every respect."   Why they had changed their mind by June is unanswered.—Journal of the Commons House of Assembly of South Carolina, VII, 6-7, 8, 10, 13.

[59] *Ibid.*, VIII, 146-47, 166.   The date of passage of the act was March 24, 1724/5.

they determined to allow the agency again to lapse at the expiration of the existing act.[60] Whether this was intended as a graceful way to ease Yonge out of the agency does not appear, but it is clear that when the agency was renewed on March 11, 1726, a London merchant, Samuel Wragg, was associated with him. Wragg's appointment preceded Yonge's by about two months, though the discrimination in salary was in favor of Yonge. In April, 1727, Samuel Wragg became the sole South Carolina agent. It may well be that the assembly had despaired of Yonge's ability ever to bring the long dispute with the proprietors to a conclusion.[61]

By March, 1728, we encounter the first instance in this colony of dissension between house and council over the agent, when the council chose Stephen Godin as their agent to secure proper instructions for the government on the question of paper money. Godin professed to regard Wragg as the "pretended agent for the riotous assembly." He had particular directions to "silence Mr. Wragg and the paper he offered" the Board of Trade as emanating only from the lower house. According to the view of Godin, and therefore presumably of the council, Wragg's agency ceased in March, 1728.[62] The houses differed sharply over an issue of paper currency. Despite the claims of Godin, Wragg regarded himself, and the assembly so acknowledged him, as agent for the province for four years and four months or from 1727 to August, 1731.[63]

The act is dated April 17, 1725, evidently the date on which it was signed by the governor.—*Statutes of South Carolina*, III, 251.

Although Governor Nicholson was asked on May 13, 1725, by both house and council to present an address and two petitions to the king on the occasion of a visit to England, I find no evidence that this was regarded as an agency.—*Ibid.*, VII, 200, 487. The same statement applies to the work of Governor Robert Johnson, who writing on November 14, 1731, to the Board of Trade, stated that the assembly of South Carolina in return for his long attendance in England, "solliciting the Publick Affairs of the Province, particularly the endeavouring their being put under His My^ties Immediate Government," gave him a present of £500.—C. O. 5/362, f. 57.

[60] Journal of the Commons House of Assembly of South Carolina, VII, 286.

[61] *Statutes of South Carolina*, III, 266. The president of the assembly, Arthur Middleton, wrote to the governor: "I assure you that it was not in my power to have it otherwise, had it been my Inclination. . . ." speaking of the choice of Wragg. There seems also to have been a decided change in the composition of the Committee of Correspondence. See Chapter VIII.

[62] C. O. 5/361, f. 9.

[63] The length of his agency is based on a statement of his brother, Joseph Wragg, to the house in 1734 when he was trying to collect Samuel Wragg's pay as agent.—Journal of the Commons House of Assembly of South Carolina, VIII, 67.

Peregrine Fury, a resident of London, succeeded Wragg with apparently no interval between agents, for he was appointed on August 20, 1731, under the regular provisions of term and salary. Regularly each year Fury was reëlected for eighteen years, though there developed a dispute between the two houses over his continuance in 1738,[64] and proved a capable, honest, efficient servant. The difficulty over his reëlection in the session of 1737-38 arose from dissension between the two houses. The council felt that he had failed in his duty in neglecting to communicate his proceedings to the lieutenant governor and to the council, especially "when by the Prorogation the Committee of Correspondence no longer subsisted." Furthermore, according to the interpretation of the council, he could depend on the assembly to make ample provision for him as they had faithfully done in the past. The Commons House of Assembly instantly registered their opinion that Peregrine Fury had solicited and transacted the Affairs of this Province "with great Prudence Care and Integrity and hath faithfully discharged the Trust repoſed in Him by this Province." The members resolved that the house would discharge the arrears due him and declared that the council members of the Committee of Correspondence had seen all his letters. It was their opinion that he was a "very fit and proper Person" for agent and so they declared their intent to provide for him whether the bill pass the council or not.[65] In somewhat sarcastic strain their message to the council the next day expressed concern at the postponement of action by the council, as passage of the bill was necessary to prevent the very interruption of correspondence of which the council complained; and it attributed Fury's failure to write to the governor to the fact that the dispatches lately sent to Great Britain had not passed through his hands, and his failure to write to the council to the prorogation of the session. "Besides, that Gentleman is not divine," they crushingly told the council, with expression of the hope that it would pass the bill at its first meeting after Christmas, as that body obligingly did.[66] But

---

[64] *Statutes of South Carolina*, III, 307-8; VI, 636-37; XI, 151.

[65] Journal of the Commons House of Assembly of South Carolina, Oct., 1737-March 25, 1738, XI, 151.

[66] *Ibid.*, p. 152; Journal of the Council of South Carolina. The fact that the lower house through the house members of the Committee of Correspondence ordered Fury to answer any misrepresentations in Britain to the disadvantage of the lower house during

by the spring of 1747, for some reason—possibly because of his failure to induce the British government to approve the paper money
act of June 17, 1746—the Commons House of Assembly began to
tire of Fury. On June 12, 1747, they passed an act appointing John
Sharpe, an agent for several of the sugar islands, to the post, an
action which the council amended by substituting Fury's name. By
a narrow vote the amendment was accepted by the lower house and
Fury was retained—for two years longer. Finally, in May, 1749,
a proposition to continue him could no longer muster the requisite
votes, and the Committee of Correspondence was directed to acquaint him with his dismissal.[67] Meanwhile Francis Yonge served
again to aid Fury with a special task during 1734-1736, as did Vander
Dusen during 1747-48, but these must be dealt with in the next
chapter with special agencies.

The agency of James Crockatt extended from June 1, 1749,[68]
to 1756, for a period of seven years, but could not escape involvement
in the constantly recurring quarrels between the two houses so
characteristic of colonial history. On July 6, 1753, Crockatt submitted his resignation to the Committee of Correspondence, suggesting as his successor Charles Pinckney, an ex-member of the South
Carolina council, who had just come to London to live. Crockatt
regretted that he had ever accepted the post, since it conflicted with
his private business.[69] The council accepted the resignation, whereupon Governor Glen urged the reappointment of Fury. The
assembly, however, had written Crockatt urging him to reconsider,
to the great anger of the upper body. The council called attention
to the fact that the ordinance appointing him had long since expired
and hence a new law would be necessary to give his appointment
legality. The house promptly pointed out that their last two agents

the late dispute with the council aligned the accredited agent with the house.—Journal
of the Commons House of Assembly of South Carolina, Jan. 16, 1738-June 7, 1739,
XII, 86.

[67] Public Laws of the State of South Carolina, p. 37; Smith, South Carolina as a
Royal Province, 1719-1776, p. 165; Journal of the Commons House of Assembly of
South Carolina, Mar. 28-Nov. 21, 1749, XXIV, pp. 338, 339. A faction of the lower
house had even wanted to pay Fury off as of September 27, 1746, claiming that he had
not been agent since June 17, 1746, but the majority would not lend itself to such dealing.—Ibid., XXII, 554.

[68] Statutes of South Carolina, III, 723.

[69] Smith, op. cit., pp. 165-66; Journal of the Council of South Carolina, XXII, 90-92.

had functioned for many years after expiration of the law appointing them. The council retorted that such a state could exist only by consent of all three branches of government. The conflict was renewed when the two houses reconvened in January, 1754/5 and carried over into 1756. To complicate matters, a letter had arrived from Crockatt, agreeing to continue as agent.[70] Since pay was due the agent, the issue resolved itself into the question whether the lower house could by control of money bills keep an agent in office against the will of the council. Accordingly an allowance for the agency salary of £1,400 was inserted in the annual estimate, his expenses of £159 under another head; but a revision a few days later dropped Crockatt's name and lumped the sum due him under the head of writing, printing, and other public services. The council, professing surprise, asked for a bill of particulars of his services. The assembly, waxing indignant, informed the councillors that the agent was paid by the people and should be selected by the representatives of the people, though his formal appointment was legal only with the consent of the other branches of government. It then made the significant statement that no account or paper laid before the house for public service would thereafter be sent to the council for inspection. As was to be expected, the reply of the council was thoroughly angry: Crockatt was declared to have no legal standing, as the council had accepted his resignation; he had no right to correspond with either house separately. As a matter of course the council rejected the tax bill on April 12, and also a second bill a few days later. Because of the French war then in progress, the governor remonstrated with the council and thus secured passage of the tax bill without change on May 20, 1756. The dispute ended with a technical victory for the Commons House, for they thus kept their agent in office until 1756.[71] Meanwhile Mr. Pinckney was acting as agent under an authority of the governor and council.

[70] Journal of the Commons House of Assembly of South Carolina, XXIX, 458. Governor Bull relating these events in 1770 said that Pinckney had some enemies in the house, Crockatt many friends.—C. O. 5/379, f. 775. Governor Bull rehearses them in a letter to Hillsborough of September 8, 1770.—C. O. 5/379, pp. 774-75.

[71] Journal of the Commons House of Assembly of South Carolina, XXX, 97, 410; Smith, op. cit., p. 168; Journal of the Council of South Carolina, XXIV, 84, 92-93. Governor Lyttleton rehearses the whole story to the Board of Trade in a letter of June 19, 1756.—C. O. 5/375 K. 145. See also Statutes of South Carolina, IV, pp. 18-19. For a concise account of the entire controversy, see Snowden, History of South Carolina, I,

Interesting in personality, though negligible in importance as a South Carolina agent, was the next person in the list of regular agents. After the post had been tendered to William Middleton, of a distinguished South Carolina family, and rejected, it was accepted by James Wright, who arrived in London and entered upon his new duties as agent about March 1, 1757.[72] His agency was terminated in about three years by the agent's translation to the exalted post of lieutenant governor of Georgia, the appointment occurring on May 30, 1760.

The next regular agent, Charles Garth, filled the post of agent in the years just preceding the Revolution, when it was most difficult, most onerous, and most interesting. Nominally he served as agent of the colony of South Carolina from 1762 to 1775, but actually he was the agent of the lower house. Although he was chosen regularly by act of the legislature on May 19, 1762, the Committee of Correspondence of the Commons House of Assembly kept up a steady communication with the home government through him independent of the governor. Communications, though they passed through the governor's hands with his mail, were supposed to be inviolate. Nevertheless Governor Boone once broke the seal of a communication from Agent Garth and sent it with an abrupt message to the house. After this, naturally, Garth sent no more messages with the governor's mail.[73] Under such circumstances it was not strange that Garth offended the council. That he was made the instrument of protest and activity against the governor is well exemplified in a recommendation of a committee of the house that "the Agent be ordered to make the strongest Representations to

246-47. McCrady is confused in his dates. The famous statement was "that no Account Petition or other paper that shall be laid before the House for the future of, for, or concerning any claim or demand whatever for any matter or thing done or to be done for the service of the Public shall be sent to the Council for their Inspection."—Journal of the Commons House of Assembly of South Carolina, p. 411.

[72] Middleton was appointed March 19, 1756.—*Statutes of South Carolina*, IV, 26-27. Action was taken by the general assembly in regard to Wright on November 19, 1756.—*Ibid.*, p. 34. The approximate date of Wright's arrival can be fixed from a letter of Abercromby's to Governor Dinwiddie, dated Mar. 3, 1757: "Mr. Wright, just arrived as agent for So Carolina."—Abercromby Letter Book, p. 55. But a letter from the Board of Trade to Governor Lyttleton, dated Nov. 9, 1757, states that Wright has only just arrived.—C. O. 5/403, p. 208. The Board had probably not been in session all summer.

[73] See *Statutes of South Carolina*, IV, 164-65 for Garth's appointment. See also McCrady, *South Carolina under the Royal Government*, p. 362.

His Majesty of the Arbitrary and Oppressive proceedings of the Governor [Montagu], and to use his utmost Endeavors to procure the removal of His Excellency from the Government or such other Marks of His Majesty's Royal Displeasure, as may prevent Governors for the future from thus opprefsing the People by abusing those Prerogatives which were intended for their benefit."[74] Of course, it was one of his first duties to defend the assembly against the charges of the governor. Under such circumstances it was not strange that the agent did not stand high in the good graces of the council.

In the sister colony, North Carolina, the permanent agency appeared late. It is the more remarkable that it was so slow in developing because, although a proprietary province, it threw off that rule and came under royal control in 1729. The obstacle to a successful and peaceful government in the Old North State prior to 1748 was lack of a medium in England through which the people could voice their views, needs, and conditions—in other words, lack of a regular agent constantly present in London. That need, at long last, was about to be supplied.

We deal from first to last with scarcely more than half a dozen men in the regular agency of this colony. The first of the short list is James Abercromby, to whom the reader was introduced in the Virginia section of this chapter. His period of service in North Carolina antedated that for the Old Dominion, for he represented North Carolina as colonial agent in London after 1749, over five years before he began to represent Virginia. Only by October 15, 1748, did the assembly sufficiently realize, despite admonition of governors, that by the absence of an agent in London it had been often misrepresented to the "Great Prejudice of the Inhabitants" of the province. James Abercromby's term was to begin on the twenty-fifth of the next March, 1749, and his instructions were to transact all public business that might arise at any of the boards in England.[75] As a forehanded individual, he notified the Board of Trade on January 10, 1748/9, of his appointment, though there is no evidence of his assuming any of the agent's duties in advance

[74] This was dated October 30, 1772, when the colonials were approaching revolt and is found among the Board of Trade Papers.—C. O. 5/394, pp. 364-65.
[75] *A Collection of all the Public Acts of Assembly of the Province of North Carolina*, p. 278.

of March 25.[76] Obviously, Abercromby had been serving the province informally in this capacity, for the act provided a small sum to compensate him for his trouble up to that time and until March 25. His participation in the quarrel of Governor Gabriel Johnston with some of the leading citizens of the colony need not delay us long. The disturbed condition of affairs in the province had led the London merchants, Henry McCulloh among them, and a few of the leading provincials to make an effort for Governor Johnston's removal on the ground of negligence and arbitrary conduct. Abercromby skilfully delayed the proceedings by charging that the complaints had originated in England and were furthermore false. The controversy has interest for us only in that it would seem that Abercromby regarded his duties as embracing defense of the governor.[77] His appointment was renewed in 1751 for three years with an increase of salary, as the earlier pittance was recognized as inadequate; in 1754 the act was again extended for three years; but in 1757 the lower house opposed a further appropriation for this purpose because of the burden of the taxes. The notice, dated December 28, 1757, from Governor Dobbs that the assembly refused to continue his agency, did not reach Abercromby until April 13, 1758. His formal appointment had expired March 25, 1757, but he felt it incumbent to continue until he had notice of nonappointment, a fact which involved a question of salary. On April 13 Abercromby accordingly, in a copy of Governor Dobb's letter laid before the Board May 2, notified the Board of Trade and the Secretary of state that he was no longer agent of North Carolina.[78]

The membership of the lower house in December, 1758, in providing an aid bill for an agent, claiming at the same time the right to name the entire Committee of Correspondence, was hardly consistent with its action of 1757 and was provocative of friction with the

[76] *Colonial Records of North Carolina*, IV, 936.

[77] There seemed to be some criticism by the Board of Trade against Johnston, for in their report in Feb., 1749, they charged negligence in submitting journals, reports, etc. Johnston replied in Sept., 1751, that he had sent the journals regularly. Of course, there is no way to prove the point; though the journals are not extant, they may easily have miscarried.—Ashe, *History of North Carolina*, I, 272; Rapier, *North Carolina*, p. 51.

[78] *Statutes of North Carolina*, XXIII, 399; XXV, 266; *Colonial Records of North Carolina*, V, 788-89; Abercromby Letter Book, pp. 142, 96. There is some reason to suppose that Abercromby was still functioning for North Carolina in connection with the parliamentary grant as late as July 20, 1759. See Abercromby Letter Book, p. 165.

governor. They now reappointed Abercromby for a term commencing the first day of the next March. Undoubtedly their actuating motive was the keen desire to get the colony's full share of the reimbursement money for the wars, a struggle in which the agents were playing a large rôle. The measure was thwarted by the governor by "finesse" as he called it: he secured the inserting by the council, when the action came before it on March 3, of the name of Samuel Smith of London for agent. In an effort to force the assent of the council, the house refused to act on other matters, but the governor prorogued the assembly.[79]

The assembly was now about to clash full tilt with Governor Dobbs and his council in a struggle which lasted for ten years. That each should greatly desire the power of appointment, and in consequence the control, of this agent was quite natural, as upon his representations and actions depended in great degree the fate of measures concerning the colony with the governmental authorities in England. From the very nature of the agency, the assembly sensed that the colonial agent should be the representative, not of the governor, but of the opposition, so that the authorities at home should hear both sides of the question. Otherwise, it was highly likely that the representations of the governor would always decide matters. The assembly felt, therefore, that when Governor Dobbs was seeking to get control of the agent, he was encroaching on the rights of the assembly and so resisted him, very properly, as they insisted. How the interests of the province "slept" when it had no agent they were learning by the manner in which the appropriation of the British parliament for reimbursing the colonies for their war expenditures against the French and Indians revealed discrimination against North Carolina, for Virginia and South Carolina received the lion's share. The first real tilt came in May of 1759, when the assembly again tacked Abercromby's appointment and provision for his support to a supply bill for the war exactly as in the preceding December. Gover-

[79] *Colonial Records of North Carolina*, V, 1087; for the law see *ibid.*, VI, 37-39, 77.
The matter had been presented in two bills: one located the seat of government at Tower Hill but without appropriation for construction of public buildings; in the second, granting an aid to the king for the war, there were clauses for appropriating out of the expected funds money to erect the public buildings and for appointing Abercromby agent together with a Committee of Correspondence. The governor got his friends in the council to pass the first bill and to let the second go to the third reading; he then had it postponed and in the meantime prorogued the assembly.

nor Dobbs refused the bill on the ground that the action destroyed the king's prerogative at a time when the crown's service demanded the money, and again prorogued the assembly. The Board of Trade later in the year held that Dobbs had no right to insist on the nomination of an agent, that the lower house was in the main justified in insisting on the right of nominating the agent, and that the rejection of an aid bill because of a failure to agree on one point was trivial and foolish. But the Lords concurred in the view that the agency matter ought to have been in a separate act and that the Committee of Correspondence ought to include some members of each house.[80]

The ill will of the governor is clearly reflected in a letter of February 6, 1760, to Secretary Pitt, in which he says: "They would not join in an address with the Council, nor send it through me as the proper Channel, but have taken upon them to nominate an Agent of their own, whom they call a Provincial Agent, and to appoint him a Salary without the Approbation of the Governor and Council, who is to be entirely under a Junto of the Assembly, and have transmitted their Address by him, which will oblige me in Council at next Meeting to appoint another Agent to act as provincial Agent under the Direction of the Govern[t] here."[81]

Such an agency representing the governor and council alone was created by the act of March 3, 1759. The person chosen to fill it was that Samuel Smith, upon whom the governor and council had earlier insisted for colonial agent. From a letter of Abercromby to Mr. Swann of North Carolina it is apparent that Smith was functioning for the council in July, 1759; the official date of termination of his activities was presumably when the house and council and governor agreed upon Jouvencal as colonial agent. In reality he was still functioning in November, 1764.[82]

This issue over authority arose again in the first session of the legislature of 1760 with both sides unwilling to compromise. The lower house passed a bill appointing as agent a London merchant,

[80] See report of Governor Dobbs to the Board of Trade of Jan. 22, 1759, *Colonial Records of North Carolina*, VI, 2-3; for reply of the Board to Dobbs, see *ibid.*, pp. 54-55. The Board pointed out that the method of appointment by the lower house had been allowed by the crown in the case of Jamaica.

[81] *Ibid.*, VI, 9.

[82] Abercromby Letter Book, p. 165. "I am obliged much against my Inclination to go on smoothly with Smith, in order that no [dis]advantage may be taken of our not Concurring together, in getting the Money from the Treasury."—*Ibid.*, (no page).

Anthony Bacon, thus in the interests of harmony abandoning Abercromby after he had been once more rejected by the council. This
selection, though made by one of the fullest houses ever known in
the colony, shared the same fate as the earlier at the hands of the
council. As the house would not amend the bill to give the council
equal control of the Committee of Correspondence and would not
forsake their choice for agent, since no reason for objecting to Bacon
was given, there was a deadlock. The house could not conceive of
objections, especially since the "Council have never heretofore altered
the Assembly's nomination of an Agent in any Bill." They also
refused to agree to alterations affecting the Committee of Correspondence on the ground that equal representation of the two houses
might prevent a quorum and make the correspondence ineffectual.[83]
They declared that they possessed the right of appointing and instructing the agent by a committee composed of a majority of members of their own body. By a solemn resolution they appointed
Bacon agent of the assembly—not provincial agent—and designated
a committee to correspond with him. In the midst of the turmoil
Dobbs prorogued the assembly until September. The quarrel between the governor and assembly grew very hot this session and
became involved with a court bill, into which it is not here necessary
to enter but which helped to inflame feeling. In a secret session of
five hours on May 23 the lower house drew up an address to the
king to be presented by their agent in which the governor was
blamed for the lack of an agent. This action whipped the governor
to terms on the court bill but not on the matter of the agency; for
it was believed that he desired the agency for Samuel Smith, his own
private attorney in London.[84]

Both houses at the November session of 1760[85] passed after some
bickering the act for a military grant with a rider appointing Bacon
agent to lay before the home government the expenses of North
Carolina in the war. Governor Dobbs disapproved of this act and
adjourned the assembly two days that it might name some one ac-

[83] *Colonial Records of North Carolina,* VI, 434, 436.

[84] *Ibid.,* VI, 92-93, 423-24, 429, 430, 434, 436, 1136-37. For the charge that the
governor wanted Smith see *ibid.,* VI, 415-16. The address to the king is found here.
Any one divulging what was said in debate was to be dismissed from the house.

[85] Though the assembly had been postponed to September, a session had to be called
in midsummer because of trouble with the Cherokees. At this session the council tabled a
bill providing for an agent.—*Ibid.,* VI, 433, 444.

ceptable to him.[86]   The house declared that their only reason for insisting on the appointment of Anthony Bacon was their desire to be consistent, as they had already displaced Abercromby because the council objected to him, and they feared that if they yielded on Bacon, no person of character would accept the appointment from a "People so inconsistent and trifling in their Conduct."[87]   The governor then unbent enough to express his willingness to accept any person other than Bacon, but that did not prevent another prorogation.[88]

A new assembly opened at Wilmington in March, 1761, after a December session had failed to deal with the issue, with an open threat of dissolution by the governor.[89]   Both sides by this time were willing to yield something. The council in the form of a rider accepted the agency and the house named some "other person than Bacon" and in addition accepted three members of the council on the Committee of Correspondence.   And so a bill appropriating £20,000 to support 500 soldiers to aid the neighboring provinces against the Indians and naming Cuchet Jouvencal of Westminster as agent was finally passed. The council in a long explanation to the governor for its change of position urged him to assent, which he did and in the same breath dissolved the assembly. When recognition of Jouvencal came before the Board of Trade, their attorney Lamb criticized the method of his appointment by a rider, but the Board contented itself with instructing Governor Dobbs to recommend appointment for the future in a separate bill.[90]   But as a sort of period to the long contro-

---

[86] The council first rejected the aid bill because of the rider (*ibid.*, VI, 499, 500) and then accepted it (p. 502), whereupon the governor rejected it.   The commoners addressed the governor on Dec. 5, 1760, in a very spirited way on his rejection: ". . . it is matter of extreme Concern to this House, to find that his Majesty's Service in the intended Expedition . . . against the Cherokees, should be Frustrated by what must appear to us to be only some private Resentment, your Excellency has taken to Mr Bacon or any person [we] appointed agent for this Province provided we grant such assistance to the Common Cause. . . ."—*Ibid.*, pp. 516-17.   For the governor's rejection, see *ibid.*, p. 469.

[87] *Ibid.*, p. 517.

[88] Dobb's message to the assembly records: ". . . after my having Publickly declared that I would concurr in making any other Person Agent in England."—*Ibid.*, p. 515.

[89] ". . . in Case you persist in inserting that Clause I may put an end to your further attendance. . . ."—*Ibid.*, p. 515.

[90] For the statement of the house for its concession see *ibid.*, p. 692; for that of the council, pp. 633-34, where it stated that it would greatly have preferred the bill without any tack but recognized the impossibility of an aid from the people on any other terms; for the request for admission of councillors to the Committee, *ibid.*, p. 656; for the instruction of the Board to Dobbs see pp. 702-3.   The agent's name also appears as Jouvencel.

versy the house did not neglect to point out to the governor that had it been so "fortunate as to have had the Concurrence of the other Branches of the Legislature in passing a Law for an agent in London," the colony might have shared more generously in the first parliamentary grant of £200,000 for its expenses in the war.[91]

In the course of the controversy, the Board of Trade laid down so clear a statement of their view of the power of the lower house in regard to the agent that it should be recorded in the text. In a letter to Governor Dobbs on April 4, 1761, the Board writes: "It is not in our opinion the part of the Crown or its Officers either in point of Right or Propriety to interfere in the nomination of an Agent so far as regards the Choice of the person, in this Respect the Representatives of the people are and ought to be free to chuse whom they think proper to act, in whatever concerns the Affairs and Interest of the Colony here and with whom they and the Council only can correspond, the Governor being very properly restrained by his Instruction from corresponding upon matters of a publick nature relative to his Government with any other persons than those servants of the Crown here, in whose department the Affairs of America are placed." But the governor could properly interfere in the mode of appointment.[92]

While the sharp difference between the two houses over the agency matter seemed to have been amicably adjusted, the embers of dissension were still smoldering, ready to burst into a blaze at the slightest provocation. The period of Jouvencal's ministrations was by no means free from friction. While the house had accepted the addition of a few members from the council to the Committee of Correspondence, it must have been a concession observed rather in the letter than in the spirit. Already on April 20, 1762, the governor was complaining that none of the councillors on the Committee was consulted in connection with the letters written to the agent or received from him. This was perhaps not strange if the

[91] This appears in an address of Nov. 14. Though this grant is discussed in a later chapter (Chapter IX), it may not be amiss to note here, by way of justification of the comment of the lower house, that Virginia received £20,546 while North Carolina received only about £6,789 all told.—*Ibid.*, p. 477. Accounts of this long controversy are found in Ashe, *History of North Carolina*, I, 296, 298-99; Raper, *North Carolina*, pp. 58, 206-8.

[92] *Colonial Records of North Carolina*, VI, 539.

chief subject of correspondence was, as the governor declared, complaints against that official himself, nor was it strange that such letters were to be directed to the speaker, contrary to earlier practice when they were sent under cover to the governor for the Committee of Correspondence.[93] But when Jouvencal was to negotiate a petition from the North Carolina council for an allowance out of the quitrents for attendance at the Court of Chancery and Claims and for extraordinary attendance at councils, it is noticeable that the governor alluded to him as "our agent."[94] And by the close of that year the council was requesting that letters, which they understood had arrived from the agent, together with copies of the replies, be sent to that body.[95] By March, 1764, the question of the reappointment of Jouvencal was up and the bickering between the houses was renewed. On March 7 the council consented to the renewal of his agency but insisted on reinstatement of a proviso which the house deleted, namely, that a member of the council must be of the quorum of the Committee of Correspondence. "Unless a Negative is vested in us [the council]," it declared caustically, "we should in fact be Cyphers which we shall not willingly agree to." When the house refused to recede, the council rejected the bill. The lower house then resolved to continue Jouvencal agent for eighteen months, the appointment dating from October 1, 1763, and created a Committee of Correspondence of its own members. Only the lower house took action.[96]

By the November session of 1764, the two houses were again indulging in sharp exchanges. On November 14 the house resolved that "it is the necessary indubitable and inherent Right of this House as the Representatives of the People to nominate the Agent," and insisted that "the exercise of a Negative voice in the other branches of the legislature on the appointment of such Agent can no ways contribute to the service of his Majesty or the good of the Province, but on the contrary may be & for some years past has been of considerable prejudice to the Interest of both." It finally declared the refusal of a governor or council to concur in the assembly's appointment contrary to the views of the Board of Trade

[93] Judging by this letter Dobbs was not a master of the English language, but his meaning is clear.—*Ibid.*, p. 837. [94] *Ibid.*, pp. 719-20.
[95] *Ibid.*, p. 875. [96] *Ibid.*, pp. 1134, 1137, 1206, 1214.

already cited.[97]   The house tried again to have the agent selected by both governor and council. It named Thomas Barker, an eminent resident of North Carolina, but the council substituted another name. When the house reinserted the name of Barker, declaring the "arbitrary and injudicious" exercise of a negative voice by the council "of a Tendency extremely dangerous to the well-being of the Province," the council rejected the bill.[98]   The house took vengeance by refusing to appropriate £1,000 for five years' service to pay the agent of the council and governor, Samuel Smith, on the ground that "he never had been appointed agent for this Province."   It would appear that the council receded on this point.[99]

In the spring of 1765 the house was again obliged to recognize the expiration of the agent's term, which had been renewed for only eighteen months, it will be recalled. It passed a resolution on May 18 to continue Jouvencal for one year, but the governor prorogued the assembly before the council could concur—or, what is more likely, refuse to concur.[100]   On the last day of this May session the house heatedly refused to comply with the council's request for submission of all letters and papers received from the agent since the last sitting of the legislature.   Governor Tryon wrote the Board of Trade on August 15 that unless at the next session of the assembly the lower house would permit some members of the council to serve on the Committeee of Correspondence and allow full access to the agent's correspondence, he would then submit to their Lordships the question whether the agent of the assembly should be recognized by the Board.   He cited, of course, that portion of the opinion of the Board of Trade which favored his contention, as the house had earlier quoted the portion which favored their contention.   The lower body, nevertheless, maintained its right, and so the Board accepted Tryon's advice, refusing to recognize Jouvencal.[101]

No agent was appointed from this time, May, 1765, to December, 1768, but that interval was far from free from recrimination. In the

[97] *Ibid.*, pp. 1255-56.
[98] Just why they wished to change to Barker remains unexplained.—*Ibid.*, pp. 1287-88; 1240, 1290.   For good measure the house added a paragraph of eulogy of Barker.
[99] *Ibid.*, pp. 1251-52, 1313, 1316-17.   Of course the council could not force the item for Smith's pay into the accounts if the house flatly refused.   A full account of this involved conflict by a contemporary is given by Governor Tryon.—*Ibid.*, VI, 306-8.
[100] *Ibid.*, VII, 60.
[101] *Ibid.*, p. 107; Ashe, *History of North Carolina*, I, 312.

reply of the house to the governor's speech opening the November session of 1766, the house spoke in a way which may fairly be held as conveying a threat: "In every other part of his Majesty's American Dominions, where the Constitution is similar to that of this Province, the Representatives of the people enjoy the priviledges of naming an agent . . . , the concurrence of the other Branches of the Legislature being considered as necessary only to give a sanction to such nomination." The denial of this privilege by the council, it was to be feared, "may be followed by consequences fatal to the tranquility and repose of this Province."[102] The council resented keenly that address as an "indecent and unjustifiable procedure and highly derogatory of the Honor of this House," and ascribed the failure of the agency laws to the refusal of the assembly to allow the council a proper share in the Committee of Correspondence. Governor Tryon, manifesting a discretion which had not always characterized his predecessors, avoided entering the dispute. Until he could lay the matter of their grievances before the king, both bodies would find him willing to concur in the appointment of an agent, "not doubting but the nomination will fall upon fit persons, properly qualified."[103]

Now enters the last agent in the history of colonial North Carolina. Yet once more an effort to elect an agent by both houses failed in December, 1768. The governor was authorized to sanction the appointment of an agent only if elected by both houses; and the critical situation which prevailed after the passage of the Stamp Act rendered it necessary that an agent's selection should be conducted in such a manner as to vest him with unquestioned authority; otherwise the interests of the colony were doomed to disappointment. Governor Tryon later declared in a letter to the Earl of Hillsborough that he had no objection to assenting to McCulloh, the nominee of the house, and added, "I could wish it might be understood how far his Majesty would have his Council share in the nomination of the person to be appointed Agent."[104] McCulloh must have regarded himself authorized to serve under the warrant of the house

[102] *Colonial Records of North Carolina*, VII, 348-49.

[103] *Ibid.*, p. 337. This delightfully vague exposition of his views is found in *ibid.*, p. 356.

[104] Though the measure to appoint Henry E. McCulloh passed the house Dec. 2, the law was tabled in the council the fifth.—*Ibid.*, pp. 918, 924. As will be related later.

alone, for an entry in the Board of Trade Journals of April 18, 1769, shows him sending in a letter, dated the fourteenth, desiring "in behalf of the Province of North Carolina" and of the Merchants of the Out Ports of Great Britain to suspend any application of the Merchants of London relative to the proposed regulations upon the importation of naval stores from the colonies. It is significant of the position of the Board that it ordered the letter taken into consideraion when "M[r] McCulloh shall produce any testimonials of his being authorized to act in this Business either as Agent for the Province of North Carolina or for the Merchants of the Out Ports of Great Britain."[105]   The Board thus remained consistent to its declared position of April, 1761.

By the fall of 1769 the people themselves were demanding an agent as is evidenced by a petition presented by residents of Anson County to their assembly, begging that "Doct[r] Benjamin Franklin" or "some other known patriot" be appointed agent, to represent the unhappy state of this province to his Majesty, and to solicit the several boards in England. Similar petitions were presented by the inhabitants of Orange and Rowan Counties.[106]   When the legislature convened that October, the council in its reply to the governor's speech stated that "We flatter ourselves an Act will be passed this Session for appointing an Agent in England," as the necessity of such an appointment was so obvious that they believed no difficulty could arise on the subject.[107]   Clearly the high tide of feeling against the Stamp Act had overwhelmed North Carolina. The prophetic instinct of the council proved well founded, for a measure to appoint McCulloh colonial agent passed both houses with little difficulty early in November and was signed by the governor on November 6. The colony had gained this important step even though they were dissolved immediately after passage of that bill because the tone in an address to the king was disrespectful and like that of Virginia.[108]

McCulloh, a native of the state residing in England, had offered his services in 1767. For Tryon's comment, dated Feb. 25, 1769, see *ibid.*, VIII, 11.

[105] *Ibid.*, pp. 164-65; *Journal of the Board of Trade*, Jan., 1768-Dec., 1775, p. 88.

[106] The Anson petition was presented later as a part of the remonstrance of North Carolina to parliament.—*Ibid.*, p. 78. It was dated, Oct. 9, 1769. This was the time it will be recalled, of the regulator movement. See also Ashe, *op. cit.*, I, 351.

[107] *Colonial Records of North Carolina*, VIII, 92. The reply was dated Oct. 30.

[108] This was a short session from Oct. 23 to Nov. 6, 1769.—*Ibid.*, pp. 100, 104, 115-16, 151.

By January 20, 1770, McCulloh had notice of his appointment, which his previous experience before the Board of Trade had led him to declare he would accept only if it were perfectly regular. His personal attitude in the controversy with the mother country is revealed in a letter to Speaker John Harvey: "A letter from Mr Pryor acquaints me, of the dissol^n of your late Assembly and of my appointment as Agent. I am pleased to think the Assembly had virtue to *deserve* the first event; & I am sensible I am greatly to *thank you* for the second . . . and I cannot but be pleased that in my person, the unjustifiable claims of a Govr and Council to *a negative*, has been defeated."[109] At the termination of his term, in 1771, McCulloh was reappointed for an additional term, with a Committee of Correspondence composed of both houses. But in December, 1773, the agency was allowed to lapse, as, in the words of the committee recommending such action, "the purposes of this Act intended have not been fully answered, it therefore becomes useless to this Province."[110]

The last gesture from this colony on the very eve of the Revolution, 1774, was a special mission and must therefore be discussed in the next chapter.

Maryland, as the one Southern province which with the exception of the years 1689 to 1715 remained under proprietary rule to the end of the colonial period, occupies a unique position. Oddly enough, her agency had a long, and, like the agencies of the rest of the Southern colonies, a turbulent history. Maryland was undoubtedly somewhat influenced by the complaint of the home government in 1702 that for want of an agent great inconveniences arose through delay of reports and miscarriage of papers. At this time the home government was also pressing for further military aid for New York from the sister colonies. It so happened that at this very time Nathaniel Blakiston, who for two years had been the popular governor of this province, was, on account of bad health, about to retire from that position. Before departing for England he offered to serve the colony as its agent for one year without pay and thereafter for as long as the assembly cared to employ him at a modest yearly honorarium or "if you think what they have pro-

[109] *Ibid.*, pp. 171-72.   [110] *Ibid.*, IX, 785.

posed to Exceed yor Inclinacon you will make yor own terms."[111]
As the lower house had just voted £300 to New York—reluctantly,
be it said—expressing at the same time a desire that Maryland's own
need for defense be presented to the king, Blakiston's offer was
readily accepted.[112]   He seems to have arrived in England about
October, 1702, and entered upon a diligent attendance at the Board
of Trade.[113]   In April, 1704, the houses of assembly agreed to continue him in their service, the council having already expressed itself
as having "a grateful Sence of his said Exe^{ys} Careful and Diligent
endeavours to serve this Province. . . ."[114]   But in 1708 the lower
house refused to continue his agency; and when the council in 1710
urged payment of his salary to the time that his attorney was notified of his dismissal, which was fifteen months later, the house deferred consideration to the next session, as the accounts had been
closed.[115]

The house turned a deaf ear to the pleadings of the council in
1710 and 1711 of the "absolute necessity of impowering some proper
person to act as agent."   The argument that an agent was needed to
solicit a certain act for relief of grievances left them cold, as "the
shortnefs of time for wch that Act is made will difcourage any
Perfons from making any interest at home for its repeale when her
Majesty's difapprobation (if procured) cannot possibly arrive before
expirason of it, therefore we conceive the feeing an Agent to fpeak
to it to be an unnecefsary charge," and so they state bluntly on

---

[111] Blakiston was unusually modest.   "I being with God's assistance bound for England I will with the utmost of my Power Serve you as Effectually as I can, in your business of New York; but I would not have you to be mistaken to think, that I am that
Considerable Person as to have the Honour of his Majesty's Eare, but I will make my
Application to that Honble Board the Lords Commissioners of Trade. . . ."   See a letter
of Mar. 24, 1702, *Archives of Maryland*, XXIV, 227-28.   Again, he says, "I am ready
to give you my Service for the first yeere Gratis and if you think what they have proposed to Exceed yor Inclinacon you shall make yor owne terms for I am very ambitious
to approve myself.—*Ibid.*, p. 261.

[112] The council took the initiative by a communication to the house on Mar. 24,
1701/2.—*Ibid.*, 227-28.   The council voted to accept the offer March 24; the house
concurred on the next day.—*Ibid.*, pp. 261, 230.   See also Mereness, *Maryland as a Proprietary Province*, pp. 464-65.

[113] The approximate date of his arrival in England can be fixed from a statement of
the council of May 1, 1704, arranging for his first year's pay, second year's in the
agency.   *Archives of Maryland, 1700-1704*, XXIV, 393.

[114] The vote was taken by both houses on the same day, April 27, *ibid.*, pp. 338, 364.
The expression of appreciation from the council came on August 18, 1703.—*Ibid.*, XXV,
164.   [115] *Ibid.*, XXVII, 506 (Dec. 9, 1708).

November 4, 1710, that they "cannot on noe Acco^t Agree wth yor Hon^r in imploying an Agent. . . ."[116]

On October 31, 1713, however, the lower house agreed to the appointment of an agent at the former salary and was of opinion that Colonel Nathaniel Blakiston was a "very fit Person" to fill the post.[117] The consideration which swayed the house then was undoubtedly their failure to present the crown with an address from the assembly regarding the claim of Secretary Lawrence to the license money from ordinaries. When another request for the colony to pay the claim came from the crown, the house was willing to pay the cost of an agent to prove that Lawrence was not entitled to the fees in question. But the burden of the expense of an agent weighed heavily on the delegation, considering the "small Commodity and Advantage (if Any) reaped thereby," especially now that Maryland was again under the proprietor, to whom there was great ease of access, as compared with the king. Consequently on August 4, 1721, this branch of the legislature was inclined to be no longer at the expense of an agent.[118] The council, however, urged upon the other house continuance of Blakiston as agent, of whose services they were sorry the house had so mean an opinion. A gentleman of good interest at court and in parliament seemed the more necessary as by uniting his efforts to those of the proprietary they might hope for success in providing against every unforeseen emergency which might arise in England. But the house, deeply conscious of nearly £2,000 paid Blakiston and of the fact that theirs was the only proprietary province incurring such an expense, remained adamant against a second

[116] *Ibid.*, XXIX, 113. See also Black Book, I, No. 10 (Proprietary Papers, 1701-1773). This paper is dated Sept. 4, 1710. The council tried to use the Act for Relief of Grievances as a club to force the Agency Act. See also *ibid.*, no. 16, signed by R. Dallam, Clerk of the House of Delegates, and no. 17. The governor also used all "possible Endeavours" to persuade them to name an agent, according to the statement of Acting Governor Lloyd to the secretary of state on January 25, 1711/2.—C. O. 5/720, p. 115. Lloyd makes much the same report to the Board of Trade on the same date.—C. O. 5/717, p. 50.

[117] *Archives of Maryland*, XXIX, 214, 274. In 1711 the house asked the council to recommend two or three persons so that they might consider their respective merits.—*Ibid.*, p. 48.

[118] Message of the lower house to the council Aug. 4, 1721.—*Ibid.*, XXXIV, 171. Their reasons for dropping the agency are stated to the Proprietor on Aug. 5.—*Ibid.*, p. 263. Their letter of dismissal to Blakiston is in most courteous terms.—*Ibid.*, p. 264. As a result of the conversion of Benedict Leonard Baltimore to the Church of England, Charles, fifth Lord Baltimore, resumed his proprietary rights in 1715.

plea of the council and prayed their honors "to press us no farther on this Subject." The members were concerned to find the subject looked upon as so important as to take up so much of the country's time. The house, however, acquiesced in the request that the agent's salary be paid until he should receive notice of his dismissal. The fact remains that in eight years Blakiston had won no important case for the province and so the agency was discontinued.[119]

Within a few years, in 1725 to be exact, the tables were turned: the lower house was urging an agent. The Board of Trade urged that the agency which thus far had been distinctly an organ of the royal government be made permanent in order to facilitate trade and the handling of colonial affairs. Though, except when the lower house had a particular grievance, they were loath to bear the burden of the cost of an agency, their idea that an agent was no longer necessary when the colony was restored to the proprietor because of their easy approach to him, underwent a swift change. Their grievances were now against the proprietor from whom they could appeal to the king. Therefore, the governor and council, who were the representatives of the lord proprietor, already had a spokesman in England; and the members of the lower house began to insist that they alone, as the sole representatives of the people, must be permitted to appoint and instruct an agent maintained by a tax on their constituents. When the Lord Proprietor refused them such an agent, the effect was something like curbing free speech. This new attitude first appeared in 1725, when the council was presenting the petition to Lord Baltimore against the act for reduction of officers' fees and was in the midst of a controversy over English statutes. The lower house passed the first agency bill of its own initiative; now the upper house rejected it as an unreasonable measure. None the less, until the year 1774, the lower house continued to pass such a bill at every session in which there appeared real disagreement between the two houses; on critical occasions this question was presented to the crown either by an address from the lower house or by an agent supported by subscription.

The tenor of the first approach to the council by the members of

[119] *Ibid.*, pp. 175-76; for the first reply of the house to the council, p. 176; for the second plea of the council, p. 177; second reply of the House of Delegates, p. 179; request for payment of full salary, p. 180; concurrence of the house, p. 182. For Blakiston's second agency see also Mereness, *op. cit.*, pp. 465-66.

the other house in November, 1725, is interesting: "We desire to know whether your Honours will Concurr with us in Allowing A Sum of Money to An Agent to be appointed by this House for the presenting the Addresses of this House and the representing and Solliciting such their Grievances in Great Britain, as are not redrest on their proper application here, and generally to Negotiate any Affairs there, that may be found necessary by this House for the Interest and Safety of the ffreemen of this province."[120] Here is manifest a desire for a regular agency, pure and simple. And what was the reaction of the council when the proposal did not come at its initiative? It tabled it and reminded the house of its refusal to continue Colonel Blakiston as agent and showed that it penetrated the real motive behind the request: "Besides the manner of your Demands are yet more unreasonable seeing by your message you intend such Agent only to be Imployed to represent your Addresses, and Aggrievances, as if this House had not equal right to the Service of an Agent." In addition the council felt that the session was too near an end to enter into such a debate.[121]

Again on July, 1729, the lower house passed an agency law, but a reminder was necessary before the upper house replied that they were not "inclinable to concurr" until they were made "sensible that the publick Occasions require it."[122] A similar effort failed in 1731, advanced by the lower house under the plea of the need of an agent to avoid hostile legislation by the British parliament.[123] There is no evidence that the council deigned to reply to this effort.

By the year 1739 the lower house refused longer to be denied an agent. A bill to raise a fund by taxation for the payment of an agent was sent up to the council. It provided for the appointment of an agent by the lower house alone, as he was to be named by a group selected by that house, called trustees, who were vested with the sole power of paying him. Clearly, as the council charged, an agent for the lower house, rather than a provincial agent, was intended. Of course, the bill was promptly rejected by the council with a caustic message. "Although a Prettier Scheme for Power

[120] *Archives of Maryland*, XXXV, 281.
[121] *Ibid.*, pp. 286-87. [122] *Ibid.*, XXXVI, 330, 354, 361.
[123] The people in Maryland had been manufacturing a little wool and flax, as the profits of tobacco were not sufficient to furnish them with even coarse clothing. They were anxious lest parliament pass legislation to forbid such weaving.—*Ibid.*, XXXVII, 267-68.

and Profit in our little World of Politicks could Hardly be thought of," they declared, "yet far be it from us to Imagine that any Persons Either in or out of Your House had any share in this Admirable Project with a View of being Trustees; should this Ingenious Contrivance ever take effect the Trustees might play the Game into each others Hands and represent each other in England." They concluded by declaring that they would gladly have their message printed with the bill to have the world know that the council had rejected a bill of "dangerous consequences," which would render the government ridiculous and which might even draw censure from the crown.[124] Not surprised in the least by the rejection, the representatives of the lower house sought to set the matter in its proper light "so that the meanest Capacity may be able to judge of it." They resented the distortion of the word "Trustee" to "Guardian" made in the council message; it would be answered, they assured the council, except that they were determind by "Nothing you can say or do," to be drawn into a rupture which might prevent execution of the public business. "We cannot help thinking," they state, "that the denying this looks too much like an Unwillingness to have the Matter in Dispute brought to Light however we shall give you no further Trouble in it, than to tell you, the People of Maryland have Spirit enough, and We hope will find means, without this Bill, to do themselves Justice."[125] Back came another retort on June 8 from the council, which was truly astonished that "any Warmth should have transported" the members to the assertion that the council would refuse the bill unless the governor and council could nominate the agent and fix his pay. "Your message of the 6th Instant would not have been less Decent if the Extraordinary threat of the People doing themselves Justice Had been Omitted."[126]

The lower house proved itself not unresourceful. On June 9 they drew up a petition to the king, praying him to instruct the proprietary

[124] Ibid., XL, 253; for the message accompanying the bill see ibid., p. 254; for the reply of the council, p. 257. The council brought even more sinister charges against the delegates. "And when after Glutting their Vanity with a Dictatoriall Power and filling their Pockets with Money under Pretence of necessary uses and Purposes, They should Perceive an Approaching Period to their Greatness of Authority and Gain They might by their Ministers Consent Employ their Power and the money Intrusted with them to their own Private Advantage and the very Great Prejudice of this Province. Instances of this kind have not been Wanting in America."—Ibid.

[125] Ibid., p. 259; Barker, The Background of the Revolution in Maryland, pp. 218, 228-30.   [126] Ibid., pp. 263, 265.

and his governor and council in the colony to assent to a law to raise money so that the house might employ fit agents to lay their cause before the king and also to lay a petition before Lord Baltimore. By about the close of July they had engaged the services of "a man of undoubted Reputation, knowledge, and Integrity" as agent, Ferdinand John Paris, who for at least seven years was paid with money raised by subscription. He was directed to present the petition to the proprietor, but if the answer of the proprietor were wholly unsatisfactory, then to lay the address before the king.[127] The governor and council caused delay, however, in the agent's proceedings the next October by refusing to the Committee of Correspondence access to the records, even when the house offered to pay the clerk of the court for his trouble. The refusal was made on the ground that no persons could act as a committee of the house except during a session of the assembly. This further incensed the lower house. Furthermore, by the time the petition had reached the hands of the proprietor, the assembly had passed a supply bill to aid in the expedition to the West Indies undertaken in King George's War. This afforded a natural opportunity for an address to the king, in which was inserted a clause on the right of appeal. The agent saw that this petition was duly presented, and in addition had it printed in the London *Gazette*.[128]

The next conflict over the issue of an agent did not arise until August, 1745, when it took much the form it did in North Carolina of a "tack" to a supply bill. When the lower house of assembly was passing on a bill for £3,000 to support the garrison at Louisbourg at Cape Breton, it inserted or "tacked" on, to use the phraseology of the time, a clause to collect two pence on every hogshead of tobacco exported out of the province for the support of an agent. The council, running true to form, refused to pass the supply bill with the obnoxious clause on the ground that it was "foreign" to the object of the bill and to his Majesty's service in general, thus condemning the blending of different matters in the same bill as un-

---

[127] *Ibid.*, pp. 419-20. Paris acknowledged receipt of the petition, but could not present it, as he had not been supplied with authentic copies of necessary records.—*Ibid.*, p. 528. Governor Bladen declared that they raised more than £400 sterling for the cost of the agency.—*Archives of Maryland*, XLIV, 59.

[128] *Ibid.*, XLII, 205, 505; Mereness, *op. cit.*, pp. 470-72.

parliamentary, unjust, and violent.[129]   On August 22 the house
came back at the other body with a sly thrust: "We little expected
You would have given it under Your Hands that the raising a Sum
of Money for the Support of an Agent at home . . . was foreign
to his Majesty's Service in General since We always presumed it
was not only for his Majestys Service, but also from his known
Goodness and Paternal Care over all his People, agreeable to his
Royal Will and Pleasure that all his Subjects tho' ever so remote,
should be enabled in the best manner their distance would admit
as well to keep up a Congratulatory Correspondence of Praise &
Thanks for the Benefits they receive from him as on every Occasion
by Oppressions and hardships imposed on them in humble and
decent manner to lay their Compl^ts before him."   They denied that
their method was "tacking," or if it were, at least not tacking in an
unparliamentary manner and pointed to precedents in the last few
years to show that those who offer a "tack" were not always thought
"enemies or ill wishers to such a bill."   The house in its turn refused
to accept the council's amendment to strike out the clause providing
for an agent.   The council then on August 23 declared that they
could prove that the projected agency, far from securing tranquility,
would be the greatest foundation of disturbance in the province and
absolutely refused to pass the bill.[130]   Thereupon, on September 28
the governor dissolved the assembly with a stern rebuke to the lower
house.   He charged that they had taken advantage of a critical
time, thinking that the council would not dare to reject the supply
bill for military aid.   "The Money for the Agent was to be raised
on the People and applied to such Uses, as the House of Delegates
only in the Plentitude of that Power which You have declared in a
Message and Resolution you are invested with shall think fit A
Power which the House of Commons in England makes no Claim
to."[131]   The house closed the session by creating a committee to

[129] *Archives of Maryland*, XLIV, 13.   The council concluded that the house would
not have consented to the Louisbourg fund without securing the funds of an agent.

[130] See *ibid.*, pp. 15-16, for the reply of the house of Aug. 22, 1745; pp. 17-20
for the statement of the council of Aug. 23.   See also Barker, *op. cit.*, p. 235.

[131] *Archives of Maryland*, XLIV, 58-59.   An account of the conflict between the two
houses was set forth in a petition to the king from the lower house, dated August 23.
See *ibid.*, pp. 92-93.

Although the official title of the lower body of the legislature was "Lower House of
Assembly," it should be recorded that at least as early as 1745 the governor referred to it
as the "House of Delegates."

receive any communication from its agent, Ferdinand Paris, and to report to the next session of the assembly and by ordering the address to the king, drawn up in August, to be transmitted to Paris.[132] A similar effort at a "tack" to another bill in the session of 1746 failed even in the lower house.[133]

The exact date of termination of Paris' agency is difficult to determine. It is clear that he was serving as late as January 4, 1744. Certainly for nearly two decades, from about 1746 to 1766, Maryland was without a formal agent.[134] This was undoubtedly owing to the hostility of the proprietor to the agency, though his attitude toward the first regular agent, Blakiston, had been not unfriendly, as is sufficiently indicated by a message from the proprietor to the Maryland assembly on October 12, 1720: "In the Mean Timme tis our Peculiar good Fortune that his Majesties faithful Subjects of the Province have Intrusted the Direction of their Application to the Care of Coll° Nath¹ Blakistone a Person so Constantly Attached to the Protestant Interest and of such known and approved Loyalty to the King and Esteem with his Ministers that Wee take Pleasure at his Instances to make our Power Conducive to your happyness."[135] But later the Lords Proprietors directed their governors to take every possible measure necessary to prevent establishment of an agency on the plea of causing "a sea of trouble" as well as unnecessary expense. The house never carried the issue of the agency nor the two taxes of which they especially complained as illegal through to the Privy Council, probably fearing defeat at the hands of the king. With every fresh rejection of the agency bill by the council, demagogues impressed on the ignorant people that the rejection was owing to realization by the proprietor that his collection of these two duties, the tobacco duty and the port duty, was illegal.[136] We know from

[132] *Ibid.*, pp. 198-99.

[133] The attempt was made to add this to a bill to issue £4,500 from the office of Commissioners to Emit Bills of Credit to encourage volunteers for the Canadian Expedition. The vote, taken on June 20, 1746, stood 13:30.—*Ibid.*, p. 316.

[134] A record of June 27, 1746, shows that the Committee of Correspondence had not heard from Paris "of late" whether from miscarriage of letters or that "he conceives himself not adequately rewarded for his Trouble in the service of the Country."—*Archives of Maryland*, XLIV, 331. The committee declared that without a public fund to defray the expense of procuring justice to Maryland that end could not be attained. Therewith Paris disappears from the records of Maryland.

[135] *Ibid.*, XXXIV, 63. He spoke in similar strain to the council on October 20. See the Black Book, Proprietary Papers, 1701-1773, I, no. 4.

[136] A duty of 12 pence per hogshead on tobacco—one shilling later—exported had been

Governor Sharpe's complaints in letters to his brothers that Lord Baltimore peremptorily refused to allow any proposal to be heard for the appointment of an agent. That refusal weakened his case in the difficulty over the tobacco duty as well as in the question of the agency and confirmed the people in their conviction of the justice of their grievances. It also stiffened the lower house in its effort to curtail every other source of income to the proprietor. Writing to William Sharpe on May 2, 1756, the governor said: "There are several Matters about which Disputes have subsisted many years between the Lord Proprietary & the people which would His Ldp suffer them to be brought to a Hearing at home & a final Determination would I am well convinced be decided without the least hesitation in His Ldp's favour, however Some of the violent Patriots as they are called think and persuade the People to think otherwise, a Cause is not to be brought before His Majesty in Council without Money & an Agent; the People have repeatedly desired to be allowed an Agent for a short time; Granting their Request His Lordship says would plunge him into a Sea of Trouble & therefore enjoynes me to take every measure to prevent any thing of that Sort, unless the people will put their Confidence in M.ʳ Calvert nominate him their Agent. . . ." But, Sharpe adds shrewdly, "as it can be easily foreseen with what Indignation they would hear the proposal, I shall never act so impolitickly as to give them a Hint of it."[137]

---

collected since 1671. After 1739 the house boldly claimed that the duty was not warranted by law; the proprietor on his restoration was not a successor to the crown, and therefore a duty given the royal government in perpetuity in 1704 did not apply to the proprietary government. The port duty was a 14 pence tonnage duty on all vessels owned by non-residents trading to Maryland. The latter amounted in 1756 to about £800 or £900 a year, which was for the proprietary's own use; the former at the same time amounted to perhaps £1,400, the greater portion of which had to go to pay the lieutenant governor's salary.—Mereness, *op. cit.*, pp. 344-45, 347; letter of Governor Sharpe to John Sharpe, his brother, dated June 1, 1756, *Archives of Maryland*, VI, 433-34.

[137] *Ibid.*, p. 401. The letter to John Sharpe, cited above, is in a similar strain as to his attitude toward the agency. He says the Lords Proprietors have always used their "Influence & Interest to oppose such a Measure."—*Ibid.*, pp. 433-34.

It might be added here that Cecilius Calvert appeared before the Board of Trade several times, probably at the behest of the proprietor, and is loosely alluded to in the *Journal of the Board of Trade* and in the Court Calendar as agent for Maryland, but there is not the slightest proof that he was ever chosen agent by the province.

A letter of Cecilius Calvert to Governor Sharpe written in 1753 (perhaps in August or September) should set at rest the doubt as to his actual relation to the colony: "By assiduity and Attendence, I have at last with great difficulty obtain'd His Majesty's warrant to the Board of Ordnance for the Delivery of the Arms Drums, etc. belonging to

Governor Sharpe tried conscientiously to convince the lower house that submission of the assembly journals to the king's ministers made an agent unnecessary, but the members of that house insisted on the right to their own spokesman and representative. They felt that the governor could not assume to judge of the expediency of a people's having an agent to support their interests when he himself must properly be regarded as the delegate of the proprietor. In the end independence on the part of the lower house forced a conciliatory attitude on the part of the proprietor so that he made many concessions, such as renouncing his claim to license money from the ordinaries.[138]

Meanwhile the struggle for an agent went on from 1752 to 1766, though perhaps with less clamor. In June, 1752, an agency bill was again passed by the house, the cost to be met by a small duty on tobacco, and rejected by the council; in 1755 the council again defeated such a measure. In 1758 the house varied the procedure by voting down a proposal to raise the sum needed for the agency charges by an export duty on iron and then recurred to their old idea of a tax on tobacco; but the council did not vary its practice of rejection.[139] The November session of 1758 saw no agency bill introduced, possibly because the assembly was voting supplies after General Forbes's victory at Fort Duquesne and the lower house did not wish to give offense by attaching a rider. But the houses repeated their same old tactics in 1760, despite the governor's almost pathetic plea to avoid the rock on which they had hitherto split. At the spring session of 1761, the opinion of the attorney general of Great Britain was read to the lower house in which he stated the view that the upper house was right in the controversy, notwithstanding the claim of the lower house to an independent authority, and ought to be

the Province,—Borrow'd by the Crown on the Canada Expedition. . . . This transaction having been compleated with Success and at litle Expence, I trust the Province will herein deem me their ju(st) and voluntary Agent under Friendship to them."—Misc. Papers, 2, no. 6, Portfolio no. 3, Maryland MSS. He did perform occasionally the duties which an agent, if there had been one, would have performed. In this sense Lord Baltimore himself could be called an agent, for he once delivered an address of the council to the king and queen in 1762.—Ibid., Portfolio no. 4, folder 32, Maryland MSS.

[138] See Archives of Maryland, XLII, pp. 505-6 for a conciliatory reply of the proprietor read to the lower house on May 2, 1744; Mereness, op. cit., pp. 473-74. Baltimore gave up his claim to license money from ordinaries for one thing.

[139] Archives of Maryland, 1752-1754, L, 18, 41, 45, 63, 73; LII, 133, 137, 153, 161, 163, 169; LV, 593, 663-64, 665.

supported by the proprietary. A new and most interesting development of this session was the forwarding through William Franklin
of an address of condolence and congratulation to King George III
from the lower house after difference with the council over inclusion
of a paragraph on an agent. The house informed the sovereign that
Franklin "will make you acquainted with the reasons, why the
Addrefs to his Majesty, makes the irregular appearance it does."[140]
It is unlikely that this address ever reached the king. The only reply
to the severe censure in the letter of the Earl of Egremont laid before
the lower house by Governor Sharpe in March, 1762, for the small
contribution made by Maryland to the French and Indian War was
the airing of their grievance that lack of an agent prevented their
transactions from being presented in their true light.[141]

The same old bill for support of an agent led to a series of
sharp exchanges this session between the governor and the lower
house. The delegates regretted being involved in a dispute with his
excellency but felt that he had "obliquely" vindicated the conduct
of the upper house. "We think therefore your Excellency went a
little out of your Way, in supposing We intended to include You
in a Charge which is exprefsly confined to them. Although your
Excellency has not entered into a formal or exprefs Denial of the
general Necefsity of employing a Provincial Agent in London, Yet
if your Reafoning in the particular Instance you mentioned can be
supported, it necefsarily supersedes the Expediency of imploying
one on every other Contest between the Government and People. . . .
We think it amounts to little lefs than a General Denial of the
Expediency of establishing a Perfon in that Character. this We
conceive is a Doctrine of so dangerous a Tendency to the Rights of
our Constituents, that We must insist a little on your Excellency's
Patience while We explain and enforce the Right of the People to
appoint an Agent and the Expediency of exercifing that Right. . . .
We hope therefore we shall be excufed if we say it is too afsuming
in a Governor, to undertake to judge of the Expediency of the

<hr/>

[140] Black Book, XI, no. 52, p. 79. Maryland MSS; *Archives of Maryland*, LVI,
214, 229, 241-42; for the address of the house to the governor on Mar. 25, 1760, *ibid.*,
pp. 230-31; for the opinion of the attorney general, Black Book, pp. 17-18.

[141] For their reply to Governor Sharpe on the rebuke of the Earl of Egremont, Journal
of the Lower House, 1762-1768, Maryland MSS, pp. 12, 33, 53. The next volume
of the *Archives of Maryland*, covering part of the period for which references here must
be to the manuscripts, is now in press.

People having an Agent to support their Interests; when he may be considered as the Delegate of the Lord Proprietary against whom they may be desirous to exhibit their Complaints. . . ." And they added that they thought His Exccllcncy a little unhappy in his reasoning if he thought transmission of the journals informed the ministers of the nature of the dispute between the two houses. Again they said boldly: "We think it not very decent in your Excellency to pervert the Meaning of Letters from his Majesty's Ministers, by arbitrary and forced Construction, merely for the sake of throwing an Odium on our Proceedings . . . nor shall we ever be induced to deviate from what We think right, by any Suggestion from your Excellency, that his Majesty's Ministers disapprove of our Conduct."[142]

The governor then in his turn became caustic in his reply of April 22. "I hope, Gentlemen, excufs the Liberty I take in just mentioning my opinion of the Matter, nor think it afsuming in me either to judge for myself or to intimate my Sentiments. It would indeed be a little hard, if I alone, in such a Government as this, where every Subject thinks He has a Right to speak his Sentiments on every Matter, should be debarred the Liberty of thinking and judging of the Expediency, or Propriety of any Scheme whatever, or be more afraid to communicate my thoughts, than if I was at Venice under the Rule of their State Inquisition. . . . This being the Cafe, I can read without the leaft Emotion, those Parts of your Addrefs which Discontent and Disappointment seem to have dictated, nor shall I take any Notice of your ungrateful Language."[143] The governor thereupon prorogued the assembly the next day.

The bill of October, 1763, differed from previous efforts only in that it sought to lay a slightly heavier tax—four pence—on every hogshead of tobacco to support the charge of the agent, but as the council ignored it, it did not become a law. The session of December, 1765, brought forth a new gesture on the part of the council in the form of a proposal for two agents, one for each house with a sum

[142] For the entire message to the governor, which is dated April 17, see *ibid.*, pp. 55-58. To emphasize their confidence in the people's support, the house ordered its answer to the governor published in the next week's *Gazette*, which carried it accordingly in the issue of Apr. 21, 1762.

[143] Votes and Proceedings of the House of Delegates of Maryland, 1762-1768, Maryland MSS, p. 76.

of money under the control of each for his support. To such a bill the councillors would give "cheerful Afsent."[144]

Meanwhile the question of an agent had become entangled with a dispute over the salary of the clerk of the council, a matter which only inflamed the members of both houses the more bitterly. This dispute had arisen as early as 1749 when the council felt that this officer was entitled to a salary above his allowance as clerk and in addition to some emoluments settled by law for services to the executives of the government. Though up to 1747 he had received a salary, the lower house held that he should receive his income from the fines and forfeitures, and that any further pay ought to be made by the proprietor out of the twelve pence tobacco duty which had been allotted him for the support of government. They insisted strongly that the people ought not to be taxed in order to pay the clerk a fixed salary, but that at most he ought to be paid only for particular services after he had rendered a detailed account. The council objected to such an account, as its work would thus be opened to the public, and after 1756 refused to pass the journal of accounts because it omitted a salary for this clerk. The issue dragged from 1756 to 1765; no allowance was made to Mr. Ross, the clerk; no journal of accounts was passed; no public debts were paid; and Maryland's credit suffered. The council refused to agree to an agent unless the house would agree to a tax for the salary of the clerk.

Hence, when the upper house proposed an act for paying an agent for each house to lay the subject matter of the controversy before the king in council, the lower house proved decidedly averse to paying the expense of a conciliar agent to carry a case against it. The proposal that, pending a hearing in England, payment of salaries to the legislators as well as the clerk be deferred was rejected with scorn. "Your ample private Fortunes the Lucrative Offices your Honors enjoy made the daily Allowance from the country contemptible to you. Is it not wonderful you have not been pleased long ago to give up entirely to the poor people and may we not hope from the amazing Increase of your Generosity and Compafsion that a Sefsion or two more will produce a Bill in your House to repeal so much of the Old Act as gives Allowance to your Members. But the

[144] For the October session, 1763, see *ibid.*, pp. 106, 109, 123; for the December session, 1765, pp. 324, 333, 334, 335.

Case is widely different with us we confefs with Candour our private Circumstances are generally pretty strict and our Attendance here occafions great Inconvenience to ourselves and Families. We do not want to better our Fortunes by serving our Constituents we only want their Approbation quiet Consciences and an Indemnity ag^t necefsary Expenses."[145]

In view of the distressed conditions in the colony the lower house in 1766 asked the council for a conference. The three conferees of that body proposed that bills of credit be emitted not only to the amount of the public debt but also to the amount of the claim in dispute; that the further sum of £1,500 be paid to their order that the lower house might employ an agent for three years. On account of the known attitude of the proprietor, the council conferees felt obliged to reject the proposition. The conferees of the upper house then submitted three propositions, the second of which found acceptance: that appeal be carried to the king in council with regard to the clerk's salary by each house without the allotment of any money for the purpose. The lower house thereupon on December 6 appointed Charles Garth its agent, creating at the same time a committee to transmit to him a full account of the dispute over the clerk's salary as well as of their other grievances, especially the lack of an agent, to receive contributions, and to have management of a lottery to raise money to pay the agent. On this occasion, as in earlier instances, the house insisted on free access to all records in all the public offices; later access was granted them, but only as private individuals, not as officials.[146] The selection of Garth was a natural one as he was a member of parliament already serving South Carolina as agent. Most of all, he had already been asked to present the resolutions which the house had passed in September, 1765, in regard to the Stamp Act and to represent Maryland before the home government. Thus despite the consideration that the issue regarding

[145] This message from the lower to the upper house was sent Dec. 16, 1765.—*Ibid.,* pp. 341-42.

[146] *Ibid.,* p. 455; proposal for bills of credit, Nov. 20, p. 459; rejected by the council on Nov. 21, p. 460. The council's other two propositions were (1) appeal to the king with sufficient funds to cover the cost for both houses (2) all public debts, including back pay of the clerk of the council to be paid but the clerk to be paid in the future in fees.— *Ibid.,* pp. 460-61; 484; selection of Garth as agent.—*Ibid.,* p. 184; *Archives of Maryland,* 1761-1770, XXXII, 181. For access to the records see Delaplaine, "The Life of Thomas Johnson," *Maryland Historical Magazine,* XV, 183.

the salary of the clerk of the council was apparently disposed of, the matter was never prosecuted before the Privy Council. It provoked little dispute after 1766, but by 1776 it was still unsettled. The agency question also remained unregularized despite the fact that the lower house maintained Garth as agent from 1766 to 1775. Fruitless efforts to pass a bill for a colonial agent appear in the legislative assemblies of the spring and fall sessions of 1766, of 1768, 1769, and 1771.[147]

The agreement between the two houses for each to select an agent to present its side of the case in the dispute over the clerk's salary, made inevitable the existence of two agents, as in Virginia. The council agreed on March 10, 1767—less promptly than the lower house, it will be noted—to contribute to the expenses of the prosecution of their appeal to the Privy Council, and employed Hugh Hammersley, secretary of Lord Baltimore, as their agent. They then indicated four of their number to draw up a presentation of their case.[148] Hammersley reported by July 20, that he had retained the ablest counsel in England in Sir Fletcher Norton and Mr. Yorke, though he was inclined to think, from the inactivity of the house agent and the lack of success of their plan for financing him, that the delegates were hunting a pretense to drop the matter. The degree to which Lord Baltimore regarded the quarrel of the council his quarrel may be measured by the fact that he insisted on paying Hammersley the fees of the retainers.[149]

The last significant defense by the Maryland House of Delegates of the right to an agent of their own was voiced in 1773 to Lord Dartmouth: "Self defence, my Lord, whether it regards Individuals or Bodys of men is the first Law of Nature, the right of Defence includes a Right to all the means requisite and proper for that De-

[147] Votes and Proceedings of the House of Delegates of Maryland, 1762-1768, for the May session, Maryland MSS., pp. 372, 387, 394; fall session of 1766, pp. 443, 452; for 1768, pp. 501, 504, 512, 543; for 1769, pp. 17, 36, 59; for 1771, p. 231. There is no record of action by the council in 1771.

[148] Archives of Maryland, XXXII, 186. See also letter of Governor Sharpe to Hammersley of Mar. 11, ibid., XIV, 385. See also his letter of Dec. 8, 1766, to the agent, ibid., p. 356.

[149] Ibid., pp. 406, 407. The lower house instructed Garth to petition the crown for an order to permit that body to appoint and support an agent. Hammersley stated that if presented, he would make a similar application in behalf of the council.—Ibid., pp. 395, 417.

fence and consequently a right to appoint and support their own Defender, without the governor's concurrence."[150]

By this date, however, the people's grievances in Maryland against parliament and the crown had become far greater than against the all but vanquished proprietor. The agency question was lost sight of in the agitation over the Stamp Act, the Boston Port Bill, and all the other acts which led up to the Revolution.

The story of the regular agency in Georgia is relatively short. The appointment of William Knox as assistant to Benjamin Martyn on February 19, 1762, has already been noted in the preceding chapter. With Knox's appointment as sole "provincial" agent to "solicit the Affairs of this Province in Great Britain," on April 7, 1763, for a regular term, at a fixed salary, and with a Committee of Correspondence in which both houses were represented to instruct him, the agency in Georgia may be regarded as fairly constituted.[151] He served, being regularly reappointed annually without friction, until on November 15, 1765, when the Committee of Correspondence was instructed to "acquaint Mr Knox that this Province hath no further Occasion for his Service," as he had given offence by his position on the Stamp Act. The council members of the Committee of Correspondence refused, however, on January 21, 1766, to act with the house members in notifying him of dismissal. The house then instructed its members to write Knox, enclosing the resolutions passed by that body.[152] Governor Wright had already cautiously suggested that if the house should decide that it was necessary to appoint another agent, Richard Cumberland was "a Gentleman perfectly conversant in the Business of an Agent well known and respected at the several Offices and for whose Abilities and Integrity" he could vouch.[153] The house, however, had already asked Charles Garth to act as a semi-official agent "to transact the only Business

---

[150] This passage occurs in a letter from the House of Delegates of Mar. 5, 1773.— C. O. 5/762, p. 305.

It is significant of the deep interest taken in the agency question that on Jan. 1, 1767, the *Maryland Gazette* printed the following about the Massachusetts agent: "We hear the Assembly were almost unanimously for the dismission of Richard Jackson, Esq. from the Agency of this Province. The Vote in the House was carried by 81 against 6; yet the Governor has not assented. So hard is it to get rid of an Agent. This should serve for a proper Caution for the future."

[151] *Colonial Records of Georgia*, XVIII, 536-38; XIII, p. 730.

[152] *Ibid.*, XIV, 294, 336.

[153] An almost identical message was sent to both houses.—*Ibid.*, pp. 327, 503-4.

they know of"—undoubtedly presentation of a petition against the Stamp Act—and so thought it unnecessary to appoint any other person.[154] The council continued to regard Knox as the agent and several months after the house voted to dismiss him, passed a resolution of thanks for his faithful services.[155]

Formal appointment of Garth as agent of the colony as a whole was attempted by the house on March 10, 1767, but the council refused to concur on the ground that he was already serving as agent for South Carolina, and as there were then matters of difference depending between the two provinces, it would be incompatible for him to discharge his duty to both. The council insisted that Georgia had no agent at that time, could have none legally without concurrence of the council, and objected to payment of the sum already sent by the treasurer to pay Garth for his special solicitation on the Stamp Act, which it stigmatized as "irregular and unprecedented and as having a direct Tendency to subvert its essential Rights and Privileges." The house then made him agent of that body alone. Naturally, the governor's protest was soon audible. In a speech sent the last day of the session Governor Wright evidently referred to Garth as a "mock Agent" whom he would oppose at every board and declared that not one farthing of the salary provided for him should be paid.[156]

Nevertheless, the lower house again the next session on February 3, 1768, passed an ordinance reappointing Garth agent, which was virtually rejected by the upper body by postponement to the first Tuesday in July.[157] Just at this time there arrived Garth's letter of November 27, 1767, declining to act as the agent of one house

[154] The reply to the governor's suggestion of Dec. 19, 1765, was made Jan. 22, 1766, and conveyed information of Garth's appointment.—*Ibid.*, p. 337. The statement that Garth was employed to present a petition against the Stamp Act is based on an entry of Dec. 14, 1765, in the Journal of the Commons House of Assembly, showing that the speaker signed the petition of Massachusetts, Rhode Island, New Jersey, Pennsylvania, and Maryland and transmitted it to Garth with the request that he present the same.—*Colonial Records of Georgia*, II, 316-17.

[155] *Ibid.*, XVII, 269. On Mar. 26, 1767, it requested Knox to solicit at the several boards the rights of the council.—*Ibid.*, pp. 372-73.

[156] *Ibid.*, XIV, 458, 474, 511; XVII, 366-68. The council did pass the tax bill of 1767 because rejection might have been harmful to the public welfare, but it specifically warned that the action of the lower house must not constitute a precedent. The substance of Governor Wright's address, though it does not seem to be extant, can be gathered from the reply of the house on Jan. 29, 1768, of the next session.—*Ibid.*, XIV, 510-11.

[157] *Ibid.*, pp. 507, 508, 512, 527; XVII, 392.

alone; accordingly the lower house asked for a conference with the upper house at which Garth's letter was read. Since the council would not recede from their objections to Mr. Garth's appointment, and since the house found an agent necessary to secure royal approbation of certain acts, the latter fearing that a person appointed irregularly might be of little service, on March 24, 1768, waived their appointment of Garth "rather than expose the province to the evils that may arise from the want of an Agent."[158] The lower house of commons then turned to Benjamin Franklin[159] and sent up a measure on the twenty-fifth of March, to make him agent which was accepted by the council with amendments April 5, and assented to by the governor on April 4.

Governor Wright reported gloomily to the Board of Trade on June 8 that he had been credibly informed that several of the members of the assembly declared that they would compel the governor and council to order the payment of the £100 which was owing to Garth "in the way they Mean to have it." The council felt that they could not give way, and so the governor feared a deadlock at the next session in October unless "I can fall on Some Method to Remove the Obstacle in the mean time." He naturally desired instructions on the tax bill.[160] Instructions on this subject had been penned by Secretary Hillsborough July 20, 1768, before Wright's inquiry reached him. While the governor and council had no discretion as to the issuing of money the secretary hoped "from the Firmnefs, which has so generally distinguished your Conduct and that of the Council, that neither You nor they will ever again, from any Consideration, consent to a Law, by which the House of Representatives shall, under Color of appropriating public Money, set up and afsume to themselves the sole Right of appointing an Agent for the colony."[161]

Already an opinion of the members of the Board of Trade, which

[158] *Ibid.*, XIV, pp. 572-73.

[159] Franklin himself says in a letter to his son, William, dated July 2, 1768, that he could not account for his appointment as he could recall no acquaintance in Georgia. It has been suggested that the Mr. Reverend George Whitefield might have suggested him, but his distinction as the outstanding agent is sufficient to account for his selection.

[160] *Colonial Records of Georgia*, XIV, 576, 579. Wright's letter to the Board is to be found in C. O. 5/650, p. 95, dated June 8, 1768.

[161] C. O. 5/677, pp. 10-11. For an account of this controversy see Flippin, "The Royal Government in Georgia," *Georgia Historical Quarterly*, VIII, 103-4, 116-17.

the crown accepted as its own, in regard to an analogous situation in Massachusetts Bay, had been forwarded by Secretary Shelburne on February 20, 1768. Their decision was that the house of representatives had no right to appoint an agent residing in England, constituted by their sole authority and retained in their separate service and pay. This seems to have been the view of the crown officials in all precedents from 1709 when the first case of this character arose and was condemned in Barbados. The Board of Trade feared that receiving an agent so partially constituted into the various offices and departments would most probably be attended with inconvenience and embarrassment; though agents might have inadvertently been admitted under separate appointment of the assembly, yet such precedents "can not be construed to establish a Right" and the members felt that his Majesty's ministers might where they apprehended inconvenience from reception of such an agent persist in excluding him, "without any Infraction of the Rights and Privilegs of the Assembly who are his Constituents."[162] Thus was put an end to a dispute which had lasted over a year between the two houses in Georgia. The outcome seemed to establish the necessity of concurrence of the council, though right of appointment inhered in the lower house of assembly. It was, of course, a compromise.

Though Franklin was reëlected agent each year until and including 1774, elections were not at regularly stated intervals, and met with some difficulty as would be expected from the turbulence of the times. In January, 1770, he was reëlected for a term which dated from the first of the preceding June; in May the effort to regularize his terms by reappointment for the year which would begin on the first of the next month had to await confirmation of the council until the next December because of the dissolution of the assembly. Franklin continued, however, to transact business for the colony. The council agreed to reappointment September 29, 1773; but the house had also provided, since he might necessarily be absent, to appoint Grey Elliott agent during his absence.[163] Oddly enough,

[162] This entire opinion is found in C. O. 5/766, pp. 80-85. The opinion in the Barbados case was felt so applicable to the Massachusetts case that a copy was sent to Massachusetts. Shelburne's covering letter, dated Feb. 20, 1768, is found in C. O. 5/677, p. 1.

[163] He was reëlected by the house Dec. 20, 1769, rejected by the council Jan. 17, 1770, his term to date from the first of the preceding June.—Colonial Records of Georgia, XV,

Governor Wright refused his assent to the reappointment of Franklin, but assented to Elliott, appointed "a kind of Conditional Agent," but as there were several "absurdities" in the bill, he thought it would prove void and expected a new ordinance presented the next month.[164]   Unexpectedly in 1774 the council objected to Franklin when it received the house ordinance of reappointment.   Several members of a committee to inquire into his conduct could not recall ever seeing or hearing a letter from him save an acknowledgment of his appointment.   Hence on February 4 that body unanimously rejected the ordinance, having assented hitherto probably only because of his eminence but convinced now that he had never done any real service to the province.[165]   About a month later it asked the governor to request that no person in the character of provincial agent be received at any public board in England who was not duly appointed by an act of the entire legislative body.   The house nevertheless declared Franklin agent on March 2 and asserted the power of appointing an agent as exclusively lodged in the representatives of the people.[166]

The acceptance of Grey Elliott[167] as assistant agent in the event of Franklin's possible absence was natural, as he was a member of the Georgia council.   Georgia seems to have had an agent functioning later than any other colony.   On September 13, 1779, long after

---

66, 81; again on May 5 for the year June 1, 1770-1771 (p. 190), confirmed by the council Dec. 21 (p. 260); reëlected again in 1773 by the house and council (pp. 370, 378).   For Elliott's appointment see pp. 369, 492, 496, 537.

[164] Governor Wright thought that no letter had yet been written by the Committee or "like to be."—C. O. 5/652, p. 14.

[165] *Colonial Records of Georgia*, XVII, 777, 782, 785.   The British ministers departed during these disturbed times from their refusal to receive addresses except through the governor and accepted one from the Commons House of Georgia through Franklin.   The king did not weigh its contents with less attention, according to Hillsborough.—Stated in a letter from him to Governor Wright of Jan. 4, 1769, C. O. 5/677, p. 29.   The charge that Franklin had sent no communications is an odd one, for on May 3, 1770, the lower house in response to the council's request for the correspondence conducted with Franklin, ordered it laid before the upper house.—*Colonial Records of Georgia*, XV, 188. A letter was read to the house Feb. 6, 1770.—*Ibid.*, p. 108.

[166] *Ibid.*, XVII, 775.   Governor Wright's letter, sent in compliance with the request of the council, adds nothing new.   For the declaration of the house of Mar. 2, see *ibid.*, pp. 782-83.   For Dartmouth's reply of May 4, 1774, assuring the council that no person unless appointed by the entire legislature would be received as agent, see C. O. 5/677, p. 99.

[167] It must be remembered that a bill to appoint Elliott agent had appeared in the lower house on Dec. 8, 1769, but had failed Feb. 6, 1770.—*Colonial Records of Georgia*, XV, 66, 108.

Franklin had taken his departure from London, Elliott solicited the post at the same time that he reminded Georgia delicately of the arrears of pay due him. As late as June 8, 1781, by Lord Germain's order an act passed by Georgia granting duties on exports, with an extract from the governor's letter, was sent Elliott to be laid by him before the Board of Trade. And yet there is no proof that Elliott served more than the two years he himself claims, as the forwarding of acts for him to solicit may have been irregular, isolated actions.[168]

Development of the institution of the agency thus proved stormy in all these Southern colonies. Long disputes over the agency between the governor and the council on the one side and the lower house on the other terminated in dual agencies for a longer or shorter period or in an agent recognized only by one house. This situation probably arose because the Southern colonies were royal or proprietary in government. Only in the Northern charter colonies did the regular agency develop without factional disputes. Its growth resolved itself into a basic constitutional conflict between the royal or proprietary governor, often assisted by the council, against a popularly elected assembly.

[168] For Elliott's letter, asking for the post, see *ibid.*, XV, 599. The policy of soliciting the post will be treated in Chapter XI. For Elliott's statement as to the length of service see *ibid.*, p. 602. The evidence of transmission of acts to Elliott is found in C. O. 5/652, f. 57.

CHAPTER 3.

SPECIAL AGENTS

THROUGHOUT the period of the regularly established agency there were special agents sent to London. These appeared whenever there was a matter of special importance or urgency or if the colony feared on the part of the regular agent lack of knowledge or zeal for the matter under controversy. Sometimes the new envoy was sent to bolster and aid the regular agent; sometimes he was sent almost independently.

As might be expected, because of the length of time covered by the Virginia agency and the numerous problems which complicated her history, that province produced more such special agents than the others combined, while Georgia and Maryland employed almost none.

The agency of Philip Ludwell, brother of Thomas, who discharged one of the last missions before the establishment of the regular agency, occurred within the first decade after Virginia accepted the idea of the necessity of such an official on her pay roll. In the hearts of Virginia Protestants there was fear and resentment over the news of James II's Declaration of Indulgence of 1687, and also despair over the local question of securing relief from the oppressions of Francis, Lord Howard of Effingham. Within the letter of the law Effingham committed many arbitrary acts, and it was during his incumbency that the power of hearing appeals was taken from the House of Burgesses and vested in the governor and council as the court of final resort. By this time some of the most reactionary elements had turned against his lordship. After the council had refused to join them in a representation, the burgesses in April, 1688, appointed Councillor Philip Ludwell, whom Effingham had suspended in 1687, to carry their address to England. He sailed on the same ship as the governor, who left Nathaniel Bacon,[1] a wealthy,

---

[1] This Nathaniel Bacon is to be distinguished from his younger cousin who led Bacon's Rebellion in 1676.

conservative, and politic old man who had served years in the council, to act in his place. Effingham arrived in London to find his king about to face a revolution and Ludwell in a strong position to call the governor to account. Several writers indicate that James II had already fled before Ludwell arrived, but the evidence to the contrary is indisputable. Ludwell himself in a petition undated but clearly before March 28, 1689, says that he did "in September last at Windsor present their said Grievances and Petition to his late Ma^{tys} own hands, whereon nothing was done by reason of the approaching Revolution since hapned. . . ." The governor found himself charged by Ludwell with collecting illegal fees for affixing the seal of the commonwealth and for registering land surveys; with duplicity in establishing ports; with bringing personal attacks against his opponents; and with using government funds improperly.[2] Ludwell reveals in one of his petitions that the Virginia assembly had complained of their grievances to the governor and council in three successive sessions to no effect; that the house had sent an address to King James but that no reply had been made to it; and that he had presented their address to King James II in person in September, 1688, but that no action was taken, owing to the impending revolution.[3] On about March 2, 1689, however, his petition was presented to the Privy Council and referred March 28 to the Lords of Trade; on May 31 both Governor Howard and Colonel Ludwell were heard by the last-named body and the case sent to the attorney

[2] For a general account of the dispute between Effingham and Virginia see Beverley, *History of Virginia*, pp. 77-79; Bruce, *History of Virginia*, I, 251-56; Osgood, *American Colonies in the Seventeenth Century*, III, 306-8; Squires, *Through Centuries Three*, pp. 233-34; Stanard, *Virginia's First Century*, p. 308. For date of the king's flight see C. O. 5/305, f. 21.

The house was dissolved by the governor immediately after it had framed its petition.— *Journals of the House of Burgesses*, 1659/60-1693, p. 329.

[3] C. O. 5/1305, f. 21. With his own petition Ludwell submitted the petition of the House of Burgesses (f. 22), and a statement of grievances which listed among the unlawful fees:

1. Fee of 200 pounds of tobacco for the use of the government seal on patents, probates, estates.

2. Fee of 30 pounds of tobacco for recording surveys of land, when there is a fee already.

3. All fines and forfeitures are appropriated to the support of government.—*Ibid.*, ff. 23-24.

C. O. 391/63, p. 214; Minutes of the Privy Council, C. O. 5/1305, f. 20. Ludwell presented a petition to the Committee of Trade and Plantations apparently March 2, 1688, copies of which were ordered sent to Governor Howard for his reply.

general and solicitor general for their opinion.[4] On September 19, 1689, Ludwell's petition, wherein the grievances were enumerated, was again referred to the Lords of Trade. The case was set for October 16, but as late as November 20, Ludwell was complaining that he could not secure a copy of Howard's answers to his charges, though his paper of grievances had been sent to the governor for a reply.[5] At the close of the year, as the Virginia ships were almost ready to sail, Ludwell begged the Lords of Trade that "whatever report they will make may be done speedily." He pointed out that because of his long absence, his own affairs as well as the anxiety of the colony for his return necessitated his departure at the first opportunity, provided their lordships laid no "comand on him to the contrarie." March 4, 1690, the draft of a report on the case was read by the Lords of Trade.[6] Some of the grievances were redressed; others were explained because they arose from the mistakes in a point of English law; and Lord Howard was ordered to remain in England. This order was probably no punishment even though he was on half pay, but unfortunately it created a precedent for absentee governors to draw a major portion of the emoluments while a deputy did the work. Finis was written to the Ludwell agency when on May 7, 1691, the burgesses passed a resolution of thanks and pay for his services at the British court.[7]

In about two years' time William Blathwayt, secretary to the Lords of Trade, was requested to endeavor as agent to procure the royal assent to a law for ports. The Act for Ports had been passed at the spring session of the Virginia assembly of 1691. That part of it fixing a tax on skins and furs had already gone into effect; the part for the erection of towns was to have become operative on October 1, 1692. The old difficulties, however, to the erection of proper warehouses had been encountered, and many complaints had been voiced. The general assembly in April, 1692, employed as agent this distinguished Englishman to secure approval of this act by the king and queen so that there need be no doubt even on the part of the shipmasters as to its status. Reasons for its approval were drawn up and transmitted to the agent intended to convince the

[4] C. O. 391/63, p. 224.
[5] *Calendar of State Papers, Colonial*, 1689-1692, secs. 447, 451, 486, 578, 460.
[6] C. O. 5/1305, f. 73; *Calendar of State Papers, Colonial*, 1689-1692, sec. 447.
[7] *Ibid.*, sec. 1452. He had, of course, returned before this time, presumably in 1690.

home government that the act would advance religion and learning and increase trade. He seems, however, to have met with scant success, for, as the time approached for the act to go into effect, the sovereigns had not given their approval nor had they sent any word by the time the next assembly convened. Hence the act was suspended. With these scanty data William Blathwayt passes from the records as a Virginia agent.[8]

Now there treads the Virginia stage the Reverend James Blair, who served his province on special missions several times and should be honored as one of the earliest pioneers in the history of American higher education. He was first sent over in May, 1691, to secure a charter for a college in Virginia. There was at that time only one privately endowed school and a few old "field schools" in the entire colony. The Reverend Mr. Blair had talked education in such a way as to inspire enthusiasm among the inhabitants and especially among the burgesses. With the other clergymen he prepared "Several propositions to be humbly presented to the consideration of ye next General Assembly, for ye better encouragement of learning." His plan called for a college of three schools—Grammar (language), Philosophy, and Divinity. He requested the assembly to petition the king and queen for a charter, a grant of land, a part of the quit-rents of Virginia, and other small revenues for the establishment of the school.[9] Although his instructions were very full, covering some twenty articles, so great was the assembly's confidence in him that he was told to do as he should "think necessarie" in presenting the supplication. He was directed to seek the assistance of the Bishop of London and to depend upon his advice as to the best way to execute his commission. If he obtained the charter, he was to secure a "good Schoolmaster, Usher, & Writing Master," and then to use his best endeavors to secure "Lysense" to collect as many "Subscriptions, Guifts and Benevolences" as he could.[10] Setting sail in June, 1691,

[8] The lower house acted on his nomination on April 25, the council on April 27.—*Journals of the House of Burgesses*, 1659/60-1693, pp. 402, 405.

[9] The address to Their Majesties was presented to the House of Burgesses May 20, 1691.—*Ibid.*, p. 368. The Council indorsed the provision for his expenses on May 22.—*Legislative Journals of the Council*, I, 155.

[10] The article providing for the care of the money contributed is illuminating as to the persons in whom the Virginians reposed confidence. It was to be kept in such places as agreed upon by the Bishop of London, Lord Howard of Effingham, who apparently had recovered their confidence, Jeffrey Jeffreys, Micajah Perry, the merchant, and Blair himself.—C. O. 5/1306, ff. 120-21.

he arrived in London by September. King William was in Flanders
directing the war then in progress; the Bishop of London was ill;
and the Archbishop of Canterbury, upon whom the king relied in
ecclesiastical matters, was at Lambeth, and when winter came on,
he was detained there for five weeks before he could come to London; finally, parliament and the Privy Council were completely ab-
sorbed in the war.[11]

Blair wasted no time but spent the months of waiting in trying
to raise money for the college; his efforts resulted in the donation
known as the Boyle Fund and other gifts, amounting to several
hundred pounds. When the Bishop of London recovered late in
the fall, he received the colonial kindly and promised his support.
His advice was to take the project before the Privy Council and
Committee on Plantations. But Blair had planned to take it directly
to the crown, for he wished funds as well as a charter and could
scarcely hope for a grant from the Privy Council where the church
party was in the minority. Supported in his view by the Bishop of
Worcester and converting the Bishop of London to this same view,
he pursued his goal with wisdom, zeal, and indefatigable energy.
He secured an interview with Queen Mary, who graciously approved
the projected college in Virginia, secured the aid of the Archbishop of
Canterbury when he finally came to London—in a word he carefully prepared the soil. Always he laid emphasis on the great im-
pulse that such an institution would be to religion in the new world.
He played many variations on the chord that thus a nursery of piety
conducted by unswerving conformists would be created in Virginia.
As a result the clergy lent him active and powerful assistance. When
he was finally afforded the opportunity to present his project to the
Privy Council, the provincial clergyman, introduced by the Archbishop and Lord Effingham, presented it in an effective way, securing the king's promise in the end to promote the plan to the best of
his power. He was asked to submit a specific plan to the Bishop
of London for presentation to the Committee on Plantations. Toward
founding the college Their Majesties gave almost £2,000, the balance
due upon the account of quitrents, and toward endowing it they
granted twenty thousand acres of choice land as well as the revenue
arising from the penny duty per pound on tobacco exported from

[11] Motley, *Life of Commissary James Blair*, p. 27.

Virginia and Maryland to the other plantations. When Blair was sent to Attorney General Seymour with the royal order to issue a charter, the latter argued that England was at war and could not afford to erect a college in Virginia. Dr. Blair explained as usual that it was to educate men to preach the gospel, as Virginia had souls to be saved. This brought forth the oft quoted ejaculation: "Souls, damn your souls! Make tobacco." The project met also with scant sympathy from business men who feared that it would take "our planters off from their mechanical employments and make them grow too knowing to be obedient and submissive." But Blair was not to be discouraged by an oath, and he got his charter, including a provision creating him president of the college for life.[12] In the spring of 1693 he returned triumphantly to Virginia with the charter.

Blair's second agency, discussed for the sake of simplicity out of chronological order, occurred in 1697. A man who has proved himself a money-getter is always called upon thereafter to display his skill, and a college always needs money. Therefore, what more natural than to find Blair back in England in 1697 to beg more money for the college? A few hints scattered through the various records of the time show that he was temporarily added to the regular agency. A letter from the trustees of the College of William and Mary to Governor Andros found its way into the files of the Board of Trade, inclosed in a letter of the governor's dated April 23, 1697. According to the letter, the work of building and furnishing the college had been brought almost to a halt for lack of money, and so they (presumably the assembly) had desired President Blair to go home to procure what assistance he could toward furnishing the building.[13] But colonials in England could not hope to escape questioning upon American problems. Hence, we find Blair taking on somewhat the character of a regular agent, for in August, 1697, he was before the Board of Trade, giving information regarding the price of tobacco in connection with quitrents and with the pay of clergy in Virginia. As a final question on this occasion he was asked to indicate other persons in London who could speak authoritatively of conditions in the colony. He named Colonel Hartwell, who was

[12] *Ibid.*, pp. 27-30; Beverley, *op. cit.*, pp. 80, 81; Bruce, *Institutional History of Virginia*, I, 390-91. The general assembly also elected him president of the college which he had done so much to create.

[13] C. O. 5/1359, p. 57.

too feeble to go out; Mr. Chilton, who had appeared before the Board the preceding year; and a Major Wilson, who lived with Micajah Perry, and who the reader may perhaps justifiably infer was a trader of some sort. Queries were accordingly directed to two of these gentlemen on September 9,[14] as the Board could thus obtain opinions which did not reflect those of the governor and council. Later that year, October 8, the Board ordered their secretary to ask Blair, Hartwell, and Chilton to send a full, written account on the state of Virginia. They submitted their statement jointly and this became the origin of the well-known pamphlet which the three later issued under the title, *The Present State of Virginia*. The chief author was doubtless Blair.[15]

At the same time, because of the profound dissatisfaction of the Virginians with their governor, Blair brought thirteen charges against Governor Andros as an enemy to the church, the clergy, and the college. Though numerous, the complaints were not petty nor personal, but all pertained to matters of importance to the colony. The hearing of the case, covering two days, took place late in December, 1697, in Lambeth Palace. The governor had assembled powerful defenders including Colonel Byrd and Povey as solicitors, whom we have already met, in order to turn the tables and arraign Blair before the Archbishop of Canterbury and the Bishop of London. Blair successfully refuted both of the accusations brought against him—and indeed they were weak—that he had, contrary to the wishes of the people, filled the parishes with Scotchmen and that he had accepted salary as president before the college was completed. On the other hand, he sustained his charges against the governor, often forcing

[14] C. O. 391/10, p. 223. It must not, of course, be inferred that any of these men except Blair were serving as agents. The Board frequently sought information about the colonies from anyone who was in a special position to know conditions in them. They are introduced here only because two of them became associated with Blair in a document. See also *Calendar of State Papers, Colonial*, 1696-1697, pp. 606-10 for the list of questions. Chilton appeared before the Board on September 20 (see sec. 334).

The list of questions sent Hartwell, and presumably Chilton, on September 9 were also addressed to Colonel Parke (or Parks) on May 27, 1698. Later, July 11, 1698, Parke also gave data on illegal trading from Virginia to Scotland.—C. O. 5/1359, pp. 207, 232-34.

[15] The order of the Board appears in one of their Journals, C. O. 391/10, p. 300. See C. O. 5/1309, f. 83, and also Osgood, *The American Colonies in the Eighteenth Century*, I, 349-50. *The Present State of Virginia* has been reprinted recently, edited by Hunter Dickinson Farish, Williamsburg, 1940.

his opponents to admit the truth. The outcome of the hearing was the exoneration of Blair and the recall of Governor Andros.

Yet once more, as an old man of seventy-one, Blair crossed the ocean in 1726 to present an address from the general assembly to the king a part of which only was a supplication for the royal bounty to the college. He bore also a letter from Governor Drysdale to the Board of Trade, dated July 10, 1726, for their favor and interest so far as he might have occasion for their support in the negotiation.[16]

Next in logical sequence comes William Byrd II, whose several confusing agencies will be treated together. In April, 1697, as he was about to depart for London to defend Andros at the Lambeth Conference, he was selected by the assembly to deliver a document of exceptional importance to the throne, an address of congratulation for escape from a conspiracy, and was thus associated for this specific purpose with Mr. John Povey, later the regular solicitor.[17] His second agency extending from about October, 1698, to 1699 appears, as has been related in the preceding chapter, to have been the only one on which he served as official, regular representative of the governor and council. His third period of service arrived in 1702, when the government had ordered the assembly to vote funds and to send troops for the aid of New York if it were attacked. In brief, the burgesses and the majority of the council felt that the order had been obtained from the king by misrepresentation on the part of New York; that it was necessary that conditions be truthfully represented to the king; and that the best method of making this representation was by an agent. In this instance the assembly in September, 1701, chose Byrd, already in England, as agent to present their address to the king and thus obviate the demand for similar grants in the future. Lest the session be ended without completing the financial details connected with the agency, for the governor refused to concur in the provision for the agent's pay, Mr. William Byrd I was requested to forward to his son the addresses to the crown, signed by the council as well as the house, and copies of

[16] C. O. 5/1320, f. 65. Blair may have made other trips to England, but not as accredited agent for the colony.

[17] The files of the Board of Trade prove that he was associated with Povey, the appointment taking place shortly before April 24, 1697.—C. O. 5/1309, f. 51; C. O. 5/1359, p. 75.

the legislative proceedings which bore upon the quota asked of Virginia. He was also asked to assure his son that the house would be accountable to him for his expenditures and an honorarium. It is interesting that in this situation Governor Nicholson felt it desirable to have a personal agent to present the situation from his point of view, and dispatched Dionysius Wright, a lawyer and former clerk of the council who had lived in Virginia more than thirty years and who knew "ye humors of the people" very well. He humbly proposed that no encouragement should be given to the council and burgesses in their address or to the agent but that the king should signify his displeasure with the assembly.[18] Byrd prosecuted the affairs entrusted to him faithfully, first drawing up a petition to the sovereign for an audience at which he might present the addresses. He did succeed in getting the addresses before the Board of Trade. It is clear that he sought to be heard on the Virginia address on the ninth of the following April but was told that his appointment as the assembly's particular agent, when he was not soliciting complaints against the governor, was irregular, as the governor was the proper channel of communication. The Board did, however, consent to consider the address, irregular though it was. Their report, made in due time, strongly condemned the appointment of an agent by the general assembly alone, and it advised that the sovereign in a letter to Governor Nicholson take note of the irregularity. Governor Nicholson also should be directed to seek a voluntary compliance with the request for assistance to New York.[19]

[18] By the lower house, Aug. 26; Sept. 27 by the council.—*Journals of the House of Burgesses*, 1695-1702, pp. 267-68; *Legislative Journals of the Council*, I, 316-17. See a letter of Governor Nicholson to the Board of Trade on Dec. 2, 1701. He felt that "If they succeed in this Addresse, I have reason to believe yt whatever Commands shall come from his Majsty of ye like Nature, they will in ye some manner be changed; and it may cost more . . . in ye long sitting of an Assembly, and employing of an Agent than what his Majty commands shall be done."—C. O. 5/1312, f. 113.

The governor also made use of Philip Ludwell who gives some insight into the situation in a statement of March 15, 1702/3. The assembly spent £1,800 and voted their agent £300 to avoid spending £900 for the troops. When the governor threatened to keep them sitting so long that the cost of the session would make them odious to the people, they contemplated a vote to serve for nothing for the rest of the session, but the governor thwarted them by sending in fresh business. It does not appear to whom this letter was addressed, but it is found among the Board of Trade papers.—C. O. 5/1314, Bundle 15, pp. 20-21. It is interesting that Ludwell's name had been proposed for agent in the House of Burgesses. The fact that Byrd was in England and so required less expense money may have weighed with the house.

[19] C. O. 391/14, p. 404.

Byrd's next appearance before the Board of Trade was the result of the first effort of the House of Burgesses on May 27, 1718, to create by their own resolution their separate agent after the council by a narrow margin had rejected the proposal for a special agent. The body had framed an address to the king asking that the instruction which forbade the governor's assent in the future to any bill on shipping or trade without a suspending clause be withdrawn as it frequently happened in emergencies that laws should go into effect at once. They could hardly expect Blakiston, considered the provincial agent but the appointee of the governor and council, to support such a measure. Furthermore, what the opposition really desired was an advocate in London to work against Lieutenant Governor Spotswood for the interest of the burgesses. Therefore, they turned to Byrd, who had been back in London since 1715 on private business and who had been a member of their body, though latterly of the council, since 1709 in fact. He was to secure favorable consideration for the address, and, if the actions of the burgesses were misrepresented, to have "regard to their Honour." In general, he was to take upon him to "execute the said office [of agent] pursuant to the Refolves of this Houfe." Instructions had been drawn up by a committee and accepted by the house by May 30. The last paragraph of the instructions show how far the house was from any idea of a permanent agent of their own. Since the colony had no way to present their grievances but by an agent, and since the governor would hardly consent to complain against himself, Byrd was "to endeavour to obtain an Inftruction to our Governor to confent to any fuch necefsary payment when the Houfe of Burgefses fhall fee meet." Even though Spotswood vetoed the bill, the burgesses resolved to pay the salary.[20] When the item of salary arose in Novem-

[20] *Journals of the House of Burgesses,* 1712-1726, p. 210 (and *Cal. State Papers,* 1717-1718, sec. 456); his instructions are printed on p. 231; the address to the crown on pp. 207-8. See also *Legislative Journals of the Council,* II, 617, 618, 619, 657.

Through Spotswood's letter to the Board of Trade June 24, 1718, we are able to follow the moves in the upper body: "This power [to name and pay an agent] tho' strenuously contended for by such of the Council who sett the Burgesses to work, was, nevertheless so ill relished by the soberer men of the same party, and so exclaimed against by the other Gent'n of that Council who are not in their Interest, that it was at last thrown out in th Council, And soon after a Vote passed in ye Burg's's House appointing Mr. Byrd their Agent." He spoke of throwing away the country's money on such an agent when they had so little business for him to negotiate.—Spotswood, *Official Letters,* II, 277-78.

The burgesses added another clause complaining of the power of the governor to nomi-

ber, the governor, ignoring Byrd, declared himself ready to transmit any addresses or instructions to Colonel Blakiston "the Perfon his Majefty has allow'd to be Agent for this Colony," without any expense, "even tho the faid Addref doth Contain Matter of Complaint ag^t the Governor himfelf."[21]

By the time the assembly had convened for the second session of 1718 some members of the House of Burgesses, with the concurrence of the council, had determined to secure the removal of Spotswood. On November 20, when only some thirty-seven members were present out of fifty-two—many had gone home—one member proposed an address to the king which accused Spotswood of subverting the constitution and of depriving them of their ancient rights. It was adopted the following day. The instructions for the agent on this head were, however, amended until they contained no serious charge against the governor. His friends in the lower house had rallied, despite the suddenness of the attack, to his support so that the revised instructions did not direct the agent to work for his removal. But the incident did not improve the governor's love for the agent of the faction opposed to him. As early as October Spotswood had written that he knew that Byrd, "whom we have desired to appear in behalf of your oppressed Subjects of this Colony," was to procure the removal of both himself and Governor Orkney.[22] The fourteenth article in the instructions, which is the only one which concerns us, was incorporated with little change; Byrd was to try for an order obliging the governor to consent to any appropriation voted by the burgesses for payment of an agent.[23]

As a councillor[24] Byrd had free access to the Board of Trade during his years in London, but that body, true to the principles enunciated in 1697, objected to receiving addresses through him instead

nate the judges of the oyer and terminer courts and praying that the council might be the sole judges of life and death.—*Ibid.*, II, 277.

[21] *Legislative Journals of the Council*, II, 631.

[22] *Journals of the House of Burgesses, 1712-1726*, IX, 228, 230, 231. On October 22 Spotswood wrote Secretary Craggs, "to show that their Resentment is not altogether personal against Me, but that even Gov't itself is the burden they complain of, they attribute the Source of these Evils to my Lord Orkney, who doth not reside among 'em, as well as to mySelf. . . ."—*Official Letters*, II, 307.

[23] See Dodson, *Alexander Spotswood, Governor of Colonial Virginia*, pp. 183-88 for an account of this attack on Spotswood.

[24] There is evidence in the Board of Trade records of his appearance for the council.— Entry Book, Nov. 16, 1717, C. O. 5/1365, p. 14.

of the governor. He insisted that as a member of the council[25] he had a right to be heard in a matter which deeply affected the council, and on this ground the Board allowed him to appear. He wrote a fellow councillor that the assembly needed its own agent, since Blakiston was under the dominance of Spotswood. Byrd was diligent and active before the Board, but he could make little impression as it accepted the opinion of the attorney general that the governor had legally the powers which he was exercising but should use them discreetly. Byrd appealed to the crown on the basis that the governor had powers dangerous to the liberties of the people. The appeal availed nothing, of course, when the king, according to the practice, called on the Board of Trade for an opinion. Hence Byrd again returned to Virginia about February, 1720.[26]

For the fifth and last time Byrd consented to represent Virginia in 1721. In mid-December, 1720, the governor and a majority of both house and council agreed on the need of sending a special agent with an address of the assembly to the crown, and to represent to the admiralty details relating to a treaty with the Five Nations of Iroquois and "all Such other matters as may hereafter be agreed on by the General Assembly."[27] They could not, however, agree on the person to fill the post. A deciding vote in the lower house by the speaker was necessary to elect Colonel William Byrd, who was again about to depart for England. As the council was debating the house resolution, the governor submitted a message which pointed out the impropriety of "interposing a perfon of the creation" of the house, through whose hands would be conveyed particulars of the administration there. It would appear that Spotswood had expressed himself in conversation as favorable to the plan of an agent, but when the measure came before him in December for official approval, he offered an amendment[28] to the effect that instructions to the agent

---

[25] For Byrd's insistence on appearing before the Board of Trade as a member of the council rather than as the duly chosen agent of the House of Burgesses, he was to be made to suffer considerable anxiety as to retaining his seat on the council. Byrd seems to have taken considerable pride in continuing the tradition, set by his father, of service in the upper house. Spotswood shrewdly turned the tables against him. See below, p. 273 note.

[26] [Byrd], *Writings of "Colonel William Byrd of Westover in Virginia, Esqr."* Introduction, p. lxxv.

[27] *Journals of the House of Burgesses, 1712-1726*, p. 300, December 14, 1720; *Legislative Journals of the Council*, II, 654. Bassett is in error as to the number of his agencies. The writer could not determine to what treaty reference is made, unless that of 1722.

[28] See *ibid.*, p. 657 for the governor's message to the council on December 19; *Journals*

be signed by the governor and that Byrd give his bond to the governor not to meddle in Great Britain with any of the affairs of Virginia beyond those specified in the instructions. The amendment was promptly rejected by the House of Burgesses, now thoroughly suspicious of their governor. He indignantly denied that he had ever in any speech or message[29] named Mr. Byrd as a fit person.

Byrd's departure on this mission must have been long delayed, for an entry in the *Journal of the Board of Trade* of November 10, 1721, alludes to Byrd, as "late arrived from Virginia."[30] Until the close of 1725, but no later, he served from time to time as special agent, for it can be established that he was back in Virginia from his final trip to England in April, 1726.

Next came a procession of Randolphs—John, Isham, and Peyton. Virginia appointed an agent to represent her in England in an effort to secure the repeal of an English law recently passed which prohibited the importation of tobacco stripped from the stalks.[31] The planters felt strongly on this subject. Stripped tobacco remained marketable for a long time and sold for a higher price than any other. The presence of the stalk caused depreciation of the product by at least two pence per pound, as the processors manufactured the stalk and mixed it with the leaf. When forced by law to ship the stalk, the planters found that it could not be used in the manufacture of high-grade products. They found themselves loaded with freight and duty for the stalk. That lessened the consumption so that the tobacco had to be held in warehouses and sold on credit. The value of the planters' labor accordingly fell, and if they were not relieved, as their agent later shrewdly pointed out to the Board, the

of the House of Burgesses, 1712-1726, p. 314 for the governor's speech defending his amendment. On January 16th, 1720/1, he wrote the Board of Trade, pointing out that Byrd could not be the choice of the people when it required the casting vote of the speaker to elect him. Rather shrewdly he suggests that, "if his Majesty shall grant the Assembly's Request before Mr Byrd gets home, it will be a means to convince the Country that his Majesties Ministers are not (as has been represented) so regardless of the Plantations as to need the Sollicitations of particular Agents to prompt them to the doing what the Interest and Safety of his Majesty's American Subjects require."—C. O. 5/1319, p. 9.

[29] On March 6, 1720/1, he gives the Board an additional fact concerning the session of December 14, when Byrd was selected agent; namely, that there were absent various members who would have opposed him.—*Ibid.,* f. 49.

[30] *Journal of the Board of Trade,* 1718-1722, p. 328.

[31] *Statutes at Large . . . to the twenty-fifth year of the Reign of George III,* 9 George I, chapter 21.

colonists would be driven to manufacture woolen and linen, as they could not afford to buy their clothing in Britain.[32]   The two houses joined in drawing up an address to the king and a petition to parliament, setting forth their objections to the law, and appointed John Randolph, clerk of the House of Burgesses, special agent to present the two documents and to secure the result which was their aim.[33] The decision to appoint a special agent was owing doubtless to dissatisfaction with Leheup, their regular agent. Randolph sailed just after June 8, 1728, by whom Governor Gooch, who was in full sympathy with the protest against the act, sent the journals and various public papers.[34]

Randolph, after his arrival in England, very wisely set about his task. He apprehended that the greatest objection he would encounter would probably be in connection with the possible effect on the revenue from the customs. Therefore, before he approached the Board of Trade, he laid before the Lords of the Treasury a statement of the case, which that body referred to the Commissioners of the Customs for their opinion. In due course this group of officials satisfied themselves that the revenue had been in no way improved by the prohibition to import stripped tobacco. He then turned to the Board of Trade in January, 1728/9, for their aid in his application to parliament. When Randolph appeared before the Board on January 17, 1728/9, he was assured that if his proposals were found of advantage to the tobacco trade and would involve no diminution of the revenue, the Board would lend all the assistance in its power for the repeal of the objectionable clause in the act relating to stripped tobacco. Meanwhile, he had busied himself with the merchants engaged in trade with Virginia, and on February 11 he presented a petition to the Board from this influential group of

[32] Gathered from Randolph's presentation of the case to the Board of Trade.—C. O. 5/1321, f. 92.

[33] The measure to appoint a special agent passed both houses March 28, 1728.— *Journals of the House of Burgesses, 1727-1740*, p. 49; *Legislative Journals of the Council*, p. 749. See *ibid.*, for the petitions to the king and to the House of Commons.

[34] Gooch wrote several times to the Board of Trade, presenting long, strong arguments for the repeal of this regulation of stripped tobacco.—C. O. 5/1321, ff. 112-13.

Gooch strikingly exhibits the cost of postage at that time, for he sent the public papers in a box by Randolph "without the charge of Postage, which I was sensible would amount to a considerable Sum," which he was to forward by post as soon as he arrived in England.—*Ibid.*, f. 44. The date of this letter fixes the date of Randolph's departure.

British subjects for repeal of the act.[35] He attained his goal, for
the obnoxious clause touching so nearly their tobacco trade was
repealed by parliament, and he was rewarded handsomely by unanimous action of the Virginia legislature.[36]

Before we discuss John Randolph's second agency, we must note
briefly the trip to England of his brother, Isham Randolph, who
was sent home to oppose a bill of parliament in behalf of the sugar
islands, prohibiting the importation of any foreign sugar or molasses
into any colony of the mainland of America and also to oppose a bill
urged by the British merchants for the more easy recovery of debts
in the plantations. He drew up a careful statement on both cases
and had it printed in England; his memorial was read before the
Board of Trade on January 19, 1731/2. His negotiations covered
at least the period from January, 1731/2, to beyond March 25, when
he made a report of progress to the authorities in Virginia, and probably beyond June 7, for the council then made him an appropriation
of £200 for expenses to be remitted at the first convenient opportunity so that there was obviously at that time no thought of his
immediate return. It is further clear that he was negotiating this
affair with the regular agent, Leheup.[37]

John Randolph must have departed on his second special agency
before Isham Randolph had again set foot on Virginia soil. Early
in the year 1732 some of the British merchants had asked for a
change in the method of bonding though not for changing the customs on tobacco to an excise tax, but further than that no details of
the desired changes seem to have been preserved. On the other hand
the merchants had been particularly active in pressing their demands
for the act which should enable them to secure the collection of their
debts, an act regarded by the planters as unjust. The assembly,
which was heartily in favor of what became the Excise Bill of 1733,
wished to see the customs on tobacco changed into an excise and

[35] These facts are gleaned from his petition to the Board of Trade.—C. O. 5/1321,
f. 92; *Journal of the Board of Trade*, 1728-1734, pp. 5, 8. On February 11, he also
asked the Board to consider an act, passed in Virginia in 1728, for private persons to sell
some entailed land, but that seemed incidental to the main object of his mission.

[36] *Statutes at Large*, 2 George II, chapter 9; *Journals of the House of Burgesses*,
1727-1740, p. xviii.

[37] *Executive Journals of the Council*, IV, 272; *Journal of the Board of Trade*, 1728/9-
1734, p. 270. The note in the council records of the council of Virginia of April 29, 1732,
indicates letters from Randolph and Leheup in regard to their negotiations.—*Executive
Journals of the Council*, IV, 267.

drew up their scheme in the form of a petition, which was afterwards printed as the *Case of the Planters of Tobacco in Virginia.* Besides complaining of exorbitant money charges, the Virginia planters accused the merchants, or some of them, of downright fraud in the trade. They alleged that extensive smuggling occurred in importing tobacco and crooked dealings in reëxportation. They cited many specific instances of such crooked handling. In contrast with the corrupt actions of British merchants they laid emphasis on the fine provisions to guard against deception in Virginia by the inspection law of 1732. The whole movement suggests strongly a revolt against the domineering "rules of the combination of merchant creditors." The petition was dated Williamsburg, June 28, 1732.[38]

A special commissioner was charged with the delivery of this petition to parliament, and the choice for commissioner fell in late June, 1732, on John Randolph, doubtless because of his former experience and success.[39] The precise date of his arrival in England cannot be stated—probably August or September of 1732, for he left about July 23. Randolph seemed to have great hopes that his business would be one of the first debated in the new session after his arrival and thus apparently hoped to be able to return home quickly.[40] This petition never came before parliament. The Board of Trade remained silent on it; it appeared prominently in the Treasury papers, but there is no record of action.[41] In January, 1733, the *Gentleman's Magazine*[42] noted the presence of John Ran-

[38] For an analysis of this statement see Sioussat, "Virginia and the English Commercial System, 1730-1733," *Annual Report of the American Historical Association,* I, 81-85. The Proceedings of the Assembly give no clue to the authorship, but Sioussat thinks it was drafted by Randolph.—*Ibid.,* pp. 94-95.

[39] The resolve to appoint John Randolph agent to "negotiate the Affairs of the Colony in Great Britain" passed both houses on June 28 and 29, 1732, and was approved by the governor on July 1.—*Journals of the House of Burgesses,* 1727-1740, p. 167; *Legislative Journals of the Council,* II, 811. Letters from Governor Gooch to the Lords of Trade on July 18, to the secretary of state of July 20, and another of July 23 were to be delivered by Randolph.—C. O. 5/1323, f. 48; C. O. 5/1337, f. 155, 157.

[40] Stated in a letter to John Custis, dated Dec. 20, 1732; manuscript preserved in the Virginia Historical Society. He stated, "then I can have no temptation to stay here." He also added that "those who complain of this mischarge and openly avow it to be so [duty on tobacco] are raving at the folly and maddness of the Virginians to desire a new regulation."

[41] The papers on this Virginia affair at the Treasury Board are dated July 1, 18, 20, but these mark their origin in Virginia and not the date of their reception at the Treasury Board.—Sioussat, *op. cit.,* p. 84.   [42] Vol. III, p. 50.

dolph in London as agent and a generous appropriation by the Virginia assembly to get the tobacco excise and the law for payment of debts to British merchants repealed. Five days before the convening of parliament, January 12, a committee of London traders and merchants waited on the speaker of the House of Commons on the subject of a general excise. The *Craftsman* defended the merchants in their opposition, and there was general battle in the printed magazines, from this article in the *Craftsman* to the squibs of poetasters. By March, 1733, the *Case of the Planters of Tobacco* issued from the press, the first of many pamphlets. The most noteworthy is the *Vindication of the Case of the Planters*, a somewhat longer document than the one first issued. Internal evidence indicates that it must have been written in London, not in Virginia, and points to John Randolph as the author.[43] On June 7 a committee of the Commons, appointed to inquire into frauds in the revenue, reported. Among the appendices of the voluminous document appears one, Appendix IV, recording the examination of John Randolph, which holds the chief interest for us. That examination occurred on May 2. During this the agent stated his opinion that the abuses arose chiefly from the method of securing the duties by bond and the discharge of the duties by debentures which were too loosely worded. He held that if the tobacco were locked up and the other parts of the plan executed, the frauds in weighing would be prevented.[44] To the great joy of the city merchants, the excise bill failed by virtue of being postponed for second reading, the equivalent of being dropped. Though Walpole had to relinquish the project of the excise, Randolph's support must have been valued by the ministry, for before the latter's departure for Virginia, he was knighted by the king—a unique reward indeed for a colonial agent.

Of all the Randolph missions,[45] the agency of Peyton Randolph

[43] *The Vindication* quotes as absurd a letter, which appeared in the *True Britain* of March 8, supposedly written by a London merchant, and criticizes it severely. The time would not allow for transmission of the *True Britain* to Virginia, preparation of the *Vindication* and its transmission back to England.—Sioussat, *op. cit.*, p. 91.

[44] See "Report of the Committee Appointed to Inquire into the Fraud and Abuses in the Customs to the Prejudice of Trade and Diminution of the Revenue," in *Reports from the Committees of the House of Commons*, I, 603-13. (Printed by order of the House and not in the *Journal*.) This gives the body of the report; the rest appears in the appendices.

[45] If the lower house had had its will, a fourth Randolph would have entered the agency list, for on August 28, 1740, the council refused assent to a house resolve to

in connection with the pistole fee loomed largest in the minds of
Virginians. During 1753 an incident occurred to call forth the independence and *esprit de corps* of the lower house. During November
of that year the people of several western counties complained of
having to pay a fee of a pistole—a Spanish coin worth about three
and a half American dollars—over and above the fees usually demanded by the governor on the issuance of a patent at the land
office, a heavy fee for the use of the government seal. As nearly a
thousand patents were out and ready to be passed under the seal
at Governor Dinwiddie's arrival, the order brought a storm of
protest. The depth of the resentment is indicated by a resolution of
the lower house that anyone paying a pistole as fee was a betrayer
of the rights of the people. The burgesses determined to appeal
to the crown, and to send as special agent to prosecute the appeal the
attorney general of Virginia, Peyton Randolph, son of Sir John
Randolph. He was to be paid a generous sum for the mission and
in addition he was assured an income of £300 for life if his mission
cost him his government position. Two addresses to the king were
drawn up, the first of which was sent, as a matter of form, to the
council, which refused its concurrence, stating its reasons. These
documents were not spread on the *Journal*, for they doubtless contained, in addition to prophecies as to the ill effects of the fee, reflections on the motives of the governor. If this matter should first come
to the attention of the ministry through the *Journal*, the case might
be prejudged against the people, because such reflections would undoubtedly be considered disrespectful to the king's representative
in Virginia and hence to the king himself.[46] Despite the care taken
to keep the papers from the governor, he did manage to secure a
copy of the "Reasons" and a perusal of the addresses through a
"private" friend, as he expressed it, on February 8, nearly two months
after they had been adopted on December 17, 1753. He immediately wrote to Abercromby, his personal agent—soon to become the
provincial agent of the governor and council—castigating them, "as
their reasons are actually inconsistent with Truth. It surpriz'd me
that a Legislative Body c'd have the assurance to let them go under

appoint Edward Randolph agent to negotiate an address to the king in regard to an act
on Lisbon Salt.—*Legislative Journals of the Council*, II, 906.
    [46] *Journals of the House of Burgesses*, 1752-1758, pp. 155, 168-69.

their Name. They keep their two Address[es] very secret from me, tho' I have had the perusal of them privately." The house drew up a third address to the king, giving their reasons for sending the attorney general and praying that he might be graciously allowed to retain his office. The next day after this resolution was passed, the governor prorogued the house.[47] The governor expressed his anger at Peyton Randolph for undertaking the agency by appointing George Wythe as attorney general, delaying action only about a month.[48]

Randolph continued to pursue his task in England, appearing before the Board of Trade on April 3, 1754, in support of the addresses, and also "soliciting" other matters intrusted to his care. The report sent up by this Board to the Privy Council, dated June 20, approved part of the petition, but it allowed the pistole fee to the governor, probably because Dinwiddie had claimed that it would increase the king's revenue. However, Dinwiddie's victory was by no means complete when the case was finally disposed of by the Privy Council. He was held right in principle, but the Board of Trade was ordered to issue regulations to guide him in the future. These regulations when announced proved sharply restrictive in collection of the fee as to size and location of grants of land.[49] Peyton Randolph himself secured a distinct victory, for the Privy Council ordered his reinstatement in his old office. Looked at impartially, the decision seems to have given approximate justice. Dinwiddie was technically right in the dispute, for lands which had not yet been taken up belonged to the king and not to the jurisdiction of the legislative assembly. The fee was ill advised but not illegal, a fact which the

[47] The letter to Abercromby, written Feb. 9, 1754, is found in Dinwiddie, *Official Records*, I, pp. 71-72. The governor pours out scorn on the poverty of the colony as he calls attention to the grants to Randolph and to the agent he may appoint. "These are no Marks of Poverty," he tersely says. It is from this letter that we learn the date on which he secured a copy of the "Reasons."

For the third address to the king, see *Journals of the House of Burgesses*, 1752-1758, p. 169. See also for this incident, Lingley, *The Transition in Virginia from Colony to Commonwealth*, pp. 25-27.

[48] A letter from Dinwiddie to the Board of Trade of Jan. 29, 1754, announces the appointment of Wyth.—C. O. 5/1328, p. 94.

[49] For the report of the Board of Trade to the Privy Council see C. O. 5/1367, pp. 73-75. The regulations laid down by that Board were as follows: no fee might be taken for a patent issued for less than 100 acres, or from families imported, or on lands to the west of the mountains, or on land preliminary steps for which had been taken before April 22, 1752 (the date of Dinwiddie's first order for the fee). No patent should be issued for a tract of land larger than 1,000 acres.

governor himself recognized when he wrote Abercromby on April 26, 1754: "If I had known that this affair would have created so much uneafinefs to me and trouble to my friends at home, I would not have taken that fee."[50]   The restoration of Randolph to the post which he had left to serve the lower house was a step dictated by the most simple consideration of policy.

By early May, Randolph was back in Virginia after an absence of somewhat more than a year and made an oral report to the house of his agency.   For the faithful discharge of his trust he was given a unanimous vote of thanks; it is highly doubtful if he ever received anything more substantial.[51]

Before James Abercromby, already referred to, became the agent of the governor and council, he became a special agent in April, 1752, by action of both the upper and lower houses to present a special address to the king.   The governor was asked to recommend some one for this particular task and the house proved amenable to the suggestion of Abercromby.[52]

A procession of special agents from South Carolina parades before the reader, some during the early period between the lapse of the agency of Kettleby and another period of permanent agent, and some, existing parallel to the regular agents, belong to the later period of this province's colonial history.

Peregrine Fury was not left in undisturbed direction of the affairs of the agency during his long reign as agent of South Carolina from 1731 to 1749.   Early in 1733 the lower house voted to send an agent home to assist Fury in soliciting the important affairs of the province and unanimously agreed that Francis Yonge was in every way qualified for the task.   The affairs which loomed as important at that juncture were the need of fortifying the port and harbor of Beaufort on Port Royal River and of strengthening the defenses of the colony in general against Spanish and Indian aggres-

[50] *Journals of the House of Burgesses*, 1752-1758, p. xviii; Dinwiddie, *Official Records*, I, p. 137.

[51] The fact that Peyton Randolph reported in person resulted from his membership in the lower house for the College of William and Mary.   Reappointment as attorney general undoubtedly necessitated reëlection by his constituency, though there is no record.   The question of his pay is discussed in Chapter IX.

[52] The lower house acted on April 18, 1752.—*Journals of the House of Burgesses*, 1752-1758, p. 96; the council acted on April 20.—*Ibid.*, p. 97; and the governor gave his assent the same day.—*Ibid.*, p. 99; *Legislative Journals of the Council*, II, 1093.

sions. Governor Robert Johnson was in full accord with sending Mr. Yonge.[53] On April 12 the assembly felt that the embarkation of Yonge might well be delayed until a later sailing, in consideration of the dangerous situation of the province, and decreed that the dispatches which he had intended to carry over should be sent.[54]

By January 8, 1733/4, there is evidence from the fact of his appearance before the Board of Trade with Mr. Fury that Yonge had taken his departure and had arrived in London. Similar entries occur in the *Journal of the Board of Trade* for January 25, May 21, August 7, and August 14, on each of which occasions Fury and Yonge are referred to as the "Agents of South Carolina."[55] By February of the next year, 1734/5, the question of a payment to Mr. Yonge had arisen, and it was a tribute to his abilities that a committee of the house set to examine his papers reported that he had been "very assiduous and of great Service to the Province" and that he justly deserved further allowance for what he had already done and what they thought he would thereafter do in support of the appropriation and in "mending" the quitrent laws.[56]

An entry in the Journal of the Commons House of Assembly of December 17, 1736, would indicate that Yonge's period of service ended sometime after March, 1735, and that he possibly returned to South Carolina sometime that year, for on December 17 of the next year the lower house decided to employ him again to assist their agent in Great Britain for a fixed period of one year to support the money bill, referring, no doubt, to the provincial appropriation bill, and other affairs, "if he will consent."[57] And therewith Yonge finally passes from the records.

[53] Public Records of South Carolina, I, pt. 2, p. 934; Journal of the Council of South Carolina, 1734-1737, VI, Feb. 23, p. 380. This action was taken by the legislature on February 22 and 23, 1732/3. We owe our knowledge of what was disturbing the colony to the letters of Governor Robert Johnson of March 30, April 2, and April 6, 1733, to the Board of Trade, written after Yonge's appointment. On March 30 he tells the Board that Yonge will lay before them a plan of the town of Beaufort and his orders to work for its fortification. He also speaks of his efforts to build a fort on the Altamaha River.—C. O. 5/364, ff. 233, 226, 227.

[54] Public Records of South Carolina, I, pt. 1, pp. 934, 988, 1006; Journal of the Council of South Carolina, 1734-1737, VI, April 11, 13, 1733, pp. 411, 413.

[55] *Journal of the Board of Trade*, 1728-1734, pp. 369, 373, 391, 405, 406.

[56] Journal of the Council of South Carolina, 1734-1737, VI, 39, 59, 61-62, 134; Journal of the Commons House of Assembly of South Carolina, IX, p. 88.

[57] *Ibid.*, November 10, 1735-March 6, 1736, X, 322. There is no entry in *Journal of the Board of Trade* that he ever appeared before the Board during the entire year.

Any restriction or interference with colonial legislation on money or currency by the home government struck a sensitive nerve in the colonials. Hence, a proposed British statute in 1744 to prevent paper bills from becoming legal tender in the colonies instantly provoked cries for an agent to appear in England to win repeal or amendment of the statute. The council at first favored leaving Fury as the most proper person to oppose the bill before the British parliament. It was their opinion that as long as they had an agent in Great Britain, "that Agent is the properest person through whose hands the solicitation ought to go, especially in cases as this is wherein there can be no sort of foundation to suspect any inclination in the Agent to favor any other interest." The message of the council to the house shows that the names of Colonel John Fenwicke and of John Sharpe had been advanced, but the council objected to both, to the former on the score of health, as the matter was of "too great confequence to the province to be left to the chance of that Gentleman's health"; and to the latter, on the score that he was very generally employed by the merchants in soliciting their bills through parliament, and since this bill was thought to have arisen from the initiative of some London merchants, it was highly likely that he would be concerned against the province in this instance.[58] The house, however, insisted on the appointment of Fury and Colonel Fenwicke as joint agents to appear against passage of the bill through parliament as it felt that Fenwicke, from his acquaintance with the conditions in South Carolina, could be of real assistance to the Englishman Fury. The council agreed to this additional appointment on December 5 and arranged for the house Committee of Correspondence to meet the council committee to prepare a letter to the agent.[59]

Once more in 1747, this colony called on Colonel Fenwicke to serve it in the capacity of special agent to secure the acceptance by the British ministry of a South Carolina act to issue and make current the sum of £210,000 in paper bills of credit. On June 17, 1746, a committee of the Commons House of Assembly decided that the bill was most likely to obtain His Majesty's approval if some prudent

[58] For the entire message see Journal of the Commons House of Assembly of South Carolina, Oct. 2, 1744-May 25, 1745, XX, 34-35.
[59] Ibid., pp. 35, 39.

person were employed to defend it at the proper offices and recommended Colonel Fenwicke. The house added the name of James Crockatt to that of Fenwicke, and to this special arrangement the council assented on the same day.[60] We know that Fenwicke cooperated with the regular agent, for a memorial of his, desiring the Board of Trade to report the bill favorably to the king, was read before that body at their session of February 3, 1746/7, but Fury alone offered a defense of the measure at the session of February 26, 1747/8. No record can be found that Crockatt declined the appointment; however, that conclusion seems clear from the fact that he appeared before the Board of Trade on February 11, 1747/8, at the head of a group of merchants apparently in opposition to that particular measure. The hostility of the merchants and the unfavorable opinion of Mr. Lamb, attorney of the Board, was too great, however, for the agents to overcome. The bill did not receive royal confirmation.[61]

The problem of colonial defense became more pressing in 1742 in the midst of King George's War. The province of South Carolina had usually been protected by independent companies of troops paid by the home government, but for several years before 1742 no such companies had existed there. However, the assembly under the threat of the Spanish on June 3, 1742, drew up a petition to the king, begging three companies and offering some additional pay to the officers and men, provided they were made subject to the sole orders of the governor and were stationed at three posts. Attorney General James Abercromby and Captain William Livingston offered their services without any pay to press the petition. A few months later they were joined by Colonel Alexander Vander Dusen, whose private affairs were calling him to London just then. These agents, if they may be so called in the absence of a fixed return for their services, served clearly as assistants to Fury, but the two first named were fully empowered to proceed with the petition in the event of Fury's death. It would appear from a letter which the two former were to deliver to the Duke of Newcastle, one of His Majesty's secretaries, from Governor Bull dated June 15, 1742,

[60] Ibid., Sept. 16, 1745-June 17, 1746, XXI, 611, 612, 625.
[61] Journal of the Board of Trade, 1741/2-1749, pp. 225, 273, 272-73; for disallowance, ibid., 1749/50-1753, p. 110.

that Abercromby and Livingston departed shortly after June 15, 1742, and from a later letter that Vander Dusen sailed shortly after September 2. Vander Dusen fell into the hands of the enemy with the dispatches he was carrying but must have been released immediately, for he had joined his colleagues by January 10, 1742/3.[62] After five months attendance at the boards, these agents report that they were as uncertain of the issue in January as at the moment of their arrival despite the recent invasion of Georgia and threat of descent on Port Royal. At the same time they supported a petition complaining of the conduct of the commander of the royal ships of war, and urging the issue of paper money to defray the cost of armaments sent to Georgia. It was three years before the matter received serious consideration in England, but Abercromby had returned home before that date.[63] Vander Dusen arrived with some recruits early in 1746.

On the next to the last day of January, 1747/8, some months after the assembly had all but dismissed Fury and might logically, therefore, think that he would decline the appointment, the lower house directed their speaker to inquire of Vander Dusen, who was again reported as about to embark for England, whether he would be willing to follow through a petition to the king relating to their trade and expenses for dealings with the Indians in case Fury should decline that service. The speaker was further to acquaint him that it would be acceptable to the assembly if he would lend his aid to Fury, if the latter should accept the appointment, whenever attendance did not interfere with his private business. As the council concurred in such an appointment, Vander Dusen consented on February 2 to act. He pointed out, however, that as he was immediately in the king's service, he might have to report to his command before the negotiation was completed, and asked into whose hands in such event he should place the affairs of the province. The house in its reply instructed him to turn over the affairs of the agency in such case to a person whose name occurs in two cases

[62] See letter of Governor Bull to the Duke of Newcastle, dated June 15, 1742; Governor Bull to Carteret.—*Ibid.*, C. O. 5/388, ff. 276, 128; Bull to Vander Dusen of Oct. 20.—*Ibid.*, f. 299 (the governor did not know then of his capture); of Vander Dusen and Abercromby to a Mr. Stone of Jan. 10, 1742/3.—*Ibid.*, f. 307.

[63] *Ibid.*, for the report of Vander Dusen and Abercromby of Jan. 20, 1743. For an account of the episode see Smith, *South Carolina as a Royal Province*, pp. 193-94.

in all the records relating to the agency—to Mr. Francis Hutchen-son.[64] The outcome of this affair does not appear from the records.

Yet a third time, in 1754, do the records show Vander Dusen charged by South Carolina with the task of assisting the provincial agent during a stay in England. As usual, though he went partly on his own private affairs, he was asked to lay the state of the prov-ince before the Board of Trade. Oddly enough, he was hauled before the Board of Trade on June 3 to explain his absence from his duties as a member of the provincial council. It seemed to irk their Lordships that five of the council should be absent at the same time and rather sharply they wanted to know his intentions about his return.[65] There is no evidence of his functioning at this time.

By his own action one of South Carolina's most distinguished sons of the colonial period enters the list of agents. In July, 1753, when he was about to go to England, Charles Pinckney offered his services during his residence there in whatever might concern the wel-fare of the colony. The council accordingly, relying on his "known zeal and great experience," as well as "capacity and integrity," in-treated his attendance at the Board of Trade as he judged most for the service of the province, either with or without Mr. Crockatt, then the provincial agent. It did not doubt that their Lordships would "favourably admit of and receive any applications that may be made by you on the part of the province" and would hold him authorized by the governor and council to act for them.

This was, of course, playing fast and loose with the regular agent, but the fact that they empowered him to act with or without their duly accredited representative showed the greater confidence of the colonials in one of their own number. Mr. Pinckney sailed about August, 1753, and remained in England we know until after December, 1757. On the 27th of June, 1754, he appeared before the Board of Trade with a second petition, setting forth at great length the danger of the French wresting the Cherokees from the British interest and so completing their scheme of making them-selves masters of all the Indian country in America.[66] As late as

[64] Journal of the Commons House of Assembly of South Carolina, Jan. 19, 1747/8-June 29, 1748, XXIII, 89, 91, 92, 96, 99. The writer has been unable to learn anything about Francis Hutcheson which would throw light on why he was selected—or, indeed, whether he would have consented to act.   [65] C. O. 5/374, no. 96.

[66] See letter of Governor Glen to Charles Pinckney of July 28, 1753, C. O. 5/374,

December, 1756, he kept urging on the Board the need of defense in the Indian country.

North Carolina's list of special agents is even shorter. Henry McCulloh served in 1747 as agent for the six northern counties of the province to secure justice in representation in the house. This issue turned on a new election law which gave all the counties the same number of delegates whereas earlier the northern counties had enjoyed a larger representation, five from each of their counties as compared with two from each of the others. The governor's method of passing the new corrective law was particularly irritating to the northern counties, as the assembly which passed it had been summoned to meet in the south, to which session northern representatives were not sent; hence, the law had been passed by a minority, as they claimed twenty-nine members out of a total of fifty-four. The governor charged that these twenty-nine had entered into a solemn agreement to disobey the summons and thus made a meeting of the assembly impossible. McCulloh laid his case before the Board of Trade and the attorney general for their opinions.[67] This case is the nearest approach found by the author in any of the Southern colonies to the dispatch of an agent for a particular geographical portion of a colony, such as was found in New England, and as is illustrated by the sending of Mr. Francis Kilby as agent for the towns of Gloucester, Boston, and Marblehead in 1755 in opposition to an excise law passed by the Massachusetts legislature in December, 1754.[68]

At the very close of the colonial period North Carolina tried the expedient of naming two special agents when, because of the rupture with the mother country, the device of the colonial agency had virtually ended. At the legislative session of 1774 on March 24, the lower house resolved to transmit a certain bill to two persons in England and to direct them to lay it before the Lords Commis-

Bundle 91; entry of the Board of Trade, C. O. 5/375, K. 98; *Journal of the Board of Trade, 1754-1758*, pp. 48, 210, 212, 279.

[67] See letter of Governor Johnston to the Board of Trade, dated May 17, 1748, for a statement of this issue from his point of view, *Colonial Records of North Carolina*, IV, 869-70. To prove this charge of an agreement to prevent a quorum, he sent two affidavits of the many he could have sent.

[68] *Journal of the Board of Trade, 1754-1758*, pp. 154, 156. Other illustrations are to be found, as a Mr. Calet who went as agent for persons in eastern Massachusetts in 1773 about some land grants.—C. O. 5/768, p. 283.

sioners of Trade and Plantations and to secure their recommendation of the act to the king and the recall of the instruction to the
governor forbidding assent to such a law. They were to exert themselves "to the utmost" to obviate every objection that might be made
to it. This bill proposed to divide North Carolina into six districts
and to establish a superior court of justice in each district. It reserved
to the colony the right of attachment on the effects of foreigners and
yet guarded against injury to debtors residing outside the province.
In a word, it was a court bill including the power of attachment. In
1773 North Carolina had passed a bill to continue the right of attachment indefinitely, but the governor received an instruction to
put this process of attachment on the same footing as in England.
The assembly feared that this would make it hard for a creditor to
recover his debts and thus affect the credit of the colony. Those
two persons in England named were Alexander Elmsley, who had
shown interest in the measure,[69] and Thomas Barker. Both were
appointed agents to carry into execution the purposes of the resolution. The usual committee was named to furnish the agents with
necessary documents and instructions. It is significant that these
two agents were Carolinians resident in England; it was deeply
significant of a conciliatory spirit in civilian matters on the part of
the British government that a new instruction was issued extending
the right of attachment in all cases where the cause arose in North
or South Carolina or in Virginia. Unfortunately, the relaxation was
insufficient, for there was little trade for North Carolinians with
South Carolina but much with New York. A letter from Elmsley
to Samuel Johnston indicates that these agents were still serving
in April, 1775.[70]

Special agents for Georgia and Maryland were almost non-
existent. Perhaps the term irregular agents is more appropriately
applied. In 1756 Alexander Kellet, one of the members of the
Georgia council and provost marshal, gave an "effectual" representation of the late distress and circumstances thereof of that colony
to the Lords Commissioners of Trade.[71] The lower house thus

[69] See Governor Martin's letter on the subject, printed in *Colonial Records of North
Carolina*, IX, 1051-53.

[70] *Ibid.*, pp. 939-40. For the memorial of Elmsley see *ibid.*, pp. 1147-49; for Elmsley's letter to Johnston on Apr. 7, 1775, *ibid.*, p. 1207.

[71] This allusion is found in a resolution of thanks to Kellet by the lower house of

euphoniously described his services, but in bolder language the entry of the Board of Trade reveals that he was really attacking Governor Reynolds when he testified before it in July, 1756. "It is alledged as well in the private Letters as by Mr Kellet, . . . that the governor has not only industriously avoided to advise with the Council on many of the most material transactions of his Administration, but that in order to conceal from them those Instructions given to him by Governm^t by which he is directed to take their Advice and Consent in matters relative to his administration, he refused to communicate to the Council many of those Instructions otherwise than verbally and without permitting them to be entered upon the Council Book." It added that Kellet and others charged that the minutes of the assembly had been altered and falsified by the clerk, who seemed to have attested them.[72]

Speaker William Little was a second representative who served Georgia in a special capacity. The assembly, learning in February, 1757, that their presiding officer was going to England, asked him to wait on the Lords Commissioners of Trade in order to present an address from the house and to answer such questions relative to the address as the members might wish to put to him. They requested the governor to affix the state seal to the resolution so that he might appear fully authorized.[73]

The annals of Maryland yield but one special agent after the agency had become established, and he was Charles Garth, who discharged his special mission so satisfactorily that he was later retained as regular agent for the lower house. His special task was to present the petition drawn up by the Stamp Act Congress in 1765 in behalf of Maryland. The unusual colonial methods of constituting an agent can be no better illustrated than in Garth's own words in a letter to the Committee of Correspondence of South Carolina under date of February 9, 1766: "Upon my return home that Night, or rather the next Morning, I found a Packett from the Committees deputed from Maryland to the Congress at New York, containing the peti-

Georgia assembly, passed on July 20, 1757, for his "great and eminent Services."—*Colonial Records of Georgia*, XVI, 229.

[72] The above appears in the report of the Board of Trade on the charges against the governor to the king.—C. O. 5/653.

[73] This resolution was passed on February 2, 1757.—C. O. 5/646, Bundle 20. The author has been unable to learn what the occasion of the address was.

tions and Memorial agreed upon at the Congress, with a polite Letter
favouring me with their request to act upon the Great Occasion as
their special Agent, having been made acquainted with my Notions
and Ideas upon the Subject from the Gentlemen who went as Committees from New York."[74]   This mark of their approbation gave
Garth a singular satisfaction and shows the modern student how the
fame of an agent passed from one colony to another.   The point at
which even the special agency became official, however, was December
6, 1766, when the lower house of assembly appointed Garth to represent Maryland before the home government and to present their
resolutions upon the Stamp Act.[75]

[74] *South Carolina Historical and Genealogical Magazine*, XXVI, 86.
[75] See Mereness, *Maryland as a Proprietary Province*, p. 481.

CHAPTER 4.

METHODS OF SELECTION AND LENGTH
OF TERM

THE WAY in which the agent was selected varied with the type of agency to be filled and also with the varying practice of the same colony at different times. Theoretically, the regular provincial agent was the choice of all branches of the colonial government. According to the dictum of the Board of Trade the initial choice lay with the lower house of the legislature, but, since the selection must be ratified by the upper house and by the governor, the choice was limited practically to such persons as could win such ratification. In Virginia from the date of establishment of a regular, permanent agent up to 1759, when the house insisted on its own agent, the choice lay entirely outside the representatives of the people; the governor appointed with the assent of the council. Yet this choice was regarded for many decades as the provincial agent of Virginia. In those colonies—and before the provincial period was ended the group included all five colonies—where the house insisted on having control of this agent, the choice lay with that body.

The particular way in which some one particular person was thought of and presented to the electing body for actual appointment was as varied as it was for any other post of government—and just as curious. In the Old Dominion the person regarded officially before 1759 as the Virginia agent was usually suggested by the governor. He was considered even by the chief executive as agent of the council, for, although the house did occasionally send a special agent, it did not until 1759 have a real spokesman. In cases of a special mission of great importance, where there existed no controversy between the two houses, and where the special agent represented both house and council, the initiative in selection of the agent usually reposed in the lower house. Naturally, when selection rested in so small a body as the council, the assent of the governor, even when he had a deputy with the title of lieutenant governor who actually conducted affairs, might easily be more than formal, for the dispenser of offices and salaries was naturally besieged by seekers of office. Lieutenant Governor Dinwiddie, for instance, in recommending James Abercromby to be agent of Virginia, stated in a letter of June 18, 1754, to Governor Albemarle, "I hope this will meet with Your L'd's Approbation."[1]

Certainly assent by the council was far from merely formal. For example, an act declaring the method of appointing an agent to "solicit" the affairs of this colony in Great Britain passed the House of Burgesses May 21, 1718, but failed in the council May 24. Unfortunately, there has been left no record which shows what plan of appointment the burgesses had in mind.[2] A dispute arose immediately over the nomination for agent, for the council refused assent to have their affairs transmitted through Nathaniel Blakiston, the governor's nominee, even though the addresses were to be presented to the king without expense to the colony.[3] On one occasion the governor, who was then the Earl of Orkney, and the lieutenant governor agreed to allow the council to select a person for agent who was not their choice.[4] In soliciting and in sending a letter of thanks for the appointment to the post, the agent in this instance addressed his communications not to the governor but to the council.[5] The council and governor were even on occasion amenable to suggestions from their inferiors. A striking illustration is the appointment of James Abercromby in 1752 for a special service at the request of the House of Burgesses. In general the council worded its approval as follows: The council "do approve of the said ————— ————— to be agent for this Country, . . . and they desire his Honour will entreat the [Lords Commissioners of Trade and Plantations] to give him leave as agent to solicit the Affairs of this Colony."[6]

The procedure, when all three branches participated, must be a

[1] Dinwiddie, *Official Records*, I, 210; Flippin, *The Royal Government in Virginia, 1624-1775*, p. 65.

[2] *Legislative Journals of the Council*, II, 617, 619; *Journal of the House of Burgesses, 1712-1726*, p. 200.

[3] *Legislative Journals of the Council*, II, 631.

[4] *Ibid.*, 1721-1734, p. 51.

[5] *Ibid.*, 1705-1721, App., p. 12; C. O. 324/60, p. 55; Flippin, *op. cit.*, p. 182.

[6] This is the form under which James Abercromby was elected June 20, 1754.—C. O. 324/60, p. 241.

formal act of legislation, if the act were to meet with the approval of the Board of Trade. Apparently appointment by a mere resolution had earlier been accepted in England as empowering an agent to act, but late in colonial history the Board found that method of appointment unacceptable. In 1769, for instance, Agent Henry Eustace McCulloh conceived it to be his duty to inform the lower house of North Carolina of the position Lord Hillsborough had taken towards his appointment by a resolution. While that mode had formerly been admitted in some cases, a stricter regulation had been enforced for some time; the ministry had determined that the assent of the governor, council, and assembly, formally expressed by an act of the whole legislature, was necessary to invest a person with the character of a provincial agent; McCulloh appointed by a "resolve," could be considered only as agent for the lower house of assembly and for such matters as that body was particularly interested in. Though McCulloh boldly insisted that a negative in either of the other branches would destroy the right of appointment in the lower house and that he must continue to consider himself attorney or agent of the province, he still recommended to the house the mode which the British ministry declared necessary.[7]

So strongly did Hillsborough feel on the subject of varying procedures that he laid down a rule to Governor Tryon at about that same time in the following words: "The inconveniencies that daily occur, from the Colonies not adhering to some certain & regular mode of appointing their Agents, are many & great & it would be very satisfactory, and prevent many difficulties that occur in the transactions of public Business, if all the Colonies would conform to that rule which has been prescribed by the Crown, of appointing their Agents by Act of the Legislature, which, as it originated in the House of Assembly, it follows of course that the name of the Person must be inserted by them, altho' the other two Branches of Legislature have each respectively a negative upon the Bills."[8] With this statement should be compared the decision sent to the Barbados government early in the century on this very question of just what the procedure for selection of the agent should be. It shows how

[7] Stated in a letter from McCulloh to the Committee of Correspondance of July 14, 1769.—*Colonial Records of North Carolina*, VIII, 55, 56-57.
[8] *Ibid.*, p. 51.

remarkably consistent the home government had been for over half a century. To Barbados, where ever since the year 1660 there had been frequent disputes between the council and assembly over the nomination of agents, went in 1709 this clear-cut reply to the argument for an exclusive right of appointment in the lower house as custodian of the rights of the people: "Among the several Reasons given for allowing an exclusive Right in the General Afsembly, some of them are very extraordinary, they being founded upon unjust suppositions; That the Governor and Council will refuse or neglect to employ their best offices for procuring from your Majesty a Concefsion of whatever may reasonably be desired for the Ease, Safety, or Benefit of the Island; And that they will in all matters be inclined to support and maintain the Prerogative without having a due Regard to the Rights and Privileges of the Subject.

"This is to suppose, not only that so many of the Principal Inhabitants as constitute the Council, have no Share in, or Concern for the good of their Country; But that both Governor and Council will act contrary to the exprefs Trust reposed in them; And we look upon any Insinuation, as that the Interest of the Crown were separate from that of the Subject, to be false and of dangerous consequence."[9]

It followed then, of course, that no lower house of itself could constitute a colonial agent—only a personal agent, if they wished the name—to transact partially the affairs which concerned the house only.[10] The home government did not, however, refuse to deal with such partial agents. This fact itself was a concession, for the implication in the statement advanced in 1709 was to the contrary. It then argued that if the assembly could appoint its agent, the governor and council could claim a like power and concluded, "What Mischief and Confusion in Businefs such distinct Agencies may occasion by their interfering and clashing one with another, according to the several Instructions they may receive from their respective

[9] C. O. 325/1. For the entire report on the Barbados Act, dated November 9, 1709, see *ibid.* For a discussion of the whole Barbados question see Penson, *The Colonial Agents of the British West Indies*, pp. 80-88.

[10] Hillsborough definitely assured McCulloh of his readiness on all occasions to promote the interests of North Carolina and to give the kindest attention to what the agent might propose to him.—*Colonial Records of North Carolina*, VIII, 57. The Board was perfectly explicit on this point, for it declared that in its judgment the House of Representatives of Massachusetts Bay had not in themselves any right or privilege to appoint an agent or representative residing in England to transact the public affairs of that province, constituted by their sole authority, and retained in their separate service and pay.—C. O. 325 I.

Principals, is obvious." It is striking, in view of this decision, that by the time of the resolution declared by Hillsborough each lower house of the legislature in four of the five Southern colonies was maintaining an agent of its own. Even after so clear a statement by the ministry that the appointment of the agent originated in the lower house of assembly, there still seemed to exist doubt as to how far the council might share in the nomination.[11]

In case of a vacancy by death or resignation in the post of agent while the assembly was not in session, the Committee of Correspondence filled the post, but some doubt existed as to whether in case of his removal, death, or refusal to act, appointment of another person by the committee, when such committee was made up of members from both houses, must be approved by the burgesses only or by them in concurrence with the council and governor. Such a question arose in Virginia in 1760. To obviate any doubt, it was held necessary to amend the agency act; it was explicitly enacted that the new appointee selected by the Committee of Correspondence should be first approved by the governor or commander in chief and should continue in office only until the next General Assembly convened, when approval must follow by both houses of that body, or by the "General Assembly."[12]

Naturally, the choice of agent necessitated virtual confirmation by the Board of Trade, but this was largely formal. That body demanded proper credentials, which took the form of copies of the legislative act of appointment or letters from the governor or both. Ex-Governor Blakiston, for instance, wrote to the governor and council of Virginia on January 28, 1705/6, that he was to wait upon the Board of Trade "for their confirmation" and later that they "chearfully Concurred in it"—obviously with compliments on the colony's securing so distinguished a person for agent, which he was too modest to repeat.[13] Even though occasionally, the boards had

[11] See letter of Governor Tryon to the secretary of state, Feb. 25, 1769. After stating that the rule on this subject laid down to Governor Dobbs on April 14, 1761, had been his rule of conduct, he expressed the wish that "it might be understood how far His Majesty would have His Council share in the nomination of the Person to be appointed Agent," as it would settle a particular which had caused his chief difficulty in regard to the agent.— C. O. 5/308, p. 126.

[12] Hening, *Statutes*, VII, 376; C. O. 324/60, p. 250.

[13] "Miscellaneous Colonial Documents," *Virginia Magazine of History and Biography*, XIX, 14.

admitted a person improperly qualified, according to their own criteria, to negotiate the colonial affairs, such admission did not constitute a right to the status of agent. The ministers might in all cases where they apprehended any inconvenience from the reception of such an agent, persist in excluding him and act consistently with reason and justice.[14]

In the actual selection of the individual for the position of agent, suggestions were put forward by nearly every one connected with the government, British or colonial. In the very breath in which the agency was first proposed came also a suggestion as to the incumbent for the post yet to be created. This goes back to the period of 1655-1660, when the early Committee for America of the Commonwealth period, just beginning to function, suggested the desirability of the colonies maintaining an agent in London. "And (if wee may deliver our Selves freely therein) we would intimat to you that Thomas Povey of Grays Inn Esq. [their own secretary], would be a most fitt Person to befriend, and serve you in that capacitie; of whose abilities thereunto, wee have had a good experience in the afsistance he frankly gave us in yoʳ late Affaires. If therefore you shall pitch upon him, it may be convenient that you write a Letʳ to his Highnefs humbly praying that he may be admitted to represent you and yʳ Affaires from time to time, and that you write to him alsoe desiring him that he will interest himself therein, and rendering such encouragements as may be beseeming him, and the relation he is to have to you."[15]   But there is no evidence that the colony of Virginia availed itself of Povey's services. The Duke of Newcastle, one of His Majesty's principal secretaries of state, had recommended Peregrine Fury to South Carolina in 1731, as is revealed by a letter from Governor Robert Johnson, in which the latter expressed his pleasure that he had been able to obey His Grace's commands in securing the assent of the assembly to the appointment.[16]

The governors, in instances other than those in which they were expected to make recommendations to the council, did not cavil to present names even to the lower house. To cite but a few cases,

[14] See the statement made to North Carolina in 1769.—C. O. 325 I.

[15] Povey's Letter Book, British Museum, Add. MSS, II, 411, pp. 19-20.

[16] Evidently Newcastle had asked an increase in salary for Fury above what had been paid the preceding agent, but that Johnson was unable to secure.—C. O. 5/388, p. 35.

the attention of the reader may be called to the suggestion of Richard Cumberland's name by the governor of Georgia in March, 1766, during the dispute between the Commons House and the council over the reappointment of William Knox, and to the clearly manifested desire of Governor Dobbs for the appointment of Samuel Smith, his private attorney in London, to the agency of North Carolina at the time of the dispute in that colony over that issue in 1759.[17]   The House of Burgesses of Virginia in 1754 resolved that their attorney general should appoint an agent to transact the affairs which concerned that house at that time.[18]   The Lords Commissioners of Trade and Plantations even took a hand at the passing out of offices, for at their session of December 19, 1752, they ordered the draught of a letter to the Commissioners of the Treasury, proposing that Benjamin Martyn be appointed agent for Georgia.   This situation was, it must be admitted, exceptional, and they were undoubtedly thinking more of the smooth working of the affairs of Georgia than of throwing the emoluments of office to some person whom they wished to favor, for they added that he should be appointed agent "under the direction of this Board."[19]

Finally, at times when there was no competition for the post or when the remote colonials did not know to whom to turn and were casting about blindly for some suitable person for agent, they were content to leave the choice to the retiring agent.   Cases in point are the request to Peyton Randolph to name some one for Virginia, and the request to Crockatt by the assembly of South Carolina, answered by his suggestion of Charles Pinckney, available because of his removal to England.   The instances where individuals solicited the post for themselves are not rare but are left for discussion to the chapter on annoyances and rewards of the office.

The length of the term for which the agents were elected did not vary greatly from colony to colony or from time to time during the colonial period.   Usually elected for one or two years, with emphasis on two years, the term did actually in practice reach five and

[17] Colonial Records of Georgia, XIV, 505; Colonial Records of North Carolina, VII, 416.
[18] C. O. 5/1328, p. 211.   In a letter from Governor Dinwiddie to the Board of Trade of May 10, 1754.
[19] Journal of the Board of Trade, 1749/50-1753, p. 377; also C. O. 391/59, pp. 388-89.

even more years in South Carolina during the middle of the century. Nathaniel Blakiston was elected by Maryland for an indeterminate period and seems to have been continued without designation of any fixed term at first. The appointment was to continue "until the Assembly shall by their Letter signify that they have no longer occasion to make use of him." On May 2, 1704, the council and lower house resolved to "request you to continue our Agent"; in 1711 and 1713 the assembly deemed him a "very fit person to continue our Agent."[20] During the experimental period in the early decades of the eighteenth century the term was likely to be only one year. In 1722 when the Commons House of Assembly of South Carolina was considering whether it was necessary to continue Francis Yonge in the agency, it was a foregone conclusion that it would be continued for but a single year—"one year longer," as it was expressed in the debate.[21] Similarly in April, 1725, the agency act was declared to be in effect one year, but it would be lawful for Francis Yonge to return to South Carolina any time after he had completed his mission, according to his instructions from the assembly or Committee of Correspondence.[22] While Fury was serving this province in the capacity of agent, the term was still technically a year and so continued except for James Wright, who was appointed for two years.

In Virginia at the creation of the agency in 1680 the term seems not to have been specified. It would appear that a certain individual was named agent to continue in office as long as the arrangement proved mutually satisfactory. The appointment on August 16, 1705, of Blakiston, already agent for Maryland, as a gentleman of "probity, integrity, and eminent ability for the discharging that Trust," was still without limitation of time. This loose method of appointment apparently continued until about the middle of that century, when the term became fixed at two years. Abercromby was elected for a two-year term while regarded as the agent of the colony, and that term was continued after he became agent for the council only. When the House of Burgesses insisted in 1759 on creating its own agency, although it gave the agency act effect for seven years, the

[20] *Archives of Maryland*, XXIV, 228, 230; for 1704, *ibid.*, p. 393; for 1711, XXIX, 213; for 1713, p. 274.
[21] Journal of the Commons House of Assembly of South Carolina, VI, 98.
[22] *Statutes at Large of South Carolina*, III, 252.

agent was chosen for only two years. In October, 1765, before the act expired, the house voted to extend it for five years from its expiration, which thus continued the agency of the lower house to 1771. The reasons why the act for renewal was rejected in 1772 do not appear.[23] The term for North Carolina, when the agency became fully established with Abercromby's first appointment in October, 1748, was fixed at two years to date from March 25, 1749; but this agent's reappointments in 1751 and 1754 were for three years each. When the lower house created its own agency for this province, it designated Cuchet Jouvencal as its appointee for one year actually, though the appointment was made retroactive for six months; but it elected McCulloh in 1768 for two years and renewed his agency for the like period in 1771.[24] The Georgia agency may be properly regarded as for the lower house, and the term was set at one year; even the great Benjamin Franklin was asked to serve this little unimportant colony for one year. This one-year term continued to be the rule to the end.[25] For the brief period from 1739 to 1746, in which Maryland enjoyed what might by courtesy be called a regular agency, Ferdinand Paris, then acting as agent, was chosen from year to year.[26]

Irregularities in tenure and negligence on the part of the legislators in taking action are striking features connected with the agency. In South Carolina the custom originated while Fury was the incumbent—a custom which later caused considerable controversy—of allowing the agent to continue in service after the act of appointment had expired. Appointed for one year by the act of March 17, 1733, Fury served no less than five years and was regularly provided for in the tax estimate before another act on the subject was framed. Subsequently, when he was appointed for two years, he served three. The members of the legislature themselves recognized their looseness of procedure, for the Commons House in a message to the council of South Carolina of February 7, 1754, declared that they did not apprehend any necessity for an ordinance to continue Crockatt as

[23] Hening, *Statutes,* VII, 277; VIII, 118.

[24] C. O. 324/60, pp. 287, 290-91; *Colonial Records of North Carolina,* XI, 110-11; for 1751, *ibid.,* XXIII, 362-63; for 1754, p. 399; for McCulloh, XI, 229-30; for 1771, XXIII, 854.

[25] *Colonial Records of Georgia,* XVIII, 538; XIII, 731; for Garth, XIV, 497; for Elliott, XV, 492, 537; for Franklin, XIX, 14, 201, 252. See also C. O. 324/60, pp. 330, 338.   [26] *Archives of Maryland,* XL, 419-20.

agent, for not only Crockatt but Fury acted many years after the laws first passed for their appointment had expired.[27]

The slowness of communication at the time rendered it impossible for the agents to assume their duties immediately after appointment, and by the same token it resulted in their continuing in office for some months after they had been dismissed. Blakiston, to cite but a few instances, was serving Maryland long after his dismissal in 1708 and so helped add to the arrears which proved so difficult to collect; Abercromby, though he was dismissed by the lower house of North Carolina on November 1, 1757, did not notify the Board of Trade until April 13, 1758, that he was no longer acting as agent of North Carolina; and though he had been appointed agent for that province on October 15, 1748, he did not begin to function until about January 10, 1748/9, when he notified the Board of his appointment. There are a few instances, however, where the agent was busy about the agency affairs before he first appeared formally before the Board. And sometimes the term extended over an irregular fragment of time beyond a full year, as when the North Carolina assembly in 1754 appointed their agent for three years and indicated that he was to serve to the end of the session. Jouvencal also, when he was appointed to serve the lower house alone in March, 1764, was appointed for eighteen months, as his term was made retroactive from March 7 to October 1, 1763.[28]

While few of the Southern agents could rival the great length of service of some of the New England agents—Richard Partridge with his record of forty-four years of continuous service for Rhode Island, Jeremiah Dummer with his eighteen years for Connecticut, or Henry Newman with his twenty-eight years for New Hampshire —some of them did succeed in piling up respectable records of long years of service. Peter Leheup heads the list with his thirty-one years of continuous work for Virginia; second comes Abercromby, if to his seven years as so-called provincial agent for Virginia we add his thirteen years as agent for the governor and council from 1761 to 1774. Equally a veteran in length of service stands Fury who has eighteen years to his credit as agent for South Carolina. Blakiston

[27] *Public Laws of South Carolina*, pp. xxi, xxxvii; Journal of the Commons House of Assembly of South Carolina, XXIX, 124.
[28] For Jouvencal, see *Colonial Records of North Carolina*, VI, 1214.

offers a record of sixteen years of unbroken service for Virginia and fourteen for Maryland when his two periods of service for that province are computed together. Garth functioned thirteen years for South Carolina, and Montague held on to his post for Virginia for eleven years as the only agent selected by the burgesses after they took over control of the colonial agency.

CHAPTER 5.

DUTIES OF THE AGENT

THE DUTIES of the agent were so numerous, so varied, so confusing, and withal so important that it seems desirable briefly to outline them by way of introduction and then to discuss each new field of his activities in detail.[1] In brief, he was a sort of ambassador or minister from the colony to the court of Great Britain, though, as a working rather than a social representative, he came into contact with the many boards far more often than with the sovereign or his ministers. Again, his duty could be defined as looking after the interests of the colony which he represented. He was, in a sense, unofficial when, as was often true, he represented only the governor and council or only the lower house, though recognized as the duly accredited representative to deal with the governing bodies of the home government and required to present his credentials. He was expected to be, and definitely needed to be, conversant with the conditions not only in his colony but in the neighboring colonies. Indeed, in the eyes of the Board of Trade, his province was the mainland of America and its adjoining islands. He was to defend the laws passed by his colony by preventing their annulment and by following them through all the various boards to which they might be referred. He was to scent far off and prevent legislation by the British parliament which might prove hostile to the colony. To present petitions to the king, the parliament, and the Board of Trade and bring them to a successful conclusion was his constant portion. He must watch the trade of the colonies—encourage it, win favorable conditions for it, and ward off actively every measure which would be disadvantageous to it. He had to deal with finances, troublesome at any time,

[1] Some of the writers on this subject seem to feel that a mere enumeration of the agent's duties is sufficient except where a particular task is linked up with some historical event. This author conceives, however, that for any adequate picture of the agent, it is necessary to see him in action; consequently she has not hesitated to undertake a rather elaborate recital of his duties, of his work, as the very heart of the study of the colonial agency.

but doubly annoying when infant colonies, poverty-stricken but ready for experiment, were always trying to yield to the lure of paper money. Accepting bills of exchange drawn on him, obtaining appropriations for presents to the Indians, and the securing and handling of the funds appropriated by parliament for military expenses of the colony and for reimbursements for the colony's expenses during the wars were hurdles which he must take in his stride. Questions of military supplies, of the erecting and provisioning of forts, of sending quotas to other harassed colonies, or of defending the colony for not obeying the ministerial order for a quota when his own colony was reluctant to raise troops for distant defense, and questions of applications for regular British troops to protect the colony against the Spanish, French, and Indians were problems with which he had to grapple. Land grants and disputes over boundaries; bounties on military stores; convoys for ships between the colony and England for defense against enemy ships or pirates and guard-ships for the American coast; import and export duties; appointment of colonial officials; relations with Indians—presents, disputes, settlement of encroachments on their hunting grounds; presentation of colonial grievances with the fervor needed to wrest sympathetic consideration from a board of Britishers who had long before decided against the colonial—all must be grist for his mill. He must be the medium for transmission of papers, journals, and documents *ad infinitum*—and the reader doubts not, *ad nauseam*.

Drafting and Presentation of Petitions

The necessity of having some one to discharge this duty was, first and last, one of the reasons for creating an agency. This was one of the earliest reasons for wanting an agent, and remained one of the last duties before the Revolution put a period to the duties of any agent. The sacred right of petition was asserted by the colonial at any crisis.

There was a certain type of address which was purely routine, requiring of the agent nothing but the time for presentation, possibly giving him a certain pleasure rather than pain. This type included addresses of congratulation, gratitude, or condolence. Congratulatory addresses appeared at the accession of a new sovereign,[2] with

[2] Such a message was sent by Maryland on April 20, 1762, to Franklin as agent to be presented to George III.—Journals of the Lower House, 1762-1768, pp. 83-84.

which was sometimes combined condolence on the death of a predecessor, or congratulations on the birth of a child to the royal family[3] or on the occasion of military victories. Such instances occurred when Colonel Blakiston was to lay a felicitation from Maryland's assembly before Queen Anne on Marlborough's victories in 1704, and when the delegates of Maryland asked Ferdinand Paris to present congratulations for the successful campaign in the West Indies in 1740 at the outset of King George's War.[4] In the same category fall the addresses of thanks which a number of the colonies sent after the repeal of the Stamp Act. Let one example from Maryland suffice. The assembly, filled with gratitude to the Englishmen who denied parliament's right to tax the colonies, after expressing its appreciation to the Earl of Chesterfield, Lord Shelburne, Secretary Conway, General Howard, Colonel Barré, Sir George Seville, and Alderman Beckford, sent separate messages of grateful thanks to the king.[5] Such messages were always graciously received.

Usually, however, petitions conveyed requests for a certain action or withdrawal of certain action about which the colony was concerned and were often far from acceptable to the ministry unless, as was the case when South Carolina requested to be taken under royal control, the supplication were in accord with the royal pleasure.[6] It seems that at times the king's subjects on this side of the water pressed the ancient right of petition very far, claiming the royal ear

[3] The council and burgesses of Virginia sent a congratulation to George III on the arrival of his Royal Highness the Prince of Wales and on the conclusion of peace with Spain. Governor Gooch sent the original to their agent to be presented to the king by Lord Orkney.—C. O. 5/1322, ff. 63, 64.

[4] For congratulation on Marlborough's success, see *Archives of Maryland*, XXVI, 216; for the success in King George's War, *ibid.*, XLII, 198. Even such formal addresses were subject to the hazards of war, for two addresses sent to Queen Anne during the War of the Spanish Succession, one from each of the houses of the Virginia assembly, were taken at sea so that Blakiston had to present copies to be transmitted to Anne through Lord Dartmouth. The Virginians expected to present the addresses through Lord Orkney; but if he were not in town, the agent was to go to the Board of Trade for orders as to the presentation.—C. O. 5/1316, f. 222; C. O. 5/1363, p. 303; *Journal of the Board of Trade*, 1708/9-1714/5, p. 282. See also "Garth Correspondence," *South Carolina Historical and Genealogical Magazine*, XXVIII, 227, for the expression of gratitude of that colony.

[5] *Archives of Maryland*, XIV, 358.

[6] The petition of Joseph Boone of September 27, 1720, in behalf of several gentlemen of South Carolina was really a request that the government of Governor Moore be not disturbed till the entire question was settled.—C. O. 5/358, f. 59.

for many petty affairs.[7]   Such matters as the currency and a bounty for encouraging speedy settlement of the frontier counties of Brunswick and Spottsylvania in Virginia by exempting the settlers from payment of quitrents were thought worthy of royal consideration.[8] Agents not infrequently were required to prosecute petitions both before the king and parliament, a task which required separate and different procedures and, therefore, entailed much work.   The regular mode of presenting petitions to the throne was through the principal secretary of state.   In case of refusal by a secretary to act, the extraordinary mode of private presentation was invoked.   The royal reply was given through the proper governor, who duly transmitted it to the assembly.[9]   The manner of presenting a petition to parliament was for the agent to deliver it to a member of parliament selected with a view to his influence upon groups interested in the question at issue.[10]   When John Randolph was sent over from Virginia to secure change of the customs on tobacco into an excise, he was charged with petitions bearing a full enumeration of grievances for both the king and the House of Commons.[11]

While petitions were many throughout the colonial period, they were especially numerous and insistent during the crises over the Stamp Act, beginning in 1765 and scarcely ceasing up to 1775. After that date the colonists properly regarded them as useless, for when Richard Penn and Arthur Lee, after waiting for some time, had expressed their earnest desire for a reply to the petition from the First Continental Congress, they were informed by Lord Dartmouth

[7] The petition sent in 1733 by Governor Gooch to the agent for Virginia, Peter Leheup, for pardon to a young man who killed a sailor by accident does not fall in this category. The right of appeal for royal clemency was historic.—C. O. 5/1337, f. 59.   No one would question the propriety of appealing to the king for aid for the inhabitants of Charleston after their fire in 1740.—Journal of the Commons House of Assembly of South Carolina, Nov. 18, 1740-Mar. 25, 1741, XIV, 16.

[8] Abercromby was directed to try to secure exemption of South Carolina from a parliamentary statute to abolish paper currency in America.   See Journal of the House of Commons, Nov. 21, 1749-Nov. 13, 1750, XXV, 171-72; for a petition about currency in South Carolina in 1727, see C. O. 5/360, f. 2; for a bounty for exempting settlers in western Virginia from quitrents see Executive Journals of the Council, IV, 28.

[9] This red tape about methods of presenting petitions to the king is explained by McCulloh in a letter to the Committee of Correspondence, of July 14, 1769.—Colonial Records of North Carolina, VIII, 55.

[10] An illustration was an address of the Virginia legislature sent to Leheup with directions to deliver it to Micajah Perry, a member of parliament for the city of London, but, more important, a leader among the merchants trading to Virginia.—C. O. 5/1321, f. 34.

[11] C. O. 5/1323, f. 28.

that "no answer would be given."[12]   From Virginia, even before
the Stamp Act had been enacted into law, in the summer of 1765
came a protest against the proposed plan of taxation as a violation
of the "most vital principle of the British constitution."   In 1766
came the formal addresses of Virginia to the king, peers and commons, presented through their agent; then followed the addresses of
the lower house of Georgia through Benjamin Franklin and the
memorandum of North Carolina protesting and asking for repeal
of the acts which imposed duties for the purpose of revenue.[13]   So
long as proprietors stood as their immediate overlords in the Carolinas, Maryland, and Georgia, petitions were in order in these provinces, and they were usually received with gracious words and little
more, for the proprietors were in no position to lend the type of aid
and military protection which only government could grant.[14]

Many were the hours which agents must have spent drawing up
petitions.   Isham Randolph drew up a lengthy petition which was
received by the Board of Trade on January 19, 1731/2, on the
famous Molasses Act.   John Randolph drafted his memorial relating to the prohibition on stripped tobacco in language which could
never be mistaken for the sober language of a legislative committee:
"Now that the Temple of Janus is shut by your Majesty's wise
Councils we have reason to hope that the Commerce of your Kingdom will revive their Navigation flourish and their Manufactures
prosper. . . . That Commodity (tobacco) is now fallen so low
That it will hardly Purchafe Raiment for the poor Planter that
Makes it."   So many and so long were the petitions drafted by
Charles Garth for South Carolina and Maryland that one wonders
how he could command the time for them.   They were, of course,
formulated according to instructions from the governor or the house

[12] Lee, *Life of Arthur Lee*, pp. 44-45.

[13] C. O. 5/1331, p. 1; *Colonial Records of Georgia*, XV, 25; C. O. 5/1333, p. 95.
See also Andrews, *Virginia, the Old Dominion*, p. 242; Moore, *History of North Carolina*,
I, 122. Knox also presented a petition for repeal for Georgia through a member of the
British House of Commons, Garth—"Garth Correspondence," *loc. cit.*, XXVI, 73.

[14] Lord Baltimore replied to the lower house of Maryland on August 12, 1743: "I
have Received your Address from Mr. Paris, and you may be assured of my having
your Welfare sincerely at Heart, and of my promoting it upon all Occasions to the utmost
of my power."—*Archives of Maryland*, 1740-1744, XLII, 505. See also Boone's petition
to the proprietors of Carolina, dated Oct. 17, 1709, Journal of the Commons House of
Assembly of South Carolina, III, 443-46.

through their Committee of Correspondence. Copies naturally had to be sent to his constituents.[15]

Forwarding of Papers, Documents, and News

Naturally, the agent was the medium through which documents and papers were forwarded to the governor and papers relating to the colony passed on to the Board of Trade.[16] Regularly the acts of assembly, proceedings and journals of both houses, petitions, minutes of the council, letters, and other public papers which might be sent by the Committee of Correspondence reached the Board of Trade through the agent.[17] So well recognized was he as a medium that the Board itself on occasion asked the agent of a given colony to bring such public papers as had not yet been transmitted to their office.[18] The variety of papers from South Carolina passing through the hands of the agent is admirably illustrated in a letter from Crockatt to Secretary John Pownall in 1753, in which he states that he is transmitting from the Committee of Correspondence an address to the king, sundry letters and other papers from the governor, a draft of fortifications, and likewise three reports from several officers of the forts near "Charles Town."[19]

The agent, likewise, was expected to send back to the colony copies of papers, pamphlets, and newspapers which were likely to interest the officials there. In 1732 Fury sent Governor Robert

[15] A partial list of the petitions drafted and presented by Garth, compiled with no thought of completeness, suggests the extent of his labors in this one respect:

Memorial regarding the Judges of South Carolina; Nov. 12, 1766; 2 pages.

Petition for Revocation of the Additional Instruction to the Governor of South Carolina of Apr. 14, 1770.—C. O. 5/408, pp. 52-53.

Petition for William Prince of Chelsea, starchmaker. *Ibid.*, pp. 271-72.

One about June 1, 1772, on the Result of the Additional Instruction on Money Bills.—"Garth Correspondence," *loc. cit.*, XXXIII, 240-43; 3 pages.

Petition of Nov. 22, 1770, on same subject.—*Ibid.*, pp. 120-23; 3 1/2 pages.

Petition for replacing provost marshals by sheriffs.—*Ibid.*, XXIX, 301-4; about 3 pages.

[16] The author makes no effort to reconcile what was clearly the practice with a letter of Governor Nicholson of South Carolina to the Board of Trade of October 10, 1723, in which he apologizes for having sent public papers to Mr. Yonge, the agent, since the Board did not approve of that practice. He had done so in order to add supplemental information if desired.—C. O. 5/359, p. 49. That this was also the regular practice in the Northern colonies is attested by a letter from the governor of New York to its agent, Champante.—Rawlinson MSS, A 272, ff. 151-52, Bodleian Library.

[17] C. O. 5/360, f. 15; C. O. 5/387, f. 75; C. O. 5/359, p. 41; C. O. 5/360, f. 97; C. O. 5/362, f. 193; C. O. 5/365, f. 70; C. O. 5/374.

[18] *Journal of the Board of Trade*, Jan., 1728/9-Dec., 1734, p. 55; *ibid.*, 1749/50-1753, p. 414.

[19] Dated Mar. 27, 1753, C. O. 5/374 K, 69.

Johnson a copy of a memorial which an opponent of the latter had told him that he intended to present against the governor; Abercromby sent Governor Dobbs a copy of the vote of the House of Commons on the king's address from the throne in 1758 to show the drift of British sentiment on public policy.[20] London newspapers forwarded by Abercromby to Governor Fauquier were welcome, and as the pamphlets began to pour out over the issue of the right of taxation, they were sent back by Franklin, Garth, and others.[21]

Newspapers conveyed some news in convenient form, but the agents did not spare their pens, especially if they could give their constituents timely notice of a new step under contemplation. From Abercromby's letters of 1757 one can construct a fair picture of the state of European politics as well as obtain an intimate glimpse of the English political situation. On May 13, 1757, he wrote: "My former letters told you of the resignation or rather Dismifsion of Mr Pitt. Ever since that there has been by all accounts strong Contests concerning an arrangement for a ministry and now from all appearances the administration will be framed through a Coalition of the Duke of Newcastle with Mr Pitt, and their friends, and these lately remov'd . . . and from hence I may expect the execution of such meafures as I had reafon to hope for from Parliament in favor of the Southward Colonys; I have heretofore told you, that Mr Pitt had procured the King's orders for marching out and if necefsary two thousand of Lord Loudon's Pounds [two words undecipherable] toward the Protection of Virginia to be at hand to protect that and the Northward Colonys and that a grant of Money from Parliament had been agreed to in the Cabinet Council, . . ."[22]

[20] C. O. 5/364, f. 151; Abercromby Letter Book, p. 83.

[21] Garth also sent a number of pamphlets on American potash at the request of the Society for the Encouragement of Arts & (Full name not given).—"Garth Correspondence," loc. cit., XXX, 170. Franklin states that he was sending to the Georgia assembly a pamphlet which he thought very well written in "our Favour," of which he had distributed many.—Colonial Records of Georgia, XV, 28.

A list of papers dispatched to South Carolina by Garth on May 14, 1770, is illuminating: 1. Votes of Parliament; 2. Petition of the New York agent to allow paper bills to be legal tender; 3. Copy of opinion of the Attorney and Solicitor General on the New York bill; 4. Copy of the Preamble of the same.—"Garth Correspondence," loc. cit., XXXI, 285-88, 289.

[22] Abercromby Letter Book, p. 25. Speaker Swann must have rejoiced that Abercromby felt obliged to write of the Seven Years War when he had nothing really to write to the Committee of Correspondence on May 13, 1757: "The King of Prussia threatened

All of this must have been grateful news to Dinwiddie and the people of Virginia. The heavy cost of postage from London to Bristol for the bulky newspapers which Abercromby had collected drove him to "take notice," as he stated in his letter of April 26, 1758, only of the "most material events."[23] The other prolific letter writer, Charles Garth, wrote intimately of actions in parliament and sent the votes for the pending session of parliament up to November 24, 1770. Except for the timely information sent by their agent to the speaker of the South Carolina lower house that an additional instruction of which they had complained bitterly had been withdrawn from instructions to the new governor Bull, the delegates would have been at a disadvantage at the new session in January, 1775.[24] In the early days of the agency, news from an agent must have been particularly welcome, as when Blakiston wrote Ludwell on January 8, 1711: "You will by our publick prints and papers see ye unhappy dissensions that are fomented and Keep [sic] up by ye contending parties. I must confess ye turning out of ye^e Duke of Marlborough gives me but a very Indifferent Impression, for those who have been ye chief agitators could not oblige ye King of France more thane ye Disgraceing ye person who has been such a Terror to that successful Tyrant."[25] The South Carolina assembly, warned by their agent that application was being made for a law that all debts in the American plantations should be paid in proclamation money, protested to the Board of Trade in 1723 that such a step would ruin the province.[26]

---

from all the greatest Powers of Europe combined together is clearing his way gloriously having forced his way into Bohemia, from four different paſsages, one of his armies under Prince Bavern having gained a compleat victory over Count Kenningsegg tho strongly posted and Intrenched with a superior Army. . . ."—*Ibid.*, p. 33.

[23] *Ibid.*, p. 98.

[24] "Garth Correspondence," *loc. cit.*, XXXIII, 119-20; see also C. O. 5/396, p. 225, address of the house to Governor Bull, dated Jan. 26, 1775.

[25] "Some Colonial Letters," *Virginia Magazine of History and Biography*, IV, 21. A portion of Blakiston's letter has such applicability to the present time that the author cannot refrain from quoting it: "we are yet in ye Darke whether we shall have peace or war, except it be a few of those who steers ye Helme. All mankind who feels Interest in theire Country wish for a Solid and good peace, and wthout that we had better risque being undone by a just war."—*Ibid.*

[26] They had to give large advances on the merchants' goods.—C. O. 5/359, p. 103. The avidity of the colonials for news from their agents is expressed fully in a terse comment by Governor Moore to Agent Boone on May 11, 1721: "Continue to give me Constent Accounts of the proceedings of our Affairs at home."—C. O. 5/358, f. 85.

Defense of an Attack on the Governor

When the agent was the appointee of the governor and council as in Virginia, he naturaly defended the governor, even against the lower house. He passed the governor's commission through the proper offices and rendered the governor other little services; Leheup, for example, applied to Lord Orkney and then to the proper offices for leave of absence for Lieutenant Governor Drysdale in 1726; Abercromby in June, 1757, secured leave for Dinwiddie to return to Great Britain for the recovery of his health.[27] Certainly it was not strange that ex-Governor Blakiston as agent espoused strongly the right of Governor Spotswood to appoint courts of oyer and terminer in Virginia against the complaint of the Virginia council.[28] When charges of confusion in the North Carolina government were brought against Governor Gabriel Johnston in 1748 and 1749, Abercromby, in vindication of the executive, declared to the Board of Trade that the charges had originated in England and that they were false. He also, later, as agent for the governor and council of Virginia, defended Governor Dinwiddie during the controversy over levying the pistole fee for land grants in 1754.[29]

When, however, the agent was the representative of the entire colony or of the lower house of assembly, he was very likely to be opposed to the governor. This happened in Georgia in 1756 when even a majority of the council turned against Governor Reynolds. In North Carolina the assembly in 1763 became involved in a quarrel with Governor Dobbs over an Act for Erecting Superior Courts, the clauses of which for the qualification of judges and duration of their commissions the governor held subversive of the constitution. Agent Jouvencal answered the charges against the lower house and insisted that the assembly was merely extending the jurisdiction of the courts.[30] Charles Garth defended the petition of the lower

[27] This appears in a letter from Orkney to the Board of Trade, July 9, 1726.—C. O. 5/1320, f. 27; Dinwiddie felt that the only remedy was the baths in England.—C. O. 5/1329, p. 69.

[28] Letter of Blakiston to Secretary Popple, Nov. 15, 1717, C. O. 5/1318, p. 253.

[29] There is some internal evidence that Abercromby's statement was in part true. See the two complaints of Dobbs and Child, *Colonial Records of North Carolina*, IV, 928-30. See also *ibid.*, pp. 936-43. For Dinwiddie and the pistole fee see Dinwiddie, *Official Records*, I, 373-74.

[30] The regular agent laid the letters of complaint against Governor Reynolds before the Board of Trade.—C. O. 5/653. For the case vs. Dobbs, see *Colonial Records of North Carolina*, VI, 986-88.

house of the sister colony in 1764 when they complained to the home government of Governor Boone's dissolution of their body and re- fusal to administer the oath to one of their members. This struggle extended so far that in 1772 we find Garth engaged in attempting to carry out the desire of the house to have Boone removed or other mark of royal displeasure shown against him.[31]   In the stress of the bitterness between governor and assembly in the years from 1770 to 1776, the agent was invariably the servant of the lower house and their spokesman. The degree to which the agent became the spokesman for the opposition to the governor is strikingly illustrated in Virginia by Abercromby in 1755 when he supported the council in opposition to the governor. The English government had directed Dinwiddie to give South Carolina £2,000 out of the public money of Virginia which was subject to the governor's warrant. This use of colonial funds without their consent called forth a strong pro- test from the council. Abercromby obeyed the peremptory instruc- tions of the council to present and support their address with every consistent argument. Abercromby's support was certain to arouse resentment by calling in question what had been fully deliberated and resolved on by the king in council.[32]

Securing Acceptance of Colonial Legislation

One of the most important tasks with which the agent was charged was what the colonials termed "soliciting their laws" or winning approval of them by the British government, for disallow- ance of a law which a given province had passed as important for its welfare had been a prime motive in the very creation of the agency system. Disallowance of colonial acts led, indeed, directly to the insistence of the House of Burgesses in Virginia for their own agent. In his speech opening the assembly of October 6, 1760, the governor of Virginia proclaimed the repeal of laws passed in 1753, 1755, 1758, and 1759. Yet the laws of 1755 and 1758 thus repealed had been

[31] C. O. 5/404, pp. 222-23; "Garth Correspondence," loc. cit., XXXIII, 264.

[32] For an account of this controversy see Virginia Magazine of History and Biography, XVII, 274-76; Abercromby's letters to William Fairfax, president of the council, September 5, 1755, ibid., pp. 384-85. The instance where Governor Fauquier actually asked an agent of the lower house to defend him may be cited by way of exception. The governor was in disfavor at home because he had ignored some instructions forbidding him to sign amend- ing or repealing bills in order to favor the colonists. The Committee of Correspondence urged the agent to do what he could to excuse the governor.—Ibid., XI, 12-13.

limited to a duration of ten months and one year respectively. Furthermore, in regard to unlimited acts it was difficult to know which acts were in force, and which were not. The governor, council, and house were united in their opinion of the value of the legislation which had thus been mutilated. The burgesses, therefore, turned to the obvious remedy—an agent of their own. To struggle against all the objections which the numerous boards in England could advance and against the opposition at times of other American colonies required of the agent a tremendous versatility—information on a vast range of subjects. In a word, he needed knowledge on the entire field of colonial legislation, some of it on subjects out of the range of the average Englishman's experience. Sometimes he needed to work up half a dozen subjects at the same time. It may perhaps be sufficient to say that twenty-five laws passed by the Virginia assembly in the April session of 1767 came before the Board of Trade on July 14, 1768, with Attorney Lamb's report on them. Agent Montague could not know on which one of them he might be grilled by some one of the Lords sitting on the Board when he was summoned to appear on July 18.[33] That the crown passed upon all legislation made more difficult the task of the agent as general lobbyist. The fate of the act depended very much on the report of the king's counsel to the Board of Trade; he was greatly influenced by his impression of the circumstances under which the colonial assembly had passed the act, the evils it was designed to cure, and the effects it would have in its operation. The agent needed to be able to explain these things and thus lead the counsel to make a favorable report. When the act came back with the counsel's report and was before the Board of Trade for its decision, the agent must again be ready with his arguments. Often this procedure called for a knowledge of the entire past legislation of the colony on a given subject.[34] At times the agent was obliged to ask for postponement in order to secure the necessary information from the colony. A case in point occurred on November 7, 1750, when the Board of Trade considered an act passed in South Carolina in 1721 for nominating

[33] *Journal of the Board of Trade*, 1768-1775, p. 39.

[34] William Byrd II attended a session of the Board of Trade on May 10, 1717, in order to defend a memorial which had been presented. The discourse turned to an act passed in 1663 concerning foreign debts.—*Journal of the Board of Trade*, 1714/5-Oct., 1718, p. 229.

a public treasurer. Mr. Crockatt, the agent at the time, when confronted with some objections of the Board, asked postponement until he could write to South Carolina to learn what reply his constituents might have to offer.[35] The power to disallow an act could, of course, work great hardship. Francis Yonge, for instance, appearing before the Board on May 30, 1723, for an act for the better government of Charleston, begged it to amend rather than void a law which had already been in force more than a year.[36]

The importance of this phase of the agent's duties appears again in connection with North Carolina in 1749 at the time of the dispute over equalization of the representation. On October 17, 1749, the agent was instructed diligently to use his best endeavors to prevent all attempts for the repeal of any of the laws of this province and to get a confirmation of some half dozen laws passed when no representatives were present from the six northern counties.[37]

Occasionally, an agent sought repeal of some provincial legislation. Such was the case with a Virginia law passed in 1663 which defrauded all creditors in England of debts due from persons going to Virginia unless that person carried over with him effects equal to the value of the debt. In 1716 Byrd represented it to the Board of Trade as so "notoriously unjust in itself" and so "infamous to the Colony" that he urged its repeal. After the usual amount of red tape it was repealed. The other case which might be noted reflects the partial view of the South Carolina council as presented by their particular agent, Godin, in order to uphold "his Maj^s authority and prerogative, wch by Impunity, hath been most notoriously Invaded and disregarded by a sett of People who have no other views to pay their debts but out of ỹ Property of his Maj^s good British traders and inhabitants." By riots for these two years they endeavored "to distrefs ỹ̃ at ỹ hazard of ỹ whole Province (should warr break out) by refusing to provide for ỹ support of ỹ Garrisons & ỹ Civill

<hr>

[35] *Ibid.*, 1749/50-1753, p. 112.   [36] C. O. 5/358, ff. 260, 262.
[37] *Colonial Records of North Carolina*, IV, 1020-21. Interesting, though perhaps not important, was the opinion of the Virginia Committee of Correspondence with regard to the relation of their agent to private acts of the assembly. At a session on June 11, 1761, it was recorded that while he was not to look upon himself as concerned in procuring the king's assent to any private act, it was left to the parties concerned to employ whom they pleased, and he was at liberty on application to solicit any such acts.—"Proceedings of the Committee of Correspondence," *Virginia Magazine of History and Biography*, XI, 22.

Governm^t." To redress these grievances he proposed the repeal of four acts and the revival of one act.[38]

Equally important with safeguarding colonial legislation so that it should not be annulled in England was the task laid upon the agent of trying to prevent action by parliament which would be adverse to the interests of the colony. Garth illustrates well this burden of following British legislation as it came before parliament in a report to South Carolina: "I have omitted to make any charge for my time and trouble in and out of the House and with administration touching the several Matters in agitation in the Course of last Session; The Continuation of the Rice Act, and the like of the Indico, the New York Act, the Custom House Act, and the Duty Act in particular touching the Clause of Appropriation, all severally engaged not a little of my time and Attention; how far and in what Degree deserving, I beg leave to submit to the Consideration of the House of Assembly."[39] While individual agents had been concerned about special acts of parliament during all the decades that agents had existed, concerted action by these officials in regard to the Stamp Act and the taxation measures which followed its repeal focused attention sharply on this aspect of the agents' work. They became then the center of the opposition to the oppressive measures of England. The agents labored to prevent the passage of the obnoxious Stamp Act but, strangely enough, had no idea but that it could be carried into operation successfully. Ingersoll, agent of Connecticut, was willing to return to his colony as collector for these duties, and even the great Franklin recommended the post to certain of his friends. But when the Act was a *fait accompli*, and the agents learned of the depth of feeling it evoked in America, they worked indefatigably for its repeal. The sincerity of some of the British-born agents for repeal is touching. Charles Garth, for example, as a sitting member of parliament, presented to that body the petition prepared by Mr. Knox, the ex-agent of Georgia, and rejoiced that it concluded with a prayer for repeal of the Stamp Act, for he wished the House of Commons to understand that repeal and not any mere modification of the Act was the immediate objective of America.[40]

[38] Letter of Byrd to the Board of Trade of May 1, 1716, Entry Book, C. O. 5/364, p. 293; Memorial of Stephen Godin for the council, C. O. 5/361, p. 7.

[39] "Garth Correspondence," *loc. cit.*, XXX, 171.

[40] Letter of Garth to the Committee of Correspondence, Jan. 19, 1767, "Garth Correspondence," *loc. cit.*, XXVI, 73.

Promotion of Trade

British officials in behalf of the English merchants and traders were deeply interested in the produce of the colonies as sources of raw materials and in the colonies themselves as markets for British manufactures. This thought of trade also loomed large in the minds of colonials in appointing agents, even in undeveloped Georgia. Witness the instructions sent Franklin at his appointment of May 19, 1768: ". . . and solicit against what you May think may be injurious to our Trade and future prosperity of which you will please to advise us that you may receive our Instructions thereupon. This Province if it meets with no Ill-advised Check we are persuaded must soon become very advantageous to the Mother Country and Considerable in itself." Even as early as June 28, 1716, when Boone and Beresford appeared before them the Board of Trade was deeply interested in the products of South Carolina. It wanted the agents to prove its claim that the value of South Carolina produce amounted to £709,763 before the Indian War. To do this the agents produced a sample of cochineal which the Board desired proved by some dyes, pound for pound. It proved as good as that from Mexico; Mr. Boone had "gathered of it" himself. South Carolina indigo, which had been planted twenty years before but had been discontinued until recently, owing to the war, was as good as that from Jamaica, though seed was brought yearly from Jamaica to prevent degeneracy. Beresford had seen cypress sixty feet long, clear of any knots, with a diameter of four feet at the base; many of these trees grew near swamps and rivers, convenient for transportation. He also conjectured that there might be several mines in the province.[41]

The Navigation Act bore hard on rice. Under it, as will be recalled, ships from the colonies were obliged to stop at a port in Great Britain before they could take cargoes to foreign ports. In 1720 Boone dwelt on the loss of the rice trade until the Board in its report of 1721 stated the case fully and recommended granting the right to export rice directly from South Carolina to southern Europe. But there was no action, and so South Carolina con-

---

[41] Habersham, *Letters*, in Georgia Historical Society *Collections*, VI, p. 73; *Journal of the Board of Trade*, Mar., 1714/5-Oct., 1718, pp. 158-59.

tinued to press her arguments for more than four decades longer. Rice was exempted from this rule in 1730 only in case of a shipment to European ports south of Cape Finisterre in Spain. Shippers had to give bond in double the value that they would land goods in Great Britain or one of the British plantations. In December, 1722, in response to a request from the Board, Agent Yonge sent an account of the exports of his colony for the preceding three years together with statistics of the total production of rice and its price. The planters, in his view, were not getting sufficient profit to encourage planting of rice. He was, of course, trying to get rice off the enumerated list so far as Spain and Portugal were concerned.[42] In 1745 Fury and Special Agent Fenwicke urged greater liberalization. But any liberalization of the law at that time was blocked by the Commissioners of Customs, who reported that it would require such alterations in the laws of trade and plantations that they could not presume to judge how far it might affect the general trade of the kingdom.[43] As late as the sixties agents were still laboring to secure some modification of the law, this time to carry their rice to the Madeira Isles, islands off Africa, and to any port of America. They urged that its increased exportation would benefit the mother country as well as the colony. Under the existing laws the tenderness and bulkiness of the grain rendered it impossible to supply the Madeira and African Isles in competition with foreigners who carried rice of an inferior quality to those parts from the "Levant Sea." As additional arguments, Garth urged that a change in the law would enable the planters to dispose of great quantities of rice "broken too small" for a European market; that it would create a larger demand for British shipping; and that it would furnish employment for more seamen and marines. In vain. In July, 1766, the Committee of Correspondence was still supplying Garth with arguments. They could not see why ships from America laden with rice should not be exempted from touching at English ports as well as those laden with corn from the Northern colonies, or the fishing ships on their

[42] Entry Book, C. O. 5/400, p. 155. His report appears in C. O. 5/358, ff. 200-1. This report was no doubt the foundation for his "View of the Trade of South Carolina," presented in 1723.

[43] *Journal of the Board of Trade*, Jan., 1741/2-Dec., 1749, pp. 180, 204, 184, 178; C. O. 5/402, pp. 107, 104-5, 120-22; C. O. 5/371, H, 84.

return to America. They insisted that any loss to the British merchants would be amply compensated to the nation in general by increase in the demand for her manufactures, adding tactfully that they
would not "be desirous of anything to the prejudice of the Mother
Country."[44] The Revolution came before relaxation of the law had
been completely won.

Closely related to the subject of the export of rice was that of
starch made from rice and the question of an appeal to take off the
duty on rice in order to benefit that industry. Garth wrote his constituents in South Carolina that the starchmakers were in general interested in preserving so profitable a monopoly as starch made from
wheat; hence they alarmed the landed interests by suggesting the
danger to them from competition in a manufacture depending on the
wheatgrower at the same time that they belittled the proposition
as visionary. Then they worked on the Lords of the Treasury by
insisting that they would be renouncing a solid annual revenue of
£6,000 for an uncertainty, an argument always touching a tender
point with the government.[45] Hence starch from rice remained a
dream as far as Britain was concerned, until 1769, as told later.

Indigo became a matter of solicitude to the agents of Virginia
and South Carolina and begot some jealousy on the part of the latter
colony. Virginia began the raising of this product in 1757, whereupon the sister colony to the south applied to the home government
to make this difficult. While making light of the thrust, Dinwiddie
thought it well to warn his agent, Abercromby, that he was to ward
off any move of South Carolina in that direction. On the other
hand, there was coöperation between Knox and Garth in 1762 for the
continuance of the bounty on "indico." It had been first granted in
1748, continued in 1755, and were continued on March 25, 1763. In
January, 1770, Garth, as agent for South Carolina, renewed the plea
for continuance of the bounty as the chief means for promoting the
culture of that plant in that colony. As inducement he held out the
hope that its culture might be extended to East and West Florida
and thus in time exclude any foreign importation into the American
plantations. Evidently the making of the indigo cubes from the

[44] C. O. 5/377, p. 337; "Garth Correspondence," *loc. cit.*, XXVIII, 229.
[45] See Garth's report to the Committee of Correspondence of Dec. 19, 1772, *ibid.*,
XXXIII, 269.

plants offered no real competition to British manufacture, for Garth had no particular difficulty in securing incorporation of the Winyaw Indigo Society.[46]

Duty on slaves became a subject of negotiation for the agents of the Southern colonies. As early as March 24, 1729/30, Godin, acting for the council, petitioned with some merchants for removal of the duty laid on importation of Negroes into South Carolina. The Board of Trade agreed to insert an article in the governor's instructions for him to secure an act transferring the duty from the importer to the buyer. Our curiosity as to the reaction of the councillors, usually wealthy planters, is not satisfied by the records. Wright, appearing as agent for South Carolina in February, 1759, experienced little difficulty in securing rejection of a petition from one H. Mure, a merchant, to be allowed to exchange slaves in the French colonies in America for indigo. Since Wright's position was in line with the general government policy, the Board found such a practice would be "impolitick" and dangerous to the commercial interests of the country and its colonies. It is interesting that at that early date the agent should have to deal with questions of quarantine. In 1767 Virginia had passed an act to compel ships importing convicts, servants, or slaves infected with "gaol fever" or smallpox to "perform" quarantine. The British government objected to some of the restrictions of the act, probably because they hampered trade unduly. The governor directed Abercromby to learn from the Board of Trade how the act could be made acceptable, as the colony was thoroughly alarmed by the loss by one planter of over fifty slaves in one epidemic.[47]

Salt proved a subject of special solicitude for colonists and their agents. The first record relating to this commodity of 1713 concerned the agents of Massachusetts, Virginia, and Barbados, for the Spanish had seized several New England ships which were loading salt at Tortugas, north-east of Cuba. Dummer, agent for Rhode Island, presented an address to the Board, praying inter-

[46] See Dinwiddie's letter to Abercromby of Jan. 4, 1757, in *Official Records*, II, 580; for the petition of Knox and Garth, C. O. 5/377, pp. 321-22; for Garth's petition of January 29, 1770, C. O. 5/379, pp. 147-48; for the Winyaw Indico Society, "Garth Correspondence," *loc. cit.*, p. 135.

[47] *Journal of the Board of Trade*, 1728/9-1734, p. 103; C. O. 5/1322, ff. 203-4; C. O. 5/1337, f. 151; *Journal of the Board of Trade*, 1754-1758, p. 371; C. O. 5/1351, p. 127.

position at the court of Spain. Ludwell, for Virginia, and the Barbados agents agreed that if the American ships were seized for gathering salt there, it would be a great disadvantage, as planters could not maintain Negroes without salt mackerel and scale fish. Most of the pleas of the agents concerned with salt related to greater ease in securing this necessary commodity. In 1749 Crockatt was memorializing the Board of Trade for the right to bring salt directly from Europe. He sought to move their hearts by pointing out the great abundance of bass, sturgeon, and herring along the coast and in the rivers of South Carolina, which would support a large fishing industry, but its development had been prevented by the problem of salt. There were no saltworks in the province, he reminded the Board, and colonists were prevented from importing salt from Europe unless it were first landed in England. English salt was not suitable for curing fish as was the coarse salt made in other parts of Europe, a kind allowed to enter New England and the central colonies directly. Salt, being a bulky commodity and perishable on ship board, could not bear the charges of transportation. He suggested logically that the ships from England, after unloading their corn in the very European countries where the best salt was made, might come to South Carolina ports loaded with salt instead of in ballast, as was then the case, thus leaving the freight on the salt as pure gain, as well as saving the expense of the ballast. It is interesting that an almost identical petition, even to the phraseology, was presented in 1763, nearly a decade and a half later, by Montague and Garth jointly in behalf of Virginia and South Carolina. Virginia resented keenly the rule that though she shipped some of her products direct to Lisbon, the vessels must either take the salt to Pennsylvania or other Northern colonies and go empty to Virginia, or take Lisbon salt to England and pay duty on it before sailing for home, or go in ballast from Lisbon to Virginia. The Southern colonies, naturally, wanted the same privilege as the Northern, but the Liverpool merchants were strong enough to prevent it; even in 1771, when through their agents North Carolina sought joint action with Virginia, Lord Hillsborough reported that the Board of Trade had not "thought fit to take any immediate Resolution thereupon."[48]

[48] *Journal of the Board of Trade,* 1708/9-1714/5, p. 486. The evidence of one of the mariners taken captive by the Spanish brought to the Board on December 22, 1713, gives

And at one time all three of the Southern colonies most concerned, the Carolinas and Virginia, had to struggle by repeated hearings before a committee of parliament to prevent the grant of a salt monopoly to some British merchants.[49]

Bounties on naval stores engaged the attention of the Southern agents, though perhaps not in equal measure, with that of the agents for the New England colonies. But for the Carolinas and Georgia with their pitch and tar, rosin and turpentine, the question of bounties bulked fairly large. Landgrave Kettleby was charged at the outset of his agency with securing a continuance of the bounty on naval stores exported to England, and as an inducement to valiant efforts, he was offered £150 besides his salary when parliament passed an act continuing the bounty. Boone and Beresford, to prove the quality of the Carolina tar, brought with them to the Board of Trade on February 25, 1716/7, two merchants in the trade and two ropemakers, together with several samples of twine which had been made up, some with Swedish tar only, some with a mixture of Swedish and Carolina tar, and some with Carolina tar alone, to display to their lordships. The discussion brought out the fact that New England and the West Indies were supplied with Carolina tar, and that there was then made in the Carolinas enough cool tar fit for cordage to meet the needs of Britain. One of the merchants present, Crane by name, affirmed that he had lately had one hundred barrels of tar from Carolina; Allen, one of the ropemakers, testified that there were not at the time 100 barrels of Swedish tar to be had in London, the amount which could be worked up in seven days, and that the trade did use plantation tar in the royal yards and elsewhere, whatever was pretended to the contrary. Allen also testified that the tar imported by Beresford was better than had yet come from Carolina and was quite equal to Swedish tar, though dealers would not admit the fact in order to keep down the price. The other rope-

a vivid picture of the times. He had been taken while the ship was at anchor, carried with most of the crew to St. Domingo, where they were threatened with being sent to the mines as slaves, if caught again gathering salt.—*Ibid.*, p. 494. For Crockatt's memorial, see C. O. 5/372, I, 50. For the joint petition of 1763 see C. O. 5/1330, f. 515. This controversy limited the privileges allowed the Northern colonies. For Hillsborough's report to Governor Botetourt, Feb. 17, 1770, see C. O. 5/1348, pp. 96-97; for the effort at joint action by North Carolina, *Colonial Records of North Carolina*, IX, 208-9.

[49] This was in 1758. See Abercromby Letter Book, p. 97; *Journal of the Board of Trade*, 1754-1758, p. 390.

maker had known Carolina tar for sixteen years and agreed that it was equal to the tar from Stockholm. Both agreed that the thinner sort was more properly used on wood and the thicker for ropes. It was noted also that Finland, whence had come most of the Swedish tar, was then almost depopulated from the wars of Charles XII and Peter the Great. The Board, obviously interested, still desired proof whether plantation tar were really approved in the navy yards or used only from necessity.[50] About a week later the agents produced their proof: a certificate from several ropemakers as to the quality of Carolina tar. Crane stated that there was scarce a ropemaker in London but used Carolina tar and raised no objections to it. Sir Thomas Johnson, member of parliament for Liverpool, told the Board that Carolina tar had been used for cordage for four years without any type of complaint. At first coerced by necessity to its use, the trade then held that plantation tar was just as good as any other. The proof of their sincerity was given when the individuals who had testified signed a petition for continuation of the bounty.[51]

Byrd had an opportunity to testify to the quality of another product required by the navy, the hemp raised in Virginia. Appearing before the Board on March 13, 1716/7, he told them that he had raised hemp for his own use for some six or seven years; that the ropemakers there declared they never had seen better fibre, for it had a fine grain and took tar as well as any hemp; and that the soil in Virginia suited to the growth of hemp was not fit for tobacco.[52] In 1723 Francis Yonge was still seeking continuance of a bounty on pitch and tar for South Carolina; James Crockatt in 1751 renewed application for continuance of the bounty; and in 1770 the agents of Virginia and the Carolinas joined in a memorial against any reduction in the bounties on naval stores.[53]

The first plea for a bounty on silk came from a source and at

[50] The account of this interesting session is found in *Journal of the Board of Trade,* Mar., 1714/5-Oct., 1718, pp. 212-13.   [51] *Ibid.,* pp. 214-15.

[52] *Ibid.,* p. 218. Byrd also testified to the presence of a good deal of iron ore in his native state, though not rich enough to mine. Very good ore, however, was found in Pennsylvania.

[53] C. O. 5/358, f. 277; Journal of the Commons House of Assembly of South Carolina, November 15, 1750-June 16, 1759, XXVI, 285; *Journal of the Board of Trade,* 1768-1775, p. 175.

a date which will probably surprise the reader. As early as 1723 the Committee of Correspondence was directed to write Francis Yonge in England to solicit for a bounty on silk made in South Carolina.[54] No evidence appears that it was granted; perhaps the likelihood of its producing results appeared slight. Quite different, as everyone knows, was the tale in Georgia. Money had already been appropriated for silk culture in this province long before there was a provincial agent. When Benjamin Martyn raised questions about the silk bounty, it was rather in his capacity of a royal officer than of agent. On February 6, 1753, when he was called in before the Board, he told them that the Lords Commissioners of the Treasury had agreed that the sum of £1,000 be advanced to pay any outstanding bills for encouragement of the raw silk culture until a plan of government for the colony should be agreed upon. The Board advised Governor Reynolds on May 5, 1756, that £700 being transmitted in copper coin and milled dollars should be applied to demands on account of the silk culture for the year 1756.[55] Naturally, their lordships sought information on this all-important subject from William Little when he appeared in London in 1758 as special agent. He felt that an immediate bounty on the trees, not on the cocoons, was necessary for the progress of the industry, as it is a long time before mulberry trees produce leaves fit for the silk worms, and the people could not live on future grants.[56] By December, 1762, Georgians were apparently concerned about the bounty, for the assistant agent, William Knox, was lauding the advantages of the silk culture and praying continuance of the bounty by parliament without alteration in the method of applying it; i.e., bounty paid on the cocoons brought to the public filature. It was granted. The next year, May 6, 1763, Knox secured what amounted to an additional bounty in the form of an allowance to Ottolenghe, director of the silk culture in Georgia, to instruct a person to carry on the silk works in the event of his death. By the close of 1764 the Board was evidently concerned about the amount expended on

[54] Journal of the Commons House of Assembly of South Carolina, 1723, VI, 162.
[55] *Journal of the Board of Trade*, 1749/50-1753, p. 393; C. O. 5/672, pp. 28-29, 378.
[56] He also urged the necessity of allowing the women to reel off the silk in their own homes because of the expense of going to Savannah and living there.—C. O. 5/646, Bundle C, 36. This paper is not dated, but it was read at the Board April 12, 1758.

bounties and agreed that the price paid for the cocoons should be reduced in order not to exceed the parliamentary grant.[57] The long conference which the Board of Trade held with the Georgia agent sometime in December, 1768—the exact date does not appear—resulted in a long document about the silk culture in Georgia, presented at their request. He gave from vouchers in his hands the amount of silk exported for 1765 and 1766—the silk produced in 1767 was lost, and that for 1768 was not yet fully in. The report shows what sums the agent had received for the industry and what he had expended. He showed its value to England and praised it as a fine thing. He suggested that the Board consult experts, three of whom he named.[58] Finally, the last gesture of parliament on the silk bounty seems to have been a bill ordered in 1769, granting an ad valorum bounty and extending it to any of the colonies. Garth felt this much more just than the old bounty confined to Georgia, when the government paid at the filature at Savannah three shillings a pound for Georgia cocoons but only eighteen pence for those brought in from South Carolina over a greater distance.[59]

If bounties were to be paid on naval stores and silk, why not on oak staves? In June, 1769, Agent Garth sent over to South Carolina a proposal from the London merchants for an alteration of the bounty on pitch, tar, rosin, and turpentine, with which was combined a proposal for a bounty on importation of staves and headings. Finally in 1771 after a number of audiences with various merchants, proprietors, and British manufacturers of casks and after much inquiry by the Lords of the Treasury, an act passed parliament granting a bounty on white oak staves and headings from the American colonies.[60]

[57] C. O. 5/648, Bundle E, 52; *Journal of the Board of Trade*, 1759-1763, p. 312; p. 361; *ibid.*, 1764-1767, pp. 127, 129.

[58] The name of the author of this memorial does not appear. According to the dates Franklin was agent at this time. The style of the report sounds like Franklin but not the tone. The document shows such conversance with the subject as would be difficult to acquire in a few days or weeks of reading. Possibly the word "agent" here refers to an expert connected with the filature who was then in London.—C. O. 5/650, p. 147, ff.

[59] Garth was by this date, April, 1769, agent only for South Carolina, but he was consulted by the Board of Trade and was told the plan they meant to present to parliament, which is not here divulged. He wished the continuance of the old yearly allowance for a few years to be applied in premiums to encourage planting of mulberry trees.—"Garth Correspondence," *loc. cit.*, XXXI, 58.

[60] *Ibid.*, XXXIII, 134. It is amusing to find McCulloh claiming credit for this bounty in a letter of July 10, 1771, to the North Carolina Committee of Correspondence.—

The activities of the agents to forward tobacco culture go far back into colonial history. The agent of Virginia in England in 1664, Moryson, aided by Chicheley, Jeffreys, and Digges, urged the Privy Council on November 16 to issue an order restricting the raising of tobacco. They estimated the importation of English manufactures into Virginia at £200,000 sterling, while the colonists raised only 50,000 hogsheads of tobacco, a difference which left them in debt to the amount £50,000. But any effort at restriction was opposed by Lord Baltimore, and so no action was taken.[61] About 1728 Virginia undertook herself to restrict the cultivation so that she should not be burdened by overproduction of tobacco. The law limited the number of plants to be tended by each tithable person to 6,000 except that an indulgence was shown to those without slaves, allowing them to cultivate 10,000 plants. It will be readily recalled that the occasion for the sending of John Randolph to England on a special agency in 1732 was tobacco—the desire to change the customs on that article into an excise, and to end the frauds practised in the customs.[62]

The making of potash seemed to require encouragement at the hands of the government. Samuel Wragg, agent for South Carolina, and a Mr. Deane, both London merchants, in partnership with others had expended over £1,500 to transport about thirty "artificers" from Holland under a two-year contract to erect saw mills and works for potash in South Carolina. Since these experts were taken away by the governor to serve in the Indian war of 1715 and insisted on leaving at the expiration of their term of contract, the petitioners asked for aid in their projects in 1735. Fifteen years later James Crockatt, agent in 1751, supported proposals to encourage the making of potash, pearl ashes, and all other wood ashes in the British colonies in America. Meanwhile an effort had been made by the South Carolina agent to get the entry of potash from the American plantations into England duty free.[63]

Colonial Records of North Carolina, IX, 10. He had probably been consulted by the Board of Trade.

[61] Neill, *Virginia Carolorum*, p. 305. Neill is in error in calling all four agents.

[62] C. O. 5/1321, f. 74; C. O. 5/1323, f. 48.

[63] For Wragg's petition see C. O. 5/365, f. 74; *Journal of the Board of Trade*, 1749/50-1753, p. 169; Journal of the Commons House of Assembly of South Carolina, Nov. 26, 1749-Dec. 13, 1752, XXV, 174.

When one recalls the keen interest of Governor Spotswood in the mines of western Virginia, it would seem a foregone conclusion that the agents would give some thought to the mining industry, though in its infancy. A letter from the Earl of Orkney about some mines in Virginia led the Board of Trade to summon the agent, then Colonel Blakiston, and the merchant prince, Micajah Perry, on March 12, 1713/4, for further information. They had little to tell except that several miners had already been sent from England at a great charge. Since the backers of the enterprise must be at considerable expense before there could be hope of a return with possibility of profit for the crown, the agent proposed that the undertakers of the plan be encouraged by a patent securing to them sole benefit for the first twenty-one years from all the mines they might discover. All that Blakiston and Perry won for their pains was the command to put in writing a specific plan of what they desired, a statement which was prepared on March 17 and read at the Board meeting of May 11, 1714. What the agent really suggested was exemption for twenty-one years from paying the crown any part of the treasure found and exemption from quitrents.[64] He and Perry were probably reveling in dreams of glittering gold and silver, whereas such wealth as was ever dug out of the Virginia mountains was black iron and coal.

Land Problems: Land Grants and Boundaries

In both Carolina and Virginia land grants early presented agents with difficult problems. In the former, for instance, in 1724 the agents were charged to lay before the Board of Trade the grievances felt by the inhabitants of South Carolina at the proprietors' order prohibiting the sale of lands, which was naturally a great disadvantage to the development of the colony. When their solicitations seemed to be making little headway, the governor and council tried to support their agents by a direct plea to the Board. At a later period, in 1752, in order to encourage settlers, the agent was directed to apply to the king for an order to the governor, directing the royal officers in South Carolina not to take any fees for the passing of grants to such poor foreign Protestants as should come

---

[64] *Journal of the Board of Trade,* 1708/9-1714/5, pp. 519, 533; for his statement of Mar. 17, see C. O. 5/1316, f. 451.

over to settle in that colony.[65] The problem of the Northern Neck, which harassed Virginia so long, arose again to torment Leheup long after Smith, Moryson, and Ludwell were supposed to have settled the matter. By the patent issued by Charles II and confirmed by James II the general assembly of Virginia had been given full power to impose taxes on the territory of the Northern Neck and to execute laws for the people of that section as for the rest of Virginia. It was never a palatinate or independent area; the proprietors simply owned the land and were entitled to the quitrents from them. Still in 1726 or 1727 the proprietors of the Neck were claiming the fines, forfeitures, deodands, and goods of felons within the territory. Hence the colony was soon sending their agent a statement of the case to digest. He was also to settle the boundaries of Lord Fairfax's grant. Made to his great-grandfather, Lord Culpeper.[66]

In 1770 there was made an effort to take from Virginia a large tract of land in the Northwest in connection with a plan for establishing a new colony on the Ohio. This was the renewal of a scheme proposed in 1763, and the controversy continued for some years, since it included land which Virginia believed to be within her borders. Montague, agent for the House of Burgesses, opposed this grant with vigor and his letters have many references to the subject, as do the records of the lower house. He naturally conceived it his duty to protect the rights of persons with land grants from Virginia. He understood that no less than 1,350,000 acres of land had already been granted, partly, he understood, to a society of gentlemen called the Ohio Company, partly to individuals who had made some progress in the cultivation of that land before the outbreak of the French and Indian War. In his petition he submitted to the Board whether before proceeding further Virginia should not have notice and opportunity to object to such grants. In his letter of February 6, 1770, to the Committee of Correspondence he gives an insight into one aspect of an agent's problems. "Very great & opulent Perfons are combined in this Attempt, & it has been conducted with fo much Secrecy,

---

[65] C. O. 5/359, p. 230; Journal of the Commons House of Assembly of South Carolina, Nov. 14, 1751-Nov. 21, 1752, XXVII, 544.
[66] "Miscellaneous Colonial Documents," *Virginia Magazine of History and Biography*, XVII, 263. The letter to Leheup is undated. Internal evidence fixes it approximately as 1726 to 1727, but an entry of February 21, 1739, shows that he is still troubled with the grant.—*Journal of the Board of Trade*, 1734/5-1741, p. 270.

that till this Treafury, had agreed on the Confideration, no body knew of the Negotiation. The Inftant I difcovered it, I enter'd my Caveat at the Board of Trade."[67] The dispute over these western grants is a part of history too well known to require repetition here, but the story of the agent's relation to them requires this brief mention.

While the question of boundary lines and disputes between the colonies did not engage the time of the agents of the Southern colonies as it did that of the Northern agents, they were far from being free from its vexations. Governor Middleton of South Carolina sent Francis Yonge in September, 1725, orders to wait on the Duke of Newcastle with papers lately sent Middleton by the Spanish governor of St. Augustine. Among other papers was a copy of a letter from His Grace to the Spanish ambassador in London, informing him that orders would be dispatched to Carolina to settle the boundary between the two governments with the governor at St. Augustine and that if the fort erected on the "Allabamahaw" River should prove to be within the Spanish territory, it should be demolished immediately or a fair equivalent be given in exchange.[68]

Crockatt was called upon to deal with one of the really annoying land problems. A proposition to annex Georgia to South Carolina after expiration of the charter granted to the Trustees was under consideration in 1750-1751 by the ministry of Great Britain. It was held injurious by both colonies. The governing officials of Savannah stated their opinion to the Georgia Trustees; the assembly of South Carolina charged their speaker to inform their agent, Crockatt, of the assembly's view. The only arguments in favor of such annexation which they could find were a possible better regulation of the Indian trade with the Creeks and Cherokees and restraint of the escape of criminals from South Carolina to Georgia. But these arguments were more than offset by the arguments against: the necessity of forts on the frontiers and the burden of salaries for rangers, scouts, and lookouts, which must fall on South Carolina, as but little contribution could be expected from the people of Georgia. The paper

[67] "Proceedings of the Virginia Committee of Correspondence," loc. cit., XII, 159-63, 164, 227; C.O. 5/1332, p. 323; Journals of the House of Burgesses, 1770-1772, p. xviii.
[68] See letter of Middleton to the Duke of Newcastle of September 10, 1725, C. O. 5/387, p. 79.

ends by charging Crockatt to oppose the proposition with all his power. The issue dragged through 1751 and 1752, calling forth a long petition from Edmund Gray, as agent for Georgia, adverse to such annexation; but ended, as is well known, with leaving the colonies separate.[69]

In 1763 the king decreed that Georgia should extend to St. Mary's River. This instantly meant trouble with South Carolina, as she claimed the region south of the Altamaha River. Governor Wright protested to Governor Boone of South Carolina, but no heed was paid to the protest. Then he turned to the Lords Commissioners of Trade and Plantations without satisfaction. Georgia appealed next to William Knox, the special agent in England, and asked that he have the South Carolinians dislodged. Knox was informed that South Carolina was preparing to make grants of large tracts of land south of the Altamaha River on the ground that this area was not covered by the charter given to Oglethorpe, and so he laid before the Board of Trade a *caveat* or protest, which the governor of Georgia had sent to the governor of the neighboring state against such grants. Georgia, expecting that those lands soon would be annexed to the neighboring province, directed its agent to use his utmost endeavors to stop proceedings so fatal to its prosperity and to retain the king's attorney and solicitor general and such other counsel as he might deem proper, and in the meantime till authentic proofs could be obtained to take such steps as he thought expedient. Garth, speaking for South Carolina, pointed out that the remote inhabitants of the region, often lawless, contributed nothing to the support of government under pretense of uncertainty as to the government to which they owed allegiance. Some check must be put to those evils and an effectual regulation of police set up. Knox was not successful; the grants already issued were legalized, but no more were to be permitted. By 1766 the South Carolina executive had made grants up to around 400,000 acres—usually to speculators—and so Garth entered another caveat to prevent royal confirmation of an act recently passed by the Georgia legislature in relation to the grantees of those lands. As he heard nothing from the Plantation

[69] See C. O. 5/373 for Speaker Rutledge's letter to Crockatt of June 6, 1750; for Gray's petition, see C. O. 5/657. Habersham was much opposed to the union of the two colonies.—*Colonial Records of Georgia*, XXVI, 375.

Office for sometime, he was inclined to think that the act would repose there without any further attention from the Board.[70]

A dispute over the boundary line between North and South Carolina seems to have been the most serious of the boundary disputes with which the colonial agents had to grapple. It arose in 1735 and dragged its slow length to 1772.[71] Garth assured the Committee of Correspondence of South Carolina on February 5, 1770, that he had taken all possible pains to inform himself upon the subject in order to present in the strongest possible manner the claims of South Carolina, and sent a copy of his memorial to the Board of Trade. He encountered the usual difficulties with conflicting and inexact maps.[72] A year later he was urging on that body determination of the boundary lines and had secured the promise of Governor Lord Charles Grevill Montagu to intercede for its conclusion before the latter left England. Another petition dated April 24, 1771, reveals the exact line on which he was insisting.[73] On April 12 Lord Montagu made good his promise by appearing with Garth at the session of the Board, but the agent for North Carolina, Mc-Culloh, to Garth's distinct annoyance, secured a further postponement. By July, 1771, the king issued to the governors of the two colonies instructions on the dividing line which threw many settlements on the Broad River into South Carolina. Great dissatisfaction was expressed, naturally, on the part of the other province and

[70] *Journal of the Board of Trade*, 1759-1763, p. 366; *Colonial Records of Georgia*, XVII, 51-52; "Garth Correspondence," *loc. cit.*, XXVIII, 233; C. O. 5/377, pp. 291-92; Johnson, *Georgia as Colony and State*, p. 112.

[71] There is hint of some questions over the line in 1735 when the Board of Trade summoned ex-Governor Burrington of North Carolina, and Fury, agent for South Carolina, before them on June 27. But since little more appears, the controversy could not have been serious until 1769.—*Colonial Records of North Carolina*, IV, 28. Fury and Yonge were both present on June 20. See also Skaggs, *North Carolina Boundary Disputes involving her Southern Line.*

[72] In a letter of April 18, 1771, he says: "I since find that the Board are not of Opinion to recommend either Branch of the Catawba River for a Boundary, by Wm. Cook's Survey of that River the South Branch appears therein to lie in an East and West Direction, and their Lordships were inclinable in that Case to have recommended the So. Branch, but as the same Direction does not appear from other Charts before the Board, the Direction of this Branch is doubtful, and therefore they have though fit to recommend a Line which may be run without delay."—"Garth Correspondence," *loc. cit.*, XXXIII, 133.

[73] *Ibid.*, p. 124. Montagu was absent from his province from 1769 to 1771. Garth's line beginning at the sea, 30 miles southwest of the mouth of the Cape Fear River, followed the direction in which it had already been marked to the Salisbury Road near the "Catauba" Lands, to be continued from the station point on that road to the Cherokee line.—C. O. 5/404, pp. 445-46.

its agent, who refused to take out instructions from the offices, especially as there were heavy fees, and in 1772 tried to secure a revocation of the royal instruction. The story passes from the agency records with Garth's assurance on April 21, 1772, that he would exert himself to prevent any revocation.[74]

Naturally, agents were consulted when settlements were projected. One of the earliest was William Byrd II, who was requested in April, 1700, by the Board of Trade to assist the Marquis de la Nuce and M. De Seuilly, who were leading a band of French Protestant refugees to Virginia, with his advice and a letter of recommendation to his father. Colonel Blakiston was consulted in 1709 upon the proposal of M. de Graffenried and Mr. Louis Michel to settle a colony of Swiss at "Potomack." A few years later, at the Board meeting of March 5, 1717/18, that same agent was consulted as to the probable effect on Virginia of a proposed settlement in the southern part of Carolina. He replied that if it were directed by good men, it would be a public advantage.[75] In the spring of 1732 the Board was considering a project for settling six hundred Swiss in South Carolina, combined with a proposal for a grant of 48,000 acres, as security for those persons who were to advance the money to defray the cost of transportation. Naturally, the agent of South Carolina, Peregrine Fury at the time, was called in. The Board, however, by the very close of 1733 had only reached the point of instructing Governor Johnson to grant a proportional part of the huge acreage sought.[76]

Indian Affairs

The solicitation for a sum for purchase of presents for the Indians fell rather naturally upon the shoulders of the agents. During 1731-1748 the expense of these presents had been defrayed by sums granted by parliament to the Trustees of Georgia and afterwards out of extraordinary expenses allowed a regiment. These

[74] "Garth Correspondence," *loc. cit.*, XXXI, 127-28, 142; XXXIII, 131-32, 133, 237; C. O. 5/381, p. 364; *Colonial Records of North Carolina*, IX, 11.
[75] Entry Books of the Board of Trade; C. O. 5/1359, pp. 396-97; *Journal of the Board of Trade* for Feb., 1708/9-Mar., 1714/5, p. 55; *ibid.*, Mar., 1714/5-Oct., 1718, p. 347.
[76] *Ibid.*, 1728/9-1734, p. 292; C. O. 5/381, pp. 96-97. When Stephen Godin was consulted in 1729 about a possible settlement of some French for a cod fishery on Gaspé in Newfoundland, it would appear to have no connection with his duties as agent of South Carolina.—*Journal of the Board of Trade*, 1728/9-1734, p. 63.

charges for Indian presents for Georgia alone ran to £7,000 or £8,000 a year, but they seem to have been reduced in 1748. A special agent for South Carolina reported back in April, 1748, that the king had granted £3,000 annually for Indian presents to be distributed by the governor, council, and assembly of that province in conjunction with one person to be appointed by the Trustees of Georgia. Crockatt reported to the Duke of Bedford in November, 1749, failure to achieve the ends for which the grant was intended, owing to the method of using the money. He had been instructed to petition that whatever future sums were allowed for South Carolina might be entirely under her own direction, separated from those granted Georgia. The method practised by South Carolina was to give presents to Indians only on special occasions or when they came to the centers expressly to renew their treaties of friendship. There was no fixed time or annual distribution of gifts, for that method would, in the judgment of those who had resided in America and understood the Indians, have disastrous results and involve a very great expense. Crockatt presumed that the inhabitants there were the most competent judges as to the goods proper for Indians and of the sums to be so applied, since a considerable part of the expense consisted in articles other than merchandise. Hence he proposed that some proper person in London be intrusted with their portion of the £3,000 to supply them with the proper assortment of goods. But government pursued its own method and appointed Jermyn Wright and Harman Verelst, who should probably be regarded as crown agents, and issued to them £3,000 from the pay office in October, 1749. But by October, 1750, South Carolina had received no goods for the Indians, though Crockatt had exerted himself by waiting on the Honorable Henry Fox, Secretary of War, to remove objections to the agent's plan of handling the Indian fund. It seems that Wright did ultimately purchase sundry goods and consigned them to Governor Lyttleton, but the consignment was only a partial one. Great difficulty must have been experienced, for in November, 1757, and again about two months later we find Crockatt once more petitioning at various offices for a grant of £3,000 for presents for the Indians contiguous to South Carolina and Georgia. He pointed out that the numerous tribes of Indians adjoining those provinces instigated by the French at Mobile and the Spanish

at St. Augustine had harassed the inhabitants, and that they had
been virtually bought by the large presents given annually at the
expense of their sovereigns. The situation was not improved by the
fact that Georgia Trustees at public expense gave more lavishly than
South Carolina and prompted even larger gifts for the Indians!
A frontier province, like South Carolina, could not sustain so heavy
a charge. As many of the articles sent were utterly improper, they
lay long after undisposed of and "rotting" in South Carolina. He
hoped for instructions which would enable the governor and council
to sell them and apply the sum yielded to proper presents for the
Indians. He added a personal plea: as a private subject he had
perhaps more to fear and more to lose by a rupture with the Indians
than the average private citizen, though he declared at the same
time that he was neither directly nor indirectly concerned in the
Indian trade. He was probably referring to his large land grants.[77]
Thoroughly wearied by his fruitless applications to the numerous
boards by March, 1752, he complained to the South Carolina lower
house that it was "not easy to describe the trouble he had had about
the Indian Present Money." In October, November, and December, 1751, he had many times attended the secretary of state who
told him that the warrant must "rife on a new Channel," the Treasury Office, but when he gave in a memorial to the Treasury, by
which it was referred to the Board of Trade, and when he attended
that group with Martyn, then secretary to the Georgia Trustees,
still nothing was done. He could see that on no account would they
agree to any money being drawn, but the whole amount must be
sent in goods. On November 25, 1752, he was ready to declare
that the Indian money had proved "the most tedious and troublesome Job" he ever met with.[78] When the Board of Trade finally

[77] C. O. 5/374; Journal of the Commons House of Assembly of South Carolina,
Mar. 28-Nov. 21, 1749, XXIV, 329. A list of his petitions serves to show how indefatigable he was: Petition to the Duke of Bedford, Nov. 9, 1749, C. O. 5/374 (no folio
number); to the Duke of Bedford of Oct. 22, 1750, C. O. 5/374; to Secretary Holderness,
Nov. 14, 1751, C. O. 5/385; to the Treasury Board, Jan. 22, 1752, C. O. 5/375; to the
Board of Trade, Nov. 10, 1752, C. O. 5/374. Also in Commons Journals, XXVIII, 330.
For the fact that Wright had made purchases see his report to the Board of Trade, C. O.
5/376, L. 16.
[78] Journal of the Commons House of Assembly of South Carolina, XXVII, 570;
XXVIII, 28. At his appearance with Martyn before the Board of Trade on June 24, 1752,
he proposed that the £3,000 be given South Carolina in partial recompense for her expenses
for the Indians, and that all the money should not be sent in goods, but a part be drawn

rendered a report on July 12, 1753, they saw no reason to comply with the request of South Carolina, for "it would only encourage other colonies to make similar demands," whereas the charge of Indian services had always been met by the colonies, except in times of imminent danger. It reserved decision as to Georgia, to which it might be necessary to grant a sum as that colony was in its infancy.[79]

The Board had evidently been clear in its own mind that the policy of grants for Indian presents must be continued in Georgia, and they were well advised to allow themselves a loophole, for in June, 1754, when the petition of Martyn, as agent, setting forth the number of Indians within the province of Georgia in alliance with the British crown, the importance of their friendship for the colony's security, and the expediency of sending some presents to them was presented, the Board recommended that £1,500 be allowed for that purpose. As late as 1760 the Board issued a warrant for Martyn to apply £48 for the freight of goods ordered by the king to be sent to Georgia for this purpose.[80]

The Board of Trade was not mistaken about the danger which lay in precedents. Only a few years before, Abercromby in behalf of Virginia had proposed that the sum of £3,500, which had been granted by the crown for presents to the Indians south of Virginia be also granted to the Ohio tribes and other Indians to the westward as a means of promoting "what further operations may be thought necessary" in the interior of the continent. No statement of action appears in the records.[81]

The regulation of the trade with the Indians was also a subject for solicitation by the agents. The laws and the actual conduct of the trade were matters of deep concern to the home government, for on them might turn her foreign relations with France and Spain. Colonel Blakiston in 1716 had to defend an act passed by Virginia to control the Indian trade. Francis Yonge in 1722 was particularly zealous to defend an act of South Carolina of that character to pre-

---

on by South Carolina to defray the cost of distributing the presents and the cost of other Indian services.—*Journal of the Board of Trade,* 1749/50-1753, pp. 334-35.

[79] Report of the Board of Trade to the Treasury Board, C. O. 5/402, pp. 427-30.

[80] *Journal of the Board of Trade,* 1754-1758, pp. 49, 53; *Colonial Records of Georgia,* XXVI, 448-51; C. O. 5/672, pp. 52, 57; C. O. 5/673, pp. 265-6.

[81] C. O. 5/1329, p. 221.

vent people of the vilest sort by fraud and abuse from stirring up the natives to revenge their injuries on the innocent. He relates how Governor Spotswood had proposed to the Cherokees in October, 1721, a peace between them and the Iroquois. Carolina objected as the Cherokees lived in the western Carolina mountains. Yonge, therefore, asked for instructions to the American governors not to propose or mediate a peace between Indians not actually residing in their own provinces without previously consulting the governor of the colony in which they lived, and also to urge the governors to pass laws to restrain their traders from misusing the Indians as the ill practice of Virginia traders might be avenged on Carolinians. A really ambitious effort of South Carolina to put an end to the abuses in the trade did not come until 1762, but she did then try to take the trade with the Cherokees into her own hands and to secure its value to herself and their friendship for the British by ending all fraudulent dealings. To Garth fell the task of winning royal assent to this bill.[82] Slightly different was this from the aim of Fury when in December, 1736, he had supported the petition of the council and assembly of South Carolina against the inhabitants of Georgia for obstructing their trade with the Indians.[83]

Despite the basis which Oglethorpe laid for relations with the Indians, Georgia was not free from harassment from the natives. Both she and South Carolina felt that the most effective check could be administered by cutting off trade with them. This was the view which some held toward the military expedition of the governor of South Carolina against the Cherokees in 1759—that the right step would be to stop all trade until ample satisfaction was secured. Likewise, in 1764, when the demand of the superintendent of Indian affairs for satisfaction for the murder of some whites by the Creeks had brought only an evasive answer, Habersham felt that the least expensive way to humble the savages was to stop all trade and communication with them and to persuade Virginia and the Carolinas to join without reserve.

[82] *Journal of the Board of Trade*, Mar., 1714/5-Oct., 1718, pp. 163-66; petition of Francis Yonge of Mar. 22, 1722, C. O. 5/371, H. 56; C. O. 5/377, pp. 288-89.

[83] *Journal of the Board of Trade*, 1734/5-1741, p. 153. Interesting, no doubt, would be the criticism directed by the House of Burgesses against John Stuart, Superintendent of Indian Affairs, which Agent Montague was directed to bring to the attention of the home government, but not enough appears to justify inclusion in the text. Just another task for the agent!—*Journals of the House of Burgesses*, 1770-1772, pp. 76-77.

The appearance of three Cherokee Indians before the Board of Trade must have been one of the most dramatic of the many and often dull sessions of that board. They had been taken over to England by the trader, Aaron Truehart, because of the discontent of that tribe with the encroachments on their hunting grounds. When Truehart died, the responsibility for these Indians fell on one Timberlake, who evidently desired reimbursement for their traveling expenses. Brought over against the consent of Governor Fauquier, the king decided that they should be sent back to Virginia, since they were in danger of being deserted and exposed to distress. The Virginia agent, Montague, found himself ordered to contract for their passage, their good treatment during the voyage, and their safe delivery to the lieutenant governor. The crown ordered passage money and some small presents at their departure paid out of the treasury. The Board of Trade did not propose, however, to deny themselves sight of the red men, and so they interrogated them at the session of February 12, 1765, at the Plantation Office, whither they were escorted by Montague. When the Cherokee leader was asked "if he had anything to offer on the part of his Nation," whereby the modern reader would infer any complaints to make, he said that he was to represent that there were valuable mines of yellow and white metal and of iron in their nation, which they wished the English to work [sic] and that they wished proper persons to teach their youth religion, and to read and write. They added that they had been troubled by European stragglers settling on their lands. When Montague had prepared an estimate of their expenses and had seen them safely aboard a vessel on March 1 his unusual task was completed.[84]

Military Affairs

As might be expected, plans for forts were early forced on the agents for consideration. Just emerging from a serious Indian War and menaced by a possible invasion by the Spanish neighbor to the south, it is not strange that Boone and Beresford even in 1716,

[84] C. O. 5/1345, pp. 155-56; *Journal of the Board of Trade*, 1764-1767, pp. 145-46, 147. The Board in a letter of March 1, 1765, approved of Fauquier for discouraging their departure.—Entry Books, C. O. 5/1368, p. 257.

It might be noted in passing that this was not the first time that the Board session had been enlivened by the presence of Indians. Two Mohawks were present at the session of April 9, 1697, brought by Agent Nicoll of New York.—C. O. 391/10, p. 65.

though sent over primarily to appear against the proprietors, still could take thought for the fortification of South Carolina. They suggested forts on both sides of the "Gulfh of fflorida at Providence, at Port Royal and on the Banks of the Isthmus of fflorida towards Mobile on the Borders of Our Frontiers." Progress in securing their defenses was slow, for not until four years later do we find the Board interested in receiving an "Account of the proper places for garrisons in Carolina." The last words of the title were probably appended at their initiative—"and the absolute necefsity of doing the Same Speedily."[85] By 1722 a committee of the Commons House of Assembly reported accounts for the building of Fort King George and barracks as amounting to £960 and as being sent home by Yonge for repayment. More than a decade later in March, 1735, this same agent now acting as special emissary to assist Fury, submitted, in response to a Board request, his opinion of what defenses were further needed in case of war with France or Spain: first, Georgia should be encouraged to erect forts; and, secondly, the government should help fortify Port Royal.[86] As the century progressed, the cry for more and better forts increased, if anything. First came the cry from Charleston in 1752 for the agent to secure royal aid to repair the damage to its fortifications from the hurricane; Charles Pinckney on his special mission in 1754-1756 urged on the Board of Trade the necessity of anticipating the French by building forts in the upper Cherokee country. On September 1, 1755, when he found the Board of Trade adjourned, he laid before Sir Thomas Robinson, a principal secretary of state, the dangerous situation of his province resulting from the designs of the French and the Creek Indians. On February 4, 1756, he divulged important information that 150 Cherokee chiefs and warriors had come to Charleston to demand a fort in the upper Cherokee country. When asked if there would be war in Virginia in the spring, their answer was "No." "My Lords

[85] Entry Books, C. O. 5/1293, p. 7. This document is not dated, but was received by the Board, Aug. 23, 1720.—C. O. 5/358, ff. 13-20. Beresford's sweeping survey of the danger from the French as seen on June 23, 1716, is perhaps worth quoting. "By many former circumstances as well as by the late Letter from the Assembly of Carolina there is too much reason to be assur'd that the French (who live and trade with the Indians from Quebeck and along the Lakes of Canida and Southward too and down the great river of Messisippi to Fort Morilla scituated on a River near the Mouth of the said great River with the Bay of Mexico) have stirred up and encouraged severall Nations of Indians to this War."—*Colonial Records of North Carolina*, II, 231.

[86] Journal of the Commons House of Assembly, 1722, VI, 83-84; C. O. 5/364, f. 255.

from this spirited, and I humbly prefume your Lordpps will think reasonable, demand of thefe people, you will perceive the danger there is, of their delivering up their Country and throwing themselves wholly into the hands of the French if it is not without further delay complied with; the fatal Confequences whereof to his Majestys interest and to the very existence of the Southern British Colonies on the continent of North America, I will not presume to repeat. . . ."[87] The story of Fort Duquesne transformed into Fort Pitt proved that this Southern colony was well advised to expend some £7,000 on the fort in the Upper Cherokee country and one in the lower Cherokee country, for which Agent Wright sought reimbursement in the fall of 1756.[88]

When immediate war threatened, the agents pleaded for troops, of course. In 1715 Kettleby, aided by Beresford, represented how hard pressed were the people of Carolina, how the Indians had burned and destroyed most of the outlying settlements and so harassed the settlers that the women and children had retired into Charleston, while the men, not above 1,400 in number, were all in arms on the frontiers but so fatigued that unless succour of men and arms were sent promptly, they would be obliged to desert the province.[89] In 1717 the agents were asked the number of troops thought necessary to subdue the Indians. They replied that less than 600 with 200 to remain for a period of two years would be ineffectual, but entries of May, 1718, show that effective aid had not yet been dispatched. In 1742, in the midst of King George's War, Governor Bull through the agents Abercromby and Livingston, who were aiding Fury, begged for three independent companies to be garrisoned on the frontier. In 1740 Fury was directed to apply to the ministry for six galleys for the defense of the South Carolina coast. Again in 1761 Montague was directed to ask for a man of war to protect the coasts and harbors from the "Insults of

[87] Governor, council, and assembly petitioned the king for money to repair Ft. Johnson at Charleston.—C. O. 5/385; also Journal of the Commons House of Assembly, Nov. 14, 1751-Nov. 21, 1752, XXVII, 598, 607-8. For Pinckney's mission see C. O. 5/386. The Board indorsed his suggestion June 20, 1754.—C. O. 5/402, pp. 443-44; June 27 he presented further data on the French designs.—Journal of the Board of Trade, 1754-1758, p. 54. Feb. 17, 1756, Governor Lyttleton was ordered on his arrival in South Carolina to inquire what steps had been taken to build a fort.—Ibid., p. 213. For Pinckney's address of Feb. 4 see C. O. 5/375, K, 128.

[88] For Wright's petition, dated Nov. 22, 1756, see C. O. 5/375, K, 177.

[89] Journal of the Board of Trade, Mar., 1714/5-Oct., 1718, pp. 64-65.

the Enemy's privateers." The coast of Virginia had for a long time had a guard ship or two until the five years preceding 1761 when it had had none except now and then a convoy for a brief period.[90]

No service, however, antedated that of procuring ammunition and other military supplies. The earliest examples come from Maryland and Virginia; one entry in the minutes of the council of the latter colony is sufficiently suggestive. On April 28, 1699, the record reads: "No arms had been sent into the colony since 1692, when 200 were sent in by Jeoffrey Jeffrys, which were all burnt in the State house" last fall. And one of the few items preserved referring to Thrale's work shows an order for him to solicit the Board of Ordnance for dispatch of the arms now ready to be sent to Virginia by the first ships. Blakiston was employed to purchase more arms and ammunition for Maryland.[91] Other instances will be cited under financial aspects of the work.

In the conflicts with the Indians and Spanish in the early decades of the 1700's the agents of South Carolina, Boone, Beresford, Barnwell, and Yonge, set forth repeatedly and at great length the outrages of the Spanish and the designs of the French for a continuous communication from Canada to Louisiana behind the British plantation, and to further this plan they had built a chain of forts for nearly 3,000 miles.[92] The agents asked earnestly for aid and supplies. Fury alleged that South Carolinians were unable in 1738 to provide themselves with sufficient small arms and stores; Livingston and Vander Dusen, joining Abercromby for this purpose in fear of another powerful attack from the Spaniards, renewed their application in May, 1743, to the ministry for the assistance of men and arms, without which many of the inhabitants would leave the province, as they were awaiting only the outcome of this application. James Wright in the midst of the French and Indian War did not hesitate to petition for a large quantity of naval stores for the several

[90] *Ibid.*, pp. 228-29; Entry Books, C. O. 5/1293, p. 151; Journal of the Commons House of Assembly, Nov. 18, 1740-Mar. 26, 1741, XIV, 39; *ibid.*, XXIX, 450-51; C. O. 5/368, G, 80. For the situation of the coast see "Proceedings of the Virginia Committee of Correspondence," *loc. cit.*, XI, 21. Abercromby urged regular convoys on Governor Dobbs in 1757.—Abercromby Letter Book, p. 31.

[91] *Calendar of State Papers, Colonial*, 1699, sec. 306 and Addenda; C. O. 391/15, p. 393; *Archives of Maryland*, XXVII, 112-13.

[92] The memorial by Beresford in which the French purpose is so clearly set out is dated Dec. 12, 1717.—*Journal of the Board of Trade*, Mar., 1714/5-Oct., 1718, p. 311.

forts of South Carolina—seventy pieces of cannon of different calibres, together with a generous quantity of powder, shot, flint, bomb-shells, and musket balls in addition to a garrison for the fort, and a company of gunners and "matrofses" from England. Lack of precise data on the part of the agent lessened the hope of getting supplies for Fort Johnson, toward supplying which the Board of Trade was favorably inclined, though they did not hold them necessary for Charleston. North Carolina, in turn, in 1754, sought through Agent Abercromby, with the aid of Governor Dobbs on the eve of his departure for America, ordnance and stores for the fort at Cape Fear.[93]

While we know that no part of the colonial period was free from piracy, the agents' connection, except for a brief mention in the *Archives of Maryland* seems to have come largely after the turn of the century and to have been mainly advisory. As early as 1720 pirates were tried by commissioners. Boone and Beresford were asked on October 11 to propose names of persons suitable for commissioners to try pirates in South Carolina. The agent of South Carolina found himself in May, 1754, directed to apply for a royal commission to try piracies and other crimes committed on the high seas by offenders brought into that province. A commission, for which he accordingly petitioned, was apparently set up for the trial of pirates in America, but its authority did not extend to murderers, who had to be sent to England for trial, as is indicated in a letter from Secretary Pownall of the Board of Trade to Agent Montague in 1771.[94]

[93] C. O. 5/381, p. 294; C. O. 5/388, f. 149. A list of Wright's demands might be appended (see C. O. 5/375 K, 177): "20 pieces of canon for 30 lb. shot; 20 pieces of canon for 24 lb. shot; 30 pieces of canon for 18 lb. shot; Sufficient shot, carriages and implements for the same. If they take the field, 10 pieces of canon, completely equipped; 15,000 18 lb. shot; 30,000 12 lb. shot; 30,000 9 lb. shot; 13,000 6 lb. shot; 400 bomb-shells for 10-inch mortars; 500 cahorn shell; grape-shot, musket balls, flints, cartridge paper and match."
Wright was expected to know the number and size of the guns at the different forts, to produce a plan of the works and a report of the surveyor.—Report of the Board to the Committee of the Privy Council dated Jan. 12, 1758. C. O. 5/403, pp. 222-30. For the report of Abercromby's effort see *Colonial Records of North Carolina*, V, 168; *Journal of the Board of Trade*, 1754-1758, p. 13.
[94] *Archives of Maryland*, XXVI, 595; C. O. 5/358, f. 46; Journal of Commons House of Assembly of South Carolina, XXIX, 318; for Crockatt's petition, C. O. 5/375 K, 106; for Hillsborough's statement of 1771, Entry Books, C. O. 5/1375, pp. 150-51.

Appointment and Removal from Office—Salaries

Since appointments to seats on the colonial councils were made in England, it is not strange that notification of vacancies and appointments passed through the agent's hands. Among the numerous instances which might be cited let a few from Virginia suffice. In one of the early cases on record the agent seems to have acted on his own initiative. When Major Lewis Burwell wrote to Jeffreys, the agent, to be relieved of his post as councillor because of his health, the agent in transmitting his request to the Board of Trade, recommended Colonel Dudley Digges to the vacancy. Blakiston as agent was complaisant enough to petition in 1705 that Byrd be given the seat in the council which had been held by his father, but it was not granted, as the Board felt that others had better claims, and so the young Byrd was kept waiting for this honor until 1708. On April 28, 1713, Colonel Blakiston, accompanied by Micajah Perry—and it requires no great imagination to realize that the latter had been asked for his good offices in behalf of the new appointee—attended the Board of Trade to inform that body of the death of Colonel Harrison and to recommend Mr. Cocke, secretary of that colony, for the resulting vacancy in the council. To indicate how sought were the posts on the council it should be recorded that on January 5, 1713/4, the agent had to present a letter from Governor Spotswood, recommending Nathaniel Harrison to succeed to his father's seat in the council. The governor's appointee won the appointment.

On June 5, 1729, Leheup was summoned before the Board of Trade to be consulted about the list of councillors recommended by Governor Gooch for vacancies on the council. With the discretion befitting an agent, Leheup merely told them that the governor had objected in a letter to Thomas Corbin and that his only instruction was to recommend Mr. Harrison to a vacancy caused by the death of Mr. Beverley. By this period it seems to be pretty clearly established that the governor should have a considerable, if not determining voice in appointments to his council, for Governor Gooch wrote to Leheup on October 5, 1732, in making some recommendations: "As I am apprehensive there will be some Pretenders to this Honour I must beg of you to be prefsing that before any Appointment is made contrary to my List and Recommendation, I may be allowed to give my reasons for opposing the Promotion of those who are for making their way to it by the Interest of Gentlemen at home who know nothing of their Lives and Characters here." Abercromby, speaking for the governor as late as 1774, recommended Mr. G. Corbin to Lord Dartmouth for the council of Virginia.[95]

Of course, the posts on the council were far from the only ones to be filled in London. In 1711, Secretary Jennings left Virginia for England, disregarding Spotswood's suggestion that he commission Philip Ludwell as his deputy. Spotswood thereupon recommended to the Board of Trade that Dr. William Cocke, a physician of Williamsburg, supersede Jennings. Blakiston supported Cocke, thus incurring Jennings' ire for not soliciting Cocke's appointment merely as deputy. Whether the agent in the late colonial period actually had much influence in the choice of the governor or not, the impression that he was a factor must have prevailed, for we find an entry in Abercromby's Letter Book for December 9, 1757, in which he reports to a certain Lieutenant Colonel Yonge, that, despite the agent's personal acquaintance with Lord Halifax, the difficulties in his path because of the existing system of appointment to the governorship could not be overcome.[96]

In cases where the agent was representing the interest opposed to the governor, discretion played little part. For instance, William Byrd II in 1717 boldly presented a memorial containing reasons against the governor joining other persons with the council in com-

[95] Jeffreys' letter is dated Jan. 1, 1701.—C. O. 5/1312, pt. 2, ff. 414, 415; for Blakiston's memorial for Byrd, dated Dec. 4, 1705, see Entry Books, C. O. 5/1361; *Journal of the Board of Trade*, 1708/9-1714/5, pp. 426, 495; *ibid.*, 1728-1734, pp. 41, 42; *ibid.*, p. 328.

The practice seemed to be for the governor to send a list of suitable persons for the council to the agent, which upon presentation to the Board of Trade was entered in the book of councillors. See entry of Feb. 3, 1735/6, *Journal of the Board of Trade*, 1734/5-1741, p. 87.

When McCulloh was told to get some men from the Northwest on to the North Carolina council, he thought it would be a "lessening of its dignity."—*Colonial Records of North Carolina*, VIII, 184.

[96] Dodson, *Alexander Spotswood*, p. 159. It is not entirely clear whether at an early period the agent had the choice of a minor officer, but more likely, he could merely recommend to the Board of Trade. In 1705/6 Blakiston was directed to find a storekeeper of the public arms to be sent over to Maryland, as the crown had approved appointment of such an officer.—*Journal of the Board of Trade*, Apr., 1704-Feb., 1708/9, p. 209.

Abercromby's effort to get appointment for Peter Randolph as Indian Commissioner in 1759 seems to have been a personal matter, but it argues that the agent had considerable influence in appointments.—Abercromby Letter Book, pp. 157-76.

missions of oyer and terminer, though the regular agent Blakiston remained cautious.[97]

If the agent were concerned with appointments, he would naturally be concerned with removals. So strong ran the feeling in South Carolina against William Rhett that it may be pardonable to quote from a letter sent Agent Boone in January, 1720/1: "We Desire you to ufe the most pressing Instances to get That Enemy to his Country and detested Reviler of Mankind removed from his office of Surveyor and Comptroller of his Majesties Customs not only that such a wretch may be Divested from any Colour of power amongst us, But alfo his Majesty be better served and the Comiffion[rs] of the Customes eased of such Impositions as he hath so long laid on them." Since success did not crown Boone's efforts, the same charge for removal of Rhett was laid on Francis Yonge a year later. Byrd naturally defended the members of the council of Virginia whom the governor had proposed to remove, insisting that they were "as able men as there are in Virginia."[98] Garth was charged in 1767 by the Commons House of Assembly of South Carolina to secure confirmation of the suspension of the chief justice, who had attacked the assistant judges, as is related elsewhere.

Similarly, the agent became naturally concerned with salaries. The first case to arrest our attention occurred in South Carolina in 1725 when Chief Justice Wright petitioned for his salary and the arrears thereof. When the case came to the Lords Commissioners of Trade and Plantations, they were attended by an ex-speaker of the Commons House of Assembly, Mr. Shelton, onetime secretary to the proprietors, and by "Fury," agent for the province, evidently to be consulted on the justice of the claim. In 1727 John Carter, Secretary of State of Virginia, sought the agent's assistance for an increase of salary. In March, 1752, Crockatt was instructed to assist George Hunter, surveyor-general of the king's lands and controller of rents, in his application for obtaining a salary from the Crown. In 1773 the council of North Carolina directed the colony agent to petition the crown for a salary for each councillor out of the quit-rents. Though the measure was proposed by Governor Tryon, it

[97] *Journal of the Board of Trade*, Mar., 1714/5-Oct., 1718, pp. 291, 292.
[98] C. O. 5/387, f. 70; C. O. 5/358, f. 208; Byrd presented a petition dated December 5, 1718, for the councillors who were to be removed and asked that they be not removed until they had a copy of the accusations against them.—C. O. 5/1318, p. 519.

was objected to by his successor because the crown revenue was insufficient for charges already laid on it.[99]

Financial Affairs

The colonial agent needed to have more pleasure in dealing with economics and financial matters than perhaps the modern research worker, for much was expected of him in these fields. Crockatt had to have or secure a knowledge of the wholesale prices of rum and molasses in South Carolina for nineteen years; and Wright had to prove a master of the British transactions for the reimbursement of the colonies for the wars. The agent frequently was expected to pay bills drawn on funds placed in his charge, and, in the early days, on funds which had not yet been transmitted to him. Peter Pagan, that early agent for Maryland who cannot be regarded as a regular agent, became a sort of banker or colonial treasurer in England to whom bills of exchange were remitted and on whom bills were drawn for payment. This idea was implicit in the very terms of Blakiston's appointment in 1704; it was proposed that some person in England be appointed to whom the treasurer might remit bills of exchange. It could hardly have been agreeable to Pagan when a bill to Captain James Bowling for £23 drawn on him was not allowed by the council in April, 1698.[100]

One of the strangest financial measures handled through an agent fell to the lot of Leheup when in 1741 the assembly, after refusing to grant any money to equip recruits or make provision for defense despite the governor's entreaties, appropriated £3,000 colonial currency to be paid into the royal exchequer by their agent in consideration of the taxes which their fellow-subjects in Great Britain had to pay.[101] In supporting an act of the South Carolina

[99] Based on drafts of letters in the archives of the Board of Trade, C. O. 5/381, p. 187; Journal of the Commons House of Assembly of South Carolina, Nov., 1751-Nov. 21, 1752, p. 206; Entry Book, C. O. 5/329, p. 237. Martyn's work in securing salaries for Georgia officials was so incidental to a time of change from the proprietorship to a regular government that it can hardly be included.—C. O. 591/60, pp. 53-54; C. O. 5/672, pp. 26-27.

[100] *Archives of Maryland*, XXIII, 474; *ibid.*, XXVI, 111; *ibid.*, XXII, 62. The writer again refuses to include a discussion of Martyn's work on finances, as his work in this connection seems more that of a crown agent than of the provincial agent. Even in July, 1764, after Garth's appointment, he secured leave to make the usual issues of money for salaries of crown officers.—C. O. 5/648, Bundle E, 103. He once declined a warrant drawn by the attorney general of Georgia until he had the order from the Board of Trade.—C. O. 5/649, p. 1. Garth seems to have acted as crown agent for Georgia in 1764.

[101] C. O. 5/1234, Bundle 97.

assembly of 1744 to enable the revenue officers to make a more perfect roll of the quitrents, and to discharge from payment of future quitrents such persons as transferred their property with proper record in the auditor's office, Mr. Fury had to discuss in his memorial the whole question of quitrents.

Wragg, McCulloh, and others of the agents had to understand fully the question of paper money and emission of bills of credit. Bills for paper currency, as any student of the colonial period of our history knows, were the *bête noir* of the governors and the ever-recurring remedy for the legislators harassed by bills but with a deficiency of metal money. Montague, to cite one illustration, transmitted before May, 1768, a petition from Virginia to issue paper money. Before June 2 he handed Hillsborough an elaborate scheme for emitting paper currency in Virginia for £200,000 redeemable in October, 1783.[102] McCulloh, to cite a second instance, probably put the problem as clearly as it could be stated. In reporting back to the Committee of Correspondence on July 14, 1769, promising to exert himself to the uttermost to obtain leave for North Carolina to issue notes of currency, he stated the position of Lord Hillsborough. "I am sorry to acquaint you, I have reason to fear that Lord Hillsborough is at present of opinion, that giving the American Assemblies a power to make their Notes a Tender is repugnant to the Idea of a Paper Circulation and highly improper." He adds that he would try to impress his lordship with the reasons why this was necessary with North Carolina's paper emissions and show that no injustice would result, but rather a great good to all from granting the request. He had great hopes of assistance from the merchants of Britain—which any one familiar with their constitutional aversion for paper money would doubt. "A general Repeal of the restrictive Act is not what I have at present in view, but rather the obtaining an Act of Parliament for the particular purposes required by you. Many and great objections which would lay to the first mode, will not to the other."[103]

The financial task which overshadows all the others and was pursued with ardor by all the agents of the American mainland was

[102] See letter of the Secretary of the Board of Trade to the Secretary of the Treasury, Dec. 8, 1747, C. O. 5/402, p. 140; for Montague's petition and scheme, C. O. 5/1332, pp. 57, 59, 69.
[103] *Colonial Records of North Carolina*, VIII, 56.

the negotiation for reimbursements for expenses incurred for King George's War and the French and Indian War. The British government under the leadership of Pitt the elder had decided in consideration of the heavy sacrifices made by the poverty-stricken colonies to put troops in the field to help fight continental wars to reimburse the colonial governments in order to encourage them in future efforts. But the appropriation by parliament was but the beginning, for the colonies and for their agents, of the pursuit of the money. In the agents' correspondence with the several colonies can be traced the slow, nerve-wracking story of this pursuit from 1754 to 1761 of a pot of gold. Abercromby in a letter of January 16, 1755, probably to the governor of Virginia, tells of the great stress laid on the execution of a warrant to prove the exact expenses of each colony. He entreated the executive to adhere to the spirit of the orders without raising a particle of opposition. In the course of the opposition in Virginia to the warrant, a remark had been dropped suggesting that the governor and council challenged the right of the crown to apply the money to the purpose indicated. He suggested that the warrant be issued in the general terms of the king's warrant.[104]

In 1756 the House of Burgesses scenting the booty afar off from a rumor, petitioned for Virginia's share of a sum to be granted by parliament to pay the great expenses and services incurred for defense. South Carolina and the other colonies followed suit. The Board of Trade in its report to Pitt on January 21, 1757, revealed itself as very skeptical in regard to Virginia's efforts to defend herself and went into a detailed examination of them. This is considered the more necessary "as the Agent is not able to give any precise account of these Services, and as those performed by Virginia are very imperfectly and very partially stated in the Addrefs. . . ." But the Board concluded with a recommendation that the Southern colonies be given a grant that session, not as a reward, but as an encouragement to future efforts.[105] Finally parliament was able to allot the proportions of the £50,000 granted in the year 1757 for the Southern colonies and the larger sum of £200,000 granted

---

[104] Abercromby Letter Book, entries for Jan. 16, 1755, and May 10, 1760.
[105] C. O. 5/1367, pp. 295-312, Entry Book.

for the colonies in general in 1758 when confirmed by the Treasury
Board as follows:

For 1756 services	For 1758 services
To Virginia £32,268 19s. 4d.	£20,546
To South Carolina £9,941 19s. 10d.	£12,183 9s.
To North Carolina £7,789 (for both 1757 and 1758)	

Virginia's quota was to be paid to Abercromby, when the warrants were properly executed, to be handed by him to such person
as should be authorized by the Virginia assembly to receive it.
Finally, the money for the first grant became available on May 8,
1760. Promptly the Virginia assembly drew £20,000 by bills of
exchange on Abercromby to be delivered to the colony treasurer, and
then drew on the agent for the rest of the sum, which was to be
applied on the debt. As has been related earlier, Montague was
created an agent for the lower house to receive any future sums.[106]

North Carolina's modest quota shrank greatly before it was ever
paid over to her colonial agent. The royal paymaster for the king's
forces in North America informed Abercromby of a demand on him
for £500 advanced by General Shirley's warrant and of another
£500 advanced by warrant of Lord Loudoun for the use of North
Carolina troops, which must be deducted from the quota according
to Governor Dobb's engagement, in addition to some demands of
General Forbes. In addition, Abercromby, Smith, and Jouvencal
tried to lay hands on this hard money grant in order to receive
the commission due them for negotiating the affair to a successful
issue. In the end the assembly voted to sue these agents for the
amount from the parliamentary grant still in their hands, some
£1,660.[107]

The purchase of arms and clothing for colonial soldiers imposed
yet one more financial burden. The earliest examples come from
Maryland where in 1694 Agent Pagan's chief function seemed to be
the purchase of arms. Maryland's collector and receiver-general
was ordered to write Captain Pagan, merchant in London, to provide and send by the first conveyance in a man of war, if one were

---

[106] *Journals of the House of Burgesses,* 1758-1761, pp. 171-72; Hening, *Statutes,* VII,
374-75. For North Carolina's share see Abercromby Letter Book, Entry of May 10, 1760.
[107] *Ibid.,* p. 143; *Colonial Records of North Carolina,* VII, 666, 670. For the sums to
South Carolina, T 1/376, E 201; Abercromby Letter Book, p. 137.

sailing, arms to the value of £250 out of the quarter part of Their Majesties' revenue now remaining in his hands but "to be Silent in the doeing thereof by Reason the Governm^t have not had time to Send at p^{sent} Sev'll Journalls home wch are now preparing." The order of arms which he was to send in 1695 was by no means negligible, including carbines with balls and swivels, pistols "plain and strong," 20,000 flints for horse and foot, 2,000 weight of bullets for muskets, 200 "Granado shells more, Answerable (fitted) to the Mortors sent for," dragoon drums, and 6 brass trumpets and two Union flags, with ten budge barrels in which to carry powder.[108] It is suggestive of the time then required for delivery to record that something over £305 was remitted Pagan on August 24, 1695, that the goods was shipped December 18, 1695, and received by June 22, 1696. The agent was paid by a commission of two and one half per cent, which amounted to a trifle over £10.[109]

When Pagan in 1698 notified the council that his private business obliged him to "commit the Affairs of his province to wit purchasing Arms"—which clearly shows the nature of the agency at the time— to Mr. Isaac Milner, bills to the value of some £249 were sent that individual. His first commission seems to have been to send twelve "rheams" of large ruled paper like the sample sent. But purchase of arms had obviously been ordered, for he was informed that a pair of long bullet molds was being sent him so that the barrels of the arms he should buy would be of the same "boar" as the bullets; and he was directed to send five pounds of bar lead for every pound of powder, the powder to be sent in small quarter barrels, containing twenty-five pounds in each "barril."[110] This function seemed still to loom large in the agency by the time of Blakiston, for he was directed by the council on April 18, 1706, to "hasten away" the arms and ammunition for which the governor had written. He was also to press an address to Queen Anne for a certain specie of copper "coyne" to be made current in the province of Maryland with "all possible vigour." By September of the same year he had purchased and sent over 100 "musquetts," 50 carbines, and 2 halberts. Blakis-

---

[108] *Archives of Maryland*, XX, 140, 248-49. The writer recognizes that this subject is as much a military as a financial affair. In such a case she must classify somewhat arbitrarily.   [109] *Ibid.*, pp. 299, 447, 460.

[110] *Ibid.*, XXIII, 462. Though this passage refers to a Mr. Isaac, other references are to a Mr. Isaac Milner. See above, Chapter I.

ton's last recorded purchase came in 1715 when he presumably obeyed the governor's instruction to buy £500 worth of arms and ammunition.[111]

It will be recalled that Colonel Blakiston was also serving Virginia as agent in 1702. He was called upon to pay the treasurer of ordnance for eighty barrels of powder, which with other stores were sold in obedience to an order in council for the use of Virginia. As late as 1711 the agent was negotiating for the exchange of some defective powder in that purchase.[112] In 1760 we find the agents handling large sums for the purchase of military supplies. To cite a single instance, the agent for South Carolina, had £2,000 put in his hands to purchase clothes and other articles for the Carolina regiments.[113]

Consultation with Merchants and Traders

Learning the reactions of British merchants to many propositions which concerned the colonies and endeavoring to secure their cooperation in measures intended for the weal of the provinces constituted an important part of the agent's work. Since, however, an entire chapter is devoted to this subject, no comment will be made here other than to list the activity as one of the agent's numerous duties.[114]

In Appeal of Cases

It is obvious that the agent would be asked to act as the medium for transference of papers in legal controversies. Illustrations are selected from the late colonial period. Not sufficient that the famous Wilkes case should reverberate through the kingdom, it must also echo in the colonies. South Carolina saw fit, in the ardor of defiance born of the Stamp Act, to advance £10,500 to support the Wilkes cause in the courts. Naturally, the government in England resented the act. The Commons House of Assembly in the colony in a long

---

[111] *Ibid.*, XXVI, 555-56; XXV, 210, 312. Allowing for the long delay in mail and freight, it is perhaps logical to infer that an invoice for arms and munitions sent mostly by the agent under date of April 21, 1716, was for goods to fill the order sent him on July 12 the preceding year.—*Ibid.*, XXXIII, 14. The reader will note that we are here discussing the purchase of arms by the agent and not his petitioning the government for a grant of arms.

[112] C. O. 5/1316, f. 299.

[113] Journal of the Commons House of Assembly of South Carolina, XXXIII, 206.

[114] See Chapter X.

series of resolutions asserted their right to control and dispose of the people's money. A copy of the resolutions was sent to the lieutenant governor, and the London agent was instructed to represent this matter to the king in its true and proper light and to "undeceive their most gracious Sovereign and convince him how much he had been imposed upon by misinformation, thereby to avert the Royal displeasure from his dutiful loyal subjects the Commons House of the province." No small task to lay upon the shoulders of Mr. Garth![115]

The dispute between the governor and assembly of that same province in 1762 as to control over the election of members of the lower house was carried to England. The governor insisted on his executive right to scrutinize the election of members, a claim which brought such a sharp dispute that the house finally refused to do any further business with him. The interchange of communications with the governor on this subject were sent by the committee to the agent with instructions to print them and to submit the entire controversy to the home government. Furthermore, to carry the appeal yet a step higher than the ministry, the assembly adopted an address to his Royal Highness, setting forth their unfortunate differences with the governor, and claiming that his insistence on the power of interfering in their popular election was a gross usurpation which not only violated the charter of the province but also destroyed their personal rights as British subjects. Of course, this sudden adherence to the charter of the proprietary government, which they had been so anxious to overthrow nearly a half century before, as still in force so far as rights were concerned, was an anomaly with which they did not feel themselves concerned. They forwarded this address to Garth, who presented it at a meeting of the British cabinet, which referred it to the Board of Trade. In due course of time Garth reported that the government, not able to act upon an ex parte statement of the Commons, had granted Governor Boone leave of absence that he might be heard in England in his own behalf. This case did not come to a determination because Governor Boone would not take advantage of his leave to go to England and in his absence

[115] For the Wilkes controversy see Cross, *A History of England and Greater Britain*, pp. 744-46; McCrady, *South Carolina under the Royal Government*, pp. 683-90.

the Board of Trade would not proceed with the inquiry into his action.[116]

A dispute between the two houses was likely to terminate the same way—with appeals to the home government. In 1773 the council of South Carolina committed a printer to gaol for printing a protest as a part of the proceedings of their journals without their order. He brought a writ of habeas corpus returnable before two justices. They discharged him. The council thereupon sent a message to the house that the privileges of the two justices, who were also members of the lower house, should be suspended. The assembly refused to comply and issued formal thanks to the justices for their action. It further asserted that the council was not a house of legislature and therefore had no power to commit for a breach of privilege, but was only a privy council to aid the governor with advice. The lower house asked the governor to suspend the members of the council who had voted to commit the printer. The council forwarded an address to the king, thus adjourning the controversy to London. Garth, in pursuance of directions from the Commons House waited on Lord Dartmouth to inform him of the orders he had received and to ask that the address of the council should not be presented until he could prepare a petition to the king on the part of the commons. Lord Dartmouth intimated that if the petition were framed upon the principle that the council was not a full branch of the legislature, there could be no proceedings, as the Privy Council could never admit that the established constitution of the colony should be brought in question. On December 15 Garth filed for the Commons House of Assembly a petition to the king in which he requested His Majesty to remove those members of the council who had ordered the commitment of the printer or to show such other mark of royal displeasure as might prevent for the future an encroachment on the liberties of the people.

In 1766 this same agent presented a memorial to the Earl of Shelburne about the case between the chief justice of South Carolina and the assistant judges. The chief justice, Charles Skinner, had presented to Governor Montagu a charge against the conduct of the assistant judges. When the governor transmitted the memorial to England, the assistant judges begged for a speedy hearing of the

[116] *Ibid.,* pp. 359-65.

case but complained that they had been unable to secure a copy of the charges against them and thus were in no position to offer a proper defense. Garth, therefore, prayed in behalf of the latter that the case might be remitted to the governor of Carolina to be finally determined by him.[117]

Aid to Individuals

Though appeals by officials for help in behalf of American colonials coming to England and by individuals themselves probably claimed considerable time, they can be dismissed here rather briefly. First in order, perhaps, come the requests to the agents from the governors in behalf of some individual in whom the executive was interested or to whom he felt the colony indebted. A case in point was a Francis Kennedy, for whom Governor Spotswood bespoke the good offices of Agent Blakiston. Virginia had employed Kennedy to approach South Carolina for recompense for the forces sent by the former colony in 1716 to aid the latter. Spotswood, at the request of the council, recommended Kennedy to the Board of Trade for some recompense for his services and asked Colonel Blakiston to assist him. He pleaded the poverty of the colonial treasury and stated that Kennedy had received only the public thanks of the Virginia government for his time and expenses.[118]

Sometimes the request came from the house of assembly through the Committee of Correspondence. Such a request came from South Carolina when the assembly ordered its committee to write to Charles Crockatt in 1749 to aid one Charles McNaire in his efforts to secure from the British ministry some recompense for his services in bringing over a great part of the Choctaw Indians to British allegiance. The colonial governor wrote the agent mildly in his interest, stating his conviction that he should have £500 sterling, which was £350 more than the assembly had voted him. The Committee of Correspondence of North Carolina likewise wrote their agent, Abercromby, out of a sense of obligation to McNaire for his services

[117] For the case of the printer see *ibid.*, pp. 715-23. For the petition of the council see C. O. 5/395, pp. 143-44; for Garth's petition, C. O. 5/395, pp. 193-94; for the Skinner case see C. O. 5/390, pp. 321-24. A case is recorded in the Minutes of the Board of the Treasury in which it appears that Garth presented a memorial against Daniel Moore, Collector of the Customs at Charleston, containing charges against the latter, but the record is too scanty to permit discussion.—Treasury Papers, 29/39, pp. 153-54.

[118] Spotswood, *Official Letters*, II, 242.

with the Choctaws. It would appear, so far as the records reveal, that Crockatt wrote an indorsement at the foot of McNaire's petition. He certified to the application and proceedings of the assembly and recommended the case to the Duke of Bedford.[119] A similar case was that of Colonel Mercer who brought a recommendation to Agent Montague from Virginia in 1763. The Committee of Correspondence stated that in consequence of distinguished gallantry he had been promoted to a lieutenant colonelcy, and was going home to seek reward in some manner for his faithful services. Montague was to introduce him properly and to use his best influence in his favor.[120]

Of an entirely different character was the aid besought for one Captain John Rains, master and owner of several vessels trading to Charleston for thirty years, who had been represented to the Commons House of South Carolina as able by certain discoveries to fix latitudes at sea more easily and exactly. By laying his discoveries before the proper persons in England, he hoped to gain some reward for his labors as being of general value to navigators. The lower house, ready to lend a sympathetic ear to every invention likely to promote the arts and sciences, and solicitous for Rains, who had never been in England, requested Garth in March, 1772, to put him "in the proper Channel for communicating his Discoveries and obtaining such a reward for his Ingenuity, as the proper Judges of such matters shall think just and reasonable." Garth seems to have done his duty by him nobly, for within a month he reports that he had mentioned him and his business to Lord Howard and several of the admirals and had even consulted Mr. Stevens, a secretary at the Admiralty Office, in regard to the proper steps for Captain Rains to pursue. He was advised that the latter must apply by petition

[119] For the letter of the Committee of Correspondence to Crockatt, dated Sept. 15, 1749, and the governor's recommendation see C. O. 5/373; for papers presented to the lower house of the South Carolina legislature, see Journal of the Commons House of Assembly, XXV, 103.

A certain merchant of Charleston, Samuel Eveleigh, who had had a sloop and cargo condemned in "Bermucies," applied in 1724 to England for redress. The lower house of South Carolina directed that the agents be instructed to render him what service they could, but nothing further appears. Presumably Yonge and Lloyd were the agents referred to in 1724.—Journal of the Commons House of Assembly of South Carolina, VI, 406.

[120] "Proceedings of the Virginia Committee of Correspondence," loc. cit., XI, 350-51. George Mercer was a son of John Mercer of Stafford County, Virginia. In 1769 he was appointed lieutenant governor of North Carolina.—Ibid., p. 350, note.

to the Board of Longitude or Latitude, from which, if his discovery offered promise of merit, a recommendation for a bounty or other compensation would proceed to the proper department. Admiral Sir Thomas Frankland was so obliging, Garth reports with satisfaction, as to procure a letter in Rains's favor to a resident of the Board of Longitude, who was a very near relative of Lord Clive. A few weeks later, on April 24, Garth reported that the secretary alluded to above did not think highly of Rains's method of calculation. The inventor had meanwhile been introduced to an East India director and been invited to explain his scheme to a committee of directors of that company to the chairman of which Garth obligingly wrote a letter of "credence" and recommendation.[121]

Somewhat similar were Garth's activities in 1772 in behalf of Mr. Louis St. Pierre and William Prince. The former was in London soliciting either a government grant or private loans and subscriptions in order to establish the production of wine in South Carolina. He had brought over a letter from Governor Bull to the secretary of state with a certificate of good conduct and "application to the Culture of the Vines" under the provincial seal, but had not brought with him vouchers of a private nature sufficient, according to Garth, to encourage private subscriptions, by which was probably meant evidence of financial standing. Garth promised his assistance at the offices of government, and, if he met with sufficient encouragement, to apply to the House of Commons for aid. As the agent was aware that several other persons were devoting themselves to that culture, he thought that parliamentary encouragement should be of a general sort, not confined to an individual. He intimated an unusual degree of interest in the subject and the likelihood of future government aid even if St. Pierre failed at that time.

The case of Prince differed because it represented an effort to benefit a starchmaker who held a patent to make starch from rice, an activity commended to Garth by many planters and merchants deterred from its manufacture by the high duty on it. The agent consulted with him and undertook to give him all the aid in his power to secure the entry of rice free of duty for seven years and free exportation of rice starch, if he would waive his exclusive

[121] "Garth Correspondence," *loc. cit.*, XXXI, 290-91; Garth's first letter was dated Apr. 4, 1772.—*Ibid.*, XXXIII, 233-34; letter of Apr. 21, *ibid.*, p. 237.

patent. He then suggested the proper form of petition to parliament and agreed to attend him at the Treasury and Plantation Boards. He requested for him an audience of Lord North and Lord Dartmouth, as he was convinced that this was a measure beneficial to Britain and to South Carolina. It is pleasing to record that Prince won a patent for the right to make starch from rice for fourteen years, beginning in 1769, and Garth the entry of rice duty-free till May 1, 1780.[122]

Miscellaneous

Obviously, there would be a host of duties falling to the lot of the agent, of greater or less importance, which defy regular classification. It would be useless to pursue every possible task which this research has turned up, but a few illustrations will be rewarding to the reader. In a few cases a special agent was selected to deal with religious matters; in other cases the regular agent looked after them incidentally. Jeffrey Jeffreys was desired by the whole body of the clergy in Virginia in 1691 to lay before the king their miserable state of poverty. Their salaries, fixed by an old law at £80 a year, to be paid in tobacco at a shilling per hundred pounds, no longer proved sufficient with tobacco a drug on the market, so that the colony was losing many of her clergy. He also asked in the name of the governor the appointment of a commissary over the clergy.[123]

Further incidents connected with religious problems arose during the genesis of the agency as duly recorded in the chapter which dealt with that period.[124] Occasionally the regular agent dealt with the sovereign as "Supreme Head of the Church in England" or with a bishop. When the governor of South Carolina in April, 1751, denied his assent to a bill for dividing the parish of St. Philip at Charleston and for building another church and parsonage, the lower house of assembly charged the Committee of Correspondence to consider the most effectual method to obtain an instruction from "our most gracious sovereign to this Governor here to pafs an act for the purpose." Later in June, the committee was directed to

[122] *Ibid.*, pp. 234-35, 265, 271.
[123] *Calendar of State Papers, Colonial*, 1689-1692, sec. 1939.
[124] Raper, *North Carolina, A Study in English Colonial Government*, p. 11; Hawks, *History of North Carolina*, II, 508. See above, Chapter I.

countermand any such directions. Of course, the only effectual way to reach the throne was through their agent Crockatt.[125] To Abercromby it fell to deal with the Bishop of London and odd it is to come across an entry in his Letter Book, otherwise filled with mundane business matters, which reveals this businessman as an emissary of the Virginia clerics. "I thought to have found the Bishop of London at his house in the Temple, but to my disappointment this morning, I was there informed, that his constant residence is at Fulham, and there I shall attend him, with your packet; the addreſs to you from the Clergy is really a good performance, I showed it this morning to Lord N-ᶜ & to Lord G-ᵘ and they both declared their approbation thereof; Your reply is also much to the purpose, both these I shall take upon me to have inserted in the newspapers, which shall, according to your desire, be transmitted to you."[126]

Along with the New England agents the emissaries of the southern colonies dealt with the Society for the Propagation of the Gospel in Foreign Parts. The burden on Francis Yonge could scarcely be considered onerous when he was directed on February 15, 1723, to return the thanks of the South Carolina assembly to that society for appointing a school master for Charles City and for some other undisclosed service.[127]

Requests for "passes" or licenses for ships and for convoys were surely a natural duty to expect of agents. The Board of Trade at its session of February 8, 1715/6, heard Colonel Blakiston, then serving both Virginia and Maryland, along with John Champante, agent for New York, a Colonel Jory, and a Mr. Duport, on the subject of passes for the security of ships and vessels trading to the "Algerines." They were asked what number of passes might be necessary for the plantations; Blakiston thought forty might be sufficient for Virginia and thirty for Maryland. As indicative of the relative importance of trade in the Northern and Southern colonies, it might be added that Champante suggested that forty passes placed

[125] See Journal of the Commons House of Assembly of South Carolina, XXVI, 317, 615-16.

[126] In a letter, probably to the Governor of Virginia, dated January 16, 1755. The subject matter of the address from the clergy to the Bishop of London does not appear. The two noblemen may have been Lord North and Lord Granville, despite the last letters, for the vagaries of Abercromby's writing and spelling render his pages often almost undecipherable, as is stated elsewhere.

[127] Journal of the Council of South Carolina, 1722-1724, II, 200.

with Governor Hunter might suffice for both New York and New Jersey.[128] In 1747 Fury was directed to seek convoys for ships to South Carolina. In 1749 Vander Dusen presented a petition from South Carolina to the king for convoys for trade, and in May, 1757, James Wright was again proffering a request for the same province for a yearly convoy for the trade to England. The requests, it will be noted, coincide with a period of war; and the state of piracy would justify requests for convoys at any time. Requests from the agent for a sailing boat or scout boat or man of war to guard the coast of a given province were not uncommon.[129]

Those who recall the pressure for indentured servants to supply labor for the colonies will find the recommendation of a committee of the upper house of South Carolina in 1723/4 to their agent to inquire how practicable it might be to bring over a number of "charity boys" from Bristol, Pool, (Liverpool?), Plymouth, and Biddiford only natural. There were all sorts of odd commissions. The provincial seal, for instance, might pass through the hands of the agent. Governor Seymour sent the old seal of Maryland by the hands of a clergyman of Philadelphia to Blakiston in August, 1706, to give to the Board of Trade. Again, an agent was to point out to the Board the excessive charge which arose from transmitting the many duplicates of the colonial journals and temporary laws.[130] Francis Yonge was charged in 1712 to find some "sober, able person, who should be a printer and book-binder," to bring with him "a plain, handsome set of letters, with a press, tools, paper, and other necessaries." The agent was authorized to advance a sum, not exceeding £1,000 currency to such printer to buy what was necessary and for his transportation, to be repaid later by his printing. Though the printer was to be allowed 25 per cent more than the usual price in Britain and was assured a monopoly of the public printing for such work, Yonge did not succeed in hiring such a printer for South Carolina.[131]

[128] *Journal of the Board of Trade,* Mar., 1714/5-Oct., 1718, p. 111.

[129] Journal of the Commons House of Assembly of South Carolina, XXIV, 329; *ibid.,* XXXI, 149. On December 4, 1758, Martyn presented a request for a boat from the governor.—C. O. 5/673, p. 194.

[130] Journal of the Council of South Carolina, 1722-1724, II, 223; for the Maryland seal see *Archives of Maryland,* XXV, 206; for the cost of the Journals, Journal of the Commons House of Assembly of South Carolina, VI, 109.

[131] McCrady, *South Carolina under Royal Government,* pp. 144-45.

Probably the unique task fell to Garth—the details connected with a statue of Pitt ordered by South Carolina as a tribute and memorial of their gratitude for his part in securing repeal of the Stamp Act. Garth took satisfaction and pride in informing Pitt of the compliment offered him from the fact that this was the first and most distinguished testimonial from America. Before he finally dispatched the statue, Garth may have lost some of his pleasure, for the details of the commission are wearisome merely to the reader of his correspondence: the search for a sculptor, the canvass for possible designs; their bids, as we would say today; and the estimate of the time necessary for the execution. After he had decided on Joseph Wilton as the sculptor, Garth found himself puzzled as to whether the statue were designed for the out-of-doors or inside of a building, and so he had the artist submit two designs.[132] When completed it was the agent's duty to see that it was shipped to the province, duly insured, and that proper workmen were dispatched on the same packet to erect it properly.[133]

As Ambassadors of Good Will

Finally, the agents were emissaries to interpret America to Great Britain and conversely to interpret Britain to the American colonies. The task called for infinite tact, for the wisdom of the serpent, and for the courage which would risk dismissal by the assembly, if necessary, while also on other occasions risking the displeasure of the government officials. Sometimes the agent kept his head on his shoulders by refusing to be drawn into colonial disputes. Abercromby, for example, wrote in 1758, when one Rutherford had lost

[132] Garth decided on Wilton for the sculptor, because of a statue of Pitt he had made for Cork. In his studio he had seen two busts of the statesman shortly to be sent to Ireland, which for likeness and workmanship were greatly admired.—"Garth Correspondence," loc. cit., XXVIII, 81. The two designs, one for an open space, and one for a niche in a room were still extant in 1835.—Magazine of American History, VIII, 215-16.

[133] For details on the Pitt statue, see Smith, "Wilton's Statue of Pitt," South Carolina Historical and Genealogical Magazine, XV, 21-23; "Garth Correspondence," loc. cit., XXVIII, 80-86, 89-93; Magazine of American History, VIII, 216-17; South Carolina Gazette, Jan. 6, 1767, May 17, 1770, July 11, 1770. The statue was erected at the intersection of Broad and Meeting Streets, near which it now stands in Washington Square. It is of fine white marble; the right hand holds a roll of parchment, partly open, on which are carved the words, "Articuli Magnae Cartae Liberatum." The left hand is extended, the figure being in the attitude of one delivering an oration. It has suffered so many vicissitudes that the head is now awry. A statue to Pitt was also erected by New York about the same time.

his seat in the North Carolina council and carried the dispute to
London: "As these matters lie between the Governor and him, I
am resolved to take no share in the Contest as provincial Agent,
which by him, I find still rests with me, notwithstanding Mr Budgens
and others information to the Contrary, which seem'd by no means
impossible, considering I have had no letters from your Govt for
many months past."[134]   This surely was the part of wisdom when
his own post was in jeopardy.   They needed to be ready with helpful suggestions.   Crockatt expressed to the Committee of Correspondence in 1752 his hope that the planters of South Carolina would
turn to the making of "pot and pearl ashes" in response to the encouragement by parliament in removing the duty and to the great
advance in price; Garth pointed out to the South Carolina Committee
that petitions signed by the speaker had more dignity and carried
more weight than when introduced into the Commons under an
agent's name; and Abercromby intimated that the governor and
council of Virginia might in their instructions to their agent note
how much the tobacco revenue was exhausted by extraordinary
service and use the money from the parliamentary grant to refund
deficiencies in case the application to the treasury on the quitrents
failed.[135]   Blakiston achieved a model of tactful suggestion when
he adroitly complained of the tobacco gauge of Virginia as "beyond
what they ought to be for they far exceed ye Law," and he would
by no means advise "y'r promoteing any Law for y'e future to
make y'e Casks bigger unless you see wise reasons for it"—and this
at a time when British merchants were complaining bitterly over an
increase of the tobacco gauge from 26 inches in breadth and 43 in
length to 30 and 48 inches respectively.[136]   Abercromby did not
hesitate to chide North Carolina for failure to acknowledge the good
offices of the king's ministers, as recommended by his letters.   "I
did them justice in my advice thereof to the Province, I did the
same for Virginia, they attended thereto and in a very handsome
manner, returned their addrefs of thanks to the Secretary of State
and Chancellor of Exchequer, I wish your Government had done the

[134] This was to Samuel Swann, dated March 4, 1758.—Abercromby Letter Book, p. 75.
[135] Journal of the Commons House of Assembly of South Carolina, XXVII, 569;
Garth to the Committee, July 9, 1766, "Garth Correspondence," *loc. cit.*, XXIX, 41;
Abercromby to Blair, Nov. 30, 1758, Abercromby Letter Book, pp. 117-18.
[136] *Virginia Magazine of History and Biography*, XIX, 16-17.

same, because the Interposition of the Secretary of State and Treaſury still absolutely necesſary to bring this Grant of Money home to you."[137]

The instances of the agents exercising discretion are legion. The agent might be warned to be discreet, as when the Virginia council ordered Byrd to be cautious as to the persons with whom he talked, especially about military aid to New York; but South Carolina had sufficient confidence in Garth to leave it to his discretion whether in efforts for repeal of the Stamp Act he would act alone or in conjunction with the other agents; and Ferdinand Paris promptly pointed out, when Maryland was criticized in 1741 at court as having sent only about two hundred men to the West Indies for the royal service, that the lower house raised money for bounties, maintenance and transportation for men, producing the acts of assembly to prove his point.[138]

The agent must, of course, be ever alert to protect the colony's interests. Blakiston used the best "artifice" of which he was capable to prevent diversion of a tax on tobacco into the British treasury in 1706 as, "if it had once found that Channel, it would have been attended with a Traine of Deficultys to have removed it againe into y'r management."[139] When Garth heard of the activity of the merchants trading to North America for a new statute in 1760 taking off the bounty on tar, he bestirred himself to get a copy of the minutes of the Board of Trade relating to that subject to send to South Carolina, with a warning that though the session of parliament was too far advanced for the measure to pass that year, it would probably be carried into the next session.[140] The moment Montague received word from one of the Lords of the Treasury in 1770 that a group of men had offered a large sum for a huge grant of land to be carved out of Virginia on the frontier with a proposal for a separate government—the so-called Vandalia Colony, he entered a caveat at the Board of Trade and in his petition appealed to their Lordships'

[137] Abercromby Letter Book, p. 78 (written to Governor Dobbs, Mar. 4, 1758/9).
[138] Executive Journals of the Council, II, 207; "Garth Correspondence," loc. cit., XXVIII, 229-30; Archives of Maryland, XLII, 199. Garth tactfully pointed out that the question of an increase in the allowance of the governor's house rent arose in the lower house of South Carolina.—C. O. 5/395, f. 53.
[139] Blakiston said that Auditor General Blathwayt and Perry had been of great assistance. —Virginia Magazine of History and Biography, XIX, 14-15 (dated Jan. 28, 1705/6).
[140] "Garth Correspondence," loc. cit., XXXI, 124-27.

sense of justice whether Virginia should not have notice and time to offer objections against such a grant.[141] Garth was solicitous that acts should be transmitted him at once, if there were the least doubt of their being allowed, so that he might present himself at the ministries at once to defend them. He relates when Dr. Franklin appeared to comply with directions from Georgia to support certain acts passed the last session, he was informed that he was too late, as the acts had already been considered and an important one repealed. Garth took the precaution, indeed, of leaving an order at the Plantation Office for a copy to be made of a certain Carolina act the moment it arrived and of a notice to be sent him. In the tense situation which prevailed at the close of 1772 it was not strange that Garth at an intimation of the calling of an assembly at Beaufort rather than Charleston hastened immediately to the Plantation Office; he was assured that no direction for the change had issued from any department of government. He then waited on Lord Dartmouth with a request for an order requiring the governor to meet the assembly at the accustomed place. Dartmouth took the trouble to notify Garth later that the assembly would sit at Charleston.[142]

To be valuable to the colony, the emissary must show considerable initiative. Abercromby secured a convoy for some ships departing for North Carolina in the spring of 1757; Garth did not literally carry out some commands from the Committee of Correspondence to press a petition for South Carolina, as he had not waited for instructions but in the pressing exigencies of 1766 had acted upon his own knowledge of the situation.[143] There were times when the initiative of the agent brought slight thanks. Abercromby complained bitterly in 1758 of his wasted efforts to prevent grant of a temporary monopoly of salt. "could I have foreseen this, I had saved myself an immense trouble and some Expence, however, it shall be a Caution to me for the future, to act by particular instruc-

[141] This was the company headed by Banker Thomas Walpole, Pownell, Franklin, Wharton, and John Sargeant. The plan was opposed by Lord Hillsborough in a report which gave Franklin an opportunity to make such a crushing reply that Lord Hillsborough felt obliged to resign. See *Journals of the House of Burgesses, 1770-1772*, p. xx.

The efforts of Virginia to protect the grants already made to the soldiers for services rendered in the Indian wars were accepted by the Ohio Company early in December, 1770.

[142] "Garth Correspondence," *loc. cit.*, XXX, 222; XXXIII, 266, 270-71.

[143] *Ibid.*, XXVI, 88; Abercromby Letter Book, p. 27.

tions only and the rather since from what is insinuated by you that the Council do not seem inclined to give me Credit for Extraordinary trouble and Expence."[144]   The agents from North Carolina, Elmsley and Barker, scored a great success apparently when they won exception of that province, along with New York, from the bill of 1775, which restricted the trade of all the colonies to England and the British West Indies.   The agents attributed their success to the fact that instead of the petition sent, they drew up another memorial "in more decent terms" and also to the closeness of their friendship with Governor Tryon.   Whether they would be thanked or censured they did not know.   In independent terms Elmsley declared that "when your Memorial was presented, we had no idea that such restraining bill was intended; on the other hand should this exemption be received favourably, give us no credit for it; for, had it not been for a tenderness we had for the reputation of your Assembly, as having been long members of it, your Petition, exceptionable as it is, should have been presented. . . ."[145]   It was not welcome to North Carolina as a whole.

Liaison officers might serve as a further definition of the agents. Garth, as a member of the British House of Commons, could scarcely fail to comprehend, though he might not share, the views of the ministry as to the serious controversy with the colonies; on the other hand, his long letter of March 12, 1769, proved his grasp of the views of his friends in South Carolina.   It was obviously the agent's duty to help the colonials to see themselves through British eyes. Garth's long report on the reaction in parliament in 1767 to the incidents in New York, Rhode Island, New Jersey, and Massachusetts should have performed just that service for South Carolina. He details the debate in the House of Commons, and the report to the colony has the greater significance when it is recalled that the debate was held behind closed doors.   "I have troubled you," he concludes, "with as few Observations as possible, that I might neither mislead nor Misrepresent a Circumstance I think that should be duly attended to in Correspondence with the Colonies at this particular Juncture more especially."[146]   A properly conciliatory tone, though it does not disregard the stand of his own country, is struck in his

[144] *Ibid.*, p. 105.
[145] Elmsley to Governor Johnson, Apr. 7, 1775, *Colonial Records of North Carolina*, IX, 1208-9.   [146] "Garth Correspondence," *loc. cit.*, XXIX, 229.

communication of December 10, 1768: ". . . being myself still of the same Mind, that they ought not to go into Parliament waiving a Point their Constituents appear to adhere to, and yet I may as I do at present think, if a Repeal of this Law can be obtained upon any Ground, it would be a right Measure for both Countries and tend to heal the unhappy Breach subsisting, as in my mind after a Repeal of a second Revenue Act, future Legislatures would be tender of the like Attempt, convinced that the Resistance was not the Passion of the Hour, or the Faction of the Day, as has been suggested touching the Ground for the Repeal of the Stamp Act, and therefore thought might be again attempted in another Shape, but which has manifested clearly the true Principle of Disapprobation of such Laws, and therefore constant Ground of Disquietude in every Instance of similar Attempts." He must even be able to understand the feeling which inspired the following irony on the part of the Committee of Correspondence on April 10, 1772: "The very ingenious Explanation you mention of the Board of Trade, with regard to the Instruction of April 14, 1770, to the governor which virtually denied to the lower house the right to originate grants, is so highly entertaining, that tho' we are under a Necessity of being as Laconic as Possible, yet lest We be thought altogether stupid and insensible, we must not pass it over entirely in Silence."[147] This same disposition to try to unite the colonies with the mother country by concessions on both sides was one of Franklin's greatest assets as an agent and is revealed in one of his letters to the speaker of the Georgia lower house after passage of the Stamp Act. He had "little hope of attaining all that he desired, or all that ought to have been granted at once, but the giving ground had had a good aspect and afforded hope that gradually every obstruction to cordial amity would be removed; it was too much to expect full repeal, considering the pride natural to so great a nation, the prejudices that had so universally prevailed with regard to the point of right, and the resentment arising from the resistance of the American provinces."

Ambassador of good will, liaison officer, shrewd business man with a knowledge of all sorts of trade, lawyer conversant with British as well as colonial legislation, diplomat with the tact and finesse of the best French tradition—all these and more the agent of one of the American colonies needed to be.

[147] *Ibid.*, XXX, 235; *Ibid.*, XXXIII, 137.

CHAPTER 6.

THE AGENT AT WORK BEFORE
THE VARIOUS BOARDS

WHILE the colonial agent was obliged in the wide range of his duties to deal with the various ministers, with practically every board in the government, with parliament, and even with the king himself, his contacts were far more frequent and persistent with the Commissioners of the Board of Trade than with all other instrumentalities of government combined. This was perfectly natural and proper, for that was the agency which the British government had created to deal primarily with colonial problems. Hence we shall start with seeing how the agent functioned before the Board of Trade. The preceding chapter dealt with his duties stated objectively and statically; this chapter proposes to deal with his work subjectively and dynamically. In other words, we want to see in motion the agents and the machinery with which they dealt.

First of all, it needs to be understood that the Board of Trade was a very real and important body in the scheme of the British government for the administration of the colonies. It recommended individuals for colonial office; it considered all the complaints concerning colonial matters; and it examined the laws passed by the colonial assemblies and made recommendations to the Privy Council upon which that body based its recommendations to the king for final action. The Board of Trade may be, on the whole, pronounced an efficient body from 1696 to 1714; inefficient from 1714 to 1748; and then under the able leadership of Lord Halifax as president of the Board a valuable body from 1748 until his resignation in 1761. From that date until the close of the provincial period of American history—beyond which date we have here no interest—it was no real force. Hillsborough, who had been president of the Board, became secretary of state for the colonies in January, 1768, and, not unnaturally, important colonial business was thereafter transferred to that office.

Proper Credentials

Clearly, the first approach to the subject is to see how the agent got through the door of the Plantation Office. Naturally, there were formalities to be complied with. The Board of Trade would deal only with the persons who had been duly and properly designated as agents. William Byrd II, to take a striking illustration, was allowed to appear before their Lordships in 1717, when he insisted on his rights, by virtue of his status as a member of the Virginia council—but only as a councillor, not as the chosen agent of the House of Burgesses, for at that time the person recognized as the official agent of Virginia was the appointee of the governor and council. Byrd put his finger on the weak spot in that position instantly: "I met with a very unexpected Rubb from an odd opinion of some of their Lord[ps] (namely, that they don't think it their business to consider any Representation concerning the Plantation, except it be transmitted to the Respective agents, and deliver'd by them) which I think I have overcome—(vain delusion). . . . Now I own this Rule is very usefull to save them abundance of trouble: but may be very pernicious to the Plantations, especially to Virginia, that has no agent except Col. Blakiston who is in truth the Lieut: Governor's Solicitor, and not the Country's for he will act nothing in the world in prejudice of the Governor, tho' he do anything never so injurious to the country." His insistence that he had a right to appear in behalf of himself and the rest of his "brethren" in the council against any innovation to their prejudice could scarcely be denied, but the incident led him thus early to the conclusion reached by the House of Burgesses only in 1759 that it would be necessary for the country to have an agent residing here, "or else I don't understand how their wrongs will ever be righted."[1]

In course of time the procedure became stereotyped. The agent handed in to the clerk of the Board of Trade a statement informing their Lordships of his appointment as agent, together with a copy of the act or ordinance which authorized it; the secretary laid the document before the Board, who then ordered it sent to their attorney

[1] For his entire letter to Philip Ludwell, dated October 28, 1717, see "Some Colonial Letters," *Virginia Magazine of History and Biography*, III, 352-53.

for his opinion on its legality. This was the routine followed in the case of James Crockatt at the Board session of November 22, 1749; in this case the ordinance of appointment went to Mr. Matthew Lamb for legal opinion.[2] In the fall of 1752 the dictum went forth that henceforth all correspondence with America was to be carried on with the Board of Trade only and not with the office of the secretary of state.[3] One is thereby forced to the conclusion that up to that date some form of accrediting also to the secretary of state had been practiced. Indeed, survivals occur after that date. In 1755 Governor Dinwiddie wrote Abercromby that he had omitted to mention the latter to the secretary of state as agent, "conceiving" it sufficient to do it to the Board of Trade and to the Earl of Albemarle, probably quite forgetting the direction of 1752 which virtually forbade credentials elsewhere than to the Board of Trade.[4] There is no evidence of an oath of loyalty being exacted.

Although the law of appointment was certainly the official credential, it must have been customary for the governor in the case of a regular agent representing both branches of the assembly to notify the Board of Trade or other boards of the appointment of a certain person as agent. In case of vacancy in the executive office or of friction between the governor and assembly the president of the council or speaker of the lower house of assembly might supply such letter of notification. Mr. Middleton, president of the South Carolina council, sent such a notification of the appointment of Stephen Godin to the Board of Trade in 1728/9.[5] Of course, where a person began to function without the proper formalities or where there was any irregularity, the person professing to act as agent was summoned before the Board. Edmund Gray of Georgia presents such a case. At the session of March 30, 1753, he was called in and

[2] *Journal of the Board of Trade*, 1741/2-1749, p. 462. This was, of course, late but only indicates that this was the regular procedure in agency history. See also for Abercromby's appointment for North Carolina, *ibid.*, p. 365.

[3] This brought rejoicing, as it relieved the colonies of the expense of double sets of journals, minutes, and laws. The agents and governors were duly notified to that effect by the Board of Trade. See a letter of James Crockatt to the Committee of Correspondence of South Carolina, Journal of the Commons House of Assembly of South Carolina, of Nov. 25, 1752, XXVIII, 40.

[4] Dinwiddie, *Official Records*, I, p. 506.

[5] His letter is dated January 23, 1728/9. Godin was to obtain proper instructions from the king on a certain matter to be sent with whoever was appointed governor.—C. O. 5/360, f. 157.

questioned as to the authority by which he acted as agent, and asked by whose orders or instructions he had presented a certain memorial.[6] In 1757, before the lower house of Virginia had appointed an agent of its own but after it had refused to regard Abercromby as a full, colonial agent, that individual was naturally apprehensive about his credentials. Though he had a resolution of the governor and council accrediting him, he said that he was under "pain" of having his credentials called in question by any of the boards or by parliament.[7] An agent was apparently subject to being held up short at any time with a demand for his credentials. At such widely separated dates as December 4, 1718, and December 18, 1754, the researcher finds an order from the Board of Trade that all persons styling themselves agents for the several colonies in America should produce to the Board as a matter of record the laws or other authorities whereby they acted as agents. By 1754 and undoubtedly earlier, the credentials were being recorded in an entry book preserved for that express purpose at the Plantation Office.[8]

Occasionally an irregularity in credentials occurred. This was especially the case with the Treasury Board at the time of paying the parliamentary grants to reimburse the colonies for their expenses in the colonial wars. Of course, the provincial authorities were filled with zeal to get the quota for their particular colonies promptly and so were probably more than ordinarily careless in regard to providing proper credentials. The case which comes to hand happens to be from a New England colony, but it is so striking that it fills a useful purpose in being introduced here. John Tomlinson, who served New Hampshire as agent from 1733 to 1753, was asked with the other agents in 1748 to leave with the Treasury Board a copy of his authority to receive the money which the Privy Council

[6] *Journal of the Board of Trade*, 1749/50-1753, p. 409; C. O. 391/60, p. 88. The rebuke administered to him will be discussed later.

[7] Abercromby Letter Book, p. 45.

[8] In 1718 Blakiston presented a copy of a minute of the council of Virginia of August 16, 1705, whereby he was made agent, a copy of which was ordered made for the Board.— *Journal of the Board of Trade*, Nov., 1718-Dec., 1722, p. 10.

On December 19, 1754, all the Southern agents appeared except those for Maryland and Georgia, where Martyn was probably still held a crown agent. Bollan of Massachusetts excused himself because of illness.—*Ibid.*, 1754-1758, pp. 89, 308. The language of the two entries, though not identical, is very similar. The order was issued December 18, 1754.—*Ibid.*, p. 89. For the record which proves existence of an entry book for the credentials of the agents, see *Journal of the Board of Trade*, Jan., 1754-Dec., 1758, p. 90.

had determined to allow the colonies. "As for my part," he replied boldly, "I cannot at present send you Copies of mine, neither have I any Letters of Attorney from my Province. But please to give me leave to say what my authority is, and I believe you will be of opinion with me, that not any Letter of attorney or any thing else can add to the authority I am at prefent pofsefsed of, and which is this; I am here agent for the said province of New Hampshire chosen and appointed such by the Governor Council and afsembly, and every act of mine is the act of the Province, and binding upon the Province as any act of their own, Especially when I act agreeable to my Instructions from them, and my Instructions from them in this Case, were to make application to H. M. for reimbursing them the Charge the Province had been at in taking and securing Cape Breton. . . ."[9] Since the sums were paid over to the agents and since Tomlinson remained agent for some years longer, presumably such an informal credential as this was accepted by the Treasury Board.

Agents Rebuked by the Board of Trade

Of course, the Board of Trade could and at times did vent its displeasure on an agent by a stern rebuke or even by withdrawal of the privilege of negotiating business before it. This seems not to have occurred during the early period when the Board felt strongly the need of a liaison officer; but later, when the agents felt themselves representatives of strong colonies, their conduct could outrage their Lordships' sense of dignity. Though not the only instance, the case of Richard Partridge is by all odds the most famous and might indeed be termed the classic instance. Serving at various dates during the long period from 1715 to 1759 as agent for Rhode Island, New Jersey, Connecticut, and Pennsylvania, he was agent for the last-named province when he became imbroiled with the Board of Trade. His offense lay in refusal to answer questions relating to the disappearance and "dispersion" from the office of the Board of Trade of a letter dated October 20, 1740, from Deputy Governor Thomas of Pennsylvania, thus giving color to the belief that he had been party to the theft; at least it was clear that he had clandestinely obtained possession of a copy of a

[9] Treasury Papers, T. I, 333, no. 160.

letter from the Board's files which was ultimately printed and
scattered broadcast over Pennsylvania. At the inquiry he could
not be prevailed upon to reveal from whom he had obtained the
copy, whereupon the Board, at its session of March 17, 1740/1, ex-
pelled him from transacting business at their board for any of the
plantations "until he shall have given Satisfaction in relation to the
said Complaint." Oddly enough this solemn prohibition of future
appearances seems to have been nothing more than a byplay, for
Partridge made light of it and was allowed to continue his appearances before the Board.[10] Jeremiah Dummer and Robert Charles,
agents for Massachusetts and New York respectively, also came
under fire from the Board and were temporarily denied access to
it. Mr. Charles had been denied a copy of certain papers by the
Board. He thereupon indulged in remarks calling in question the
propriety of the rules of the Board in regard to copies of papers,
which the Lords censured as "arrogant and indecent" and "unbe-
coming his character as an Agent," as he had no right to question
their rules and orders. The Board resolved to receive no application from Dummer after the governor of Massachusetts should have
had an opportunity of choosing another agent. His offense was that
he had abused and insulted Mr. Astell, a merchant, because the latter
had given "his thoughts to this Board in relation to naval stores
imported from the plantations." Dummer was forgiven at Astell's
request after apology.[11]

Some Southern agents did not escape rebuke. Edmund Gray of
Georgia was called in on April 4, 1753, following the questioning
of his credentials on March 30, and told that his memorial appeared

[10] Partridge served Rhode Island for no less than forty-four years and New Jersey for
thirty years. See for the Board decision, Entry Books of the Board of Trade, C. O.
5/1294, pp. 146-47; 408; 383; 392; *Journal of the Board of Trade*, 1734/5-1741, p. 375.
For a full account of the episode referred to above see Wolff, *The Colonial Agency of
Pennsylvania*, pp. 94-98. On a later occasion, February 7, 1752, Partridge was rebuked
for improper publication of an order of the Privy Council to New Jersey. This time
Partridge divulged that he had secured the paper from a clerk in the Privy Council
office.—*Journal of the Board of Trade*, 1734/5-1741, p. 375; Jan., 1749/50- Dec., 1753,
pp. 268-69; *Documents relating to the Colonial History of the State of New Jersey, New
Jersey Archives*, VIII, 29-30.

[11] Though Partridge did not serve any of the Southern colonies, the writer would not
feel justified in omitting this classic instance of discipline of an agent.—*Documents relative
to the Colonial History of the State of New York*, VII, 338 for Charles; *Journal of the
Board of Trade*, Nov., 1718-Dec., 1722, pp. 21-22 for Dummer; also Burns, *The Colonial
Agents of New England*, p. 52.

to them not only most extraordinary but also "highly disrespectfull
to this Board and to government in general, inasmuch as it presumed to point out to the Crown which persons were or were not
proper to be appointed Governors of Georgia." Such a proceeding
and behavior in an infant colony was not in their judgment "paral-
leled, and showed that a very improper and refractory spirit prevailed amongst the People there." However, the Board contented
itself with no other censure than rejecting the memorial; the people
of Georgia should count themselves fortunate that no other notice
was taken of "so indecent, so improper a Conduct." With a sym-
bolic gesture the Board returned the memorial to Gray and ordered
him to withdraw. The rebuke administered to Peyton Randolph
in 1754 when he was in England as special agent concerning the
governor's fees for land grants, was rather for his absence from his
post as attorney general of Virginia than for any act of disrespect
to the Board. When the Board demanded what leave he had to be
absent, he explained that he had declined the service as special agent
at first considering it inconsistent with his office of attorney general
but that he later had thought proper to acquiesce in the insistence
of the burgesses and had asked for leave of absence, which the
governor had refused; but he then was so deeply engaged that he
could not recede; and that, in any case, he did not apprehend that
he was acting contrary to the prerogatives of the crown. He humbly
admitted that he did not consider himself attorney general during
his absence; but, as we know, he took every step to have himself
reappointed after his return. A final example was a mild rebuke
administered to Montague on June 7, 1768, for suppressing the
hostility of the council of Virginia to a scheme for paper currency
presented by him to the Board for the House of Burgesses.[12]

Attendance at Board Meetings

First and foremost among the duties of the agent was frequent,
one might almost say, constant, attendance at the meetings of the
Board of Trade. He almost literally had to dance attendance on
their Lordships' pleasure and convenience like a lackey. No record
is more frequent than that Mr. —————, agent for —————, is

---

[12] See *Journal of the Board of Trade*, 1749/50-1753, p. 411, for Gray; for Peyton
Randolph see *ibid.*, 1754-1758, p. 26; for the rebuke to Montague, *ibid.*, 1768-1775, p. 31.

desired to attend the Board on —————————next. Perhaps the demands made by this attendance on an agent's time can be no better set forth than by a chronological record for the agent Abercromby in transacting affairs for North Carolina for a period of little more than a year on one matter only; namely, a petition against an act for a more equal representation in the lower house of assembly. The record follows the entries of the journals of the Board of Trade and shows that between March 21, 1749/50, and June 27, 1751, that agent had had to attend the Board no less than ten times.[13]

Postponements and delays, for which the Board or some agent might be responsible, were far from infrequent. Sessions of the Board were sometimes postponed for lack of a quorum or the secretary's indisposition, and some agent's time was thereby usually wasted. The reader can easily picture the disgust of two agents to find on October 31, 1729, only two of the Board of Trade present and to be directed to attend again on the following Thursday.[14] Sometimes, as in modern law cases, one of the agents would ask and secure postponement in order to have an opportunity to examine papers presented by the other side or to secure further data. Sometimes, on the other hand, to the Board's annoyance, the agent himself or a merchant might for personal reasons delay certain matters. Such a case occurred when Colonel Henry Hartwell, notified to attend the session of August 25, 1696, or as soon as convenient, on Virginia affairs, failed to be present. When he still did not appear on September 7, the Lords ordered that he should be "positively summoned to attend on Wednesday morning next." The following

---

[13] See App. II, *Journal of the Board of Trade* for the dates indicated; *Colonial Records of North Carolina*, IV, 1225-27. Many other illustrations could be cited. One of the early cases for New England might be noted to show how early frequent attendance was called for. Agents for Boston appeared against the Mason and Gorges claim:

Mar. 31, 1677	Mar. 25, 1678	Dec. 6, 1678
Apr. 5, 1677	Mar. 28, 1678	Dec. 13, 1678
July 19, 1677	Apr. 8, 1678	Feb. 18, 1678/9
July 27, 1677	Apr. 18, 1678	Feb. 24, 1678/9
Aug. 2, 1677	July 30, 1678	Mar. 4, 1678/9
Sept. 6, 1677		

—C. O. 391/2, pp. 7, 19, 89, 95, 102, 109, 225, 231, 233, 247, 262, 271, 272, 309, 313, 317. On July 30, 1678, the agents began to grow weary and to ask to be allowed to go home.

[14] *Journal of the Board of Trade*, 1728-1734, p. 69. For an instance of illness on the part of the secretary, see "Garth Correspondence," *loc. cit.*, XXXIII, 125.

morning a messenger reported that he found him too ill with gout to walk or write. He sent his promise to come as soon as he could. On September 9 the Board courteously sent him a list of "enquiries" to be answered with "what convenient speed" he could. He answered at great length on September 14, through another hand unless his gout had improved remarkably.[15] Montague notified the Board on one occasion that he could not attend on the day specified for considering a petition of the merchants for an act on bills of credit on account of illness. The Board notified the several merchants interested that the business was postponed till he was able to attend.[16] So important an agent as Garth, a lawyer and member of parliament, felt at liberty to ask postponement of the date for consideration of a Georgia law, as he had to hold the quarter session for his borough at a date which would not allow him time properly to instruct his counsel.[17] Occasionally the Board, summoning on too short notice, found the agents out of town, as was the case when Crockatt was ordered to attend on October 26, 1750.[18]

A summons on a certain agent to attend for the affairs of some other colony than the one for which he was accredited was not rare, and made claims on his time for which he presumably received no recompense. Colonel Blakiston appeared at a session of November 1, 1709, with Colonel Jory and several other gentlemen on a matter which concerned the Leeward Islands, and one wonders just what information he could have had when his personal knowledge of

[15] C. O. 391/9, pp. 69, 93, 25; letter to Hartwell from the secretary of the Board dated Sept. 9, Entry Book, C. O. 5/359, p. 89. The items on this subject in the *Calendar of State Papers*, are too scanty to be of value; recourse must be had to the manuscripts.

[16] Entry Book of the Board of Trade, C. O. 5/1368, p. 210. In a few days he felt called on to thank the Board and to notify them that he was "ready to obey them when they thought proper to command."—C. O. 5/1330, p. 273.

[17] C. O. 5/647, p. 405. His letter to the Board is dated January 10, 1767.

An agent of distinction in the early days of the Board's history did not take its orders so humbly. In 1698, for instance, Sir Henry Ashurst, agent for Massachusetts Bay, was far from dancing attendance on the Board. The attorney and the solicitor general placed their delay in reporting on a New England address to the Board on the ground that they had not been attended by Sir Henry Ashurst. The Board ordered the attorney and the solicitor general to notify Ashurst to attend them, or, "if he neglect to do it," they are to make such report as they can without him. And they also ordered their secretary to notify Sir Henry that they "expected" his attendance upon that subject.—C. O. 391/11, p. 304.

[18] *Journal of the Board of Trade*, 1749/50-1753, p. 109. Sometimes the Board would send word to agents that they desired to speak with them the next day. When agents had come over expressly for a certain purpose, as had Yonge and Lloyd in 1722, such sudden summonses were probably welcome.—*Ibid.*, Nov., 1718-Dec., 1722, pp. 368-69.

America was confined to Virginia and Maryland. When the Reverend Mr. Blair, summoned to attend on August 18, 1697, was confronted with inquiries about Maryland, he stated frankly that he had never been there and was not acquainted with that country as he was with Virginia. But he did furnish some information about the transportation of tobacco, the size of the ships used, and also about the method of taking up lands in Maryland and Virginia so that he probably did not feel that his appearance was futile.[19]

The summons to several agents to appear at the same time was probably actuated by a desire to clarify matters rather than a desire to save the time of the agents, but it worked out, doubtless, to their greater satisfaction in that respect. For instance, Blakiston was ordered to appear at the Board session of July 24, 1719, as the spokesman for Maryland and Virginia; at the some session were to be present Jeremiah Dummer for Massachusetts and Mr. Ambrose Philips for New York. As events moved forward toward the middle of the century, it became increasingly the custom to bring in nearly all the continental agents. For instance, when the sugar islands were seeking in 1750 a total prohibition of trade between the North American colonies and all foreign settlements, the agents of all the Northern colonies and several of the Southern colonies were brought in to face John Sharpe, the spokesman for the sugar islands. William Bollan for Massachusetts and Robert Charles for New York objected to the proposed prohibition and were strongly supported by Crockatt, Abercromby, and Paris, speaking for the Southern colonies of the mainland. All agreed that the proposed step would be ruinous to North American trade.[20]

In the course of their dealings with the Board of Trade, the agents seemed to feel it desirable to seek out and bring with them provincials who might be in London on private business, ship captains who had visited the colony in question, or, as indicated in the preceding chapter, British merchants who had had contact in one way or another with the subject at issue. A few illustrations will suffice. Blakiston brought to one session John Bradford, lately arrived from Maryland, who furnished some information on the

[19] *Ibid.*, Feb., 1708/9-Mar., 1714/5, p. 83.

[20] *Ibid.*, Nov., 1718-Dec., 1722, p. 86. All these agents were before the Board repeatedly at the close of 1750: on Nov. 13, Dec. 6, 7, and 10.—*Ibid.*, 1749/50-1753, pp. 119, 128, 133, 138-39. See also for the full story of these sessions C. O. 391/57, pp. 364-421.

progress toward creating towns in that colony. Meager though it seems now, British merchants, eager for new markets, probably listened with relish to the tale of ten towns being laid out in the Patuxent area, though it must have dashed their hopes to hear that the whole sum expended on the houses did not amount to £150 sterling. On another occasion he ushered in a Mr. Floyd from the same province to be interrogated on an act concerned with bonds which Lord Baltimore wished repealed.[21] Certainly, it could not have been otherwise than helpful to the Board to have first-hand contact with colonials who had sometimes helped pass the very legislation then before them for review. One can fairly feel the impression which Colonel Jennings, president of the Virginia council, must have made when the Board was considering repeal of an act declaring who might hold office in that province. Present at the passing of the act in 1705, he declared that it was not meant to restrain any one from holding office who was commissioned by persons in England with authority from the crown, but only to restrain the governors from bestowing the choice offices on favorites.[22] Amid the turmoil of Indian troubles and efforts for peace in South Carolina, their Lordships certainly would listen eagerly in June, 1717, to a man who had left the province only the preceding April, bringing, so to speak, the latest bulletins from the front.[23] Lest it be thought that these visitors were thrust upon the Board, it may not be out of place to quote the attitude of that body, which on January 14, 1714/5, told one of the agents that the "Board will be glad if he bring with him any gentleman of that province who may happen to be now in town, or others who are versed in the affairs of those parts."[24]

Information—please

The Board of Trade regarded the agents as sources of information on persons, things, events—on subjects presented to their Lordships by the agents or on subjects brought up by the Board members. They were to be fountains of information concerning the colonies,

[21] *Journal of the Board of Trade*, 1708/9-1714/5, p. 95; C. O. 391/15, p. 402.
[22] Entry Book of the Board of Trade, C. O. 5/1364, p. 228.
[23] *Journal of the Board of Trade*, Mar., 1714/5-Oct., 1718, pp. 240, 241.
[24] *Ibid.*, 1708/9-1714/5, p. 590.

their own or neighboring provinces, to be tapped at will. Blair, clergyman though he was, was brought before the Board of Trade and asked his opinion on transporting disbanded British soldiers to Virginia. As if he had long been studying the matter, he instantly suggested that they should be sent over, supplied with household stuff, wearing apparel, and tools at the king's expense; that, if possible, they were to follow the trades they knew, or hire themselves out for a year or two to learn a trade, as there was great need for varied trades in Virginia; and that a skillful overseer of transport was needed.[25] On another occasion he was quizzed on the price of tobacco, quitrents, the colonial revenue, the yield of the duty of two shillings per hogshead on tobacco, customs officers, general administration, the wisdom of exemption of councillors from the process of law, duties on imports, grants of land and conveyances, population statistics, and the growth of towns. In short, he seems to have been subjected to an "Information, Please," and to have sustained himself with the credit befitting a trained intelligence. Boone and Beresford were expected not only to reveal the status of the Indian War, but to supply data on the products of Carolina and the Bahamas,—five hundred miles from their home, if you please,— on silk, cochineal, indigo, cypress masts, coffee and drugs, minerals, and the economic value of the province as a whole. It is a trifle amusing to read that Boone pulled out from his pocket in the midst of the discussion an assessment of the whole province and a sample of cochineal.[26] The reader will not fail to note that some of the products mentioned were no nearer South Carolina than is South America. That the advice of Boone and Barnwell should be sought on the form of government desirable for South Carolina in 1720 and on the value of establishing a frontier post on the Altamaha River as an outpost against Spain merely reflects credit on the intelligence of the Board. When Governor Reynolds complained of opposition even from the council in Georgia, the Board did not scorn to interrogate Agent Martyn and to listen to the letters which he produced from correspondents in Georgia complaining of the governor and the improper behavior of Little, his secretary, in its effort

[25] C. O. 5/1359, pp. 125-28: C. O. 391/10.
[26] *Journal of the Board of Trade*, Mar., 1714/5-Oct., 1718, pp. 158-59.

to get an insight into the disordered and discontented state of that colony.[27]

Agents needed to know the history of their respective colonies. Yonge and Wragg, assisted by Colonel Robert Johnson, drew up on May 28, 1728, in pursuance of an order of the Board of Trade, an account of the settlement of Carolina and of the attempts of the Spaniards to settle there or to disturb the British subjects. It began with the "discovery of Florida by Sebastian Cabot in 1497," came down through Ponce de Leon and Navarez, and included a list of the attempts against the Carolinas made by Spain. Stephen Godin also about the same time, 1728, for the agent of the council could not let the agents for the lower house outshine him, submitted an historical account of the settlement of Carolina, equally detailed.[28] Though there is not the slightest evidence that the Britisher Peregrine Fury ever set foot in America, he was consulted, equally with Colonel Horsey, as to the several batteries and forts which the South Carolinians had erected in 1738 when they pleaded inability to provide themselves with a sufficient supply of ammunition.[29]

No person could appear or event involving a given colony occur, however insignificant, if it engaged the attention of the Board, but the agent would be sent for. Even in a case when the governor was concerned and presumably would deal directly with the proper British ministry, the agent must be sent for. An order in council brought the case of a naval officer stationed on the Rappahanock River before the Board of Trade on January 4, 1711/2. That officer, a Gawin Corbin, complained that Lieutenant Governor Spotswood had done him a great injustice by suspending him on suspicion of his having been concerned in an erasure in the royal letter of license to the ship *Robinson*. Corbin was naturally ordered to attend the Board the next Friday morning, but so was Colonel Blakiston. As one might expect, the agent does not seem to have produced any information at the Friday session.[30] Another such minor case arose in 1724 when the Duke of Newcastle had referred papers of com-

[27] *Collections of the South Carolina Historical Society*, I, 253, 254; II, 142, 143; for Georgia see C. O. 5/672, pp. 388-89.

[28] C. O. 5/360 ff. 66-67 for Wragg and Yonge's account; C. O. 5/360, f. 63 for Godin's.

[29] Entry Book of the Board of the Trade, C. O. 5/401, p. 299.

[30] *Journal of the Board of Trade*, 1708/9-1714/5, p. 325.

plaint from a certain Seigneur Couturier to the Board of Trade, evidently submitted from the office of the French ambassador. Though the agent of South Carolina, who must have been Yonge at that date, could shed no light on the matter when summoned in April, 1724, by July he had been able to write their Lordships that the said Couturier was being held in confinement at the marshal's house in Charleston under charge that he had entered the British colony from the French settlement at Mobile—he spells it Noville—together with two Frenchmen and two Indians, without the pass required of all persons who came from the French or Spanish settlements. Yonge had acquired this information from a merchant who had lately arrived from Carolina. Presumably this satisfied the Board, for there is no further entry on this subject.[31]

When the Board lacked a copy of the Virginia laws in 1697, they promptly turned to the young Byrd, who had already appeared before them as agent, for a copy. Fortunately, as a law student at the Temple, he was able to supply their Lordships with what a layman would suppose was one of the tools of their trade since regular transmission of the colonial laws, journals, and minutes had been long since established as routine.

Selection and Retaining of Solicitors

Obviously the hearings before the Board of Trade, dealing, as they so often did, with legislation, whether defense of a colonial law or the handling of trade, which was often regulated by law, or questions of land and boundaries, which rested on legal grants, became highly legalistic. Hence, the agent must have expert legal advice and aid. This appears true, naturally, when the agent was a colonial planter or a British merchant, but also, perhaps strangely, when the agent was himself a trained jurist, as was true of Ferdinand Paris and Charles Garth, the latter a member of the British House of Commons as well. This had probably crystalized into the regular and proper practice before agencies were established in the Southern colonies, as the New England agents had consulted lawyers or solicitors, as they would be called in England, in the seventeenth century when they were guarding their precious charters.[32]

[31] C. O. 5/382, Bundle 37; C. O. 5/381, p. 32.
[32] Burns, *The Colonial Agents of New England,* pp. 41-42, 46.

However, the need for expert opinion was felt comparatively early in the Southern colonies, for we find Francis Yonge dealing with a Mr. Sharpe as solicitor in August, 1726, while he was on his third agency, striving to gain South Carolina's freedom from the proprietors. The solicitor drew up and laid before the king's attorney and solicitor general a statement of the case some time before the date of the hearing. Again in January, 1733/4, this same Francis Yonge as assistant agent engaged Mr. Sharpe once more as solicitor on the question whether assistant judges had a right to vote with the chief justice in criminal cases. The author is forced to conclude that this was in all probability Mr. John Sharpe, brother of Horatio Sharpe, governor of Maryland. This conclusion seems logical as he was during his entire mature life deeply and constantly concerned with the colonies, serving continuously for some of the British West Indian islands from 1723 to 1757, and often appearing before the Board of Trade as solicitor for various of the North American colonies.[33] This same colony retained the services of a Mr. Dunning as counsel in 1764;[34] and Garth in 1767 secured the aid of that same gentleman in a contest with Agent Knox over a Georgia act concerning grants of land to the south of the Altamaha River when he learned that Knox had retained Mr. Wedderburn as counsel, as he felt he must meet Georgia "with equal ability."[35]

Immense Amount of Writing: Reports, Statements, Letters to the Colony

It would be difficult to exaggerate—doubtless, it is difficult for us to comprehend—the burden of the writing performed by the agents in an age without shorthand or typewriters. Despite the fact that "fair" copies of the rough drafts and duplicates were executed

[33] This statement is based on Miss Penson's list of agents for the British West Indies. See The *Colonial Agents of the British West Indies*, App. II, pp. 250-54. For the notice of Sharpe serving as solicitor for South Carolina, see *Journal of the Board of Trade*, 1728/9-1734, p. 369; for service in 1726, see C. O. 5/387, pp. 95, 96; for a letter of Governor Nicholson to A. Middleton of November 22, 1726, showing that the former had called on Sharpe in his chambers in Lincoln's Inn on the same subject, see C. O. 5/387, p. 120.

[34] John Dunning, eminent lawyer, afterwards became Lord Ashburton.

[35] *Journal of the Board of Trade*, 1764-1767, p. 99; "Garth Correspondence," *loc. cit.*, XXIX, 130-31. It is rather interesting that, according to Garth, it was unusual to attend the Board with counsel on boundary lines.—*Ibid.*, XXXI, 129. Wedderburn rose to be Lord Chancellor but is better known in America for his savage attack on Franklin before a committee of the Privy Council in 1774.

by clerks, the imagination can still picture Garth or Abercromby,
Yonge or Montague, perhaps crouched over a candle, or pressed
close to a window on some dark November day, writing, writing
hour after hour, for a secretary without shorthand at his command
would probably be more of a torment than aid.   Any person who
has poured over Abercromby's impossible penmanship and laboriously
worked out his fashioning of the various letters of the alphabet
ardently wishes that the day of typewriters had dawned a century
or two sooner.   And the researcher who plows through all the Garth
correspondence wonders when he slept.

First, there were the numerous letters to the colonies—to the
governor or to the Committee of Correspondence, sometimes to
both.[36]   These letters are noted here in this chapter because the
bulk of the correspondence related to hearings, attendances, and
letters to the Board of Trade.   A few reports, as Garth's during
the crucial years from 1767 to 1773, dealt with parliament; some
letters dealt with the ministry and the various other boards; but
the great bulk were on the dealings with the Board of Trade and
Plantations.   Though the work of duplication—and it must be
remembered that letters, like the colonial laws and journals, often
went in duplicate, and sometimes in triplicate—represented the labor
of hired clerks, it may not be amiss to devote a few sentences to this
subject.   The modern reader shudders for the clerk who transcribed,
probably three times, a letter by Governor Cornbury eight pages
long of close writing on large paper.   The author came across one
letter from a Virginia governor which was seventy-seven pages long!
But if the researcher is impressed with the manual labor of this
writing, he is equally impressed with the necessity of sending duplicates.   The Virginia Committee of Correspondence, for instance,
reports on April 30, 1761, to their agent Montague the misfortune
they had met in having not only the first but the second copy of
their letter to him taken by the enemy. Abercromby waxed so enthusiastic in the spring of 1760 when the parliamentary grant of that
year was finally made, that he sent three letters to carry the good
news of winning Virginia's share of £50,000: he sent an original by a

[36] Governor Nicholson on June 15, 1724, sent a letter from Francis Yonge down to the
lower house, which he asked to be returned after it had been read two or three times, but
no copy was to be taken of it.—Journal of the Commons House of Assembly, VII, 56.

ship from Bristol, the first that sailed for Virginia; a duplicate by a ship from London; and a triplicate on a Virginia ship which sailed in July in Governor Wright's convoy. In the midst of the Seven Years' War then raging he could only hope that one of the three would reach its destination. One recalls also that when Colonel Vander Dusen fell into the hands of the enemy in 1742, all the dispatches which he was carrying were lost,[37] but the duplicates had a chance of safe delivery. Sometimes the letters of the agents contained copies of important official reports or decisions which the colonial officials should see; if a clerk were not readily available or if time were precious, the conclusion is well-founded that the agent did the copying himself. Leheup's letter to the Virginia council of January 19, 1725/6, inclosed a copy of the report of the attorney and solicitor general on the queries sent by Virginia in regard to land grants in the counties of Brunswick and Spottsylvania. Abercromby inclosed in his letter of March 15, 1758, a copy of his letter to General Abercromby about the monetary grant of parliament to the colonies; a copy of his memorial to the Lords of the Treasury about the application for an aid out of the quitrents to the tobacco revenue; a copy of Governor Morris's petition for a salt monopoly which he and other agents were opposing; and a copy of the arrangements for pay made for Nathaniel Blakiston, former agent, so that the Virginia council might find an example to encourage the present agent.[38] Always the agent had to keep and send accounts of money disbursed by him, and the reader can readily imagine the laboriousness of this part of his correspondence during the years when the parliamentary grants of reimbursement were being negotiated and handled.

Again the frequency of the letters might be indicated by a brief tabulation: Garth sent the Committee of Correspondence in a period of less than six months at least six reports, an average of one a month; to Governor Montagu in a little over three years he sent

[37] "Proceedings of the Virginia Committee of Correspondence," *loc. cit.*, XI, 18; Abercromby Letter Book, Oct. 1, 1760. For Vander Dusen's capture see Chapter III.

[38] *Executive Journals of the Council*, IV, 99. It is amusing to read of a friendly rebuke to Franklin for not writing more frequently to the Committee of Correspondence in Pennsylvania, "Even if there is nothing to say," in order to show his activity and interest in his commission and to stop criticism.—Sharpless, *A Quaker Experiment in Government*, II, 86; Abercromby Letter Book, pp. 84-86.

twenty-three letters.[39] The length is as important as the frequency
of the letters.   Garth's were perhaps the longest: on March 12,
1767, he covered seven and one-half printed pages in one letter
to the Committee of South Carolina; on May 17 he was equally
lengthy; and his report on the repeal of the Stamp Act extended to
a document of twenty-four printed pages.   He also sent a very
long report to the Maryland House of Delegates relating to the
objection of parliament to the petition of Massachusetts Bay.[40] The
agents' zeal often led them to add hasty postscripts to letters which
they evidently left open till the last possible moment for mailing
to add timely information on matters of importance.   On February
4, 1771, Garth added a postscript to a letter which had been held
since February 1 to say that a bill for continuing the Mutiny Act
for America without alteration had been introduced in the House
of Commons.[41]

One is impressed, incidentally, by the type of memory displayed
by some of the agents; with Garth's kaleidoscopic memory, for instance, which reproduced for the South Carolina Committee of
Correspondence the session of the Board of Trade of March 25,
1770, with meticulous detail—all that was said or read by members
of the Board or by himself. The reader would be inclined to think
that he had consulted the notes of a clerk, except that he states that
the above was "to the best of my recollection."

Study and Research

The mass of material which the agent had to plow through and
digest before he could appear before the Board probably seemed at
times forbidding and discouraging to continuance in the post. The
list of documents which the Commons House of Assembly of South
Carolina ordered sent to the agents as early as 1716 rather staggers
one, for it indicates the range of subjects with which the post de-

[39] Gathered from the "Garth Correspondence," *loc. cit.* It must also be recalled that this
publication represents selections.   Wright's correspondence, when he was serving as agent
to South Carolina in 1728 seems much more moderate, though of course, the four letters
of February 28, May 18, June 13, and August 5, may represent only those thought important
enough to be entered in the Journal of the Commons House of Assembly of South Carolina
(see XXXII, 4).

[40] "Garth Correspondence," *loc. cit.*, XXIX, 214-21; 223-30; XXVI, 68-92; "Stamp
Act Papers," *Maryland Historical Magazine*, VI, 283-87.

[41] "Garth Correspondence," *loc. cit.*, XXXIII, 125.

manded conversance.[42]   At the time of the controversy over Colonel
Rhett in 1721, Agent Boone sent the governor a copy of Rhett's
letter to the Commissioners of the Customs.   Governor Moore felt
called upon to answer it paragraph by paragraph so that Boone might
vindicate the inhabitants of the province against the "malicious aspersions" contained in the said letter.[43]   There was to be no slacken-
ing of work for the agent.   Maryland perpetrated on Ferdinand
Paris in 1741 a dossier of papers relating apparently to one case,
which may be termed equally overwhelming.[44]   There was no
lessening of papers with the years—on the contrary, rather an increase in documents dispatched to the agent.   In 1763, when papers
were sent to Garth on "A Full State of the Dispute betwixt the
Governor and the Commons House of Assembly of South Carolina,"
it required some thirteen separate documents to present the case,
going back to the instructions issued to Governor Nicholson in
1700.[45]

Of course, full and precise information was properly demanded
by the Board of Trade in arriving at their recommendations.   Despite
such voluminous dossiers as were sent over, the agent often had to
ask for other records.   For instance, on the very question raised in
1741, in connection with which so many papers were sent Ferdinand
Paris, as detailed above, the agent found that he needed a copy of
an act relating to the revenue of Maryland, passed on April 30,
1679, which had been referred to in an order of council, dated
February 26, 1690.   As that act was not to be found on record
in England, he wrote back to the colony for it, but since it could
not be found there, a deposition to that effect from the clerk of the
House of Delegates of Maryland was transmitted to him in August,
1742.[46]

Even after the riotous proceedings in the colonies preceding the
outbreak of the revolution had disrupted the regular communications of the Committees of Correspondence, long reports went to the

[42] Journal of the Commons House of Assembly of South Carolina, V, 143-44.
[43] Ibid., pp. 486-87.
[44] Archives of Maryland, XLII, 205-9. See App. III.
[45] The list appears in the pamphlet entitled as above, p. 2. It included, of course, copies
of the Journals of the Commons House of Assembly, reports of Commons' Committee, message to the Governor, his reply, A Governor's Speech, the Commons' reply, Minutes of the
House on the Debate and Framing of the Remonstrance, etc.
[46] Archives of Maryland, XLII, 358.

agent for him to study. One illustration is sufficient. The members of the lower house of South Carolina who were in Charleston on November 20, 1772, felt it incumbent on them to give Garth an account of the governor's conduct and to include some remarks on the speech with which he dissolved them. Then followed a five-page account which concluded: "You will pursue such Means as you think best to prevent his Excellency's Information being received as true and candid, and obtain Justice for the Province."[47]

Besides the papers thrust upon the agent by the colonial authorities, he often had to make exhaustive researches of his own. For instance, when the question of repeal of the instructions to the governor of South Carolina, which forbade his assent to any money bill without an express provision that money should not be issued for any other service than that to which it was appropriated, was being agitated, Garth examined diligently the journals of the lower house. He turned up cases of orders on the treasurer without the assent of the council and governor up to March 10, 1737, and many instances after 1751. He seems to have established the rule that if the lower house ordered an advance from certain appropriated funds which proved not to be needed, it asked the assent of the council; but in the case of orders generally, it acted on the assumption of surpluses sufficient till the next tax bill. Garth insisted that these instances disproved any charge that the lower house had lately assumed illegal power and therefore asked the king to withdraw his additional instruction.[48]

Abercromby also worked up precedents in 1759 from former acts when the clergy were protesting the virtual decrease in their salary through the decline of the price of tobacco. He showed that the general assembly in 1753 had increased the allowance of the clergy when the price of tobacco was low and that in the present case the legislature had not deviated from the rule and principles of justice, nor had this act any partial tendency to the prejudice of the clergy alone.[49]

In a period when the request for transmission of papers across the Atlantic and fulfillment of the request required anywhere from

[47] "Garth Correspondence," *loc. cit.*, XXXIII, 280. For the entire account see *ibid.*, pp. 275-80.
[48] *Ibid.*, pp. 120-23.   [49] Abercromby Letter Book, pp. 168-69.

three to six months, an agent must perforce, if possible, seek his material nearer at hand. And so he must take endless copies of papers. This meant first securing the permission of the Board of Trade to examine and search their records, a task in itself, for the Board tended to the view which too often obsesses authority; namely, that records are for preservation and not for consultation. At first, such permission was easily secured. For instance, Colonel Blakiston attended the Board on May 1, 1716, to desire copies of the complaints against Governor Spotswood—two anonymous letters from Virginia. Without objection or ado he was ordered to have his copies. But by 1747 a marked change in the attitude of the Board seems to have occurred. Because this is revealed most clearly in connection with New Jersey, the writer does not hesitate to step outside the strict field of the Southern colonies, especially since the agent in the case happened to be one who also served Maryland. Ferdinand Paris laid before the Board on August 6, 1747, a paper signed by himself on behalf of the proprietors of lands in East New Jersey, praying for attested copies of several papers in that office. It was ordered that he have leave to examine the books of the office with a clerk in attendance, and to mark such papers as he should judge necessary, and that a list of the same should be laid before the Board. At the following session, when a list of the papers petitioned for by Paris was laid before their Lordships, instructions were given that copies should be made and delivered to him, but that he should not be permitted to take copies of the minutes from the Journals of the Board.[50] It is to be noted that this refusal to leave an agent alone with the records was probably inspired by the loss of a letter from the files in 1741, related elsewhere. Thereafter, it would appear that clerks of the Board, and not the agents or their clerks, made the copies.[51]

[50] For Blakiston's request see *Journal of the Board of Trade*, Mar., 1714/5-Oct., 1718, p. 134; for a request by Wragg, see *Colonial Records of North Carolina*, IV, 323; for Paris' request, *Journal of the Board of Trade*, 1741/2-1749, p. 251.

[51] One finds this entry for May 11, 1750, in respect to a request of Abercromby for a copy of a Virginia law on quitrents: "A copy was ordered made and delivered him." C. O. 391/57, p. 207. It is also printed in the *Journal of the Board of Trade*, 1749/50-1753, p. 70. A request from Garth on December 13, 1773, to have leave to examine some records of South Carolina when the crown took over the province from the proprietors and to inspect the constitution of appointment of a council went no farther; presumably a clerk of the Board did the copying.—C. O. 5/380, p. 197. Mention of a copy of a Board of Trade entry is to be found in "Garth Correspondence," *loc. cit.*, XXIX, 120.

When the colonies wished documents which were missing in the colonial records replaced, it was, naturally, the agent who must arrange for such copying from duplicates in the British offices. In June, 1764, Virginia became awakened to the seriousness of gaps in her records. Some of the original charters granted to the colony had disappeared, been lost, or destroyed by fire. Therefore, Montague was directed to search the proper offices and to have copies made of all the charters ever granted to Virginia and of any papers which might be of use to be placed among the records of the province.[52]

Papers for the Board of Trade

We have spoken of the long and numerous letters which the agent dispatched to the colony. Now we must take cognizance of the lengthy reports, briefs, and arguments which he prepared for the various agencies of the home government, especially for the Board of Trade. The papers prepared and presented by the South Carolina agents from 1717 to 1719 during the early struggle of the settlers of that province to free themselves from proprietary rule may well serve as examples. Boone and Beresford presented a long list of reasons for such action by the crown which was received by the Board of Trade on October 10, 1717, and followed at once by a supplemental paper; another petition accompanied by a lengthy argument was presented on February 5, 1717/8; and then came a letter on February 24 begging consideration by the Board of previous communications. Francis Yonge, under date of June 5, 1719, presented the proprietors of South Carolina with a lengthy narrative of the events in South Carolina,[53] obviously drawn up by himself. Another classic document has already been alluded to. In 1697, Colonel Hartwell, who had answered a list of queries because he was too ill with the gout to walk or write, was not suffered to escape

---

[52] "Proceedings of the Virginia Committee of Correspondence," *loc. cit.*, XII, 6-7. Note might also be taken of the fact that a similar petition came from William Bollan and Christopher Kilby, agents for Massachusetts Bay, presented to the Board of Trade on April 27, 1748, praying for copies of the journals of the General Court of that province, from July 5, 1737, to February 14, 1746, which had been lost by fire. They also asked to secure from time to time copies of such other papers as might help to repair the loss sustained on that occasion.—*Journal of the Board of Trade*, 1741/2-1749, p. 281. The petition was granted.

[53] See C. O. 5/1318, pp. 323, 325, 337 for the papers of Boone and Beresford. For the paper presented by Yonge see *A Narrative of the Proceedings of the People of South Carolina*, II, no. 10.

with his direct replies, but along with the real agent, Dr. Blair, and Mr. Chilton, was informed a few weeks later that the Board did not doubt but "in a more free discourse without the confinement put upon you by thos Queries, you may be able to suggest other things to them of no less importance." Therefore, they were asked to draw up in writing a "full and plain" account of the whole public state of Virginia with regard to the royal and the people's interest.[54] It early crystalized into the usual procedure in a controversy of affording one party a reply to the strictures of the other party. Such procedure appeared early in New England but occurred also in the Southern colonies. For instance, in July, 1723, several complaints against Governor Nicholson mentioned in a certain memorial were ordered delivered to Yonge for his answer; and when complaints came from the receiver general of Virginia concerning Governor Spotswood's grants of land, searching questions were sent to both the governor and Agent Leheup for replies, the preparation of which must have cost the agent much time. Similar was the demand made of the two agents of South Carolina in 1729, as of Colonel Johnson, who was governor of the province, and of Captain Burrington, late governor of North Carolina, to put in writing, as soon as convenient, their opinions on certain questions with regard to the necessity of paper currency in that province.[55] *The Colonial Records of North Carolina* yield a long paper drafted by Abercromby in 1755 entitled, "Reasons in support of the Quit Rent Bill of North Carolina in answer to the Objections taken to the said Bill by Sir Matthew Lamb's Report to their Lordships [of Trade] on the said Bill."[56]

Writing of Pamphlets

To strengthen their case with the public, the agents did some extra writing; they sometimes prepared statements for publication as

[54] C. O. 5/1359, pp. 124-25, letter of Oct. 8, 1697, to Colonel Hartwell, Dr. Blair, and Mr. Chilton; alluded to in Chapter III.

[55] *Journal of the Board of Trade*, 1722/3-1728, pp. 38, 289. For the questions on a paper currency for South Carolina, see *ibid.*, 1728-1734, p. 35. The case in New England referred to occurred in 1697. The Earl of Arran petitioned for his claim to the Narragansett country. The Board of Trade ordered that copies of the order of the Privy Council referring the case to the Board of Trade and Arran's petition be sent to Major General Winthrop, Agent for Connecticut, and to Mr. Brenton, who is the only person known to have had deep interest in Rhode Island, that they might present in writing their reasons against granting the petition.—C. O. 391/10, p. 83.

[56] V, pp. 449-56.

pamphlets or in the newspapers of the day. During the pre-revolutionary struggle when sympathizers with the colonial opposition within and without parliament might be influenced by the public prints, this would appear a natural part of the agent's labors. It may prove surprising, however, to learn how early pamphlets appeared. The political pamphlet by Leonard Strong published in England in 1655 during the Commonwealth period is recalled as one of the first of this series, even if one includes the work of New England agents.[57] The pamphlet of 1706, bearing the name of John Ash, was a collection of assorted facts which went to prove Oldmixon's sweeping assertion of wrongs against the South Carolina settlers made only two years later. Though Ash died before he had finished his pamphlet, Joseph Boone assumed the task of convincing the proprietors of the justice of the dissenters' cause. It was he who enlisted in his cause the famous novelist and journalist, Daniel Defoe. Supplied vicariously with his material by the malcontent nonconformists, Defoe prepared two solid pamphlets, one of which he called *Party Tyranny*. As stated in the introduction, it contained an abridgment of *High Church Tyranny*. Both of these effusions and the pamphlet attributed to Ash were fiery and partisan.[58] Francis Yonge during 1726, the last year in which he held the full agency, published the pamphlet, *A Narrative of the Proceedings of the People of South Carolina in the Year 1719*, which deals almost exclusively with the events of the years 1719-1721.[59] The apologists for Rhett and Trott do not, of course, hold this account in high esteem. Colonel John Barnwell, after he had arrived in London, following the fashion, published a pamphlet in 1720, *An Account of the Golden Island*, showing the title of the Carolina proprietors to the territory between St. Augustine and South Carolina. In a letter from the Carolina Coffee House, he offered his testimony to the importance of the design.[60] Commanding more attention than any of the above pamphlets was a series of questions and answers on the state of Maryland which appeared in the British capital late in the colonial period. The *Questions* which were pub-

[57] The New England agents offered a number of pamphlets: Winslow, Mather, Ashurst etc.

[58] For comment see Snowden, *History of South Carolina*, I, 147.

[59] See *ibid.*, I, 193-94 for an analysis of this pamphlet.

[60] McCrady, *South Carolina under the Proprietary Government*, p. 577.

lished in the *London Chronicle* for September 16 to 19, 1758, were thought to be by Benjamin Franklin. The *Answers* were prepared by Governor Horatio Sharpe, if handwriting were to be a criterion, but disowned, when he heard from Cecilius Calvert, secretary to Lord Baltimore, that the latter had stigmatized the *queries* as impertinent and ridiculous and not worthy an answer.

The queries which would challenge our interest are numbered 25 to 28 inclusive but we can take time only for number 25. The query reads, "Whether they have any agent here to represent their complaints and justify their conduct?" The answer bears every earmark of being written by a royal devotee. It declared that if the people wanted an agent on the footing of a regular provincial agent, the council would not object, but the truth was, whatever the pretense, the lower house wanted "an Agent to serve themselves only."[61] Garth should be recognized as at least part author of a pamphlet which appeared very late. A pamphlet had been written by Sir Egerton Leigh, attacking Henry Laurens, entitled *Considerations on Certain Transactions of the Province of South Carolina*, which was published in January, 1774. Garth agreed to furnish material for a reply and consulted with Ralph Izard, a South Carolina planter, who, though loyal to America, was in London at this time, but the reply was prepared by Arthur Lee, a Virginian, who was, however, serving as assistant agent for Massachusetts at the time of publication, April 8, 1774. Laurens bore the expense, Garth provided the material, and Lee wrote the pamphlet, the reply of an American official to a Britisher who had attacked an American.[62]

[61] The lower house wanted an agent, it was asserted, to "insert Queries in London Chronicles, misrepresent the proceedings of the other Branches of Legislature or to harass the Proprietory whenever he may happen to disoblige a Leading Member & that they under pretense of paying their Agent & supplying him with Money for necessary purposes may have the Treasury at their own sole Disposal or at least as much Money without Account as they may be pleased to say is expedient for the Peoples Service."—*Maryland Historical Magazine*, XXXIII, 243. For the whole see pp. 228-47. The original manuscript of Sharpe's replies is now in the custody of the state: no. 7, portfolio 2, Hall of Records, Annapolis. Since this pamphlet concerns a Southern colony, it is felt necessary to include it.

[62] See "Izard-Laurens Correspondence," *South Carolina Historical and Genealogical Magazine*, XXII, no. 1, p. 3, note 6. For Izard see *D. A. B.*, IX, 524-25; for Laurens, *ibid.*, XI, 32-35. Incidentally, it might be noted that Arthur Lee wrote another pamphlet. In the spring of 1775, the lord mayor and aldermen of London presented in the name of its citizens to king and parliament a remonstrance against the colonial measures of the ministry. The action produced a sensation in England. The style and spirit of the remonstrance were greatly admired and it enjoyed a wide circulation. It developed

Appearances Before and Dealings with Other Boards

As was indicated at the beginning of this chapter, the agent was obliged to deal, from first to last, with a host of officials and boards—the Treasury Board, the Commissioners of the Customs, the Lords of the Admiralty, the Board of Ordnance—the Ordnance Office, as it was more generally termed—and the Lords Justices.

It is inevitable, of course, that the bulk of the transactions between the agents and the Treasury Board should relate to the reimbursements which were voted by parliament to the colonies in return for their aid in the colonial wars. Still, there arose some other matters which carried the agent to the door of the Treasury or led him to address that Board in writing. After the serious fire in Charleston in 1740 parliament granted £20,000 for resettling and reëstablishing the sufferers. Agent Fury applied to the Treasury Board for the issuance of that sum to the proper person or persons in order that it might be effectively distributed. Though the Treasury referred the matter to the Commissioners for Trade and Plantations, it was to the former body that the agent had to address himself to get action started.[63] When Crockatt was struggling to secure the sizable sum of £3,000 for South Carolina to be used for presents to the Indians in 1752 it was to the Treasury Board that he turned, though it must have been discouraging to find his application referred to the same old Board of Trade and Plantations.[64] Though the numerous entries of Benjamin Martyn's dealings with the Treasury Board refer to him as agent after February 6, 1753, the reader must remind himself that much of that gentleman's labor was still the continuation of his activities as secretary of the Georgia trust. It is, however, perhaps indicative of the changed status of the colony that these communications, too, were referred to the Board of Trade.[65] We find Garth approaching the Lords of the Treasury several times: on March 17, 1769, following up by a personal attend-

that Lee had written it at the request of the Common Hall.—Lee, *The Life of Arthur Lee*, I, 45-46.

[63] The letter passed from the secretary of the one body to the secretary of the other and is dated June 19, 1741.—C. O. 5/368, G, 50.

[64] *Journal of the Board of Trade*, 1749/50-1753, pp. 334-35.

[65] Such an entry at the Treasury Board for February 21, 1753, shows a record for the annual services and £1,000 to be drawn for the silk culture.—*Colonial Records of Georgia*, XXVI, 385; see also *Journal of the Board of Trade*, 1749/50-1753, p. 397.

ance a memorial to continue an act granting export of rice to any American port south of Georgia; and then in 1770 with his petition for a remission of part of the high duty on rice from the colonies. He reported to South Carolina with satisfaction his success in the latter interview, for the Lords of the Treasury proved ready to unite with him for such a bill for relaxation from the strict prohibition of the Navigation Acts to allow export to the foreign West Indies. This did represent a gain. Only a few months earlier this agent had been memorializing these same Lords to secure redress for the king's loyal subjects in South Carolina against the conduct of the revenue collector. They were ready to pass by any occasional grievances, he told their Lordships, that "might have proceeded from a Want of Official Knowledge or Information" but were "impatient of submitting to repeated Insults and obstinate Oprefsion, Conscious that such their Case is." Unfortunately, the records do not reveal whether his full confidence that it would appear in this light to their Lordships was justified.[66] Abercromby carried an application from the governor and council of Virginia to this Board for an aid to the tobacco revenue out of the quitrents when the public revenue of two shillings per hogshead granted in perpetuity for the support of government had fallen short, because of the war and the departure of settlers from the colony. The petition asked that £3,079, which had been paid from time to time from the tobacco revenue to the quitrent fund, might be replaced to meet public emergencies. But, even though Abercromby was sent for and plied with questions about the loan from the tobacco fund, and though he followed the matter up with a second petition rehearsing the facts, both to the Treasury and to the auditor general of the plantations, to whom the Treasury Board referred the petition, the agent complained that he met only with difficulty and delay.[67]

An interesting bypath led from the Treasury Board to the mint and to the master of the mint for Agent Garth. The colony had mentioned to the agent its desire to have £100 in half pence fresh

[66] "Garth Correspondence," loc. cit., XXXI, 143, 54, 57; Treasury Papers, T, 1/465, no. 261.

[67] Abercromby labored with the secretary of the Treasury Board to have the petition referred to the auditor general, as he hoped thus to give it a more favorable turn, judging from precedents he had found in the books of the auditor's office, but his hopes were evidently disappointed.—Abercromby Letter Book, pp. 105, 107; Treasury Papers, T, 1/389, nos. 107, 110.

from the mint sent to the treasurers in South Carolina so that they could call in some of the bad copper coin in circulation in Charleston. The Treasury Board signed an order to Garth upon the master of the mint for that sum. Naturally, he encountered difficulty at the mint because of previous contracts to deliver to other persons; however, the master of the mint promised to accommodate him in about a month's time. The agent added as a bit of advice that he felt there would be no difficulty in securing the coins if due notice were given so that the director of the mint could contract with the copper works for the necessary amount in addition to the usual annual supply.

It is no part of the purpose of the writer to trace in detail the negotiations of the agents with the Treasury Board for reimbursement of their military expenses, but a few entries may be permitted. Of course, they were just like flies around a honeypot, as soon as word began to circulate of the possibility of a grant of £200,000 for reimbursement. Wright petitioned to the Treasury for South Carolina's share of the grant; Franklin submitted the account of £327,851 as Pennsylvania's expenses to the end of the campaign of 1758, and an impressive total it was; Abercromby showed an expense account of £52,000 for Virginia on June 19, 1759; in rolled the pleas from New York, Massachusetts, Rhode Island, and New Jersey, besieging the Treasury for a sum adequate to their expenditures; Martyn looked out that Georgia should not be neglected.[68] Only North Carolina was backward for reasons which she rued—lack of an agent to look after her interests.

When colonial legislation was likely to touch the revenues from import dues, it was referred to the Commissioners of the Customs. Two Virginia acts, one for ports, and one for the advancement of manufactures in the colony were sent as early as 1692 to that body. It heard the arguments of the London merchants objecting to the measure and of several persons in behalf of it, among others the agent. The recommendation of this body for "revisal" of the laws won the support of the Board of Trade. In 1731, on the other hand, Agent Leheup complained to the Board of Trade that he was not given an opportunity to be heard by the Commissioners of Customs,

[68] Treasury Papers, T, I/376, E, 148; T, I/388, no. 106; T, I/388, no. 172; ibid., no. 79.

though he had attended them for that express purpose before they made their report to the Board of Trade against an act passed by Virginia to amend the staple of tobacco and prevent frauds in the customs. He then presented four and a half pages of argument in answer to the objections of the customs officials. When the latter body heard of Leheup's further arguments, they, of course, sought a copy and assailed them.[69]

It was inevitable from the nature of Colonel William Rhett's position as collector of customs at Charleston that Boone and Barnwell should have contact with the Commissioners of the Customs when they were bringing charges against the collector of violating the laws of trade and navigation by selling the Spaniards at St. Augustine military stores whereby they could better fit out privateers. The attention of the customs officials was drawn to the fact that customs officers under an old law of Henry VI should not be interested in foreign trade or own a ship or trading vessels.[70]

Naturally, when the agents knew that some other board, such as the Board of Trade, had called on the Customs Board for a report such as an account of the exports and imports to and from Spain and England to a given colony from 1750 to 1765, the agent would exert every influence to secure a report favorable to his cause. Garth tells us clearly the procedure when any alterations which would affect the revenue were proposed, at least as it existed in 1770. Such matters would, of course, go early to the Treasury Board, which would in turn always refer them to the Commissioners of the Customs whose opinion would generally carry great weight in determining the nature of the report of the Lords of the Treasury. It was therefore felt by Garth important to learn the ideas of the Collector of Customs, who influenced greatly the views of the Commissioners of Customs.[71]

Dealings with the Admiralty Board had to enter into the agent's calculations. This was true of the early agents, for it was there that they had to solicit the ships so urgently needed to protect the shores during King William's and Queen Anne's Wars. Blakiston, for

[69] Entry Book of the Board of Trade, C. O. 5/1358, pp. 162, 167-68 for 1692; C. O. 5/1322, ff. 95-99 for the case of 1731. For the attack by the customs commissioners on Leheup's arguments, dated Custom House, Feb. 27, 1730/1, see C. O. 5/1322, f. 99.
[70] Entry Book of the Board of Trade, C. O. 5/400, pp. 139-40; C. O. 5/382, Bundle 23.
[71] "Garth Correspondence," loc. cit., XXXI, 141.

instance, assured Virginia on October 4, 1708, that he would not fail to use his best endeavors for a ship to guard the coasts of that colony. Indeed, he found many Britishers surprised that the *Garland* had been ordered home after a stay of only six or seven weeks, when the admiralty knew the many disasters on that shore the preceding year for want of a guard ship.[72]

The ubiquitous Abercromby, of course, had dealings with the Admiralty. In May, 1757, although his letters came from neither the governor nor the Committee of Correspondence of North Carolina, though inclosing an address from the governor and council, he took it upon himself to solicit the Admiralty Board to reëstablish the Cape Fear station by sending a sloop of war. He was given to understand that a sloop, part of the Carolina convoy, had been ordered to the Cape Fear station. As advice came that very day of her capture by the enemy, an order was issued to Admiral Holborn to send one of his sloops. As the number of captures by the enemy had produced a great demand for regular convoys, he suggested the desirability of the North Carolina merchants using the same convoys with those of South Carolina or Virginia while their agent stood ready to bring their plans before the Admiralty Board.[73]

The relations of the agent with the Board of Ordnance much as with the Admiralty Board followed a routine. One of the early examples arises with the agent of a Northern colony.

Mr. John Champante, to whom we have had occasion to refer earlier as agent of New York, had been dealing with the Treasury as well as with the Ordnance Board in an effort to secure arms to be sent as presents to the Indians of the Five Nations. The Treasury had issued the order to the Board of Ordnances to provide long "Fuzes" (guns) to the value of £400, ammunition to the value of £100, and to provide clothes to the value of £300 before May 6, 1700. But by June 12 he had not overcome the difficulty of procuring from the Ordnance Board the type of light fusil ordered and was enlisting the aid of the Board of Trade. Possibly the impatience

[72] "Miscellaneous Colonial Documents," *Virginia Magazine of History and Biography,* XIX, 19.

[73] Abercromby Letter Book, p. 27. For a petition of Joseph Sherwood, agent of Rhode Island, dated December 7, 1759, concerning a deficiency of officers in the Court of Vice-Admiralty and inconveniences likely to result in consequence, see Admiralty Papers, I/3819.

of the Admiralty to know the cargo of arms for which they must provide shipping may have accelerated the action of the Ordnance Board.[74] The books of the Ordnance office show that by the direction of the Earl of Romney in June, 1702, eight barrels of powder and other military stores were sold for the use of Virginia and paid for by its agent, probably Byrd, to the treasurer of the Ordnance Board.[75]

Last to be named in the group of boards or commissions come the Lords Justices. This writer has found no evidence of dealings on the part of the agents with the Justices until late in colonial history, though that does not, of course, preclude the possibility of such dealings. There are allusions to petitions from Edmund Gray in 1752 and from Benjamin Martyn in 1753 relative to Georgia, referred to the Lords Justices, which suggest possible relations on the part of those two agents. And there is a notation by Abercromby which shows that he had been led at least to the study of certain orders of the Lords Justices.[76]

Indicative of the way in which the agent might have to deal with several boards all at the same time is Garth's report to South Carolina of July 6, 1766, on a clause which Governor Bull had suggested for regulation of the coasting vessels. The agent drew up a clause and attended the Boards of Trade and Treasury to solicit for it, but the Treasury was opposed to it; the Board of Customs, to which his papers were sent, failed to make any report on the subject; thereupon the Chancellor of the Exchequer wished him to postpone the matter until the next session.[77]

Relations with High Officials of State, Parliament, and the King

When the colonies grew to be important as pawns in the international relations with France and Spain, and when, fully grown, they dared to assert themselves against the mother country, their accredited spokesmen asked and secured audiences with the highest

[74] C. O. 391/13, pp. 32, 70, 74.

[75] This is shown by a letter from the Ordnance Office to the secretary of state under date, Nov. 24, 1711. C. O. 5/1316, f. 299.

[76] Letter of Thomas Hill to Richard Polanger, secretary to the Lords Justices, of July 21, 1752, C. O. 5/67, pp. 4-5; for Martyn's dealings, C. O. 5/646, Bundle C, 48; Abercromby to President Blair of the council, June 29, 1761, Abercromby Letter Book.

[77] "Garth Correspondence," *loc. cit.*, XXVIII, 232. Six months later he reported that the Commissioners of the Customs had reported unfavorably, apparently not understanding the nature of the application, and so he would try again with the Chancellor of the Exchequer.—*Ibid.*, XXIX, 130.

ranking officials of state. The cabinet member most nearly concerned with the colonial problems was the secretary of state for the colonies. Interviews, however, with the cabinet officials occurred throughout the history of the colonial agency. The reader finds Governor Nicholson writing to the Duke of Newcastle and almost casually remarking that if Francis Yonge had not already left London, he would desire him to wait on His Grace in order to give a complete account of all the affairs of South Carolina, as the governor had written him fully by every opportunity.[78] When Governor Gooch was involved in some embarrassment over appointment of a resident Englishman to a post in Virginia which had always been held by prominent colonials, he ordered Leheup to wait on the secretary of state in the hope that the agent could extricate him from the unpleasant situation.[79]

These interviews multiply as we approach the Revolution. The effort to secure a repeal of the Stamp Act brought the leaders among the agents, such men as Franklin, Garth, and DeBerdt of Massachusetts, into frequent contact with the chief secretaries of state. On February 10, 1766, Garth had a long interview with Secretary Conway to present the petitions to the king from South Carolina and Maryland. The petitions to be presented to the House of Commons offered some difficulties and led to a long discussion between Agent Garth and the secretary. The one from Maryland was open to the objection that it was signed by a committee and that it blurred the distinction between the power to tax and the power to levy duties. Hence, Secretary Conway feared that it would meet defeat. From the secretary Garth went straight to Lord Dartmouth, who was kindly disposed to the colonies, to ask the favor of his introduction and patronage of the petition in the House of Lords. Since the address had been put by South Carolinians in the form of a memorial rather than a petition, as was the case with the addresses to the king and to the Commons, his Lordship feared that the distinction would give great umbrage to the Lords. On this account—and the Peers made a distinction here of which we take little account today—some one would be sure to challenge it. Dartmouth, therefore, urged the agent to extract such parts of the petition as

[78] C. O. 5/387, p. 67. This letter is dated Aug. 25, 1724.
[79] C. O. 5/1337, f. 302.

had not been passed upon in the petition from Massachusetts two days earlier, and to present it as signed only by himself but approved by six sets of committees. Feeling unable to accept this suggestion, Garth adroitly drew up a *petition* to introduce the memorial, with which he waited upon Lord Dartmouth. At another interview the next morning his Lordship urged him not to press the addresses then in order not to hazard the loss of a single vote for repeal of the Stamp Act, for even if the motion for repeal was lost, he could apply later for an alteration of the act and for relief for the lower classes in America.

In about two weeks, on February 12, he had to wait on Secretary Conway again with a petition from the Assembly of Georgia and to notify him that the sentiments of this colony were uniform with those of the rest of the continent. Again, when Maryland had unanimously passed a resolution of gratitude to be presented by Garth to the Earl of Chatham, the Earl of Chesterfield, Lord Shelburne, Secretary Conway, and many others, the agent waited upon the high officials of the government mentioned to assure them, in the words of the Maryland resolution, that "their memories will be endeared by their benevolence and regard to British America."[80] Gratitude toward Pitt went still farther, as the reader knows, in South Carolina, and expressed itself in the determination to erect a statue in his honor. When Garth informed Pitt of that fact, the latter desired to be quoted as saying that he was highly sensible of the honor and would retain a grateful sense of so distinguishing a mark of their good opinion and restated his view of the relation of the colonies to the mother country.[81]

Sometimes, as when the secretary of state was displeased with the action of a colony,[82] the agent must have been glad to make his escape from the mighty person's presence. Interviews with

[80] For Garth's detailed account of his interviews with these men see "Garth Correspondence," *loc. cit.*, XXVI, 86-87, 90. His report to the Maryland Committee of the House of Delegates dated March 5, was in almost identical language. See "Stamp Act Papers," *Maryland Historical Magazine*, VI, 289-90; Edgar, *A Colonial Governor in Maryland*, p. 226 for the resolution of thanks.

[81] "Garth Correspondence," *loc. cit.*, XXIX, 121.

[82] Such a case occurred in July, 1767, when the secretary was displeased over the suspension of Chief Justice Skinner by South Carolina. As a wise measure of precaution, Garth left with the Board of Trade a duplicate of the report of the Committee of Correspondence about this justice's conduct.—*Ibid.*, pp. 298-99.

Hillsborough are recorded by Garth, when this would appear to be the case.

Occasionally, far more rarely than with the secretary of state, audiences were secured with other members of the cabinet. Crockatt, for instance, waited several times in 1750 on the Honorable Henry Fox, secretary of war, in an effort to remove objections raised by interested parties to certain of the agents' proposals; Garth talked with the Chancellor of the Exchequer on the subject of a currency bill for South Carolina and had the satisfaction to find him favorably inclined to it, but found him averse to relaxing the restrictions of the navigation laws. On another occasion he secured an interview with that same official to discuss the coasting trade. The records also show interviews with the auditor general asked for by Abercromby, when he was soliciting in 1759 a refund to the tobacco revenue from the quitrents.[83]

Dealings with the attorney and the solicitor general were apparently more numerous than with the officials just named, as was perhaps natural in view of the fact that an important part of the agents' work related to colonial legislation. Clearly a greater informality on the part of the agent in dealing with the various boards was tolerated in the early period than later, for John Champante in 1701 was allowed to take away personally from the solicitor general's office some acts of the Massachusetts assembly, though he was agent for New York, which he delivered to the Board of Trade with the report of the solicitor.[84] It would appear that Abercromby in 1759 "took" the attorney general's opinion upon the agency law under which the House of Burgesses had set up their own agent. Undoubtedly, Abercromby was concerned about his own status as agent of the colony and was relieved to find that in the eyes of the highest legal official in England the authority of the governor and council "acting in their State capacity [by which he must have meant appointing an agent] remains entire." Hence, he could continue in their service as agent.[85] In a rare instance, Agent Knox was directed in

---

[83] See letter of Crockatt to Bedford, Oct. 22, 1740; C. O. 5/374; "Garth Correspondence," loc. cit., XXIX, 130; Abercromby Letter Book, p. 182.

[84] C. O. 391/13, p. 358, session of the Board of Trade of February 13, 1700/1. There must have been something in the laws affecting New York or constituting a precedent, for they had been passed at the session begun May 29, 1700.

[85] Abercromby Letter Book, p. 184.

1763 to consult in advance the attorney and the solicitor general as to the validity of a certain law which Georgia was considering.[86]

There are a few cases where agents appeared before a committee of the House of Commons or even at the bar of the House itself. Abercromby in behalf of North Carolina, Wright for South Carolina, and Montague for the lower house of Virginia appeared before a committee of the Commons in coöperation with the merchants of Britain against a certain petition. After the agents had been heard five times, the petition was dismissed. Even where the agents did not have dealings with the Commons as a body, they sought out individual members. Abercromby said frankly to his friend John Blair in a letter dated March 31, 1758, while opposing a salt monopoly in America, that if the group of agents which was fighting the grant were defeated in the parliamentary committee, they would apply to be heard by counsel before the House of Commons. When it was proposed to give the surveyor general of the woods the power of vice-admiralty courts, reasons against such a grant of power were placed by the agents in the hands of several members of parliament.[87]

Sir Henry Ashurst, agent for Connecticut and Massachusetts, fought an act to vacate the colonial charters, requesting the House of Lords to be heard by counsel, a request which the peers granted. Throughout the dispute he was present in person at all the hearings. Jahleel Brenton, agent of Rhode Island, bestirred himself actively against this bill so that on one occasion he along with some others was ordered to attend the House of Lords. The classic example is, of course, the appearance of Benjamin Franklin at the bar of the House of Commons in connection with the Stamp Act controversy.

[86] Habersham, *Letters*, p. 14. Naturally, the agents consulted repeatedly with the counsel of the Board of Trade who were during the period of greatest activity by the agents, Sir Matthew Lamb and Mr. Richard Jackson. Abercromby and Peyton Randolph attended Mr. Lamb in December, 1754, on an Account for docking Entails.—*Journal of the Board of Trade*, 1754-1758, p. 90, C.O. 5/1328, p. 307; Garth had a conference with Mr. Jackson in 1770.—"Garth Correspondence," *loc. cit.*, XXXIII, 118-19. The above are a few instances only.

[87] For the action of the three agents against the petition see Abercromby Letter Book, p. 97; for action against the salt monopoly, *ibid.*, p. 93; for reasons concerning extending the powers of the surveyor general of the woods, covering two pages in all, see Rawlinson MSS, C, 379, pp. 26-27, 30-31; *Journal of the Board of Trade*, 1768-1775, p. 239.

A few of the agents are conspicuous for actually securing interviews with his majesty, the king. As one recalls the long roll of some two hundred agents, including for the moment all the colonies, one is impressed with the fact that it was the agents on special missions, usually men distinguished in their own colonies, who succeeded in coming face to face with the sovereign. The list is not long. Increase Mather should be noted; during his years of service in England as agent of Massachusetts Bay, he was sent to secure relief from the administration of Governor Andros and stayed to secure a satisfactory charter. Despite the fact that he was a leading Puritan divine from the stronghold of New England Puritanism, he secured no less than five personal audiences with the Catholic King James II to present his case against Andros; perhaps he won favor by praising the king's Declaration of Indulgence. He also succeeded in having one audience with Queen Mary and several with King William, to whom presumably he might look for sympathy, as both sovereigns were Protestant.[88] Although Ashurst was influential at court, there is no evidence of his seeking an interview with the king over colonial affairs. Among the agents of the Southern colonies only three appear to have entered the royal presence. The Reverend Mr. Blair secured audiences with both King William and Queen Mary, as has been related in the third chapter. Philip Ludwell was afforded an opportunity, as he distinctly tells us, to present the address of the Virginia burgesses against their governor to the king in person. His Catholic Majesty would seem to have been unwontedly gracious in admitting colonials—New England Puritan and Virginia Cavalier alike. The only other Southern agent who seems to have made his way into the royal presence was Charles Garth, who presented a petition of humble gratitude to George III from the assembly of South Carolina for repeal of the Stamp Act. After the usual preliminaries on September 2, 1766, which included calling on Lord Shelburne in order to arrange for the audience, he had, the next morning as Garth was pleased to put it, the "Honor to kiss his Majesty's Hand," and to present the address.[89]

[88] *Calendar of State Papers, Colonial,* 1685-1688, p. 593. See also Murdock, *Increase Mather,* and Burns, *The Colonial Agents of New England,* pp. 40-41.
[89] "Garth Correspondence," *loc. cit.,* XXIX, 43-44.

CHAPTER 7.

THE COMMITTEES OF CORRESPONDENCE

TRUE to Anglo-Saxon methods of conducting legislative business, the various colonies set up committees from the parent body, the legislature, or the lower house to correspond with the agent. There were, naturally, exceptions and variations in their organization and procedure in the various colonies. In the irregular situation which existed in Virginia prior to 1759, the chief executive usually wrote and received the letters from the person who was serving as agent of the governor and council. In the early years of the agency in Maryland, the assembly ordered the Committee of Laws to prepare and send the letters to Colonel Blakiston.[1] But later on this colony fell in line with the accepted and natural procedure of all the other colonies and created a Committee of Correspondence. The committee created in South Carolina in September, 1721, continued with very little revision until 1776. During the last few years of its existence its members were drawn almost entirely from the lower house and were entirely under its control. Sometimes another committee or the entire house might issue instructions through the Committee of Correspondence. No distinction in name appears whether the committee was the organ of the entire legislature or was functioning merely for the lower house. In the late colonial period the lower house controlled the agent in South Carolina, North Carolina, and Georgia even when that body did not have a separate agent. When the Revolution broke out, South Carolina used this committee to correspond with the other colonies; no new committee or machinery was held necessary as it was, for instance, in Virginia.

The number held requisite on the committee varied greatly from colony to colony and from one period to another in the same colony. Sometimes the number was surprisingly large. Where the agent represented the entire legislature, representatives from both bodies

[1] *Archives of Maryland*, XXX, 596.

sat on the committee. The smallest number which the author has encountered was in South Carolina in 1714 where three men constituted the membership.[2] In this province the number ranged later from eight in 1724 to twenty-one in 1762. The ordinance of 1762 provided for a committee of four from the council, the speaker, and such as the lower house "might choose." It chose to appoint seventeen members.[3] In the early years the proportional representation between the two houses was adjusted with greater equality than later. For instance, in 1724 three of the eight members in South Carolina were drawn from the council while five came from the lower house.[4] As the numbers rose, an increasing proportion was claimed by the lower house. In 1762 one is almost startled at the distribution; only four of the total of twenty-one represented the council. Very often it was stipulated that the speaker must be of the number. When the membership was small, a majority constituted the quorum; three members of the five in this colony had to be present in 1712 or two of the three in 1714 to transact business;[5] but as the number rose, the quorum declined proportionately. The rule in 1762 when the membership was so very large illustrates this, for nine, or less than half, constituted a quorum. Also in 1756 five constituted a quorum when the committee consisted of sixteen men.[6] All the council members together could not constitute a quorum, though assembly members did have power to meet and do business without a single member of the council being present. This was precisely the way the committee here functioned, for there were many reports and letters dispatched to and received from the agent concerning which the governor and council were kept in ignorance. The committee probably felt that they had scored on the executive when they complained through Agent Garth about Governor Boone's conduct in the Gadsden case and when they lodged complaints with Secretary Shelburne against Chief Justice C. J. Skinner.[7]

[2] McCrady, *South Carolina under the Proprietary Government*, p. 517; *Statutes at Large of South Carolina*, II, 621.

[3] *Ibid.*, IV, 164; Journal of the Commons House of Assembly of South Carolina, XXXV, 121.   [4] *Ibid.*, VII, 147.

[5] *Statutes of South Carolina*, II, 601; III, 621.

[6] *Ibid.*, IV, 164; Journal of the Commons House of Assembly of South Carolina, XXXV, 121.

[7] Smith, *South Carolina as a Royal Province*, p. 170. The Gadsden case was a disputed election case under the law of 1721.—*Ibid.*, pp. 340-47. The assembly brought

North Carolina created committees varying slightly in number, usually eight or nine, though the number which directed Abercromby one year seems to have been only five.[8] As was the case in South Carolina, the Commons House insisted on an ever larger proportion; contented with three members in the earlier period of the regular agency, it demanded five out of eight in 1769, and seven out of nine in 1771. A majority of the entire committee was usually stipulated as a quorum, or, as an extra precaution in 1769, a majority of the survivors of those named.[9]

In Maryland, oddly enough, the number declined; a committee of nine, called trustees, was thought necessary in 1739 properly to direct Ferdinand Paris, but five and six seemed sufficient to correspond with Garth in 1765 and 1769, with three empowered to act in the latter year during a recess of the assembly.[10]

Relatively small at first, twelve in 1762, the Georgia committee rose to seventeen in 1773 and so continued to the end of the provincial period. When the smaller number prevailed, the committee included the president of the council, four councillors, and the speaker in addition to six other members from the lower house. Seven were held to constitute a quorum, which must include two councillors and five of the house. When the total membership was seventeen, the quorum was nine, to include two councillors and seven of the house. However, when the membership consisted of fourteen, as it did in 1763, 1768, and 1770, seven availed as a quorum, five of whom had to be of the lower house. The committee was thus heavily weighted in favor of the house, which was regarded as more directly representing the people.[11] The law appointing Franklin agent in 1768 provided for a quorum by curious phraseology: if any of the members "refuse or neglect the summons

---

charges against Chief Justice Skinner in 1766 of ignorance of the law and of general misconduct, but the real reason may have been that he tried to execute the Stamp Act. For a fuller discussion see *ibid.*, pp. 356-57.

[8] C. O. 324/60, p. 283.

[9] *Colonial Records of North Carolina*, III, 277 (for 1731); XI, 229-30 (for 1769). In 1731 four, or just half, of the committee was authorized to draw up an address. For 1771 see *ibid.*, XI, 237.

[10] Journal of the House of Deputies of Maryland, 1762-1768, pp. 354, 536. For the number in 1769 see *ibid.*, 1769-1774, p. 45.

[11] *Colonial Records of Georgia*, XVIII, 482-83, 537; XIX, pt. 1, p. 250; C. O. 324/60, pp. 312, 330.

to a meeting of the committee," seven were vested with power to act. The personnel in Georgia remained much the same from 1768 to 1770. In 1770 Franklin was directed in rather odd fashion to address his communications to the member first named in the agency law, James Habersham, as it happened, and to the other members of the committee.[12]

In Virginia, the Old Dominion, we are properly concerned at this point only with the committee created on April 5, 1759, when the separate agent for the House of Burgesses was created. The number was fixed at twelve. Leave was given on May 30, 1763, for a bill to add sundry persons to the committee because of the death of one of the members and because of the great problem of attendance for several of the others who resided at a remote distance from the capitol. Hence four more were added to the committee, vested with the same power and "liable for any misdemeanour to sensure of the General Assembly."[13] It is deeply significant that to direct this agent and spokesman of the lower house, the council was allowed four members on the committee, a fact which accounts, largely, for acceptance of the bill by the council.

More important than the numbers on the committees was the caliber of the men selected and consenting to serve. Without hesitation it may be asserted that they were able men, among the best the colonies afforded. From the very nature of the work to be performed, the members needed to be selected with care. The qualifications called for were severe: they needed to be men of high, strong character, not afraid to speak out for the colony; they must be broad-minded with an understanding of the economic and political problems of America and, in particular, of their own colony; they needed to know Great Britain, and, if the empire were to be preserved, to be loyal to it; they required good, sound judgment; in order to carry weight in Britain, they should be men of standing in the colony—in short, the leaders, which meant, of course, men of liberal education and men of property; and finally, and above all, they must be faithful to the interests of the people of the province.

[12] Colonial Records of Georgia, XIX, pt. 1, pp. 13, 200.
[13] Hening, Statutes, VII, 276, 646-47; Journals of the House of Burgesses, 1761-1765, p. 193; C. O. 324/60, pp. 253-54. The additional members of the committee were impartially chosen from the two houses so that now six councillors and ten burgesses sat on the committee.

Exactly the type indicated above was to be found among the delegates in the two houses of the legislative assemblies, and it was usually these leaders who were named to the Committee of Correspondence. After 1765 new men, as is well known, came to the fore, and most of the members of these committees became more radical, forwarding the revolutionary movement, which they conceived to be for the deepest interest of the people, as they had formerly sought to promote their interests by peaceful means.

To the person acquainted with the colonial history of Virginia, a bare perusal of the names of the committee members during the period 1759-1773 will suffice to reveal the caliber of the leadership. Let us start baldly with the personnel in 1763 when the number had been brought to sixteen by the addition of four men to the original committee of twelve appointed in 1759. Three of the six members from the council served at one time or another as president of the council; one of these three so distinguished, Thomas Nelson, was also at the same time secretary of state and the other two, John Blair and William Nelson, served as acting governor each at various times.[14] All six had rendered long public service. Two of the ten burgesses, John Robinson and Peyton Randolph, had presided or would later preside over the house as speaker; the former, indeed, had already, before accepting service on this committee, been both speaker and treasurer of Virginia for no less than twenty-one years. One of the other committee members, Robert C. Nicholas, was to be honored by his fellows by being made treasurer of the colony of Virginia.[15] Peyton Randolph, already attorney general, will be discussed in another chapter with the agents. Two others of this committee, Richard Bland and George Wythe, sat later in the Continental Congress under Randolph; two, Thomas Nelson and George Wythe, signed the Declaration of Independence; Wythe be-

[14] For clarity it seems desirable to list this group of men who served the colony in this capacity so long and honorably. *Members from the Council:* William Nelson, Thomas Nelson, Philip Grymes, Peter Randolph, John Blair (added in May, 1763), Robert Carter Nicholas (added in May, 1763). *Members from the House of Burgesses:* Charles Carter, Richard Bland, Landon Carter, Benjamin Waller, John Robinson, Peyton Randolph, George Wythe, Robert Carter Nicholas, Lewis Burwell (added May, 1763), Dudley Digges (added May, 1763).

[15] For the membership of that year see Hening, *Statutes*, VII, 276-77, 646-47. Robinson continued in both posts until his death in 1766, though his administration of the provincial funds ended in financial disaster to his estate, for he was found to have defaulted about £200,000, much of it loaned to friends.

came professor of law at the College of William and Mary, and Nicholas later served on the Virginia High Court of Chancery. A brief recapitulation of the scholastic training of this group of sixteen proves that they could qualify as men of liberal education. John Blair, nephew of the Reverend James Blair, had been educated at the institution founded by his uncle; William Nelson and Robert Carter Nicholas had received their training at the same place, as had Peter Randolph and John Robinson. Peyton Randolph had passed from the provincial college to study at the Temple in London; Thomas Nelson had spent three years at Cambridge. Richard Bland had polished off the best training Virginia had to offer, according to some accounts, with study at the University of Edinburgh; and Landon Carter is thought to have studied in England.[16] William Nelson and Robert Carter Nicholas were known for their earnest devotion to the church. Wythe, with a record of eleven years in the lower house of assembly, was selected to draw up for Virginia the Remonstrance to the British House of Commons against the Stamp Act and was sent to the First Continental Congress.[17] At least six of the burgesses who served on the committee during these years were members of the lower house for over fourteen years, while four of the six served twenty-seven, thirty, thirty-three, and forty-two years respectively. The requisites of experience, age, and long public service gave promise of wisdom in dealing with the mother country.[18] A committee of greater dignity and information was not to be assembled in Virginia.

A study of the membership of the Maryland committee for the last decade before the revolt also substantiates the view of unusual ability of the personnel. Outstanding in the group who served this province during the last decade of colonial history is Colonel Edward Tilghman. A distinguished lawyer of Queen Anne County, who sat for many years in the assembly, he rose to be speaker one

[16] See *D. A. B.*, for sketches of Blair, Nelson, Robert C. Nicholas, and Bland. See also the note to "Proceedings of Virginia Committee of Correspondence," *loc. cit.*, IX, 357.

[17] *Ibid.*, pp. 586-89; Herrink, "George Wythe," *The John P. Branch Historical Papers of Randolph-Macon College*, III, 283-313. Wythe's was the first chair of law in an American college. He was also chancellor of the state of Virginia.

[18] For notes on the members of the Virginia Committee see "Proceedings of the Virginia Committee of Correspondence, 1759-1767," *loc. cit.*, IX, 355-59. The four men alluded to were Peyton Randolph, Robinson, Bland, and Digges. The notes are not altogether reliable, as the statement that John Blair was educated in Scotland is not correct.

session and was sent to New York in 1765 as a member of the Stamp Act Congress.[19]   Even more distinguished was his second cousin, Matthew Tilghman, who represented Talbot County in the Maryland assembly for thirteen years and sat for Queen Anne County in the session of 1760-1761.   In 1773 and 1774 he presided over the House of Delegates.   Throughout the Revolution he played a leading part in the affairs of Maryland, heading every delegation sent to the Continental Congress until he was summoned home to help prepare a new form of government for his state.[20]   Occurring almost as often in the annals of Maryland are the names of Thomas Ringgold, who was named to the Committee of Correspondence in 1765, 1768, and 1769; of William Murdock, who played his rôle as a delegate in the lower house for many years and as a leading spirit in the protest against the British scheme of taxation;[21] and of Thomas Johnson, who served repeatedly on the committee during the years when the controversy between the two houses over the appropriation for an agent was hottest and who was to serve his compatriots during the Revolutionary period with such distinction that he was chosen first governor of the new state of Maryland.[22]

Preëminent among the members of the Committee of Correspondence, as they were in the late history of colonial Georgia, loom the names of James Habersham, Noble Jones, his more distinguished son, Noble Wymberley Jones, and Joseph Ottolenghe.   It is noteworthy that Habersham, the two Joneses, father and son, and James Edward Powell served on the committee continuously from 1768 until 1773, when Habersham ended his service.   The other two served beyond that date.   Ottolenghe is identified with the effort to build up the silk culture in Georgia and was prominent in the colony's counsels from 1752.[23]   James Habersham brought the richest pos-

[19] For Colonel Edward Tilghman, see D. A. B., article on his son, XVIII, 542; Tilghman, Talbot County, Maryland, I, 423-32.

[20] See "Tilghman Family," Maryland Historical Magazine, I, 370-71; Andrews, Tercentenary History of Maryland, IV, 859-60; D. A. B., XVIII, 543-44.

[21] Journal of the Lower House of Maryland, 1762-1768, pp. 354, 536; 1769-1774, p. 45.   For Ringgold and Murdock see National Cyclopedia, XIII, 459.

[22] For Thomas Johnson see Delaplaine, Life of Thomas Johnson, pp. 39-40, passim; Andrews, Tercentenary History of Maryland, IV, 903-7; Scharf, History of Western Maryland, I, 389-92; Williams, History of Frederick County, Maryland, I, 101-7, D. A. B., X, 121-22.   He displayed as governor such sound judgment that Washington offered him in succession the posts of secretary of state, commissioner of the Federal City, and of justice of the highest court, on which he sat until 1793.

[23] Colonial Records of Georgia, XIX, pt. 1, pp. 13, 200, 250; XIII, 731.

sible background of experience to his work on the committee, for he had migrated to the infant colony only five years after its founding, and his prominence in the colony can scarcely be exaggerated as he held many of its highest offices—those of councillor, secretary, president of the council, and acting governor during Governor Wright's absence in 1771.[24] Reared in Georgia, to which colony his father had moved early in its existence, Noble Wymberley Jones was the owner of a princely estate and so very naturally entered the Commons House of Assembly in 1755, where he served almost without interruption till the Revolution, part of the time as speaker.[25] The research student notes a few other names which still mean something in Georgia history: that of John Milledge, who appeared in the first provincial assembly in 1751, where he soon emerged as a leader; and of Grey Elliott, who was later to receive instructions as agent for Georgia instead of drafting them.[26]

In South Carolina a list of the members who served on the Committee of Correspondence is a roll call of the families prominent in the history of that province: Wragg, Pinckney, Barnwell, Fenwick, Izard, and Bull; Laurens, Guerard, Lloyd, and Gadsden. Already in an early committee, that of 1722, occurs the name of Colonel John Barnwell, himself an agent who had served the colony as recently as 1720 and who was soon to be cut off by death from further service. A similar procedure to utilize the experience of a returned agent was followed when John Lloyd, just returned in mid-January, 1722/3, from his mission, was added to the Committee of Correspondence within a month.[27] In 1724 the council contributed Ralph Izard and William Bull;[28] in 1739 the lower house selected among its group of seven to direct the agent Mr. Rutledge and Dr. William Bull.[29] Peter Manigault, placed on the committee in 1746,

[24] D. A. B., VIII, 68-70. [25] Ibid., pp. 196-97.

[26] Ibid., XI, 617 under the article on John Milledge, Jr.

[27] Journal of the Commons House of Assembly of South Carolina, VI, 25, 160.

[28] Ibid., VII, 147, 148. The Bull family contributed many outstanding figures to the political life of South Carolina. This William Bull seems to have been the one designated in genealogical accounts as William Bull I. He served in the lower house from 1705 to 1719 and in the council from 1721 to 1737, and acted as lieutenant governor from 1738 to his death in 1755, though his administration as acting governor lasted only until the arrival of Governor Glen in 1743.

[29] This William Bull is distinguished by genealogists as William Bull II, though by virtue of his medical title he is easily distinguishable. He studied medicine at Leyden but

brought to the work the rich background of study at the Inner Temple, practice of the law, travel on the Continent, and management in South Carolina of the interests of several London business firms. He was, no doubt, to profit from his experience on the committee when serving as speaker from 1765 to his resignation in 1772.[30] The services of Henry Laurens, whose name appears on the committee entries from 1766 to 1767, do not require repetition here, but the facts that he rose to be president of the Continental Congress and was dispatched on a mission to the Dutch are indicative of his caliber.[31]

After the middle of the century reappointment seems to have been rather the rule. Manigault and Thomas Smith, who served in 1754, were reappointed in 1756; Pinckney, Masyck, Manigault, Colonel Middleton, and Charles Pinckney appear in the committee list of 1762 as well as in that of 1757.[32] It is also to be noted that sometimes the method of utilizing experience in connection with the agency was reversed: instead of placing returned agents on the committee, men who had served on the committee were sent as agents. Cases in point are those of Colonel John Fenwick, who had served years before his agency as a committee member in 1723; Charles Pinckney, who served in 1746, though his agency was not until 1753-1756; and Colonel Alexander Vander Dusen, whose agencies were in 1743, 1748, and 1754, and who had sat on the committee in 1746.[33]

Among this array of legislator-committeemen, are to be found Carolina's best—a chief justice, an attorney general, speakers of the Commons House of Assembly, and a onetime lieutenant governor.

---

followed the profession of politics rather than medicine. He sat in the lower house steadily from 1736 to 1749, presiding over it for seven years, 1740-1742 and 1744-1749. He passed to the council in 1749, where he sat until he was appointed lieutenant governor in 1759. For his appointment to the Committee of Correspondence on November 10, 1739, see Journal of the Commons House of Assembly of South Carolina, Sept. 12, 1739-May 10, 1740, p. 125. For William Bull I, see *D. A. B.*, III, 252; for William Bull II, *ibid.*, pp. 252-53. The manuscript records merely "Mr. Rutledge."

[30] Journal of the Commons House of Assembly of South Carolina VI, 160; *D. A. B.*, XII, 234-35. He died in England in 1773 whither he had gone in search of health.

[31] *D. A. B.*, XI, 32-35.

[32] See *Statutes of South Carolina*, IV, 26; *South Carolina Historical and Genealogical Magazine*, XXVIII, 88; Smith, "Wilton's Statue of Pitt," *ibid.*, XV, 22.

[33] Journal of the Commons House of Assembly of South Carolina, VI, 160; XXI, 625, 614. Note, however, that Vander Dusen had had an earlier agency in 1742.

As in Virginia, these men tended to become more radical as they approached the Revolution. As a single illustration it might be recalled that John Rutledge, who served on the Committee of Correspondence in 1762 and 1766, was chairman of the committee which drew up the address to the House of Lords for the Stamp Act Congress, although all his traditions of family, study at the Temple, and admission to the English bar should have made him a Tory. His later distinguished services to his state and to the formation of the Union belong to another story.[34]

There remains judicial appraisal of the caliber of the members of the North Carolina Committee of Correspondence. Here one encounters as committee members prominent during the decade after 1748 John Swann and his brother Samuel Swann, John Starkey, and John Ashe. Eleazar Allen, who died in 1750 and hence barely enters our story, had been prominent in the affairs of this Southern province in its early days despite his New England birth because of his excellent education and business qualifications. He was a member of the council from November 2, 1734.[35] First appearing in the lower house in 1739, John Starkey soon had won a place in the leadership of that body and was placed on the Committee of Correspondence in 1748; here again is a man who served continuously in the lower house until his death in 1765, a period of twenty-seven years, and who was also treasurer for the southern counties fourteen years.[36]

It is impossible to delve far into the history of North Carolina without encountering the names of John and Samuel Swann. The former first served on the Committee of Correspondence for the lower house in 1748. His name appears again in 1761 as an appointee from the council, to which he had been transferred in 1752. Far more important, however, was his brother, Samuel Swann, who served in the lower house for forty years, as speaker for nearly

[34] John Rutledge served in the Commons House of Assembly first in 1761 and represented the colony in the provincial bodies until the Revolution seated him in the gubernatorial chair. He knew how to make himself acceptable to the many merchants as well as to the planters. For a brief account of his life and services see *D. A. B.*, XVI, 258-60.

[35] Allen died in 1750. He graduated from Harvard University in 1726 at the age of thirty-four, returning from Charleston to Boston for the purpose. He did not move to North Carolina until about 1734. See *Biographical History of North Carolina from Colonial Times to the Present*, V, 1-7. For the composition of the committee see Swann, *A Collection of North Carolina Laws*, p. 278.

[36] For data on Starkey's life see *Biographical History of North Carolina*, V, 379-82.

twenty years—until 1762, when he declined reëlection. His qualities of bold leadership are sufficiently attested when it is recorded that he was frequently chosen to represent counties in which he did not reside.[37]   Cornelius Harnett was another member of long and honorable service, sitting, as he did, in the lower house for twenty-seven years in all; there were few committees of importance on which he did not serve, few measures on which he was not consulted.[38]

In 1758, when the lower house appointed its own agent, it created its own committee to direct him and then appear new names. There could scarcely be a more striking illustration of the importance of this committee than one which the lower house constituted, consisting of Speaker Swann, his two nephews—John Ashe and George Moore—and Treasurer Starkey, stigmatized by Governor Dobbs as a "junta."   Through the agent this group really conducted the affairs of the colony in London.   Most arresting is the name of John Ashe, who succeeded to the seat of his uncle and guardian, John Swann, when the latter moved to the upper chamber.   Always active in the counsels of the assembly and rising steadily in importance, he succeeded Samuel Swann in 1762 to the speakership.[39]   In 1769 appear the names of Lewis Henry de Rossett, Alexander McCulloh, John Harvey—prominent for thirty years in this colony, first appearing in the assembly in 1746, elected speaker in 1766—and

[37] For further details on Speaker Swann see *North Carolina Colonial Records*, IX, Introduction, pp. xxxviii-xlvii. Governor Johnston complained that he told the house what to do from the chair.   He was speaker from 1742 to 1762 except for two years.   Thomas Barker was also on the Committee of Correspondence.

[38] Few early statesmen of North Carolina have a more interesting record than does Harnett.   Born in 1723(?) probably in Chowan County of an Irish father, he early became identified with the Cape Fear settlement, residing in Wilmington from 1750 to his death in 1787.   In the long contests between the governor and the assembly he was against encroachment of the royal prerogative.   In the Regulator movement, however, he upheld the governor in suppressing the disorders in the interior and was awarded £100 by the assembly for his expenses in the campaign.   He led the movement in the assembly to create a Committee of Correspondence to deal with the other colonies and became one of its nine members.   He was the master spirit in the Wilmington Committee of Safety and also of the New Hanover Committee of Safety.   He was sent by the colony as delegate to the Continental Congress from June, 1777, to 1780.   For a fuller account see *Biographical History of North Carolina*, II, 152-62 and *D. A. B.*, VIII, 279-80.

[39] John Ashe first succeeded Swann as speaker, serving from 1762 to 1765, and then Starkey as treasurer.   He became a leader in the Stamp Act agitation and in the Revolution. He also had a military career, first as an officer of militia in the French War and then in the Revolutionary War.   One of the first to begin the revolt, he died before Cornwallis' surrender.—*Biographical History of North Carolina*, IV, 36-52.

Joseph Montfort, representatives of families which have had a distinguished place in the history of the Old North State.[40]

To sum up then the evidence which justifies the conclusion that men of the first importance served on the Committee of Correspondence, thus bearing witness to the importance of the office: the speaker was pretty regularly of the membership; the service was regarded as of sufficient importance to command the attention of some members for long years of service; some colonies wisely utilized the experience of members who had served on the committee as special agents, and, conversely, placed agents after their return on the committee; and, finally, the personnel changed with the times so that more radical spirits took charge of these committees as they did of the general affairs of the colonies as matters drifted toward the Revolution.

Reappointment to the committee was, to say the least, common. In Virginia, as has already been noted, members served under reappointment for very long periods; the records of South Carolina show reëlections for four, six, and even seven terms. In Georgia, where the term was short, members were sometimes reappointed before expiration of the term of office unless there was reason for a change. In North Carolina the same names reappear again and again, not only for the representatives of the council but also for the members from the lower house.

As we approach the period of sharp conflict, the question of whether the committee could continue to function in the face of hostility and prorogation by the governor naturally becomes important. Interestingly enough, we have an explicit statement on the subject from members of the South Carolina house to their agent. Writing to Charles Garth, on November 20, 1772, they say: ". . . when the Members are nominated, they are, by the Act, a Committee, and, nothing but a Dissolution, which makes them no longer Members, or an Appointment of others by the House, puts an end to the Committee of Correspondence. Even a Dissolution, we submit, would be no Bar to the receiving a Complaint made by the express

[40] Colonel John Harvey proved another leader in the eventful times preceding the Revolution. His first appearance in public life was as a member of the assembly in 1746, but it was not until 1754 when full representation was restored to the northern counties that he could regularly represent his county. For thirty years he was a prominent actor in the struggle against royal government. He and Speaker Swann were congenial, bold spirits. In 1766 he was elected speaker, which post he filled with one interruption only until the close of the royal regime.—*Colonial Records of North Carolina*, IX, xlv-xlvii.

Order of the House, against a Governor, because it would, then, be in his Power, to prevent one ever being made against him. . . ."[41]

Much earlier that colony had tried to protect their committee against possibility of disruption by the governor or some agency outside their control. In the law of 1714 setting up the committee, the assembly explicitly declared, that it "shall cease to be such by a vote of the House of Commons"[42]—and, by implication, in no other way.

The duties of the Committee of Correspondence are fairly obvious. The genesis of instructions by a Southern assembly to the committee is to be found outlined in a statement of May 21, 1691, when four burgesses in the Virginia house were directed to withdraw and "confider of Inftructions to be given to the Reverend Mr James Blayre for the foliciting and profecution of ye bufinefe of the Colledge and report the Same to the houfe."[43]

The duties of the committee were defined simply, clearly, and as they actually existed throughout the colonial period by the South Carolina legislature in 1714. The three members were directed to transmit to the agent all orders or instructions which they received from the assembly as well as such orders and instructions as the committee (or a majority of them) deemed proper for the benefit of trade, navigation, and the common advantage of the province; in the second place, the committee was to lay before the assembly all letters, replies and other papers received from the agent which "any way" concerned the public affairs of the colony.[44] The directions by the North Carolina assembly to their Committee of Correspondence in 1748 and 1769 appear not merely to embody the earlier ideas but show the lines along which the agency had developed in a half century: they were to correspond, advise, direct, and instruct the agent in all such matters relating to this province as may be moved or solicited, or that they may think proper, to move or solicit "before his Majefty in Council, or at any of the Boards in Eng-

[41] "Garth Correspondence," loc. cit., XXXIII, 277-78.

[42] Statutes at Large of South Carolina, II, 601.

[43] Journals of the House of Burgesses, 1659/60-1693, p. 372. The instructions formulated by the committee were not presented, merely the statement that they were drafted for the agent's guidance and approved by the house and council.—Ibid., p. 374.

[44] Statutes of South Carolina, II, 621. The clauses which conferred discretion on the committee appeared first in the Act of 1712.

land." There is the added direction to the committee to lay before the governor and the assembly copies of "Difpatches, Orders, and Directions" which they sent to the agent.[45]

Virginia introduced several new principles in her agency act in 1759. No one member of the committee should act independently of the rest by sending a private letter to the agent with matter repugnant to the action of the committee as a whole or communicate any instructions before they had been approved by the whole body under pain of censure by the general assembly. More important and imperative under the conditions obtaining in relations with the mother country were the power vested in the committee to remove the agent by majority vote, though they must lay their reason before the next assembly, and the power to fill a vacancy from death, resignation or removal, subject to approval by the next assembly.[46]

If the agency was created to deal with a special issue or if the house was faced with a special problem, the committee was likely to find its duties more exactly defined. For instance, when Maryland made Garth her special agent in 1766 to protest against the Stamp Act, the committee was directed to prepare and transmit to him a full state of the dispute and other grievances.[47] Again, in a crisis, the committee might be reduced to a mere transmitting agency. Virginia presents such an instance in April, 1768, when the assembly was sufficiently aroused to draft a petition to the king, a memorial to the Lords, and a remonstrance to the House of Commons against the British views of taxation. Apparently, the council had concurred and the committee was to direct the agent of the burgesses to coöperate with the agent of the Virginia council.[48] South Carolina in 1736, disturbed because their agency law had expired with the session too near a close to permit of drawing a new bill, appointed a new committee in order that it might correspond with the agent, Peregrine Fury, during the legislative recess, especially to assure his working for approval of their money bill, by which was meant the act of emitting £210,000 in bills of credit.[49]

[45] *Collection of all the Public Acts of Assembly of the Province of North Carolina*, pp. 278-79. The directions of 1769 repeat the very language of the earlier act.—C. O. 324/60, p. 287.   [46] *Ibid.*, p. 245; Hening, *Statutes*, VII, 276.

[47] *Archives of Maryland*, 1751-1770, XXXII, 182.

[48] *Journals of the House of Burgesses*, 1766-1769, p. 174.

[49] Journal of the Commons House of Assembly of South Carolina, May, 1735-May, 1736, X, 22; *ibid.*, July 13-17, 1736, X, 73.

In the cases of the numerous disputes which clutter colonial history, the preparation of arguments and collecting of the substantiating evidence in the form of papers, often copied from the colonial records, fell to the lot of the Committee of Correspondence, often under the euphonious phrase, "furnish him (the agent) with all necessary information." Securing acceptance of bills passed by the separate provincial legislatures entailed constant transmission of arguments to the agent with which he could hope to sustain the act challenged by some board or agency in Britain. Instances are simply legion, and the records filled with long expository arguments in support of certain laws even before we encounter the lengthy denunciations of the Stamp Act controversy. The famous Two-penny Act, out of which grew the Parsons Cause, which carried Patrick Henry to fame, is a good illustration. This Virginia act decreed that the salaries of clergymen might be paid in money instead of tobacco, the value of the product computed at two pence a pound whereas the current price of tobacco was six pence. It was held that the lower price was what it was originally intended the clergymen should have. In the twelve-page letter to their agent, Montague, dated December 12, 1759, the Committee of Correspondence devoted fully half the letter to the opposition of the clergymen to the act, and accused them of abusing and misrepresenting the legislature and injuring the country.[50] The voluminousness of the correspondence considered and drafted by the committee is well exemplified in the South Carolina exchanges with Peregrine Fury from June 26, 1747, to December 2, 1748.[51]

The committee had to carry on what we designate today as research. Nowhere is this better illustrated than in connection with the reimbursement by the mother country for expenditures for the colonial wars. Each colony was, of course, eager to secure the maximum amount, but England demanded proof of the sums expended. The Virginia Committee of Correspondence began to work in May, 1759, by asking the governor for copies of the letters written by

[50] The clergy had much law on their side. It ended in their defeat but badly strained the bond with England. For a fuller explanation of this case see *Virginia Magazine of History and Biography*, X, 347, 353, and Note, pp. 353-56; also Wirt, *Life of Patrick Henry*, pp. 19-29.

[51] See Journal of the Commons House of Assembly of South Carolina, Mar. 29, 1749-Nov. 21, 1749, XXIV, 721.

Secretary Pitt on how to apply to parliament for repayment. These copies were to be sent to the agent of the lower house to guide him in gaining Virginia's share.

Again the committee in Maryland in 1767 needed access to the documents of the council, a fact which always complicated matters if there were dissension between the two houses—as there often was. The committee applied to the council for authorization to search through the journals of the upper body for the period preceding the year 1704 and also House Journals in the council's custody preceding 1693 and for the years between 1696 and 1704 in order to supply their agent, Garth, with requisite material.[52]

A perusal of the minutes of meetings of the Committees of Correspondence, which have fortunately survived in part for South Carolina and Virginia, reveals the procedure followed by the committee at ordinary meetings.

Members were summoned by the clerk or other designated person upon an order for a meeting by the chairman or in his absence by any one of the committee. Meetings seem to have been irregular, called presumably to consider letters and papers from the Lords Commissioners of Trade and Plantations and from the agent or on order of the assembly to draft communications.[53] In the early period the agent addressed his letters to the governor. But by 1760 the friction between governor and lower house had begotten distrust and suspicion toward the royal representative so that the committee of the Virginia House of Burgesses directed their agent to send his communications to Mr. Nelson, the chairman of the Committee of Correspondence, but not to address them to him as a member of the committee, for that might tempt some one to open and confiscate them.[54] The Georgia act of May, 1770, required the agent to ad-

[52] *Virginia Magazine of History and Biography*, X, 338; *Archives of Maryland*, 1761-1770, XXXII, 180-81.

[53] Certainly meetings were inspired in the early history by receipt of letters from England. In October, 1723, a committee of the lower house of South Carolina was appointed to meet a committee of the Council "to consider of the Letters of the Right Honorable the Lords Commissioners of Trade, and Francis Yonge; etc."—Journal of the Commons House of Assembly of South Carolina, 1723, VI, 292.

The wording of a Georgia minute confirms the statement made above, "that if after being summoned in consequence of an Order—from any of the Committee by the Clerk or other person appointed by them for that purpose. . . ."—C. O. 324/60, p. 312. This minute is of May 19, 1768.

[54] See the statement to the above effect in the minute of the committee meeting of

dress his letters to the chairman, "the person first named in this Ordinance." No letters were to be opened or the seal broken "upon (any) pretense whatsoever before such number of the committee aforesaid are meet," though seven were impowered to proceed with the business. The committee drafted the instructions and letters to the agent, but South Carolina as early as June, 1748, expressly forbade it to send any letter to him during a sitting of the assembly without first reporting it to the house.[55] The presentation of instructions to the house for approval before transmission certainly prevailed in all the Southern colonies. In Georgia the committee regularly laid before the house sundry letters and papers which it had received from the agent, often with the answers of the committee; in 1773, when conditions were highly disturbed, the chairman read to the house excerpts from several of the letters from Franklin which the former had received during the interval caused by dissolutions of the assembly. Sometimes the house ordered the letters and papers to be laid upon the table for the perusal of the members. A similar procedure prevailed in Virginia, where the council sent down to the house letters from Agent Montague in 1761, and where on another occasion the "register" of the proceedings of the committee were spread before the house. Correspondence between Garth and the Maryland committee was also laid before the house and let lie on the table.[56] Where the agent was a regular official for both houses, both would be concerned with the instructions. Hence, in Virginia, in April, 1759, where the agent, although called agent for the burgesses, claimed to be acting for the colony as a whole, the lower house sent up the instructions to the council for concurrence.[57]

A clerk to transcribe the thoughts and decisions and rough notes

October 7, 1760, and also the letter to Agent Montague of November 5, 1760: "This is thought a necessary Caution to secure 'em from ye Inspection of such as might be curious enough to open them."—*Virginia Magazine of History and Biography*, XI, 10, 17.

[55] *Colonial Records of Georgia*, XIX, pt. 1, p. 200. Journal of the Commons House of Assembly of South Carolina, Jan. 19, 1747/8-June 29, 1748, XXIII, 693.

[56] This was true in 1762, 1764, 1770, and 1773.—*Colonial Records of Georgia*, X, 362-63; XIII, 729; XIV, 86; XV, 194; XVI, 26. On Virginia proceedings see *Journals of the House of Burgesses*, 1758-1761, p. 193; 1761-1765, p. 9; Journal of the Lower House of Maryland, 1762-1768. "Register" means minutes.

[57] *Legislative Journals of the Council*, III, 1220.

of the committee into a legible, clear hand for the agent was obviously necessary. Experiences reflected in the South Carolina committee translate into evidence logical suppositions of what would happen. At the session of November 30, 1716, the House of Commons decreed that "a good blank paper book well-bound, be provided by the Clerk of this House at the Public charge, wherein to enter the several letters and addresses sent enclosed, and to be sent by this House, or the commissioners they appoint to correspond with our agents, and likewise what letters are sent by the said agents to the said commissioners."[58] But the "good blank book," even though well-bound, was not self-executory, for the Committee of Correspondence reported to the House on December 7, 1722, that after sending for the several papers relating to the agency, they found them "so intricate and confused" that it took much time to "methodize" them and to take abstracts. There were some letters without date; it could not be determined which committee members had signed them; and the additional instructions sent by Mr. Yonge could not be found. The committee hence concluded sanely that "this affair of the agency being of great consequence and expense, ought to be transacted regularly and with caution," that they should have a clerk to enter the proceedings of the committee, as well as all letters and orders to the agent in a book—whence we conclude that the original good blank book had been quite ignored.[59] This recommendation bore fruit, for on February 22, 1723, the house assigned a clerk to the committee to keep a book with all the instructions to and from the agent and voted him the sum of £50 for his trouble until March 25 next ensuing. The modest sum must have been intended as a year's stipend, for an entry of April 17, 1725, shows South Carolina appropriating £50 per annum for a clerk for this committee.[60] By 1759, when the Committee of Correspondence created by the Virginia assembly met on May 8 to organize, it immediately recognized the necessity of having a scribe and forthwith named one George Davenport to that post. The burdensomeness of long-hand transcribing is emphasized when it is recalled that the committee, following the customary practice of that

[58] Journal of the Commons House of Assembly of South Carolina, 1716, V, 186.
[59] Ibid., VI, 108-9.
[60] Ibid., p. 214; Statutes of South Carolina, III, 251.

time, sent three separate copies of its letters to the agent by different ships in the hope that one would reach its destination. That such duplication was necessary is attested by a reference in the minutes for the session of November 6, 1760, to two copies of one of its letters as having been captured by the enemy.[61]

The record of performance of the members so far as attendance is concerned in the colony for which we have a record, may be checked as good. The record of the sessions of the Virginia Committee of Correspondence from May 2, 1759, to September 14, 1765, shows of a membership of twelve an average attendance of eight, never rising above eleven—and that number attained but once—but never falling below seven. The two Nelsons, Peyton Randolph, George Wythe, John Robinson, and John Blair, after he came on the committee, would have to be rated as faithful attendants at the sessions.[62] Service could scarcely be deemed onerous, if one judged by the number of meetings held: in 1759, the year of organization, six were held; in 1760 but three; three likewise in 1761; only two are recorded in the meager minutes of 1762; three in 1763; and four in 1764. Incompleteness of the records after 1764 makes further pursuit of this question futile.

There remain to be considered the formal instructions drawn by the committee to guide the agents. They early became formidable instruments. The language of the instructions to Moryson, Ludwell, and Smith, sent in 1674, it will be recalled, to secure a good

[61] *Virginia Magazine of History and Biography,* XI, 12, 18. The exigencies of war even led to quadruple papers. On the date given in the text one finds the order in the minutes of the Committee of Correspondence, "That the C'lk prepare a fourth Copy of the first Lr & the sevl Papers therein mentd & refd to, to be sent home by the first Ships, the Com. being inform'd that ye two first already sent are taken."—*Ibid.,* p. 12.

[62] This brief statistical data has been computed from the Minutes. See "Proceedings of the Virginia Committee of Correspondence," *loc. cit.,* X, 338-41; XI, 7, 131 ff., 346 ff.; XII, 159 ff., 225 ff., 389 ff.

No records for the meetings from December 19, 1764, to September 14, 1765, are to be found. It is possible that legislators were waiting to see the outcome of the Stamp Act. Records are also lacking from September 15, 1765, to November, 1769. The records for the period 1769-1770 are chiefly letters from Montague and the Journals of the House of Burgesses.—*Ibid.,* XII, 157-69, 353-64. Since this was the period of the Townsend Acts and non-importation agreements, it is probable that the records are lost. Montague, it is true, does not refer to letters from the committee, but that is not conclusive that none were written, even if there was little occasion for the committee to write, as his were chiefly reports on British action.—*Ibid.,* pp. 157-69. Of course, the membership consisted of sixteen after May 30, 1763, but only seven meetings are recorded for the enlarged membership.

charter for Virginia, is interesting, not as typical of the instructions issued when the agency had become established as a governmental institution but as indicative of what Virginians conceived as their rights. The burgesses were loyal to the spirit of their whole past when they directed their agents to insist on the right to be taxed only with their own consent and to dispel any doubt on this issue before they proceeded to less important demands.[63] Very similar in their insistence on the rights of colonials as Englishmen were the instructions to Jeffrey Jeffreys in 1691, who was to secure confirmation of land grants, it will be recalled. He was to take special pains to see that the charter contained a confirmation of all lands already granted by the crown and "also all Priviledges, Immunities formerly granted or promised to be granted in [by?] all or any of their Maj:[ties] or their Royall Progenit[ors] their Charters, Liberties, Proclamacons and Instrucons." More explicit was the direction to supplicate Their Majesties "to confirm to Virginia ye authority of ye General Assembly consisting of ye Governor, Council, and Burgesses as near as may be to ye model of ye Parliament of England." Indeed, in reading the following plea, one could readily date it 1776 instead of 1691: "that no tax be laid on any of ye people of this country, but with the consent of their representatives," and that the burgesses begged that they should be governed "after the same method as Englishmen and should have the full benefit of all ye great charter, and of all other laws and statutes regulating ye liberties of ye subjects."[64]

Of the same lengthy, involved character were the instructions dispatched by South Carolina to the early agents, Boone and Beresford, in February 25, 1715, to secure a redress of grievances—and there seem to have been many—from the proprietors; to Francis Yonge and John Lloyd under date of September 19, 1721, embody-

[63] Buried under the antiquated verbiage the idea is perfectly clear: "It is humbly conceived that if his Majesty deduce a Colony of Englishmen by their own consent . . . or license or permit one to be deduced to plant an uncultivated part of the world, such planters and their heires ought to enjoy by law in such plantation, the same liberties and priviledges as Englishmen in England. . . ."—Randolph MSS, III, 331. See also Hening, *Statutes*, II, 525-26; Bruce, *Institutional History of Virginia*, II, 531.

[64] Jeffreys' instructions were dated May, 1691; *Legislative Journals of the Council of Virginia*, I, 154-55; Bruce, *op. cit.*, II, 532.

ing twenty-six paragraphs, for their work was so diverse and manifold that it approached that of the regular agent.[65]

A period of less elaborate instructions then intervened from around 1720 to the beginning of the Revolutionary quarrel. The Virginia committee spared itself by perpetrating on William Byrd the Journal of the House of Burgesses with the blanket request that in case of any misrepresentations, he was "to have regard to their honour."[66]   Instructions tended to be briefer as they took the form of letters dealing with particular issues rather than formal instructions formulated as the agent took office.   One finds, for instance, a letter from the Virginia committee to Agent Leheup, written in 1726 or 1727 on the subject of the Northern Neck; South Carolina urges Agent Fury on January 25, 1736/7, to press home on the king's ministers the defenceless condition of Georgia and also the inability of South Carolina to defend herself, let alone Georgia.[67] Agent Knox was instructed briefly to apply for a convoy for ships bound from Great Britain to Georgia and vice versa, for a guard ship to be stationed on the Georgia coast, and for some regular troops equipped with artillery and ammunition to defend the forts in the province.[68]

Then again during the period of heated controversy from the Stamp Act to the rupture come longer, fuller instructions.   South Carolina in February, 1763, involved in a tense dispute with the governor concerning the control of the house over the election of its own members, already mentioned, sent their agent a full statement of the dispute including a number of papers.   Georgia, though holding somewhat aloof from the Northern colonies in the protest against the Stamp Act, dispatched to Knox a long discussion of its effect on the export of lumber and live stock from that province and although admitting that the tax might be as just as any that could be imposed on the colonies, expressed alarm over the manner of

[65] For instructions to Boone and Beresford see Journal of the Commons House of Assembly of South Carolina, 1715, IV, 378-80; to Yonge and Lloyd, C. O. 5/358, pp. 127-33.   See also McCrady, South Carolina under the Royal Government, p. 40; Collections of South Carolina Historical Society, I, 260.

[66] These instructions to Byrd are, it should be noted, a bit earlier than the date embraced in the text; they are dated May 30, 1718.—C. O. 5/1318, p. 425.

[67] "Proceedings of the Virginia Committee of Correspondence," loc. cit., XIII, 263. Extract of a letter from the Committee of Correspondence to Fury, C. O. 5/388, p. 139.

[68] Colonial Records of Georgia, XIII, 682-83.

imposing it and fear of the precedent. In 1770 followed long instructions to Garth from South Carolina and in 1773 to its agent from North Carolina.[69]

[69] Journal of the Commons House of Assembly of South Carolina, Feb. 14, 1763, p. 5; Habersham, *Letters*, p. 32; C.O. 5/393, p. 214; *Colonial Records of Georgia*, IX, 578-80.

CHAPTER 8.

THE PERSONNEL IN THE AGENCIES

THE reader has been made cognizant of the type of distinguished person who served on the Committees of Correspondence. Obviously the effort to promote the relations with the mother country and to make them workable demanded of those committees the best ability the colony could command—and received it. Similarly, the individuals who served to effect and maintain those relations in England needed to be men possessing unusual qualities in an unusual degree. If it were the function of this study to classify and catalog the entire personnel of the agencies of all the thirteen colonies, some two hundred in number for the entire colonial period, it would be easily demonstrated that there were included among names but little known outside their narrow circles and forgotten after their brief day others which were distinguished both in their time and thereafter. From Sir Henry Ashurst and Constantine Phips, later Lord Chancellor of Ireland, to the great Edmund Burke, who deigned to serve as agent for New York; from Edward Winslow and the distinguished divine, Increase Mather, to Arthur Lee; from Jeremiah Dummer and his contemporary, Richard Partridge, the Quaker who served Rhode Island continuously for almost half a century, to the London merchant, Barlow Trecothick; from the erratic Major Joseph Dudley, who returned from his agency to no less a post than the governorship of Massachusetts Bay, to that outstanding American of all time, Benjamin Franklin, there passes in review a truly astonishing group of Britons and Americans. When one confines the parade to the agents merely of the Southern colonies, one is still confronted by some names of distinction. Benjamin Franklin's services had been enlisted by Georgia, as has been revealed earlier; a man of tested gubernatorial caliber, Nathaniel Blakiston, consented to serve two colonies in what must have seemed to him a not too humble capacity; James Wright found the agency of South Carolina no disqualification for the governorship of Georgia. William Byrd II, one of Virginia's wealthiest planters, and Grey Elliott, planter and auditor general of Georgia, were distinguished men of their respective colonies. John Randolph, thought worthy by the mother country of knighthood, Peyton Randolph, who was later twice chosen president of the Continental Congress, Francis Yonge, Charles Pinckney, and Colonel John Barnwell, Colonel Philip Ludwell and William Little, ex-speaker of the Georgia lower house, all shed luster in greater or less degree on their respective provinces. As was perfectly natural, indeed inevitable, outstanding members of the community were invariably chosen for the special mission.

The rule may probably be safely asserted that during the early years, when agents were dispatched to deal with pressing emergencies, colonials were usually selected because they were prominent and trusted by their fellow-citizens; later, when the agency was established as a regular post, the colonies, on the score of expense, preferred some one resident in England—a colonial who had gone "home" to live, or was temporarily resident in London, or a British merchant, preferably one who from a fairly long residence in the colony was conversant with conditions there; in the middle decades of the eighteenth century a solicitor, because of his knowledge of law and, therefore, presumably his ability to prevent colonial legislation from being disallowed, seemed acceptable; late in colonial history, if Charles Garth is representative, the Southern colonies, at least, looked upon a member of parliament with favor.

First to be noted is the group of governors who, as the official heads of the colonies, would be listened to with respect by the home government and who were the official spokesmen for the small group of settlers struggling for bare existence. The dispatch of Sir George Yeardley and Francis Wyatt in the early decades of the seventeenth century was not only natural but, under the circumstances, inevitable. The designation of Sir William Berkeley as agent for Virginia followed as a natural consequence when that official was about to embark for a visit to the mother country. Richard Bennett and John Coode represent the natural selection of the active head of the government to defend a revolt. Failure to use the governors, as the members of the lower houses gained strength and independence, was just as logical an attitude on the part of the colonials.   Acceptance by Maryland and Virginia of the offer of service as agent by ex-Governor Nathaniel Blakiston falls into a different category and represents merely willingness to have as spokesman a man who knew the colonial situation and who could serve at slight expense.   He had dwelt in Maryland as chief executive for over three years from January 2, 1698/9 to July, 1702. His resignation had been accepted in June, 1701, on the score of ill health after a term highly acceptable to Marylanders.   The facts that several members of his family had emigrated to Maryland and that he was not friendly to Lord Baltimore were probably in the eyes of Marylanders no disqualifications.   However, what made him really of value as an agent was his interest in mercantile affairs, for he had been made free of the Merchant Adventurers' Company of London in 1698.[1]   Possibly the fact that Captain Francis West and Edward Digges had acted as governors of Virginia added to their stature as agents.   Three of West's brothers had participated in the establishment of Virginia; he himself had resided in the colony since 1608 and was a member of the council in 1609 and continuously from 1619 to 1633.   Digges loomed so large in England that he became a member of the Council for Foreign Plantations—forerunner of the Board of Trade—during his brief residence in London just after the Restoration, but in 1664 he returned to Virginia as auditor general.

In this general group of high dignitaries should be noted also Landgrave Abel Kettleby, the first regular agent for South Carolina.   The title marks him as one of the provincial nobility of that colony and the dates 1712 to 1716 are sufficiently indicative of the fact that he was chosen before that province had manifested any strong disposition to throw off proprietary rule.   The fact that he was a barrister of the Inner Temple probably was at this early time not a factor.   It might reasonably be assumed that he would have a deep interest in the welfare of the young colony of South Carolina since he had secured five thousand acres of land there.[2]

If the agent were a colonial, his prominence usually arose from

[1] On Blakiston's mercantile interests see Surtees, *The History and Antiquities of the County Palatine of Durham*, III, 402.   See also McMahon, *Historical View of the Government of Maryland*, I, 267; *Virginia Magazine of History and Biography*, XIX, 14, note.

[2] See Smith, "The Baronies of South Carolina," *South Carolina Historical and Genealogical Magazine*, XV, 149, 151.

his holding high public office. Often he was a member of the provincial council. Examples quickly come to mind: John Pountis, the first of all agents, who was also an admiral and treasurer of a hundred in Virginia, Colonel Philip Ludwell, John Ash, Francis Yonge, the Reverend James Blair, William Knox, Colonel Fenwicke, James Crockatt, Alexander Vander Dusen, and many more who sat in the councils of their respective colonies. Henry McCulloh boasted, as one of his qualifications, of having sat on the North Carolina council.

William Byrd II and Grey Elliott represent cases where for convenience the governing authorities in the colonies took advantage of their presence in London to utilize their services, the one long before he attained the dignity of the council, the other after he had graced the Georgia council. In 1697 young Byrd, then a mere stripling, though already a member of the House of Burgesses, was about to go to England on personal affairs, and so when the Virginia assembly wished to have an address presented to the Board of Trade, this son of one of the wealthiest and most prominent men in the colony, was entrusted together with John Povey with the more or less formal mission. Since he was well born, of manly appearance, and good address in an age when maturity came early, the appointment is not so inexplicable as it would be today. It should also be recalled that Byrd had been sent over at the age of ten or eleven to be educated in England and had been under the particular care of Sir Robert Southwell. Having served once, he was a natural suggestion for the appointment the next year, October, 1698, as the regular agent on a salary. Again in December, 1701, when it was felt that some one must show the impossibility of Virginia's sending military aid to defend New York, the young man, who "knew his way about" in London and was already on the ground, was again a natural choice. In the intervals between his various agencies, he became receiver general, and in time succeeded to his father's seat in the council, so that he properly classifies here. During his fourth period of service as agent he narrowly missed losing his seat on the council because of his prolonged absence from the colony, thus furnishing an excuse for an attack by the governor when Byrd was serving the council in their conflict with the chief executive.[3] Even

[3] For the address presented by Bryd and Povey, see *Calendar of State Papers, Colonial,* 1696-1697, sec. 967. Governor Spotswood, between Byrd and whom existed a great

then, he represents strikingly the appointment of a colonial already in England, for he had been in England on his own business over three years when he was appointed on May 27, 1718, as agent for the burgesses to gain withdrawal of restrictions on the governor's right to sign bills of shipping. After the hurried trip home in 1720 to reconcile the warring factions which existed in the colony, he was named agent for the last time in December of that year because he was about to return to England on private business. There he resided for five years, until 1726.

Not many colonials had probably the acquaintanceships which were Byrd's. Favored by the patronage of Sir Robert Southwell, he was introduced to many of the first persons of the age in knowledge, wit, birth, or rank. He established an intimate friendship with Charles Boyle, Earl of Orrery. He was even chosen a fellow of the Royal Society. To all this he added travel in the Low Countries and France. By this time he represented the type of colonial who would be a logical choice for agent—a staid planter of established position, distinguished family, and wealth, a member of the council, where, indeed, he held a seat thirty-seven years, a cultured gentleman, and in addition, a man of long experience in England with many important contacts.[4]

A group of early agents who were members of the colonial councils merit more than bare listing. Colonel Samuel Mathews, a planter and member of the Virginia council for more than twenty years, who contributed during the Commonwealth period to crystalizing the agency as a regular post, won a place in Peter Force's *Tracts* and helps us to see what material considerations brought prominence in the middle of the seventeenth century. Mathews

hostility, proposed removal of Byrd from the council on the ground that he had already been absent from Virginia three and a half years, and on the score that he desired to become agent for the House of Burgesses. Spotswood also attacked him in 1716 for irregularities in his accounts as receiver general. See *Journal of the Board of Trade,* 1714/5-1718, pp. 74, 183, 187.

The Reverend James Blair and his confederates were working for the removal not merely of Spotswood but of Lord Orkney as governor, and it was to this end that the attempt to appoint Byrd agent had been made.—Dodson, *Alexander Spotswood,* pp. 256, 257.

[4] For the appointment of May, 1718, see *Journals of the House of Burgesses,* 1712-1726, pp. 194, 210, 216. For an account of William Byrd II, see *D. A. B.,* III, 383-84; *Writings of "Colonel William Byrd of Westover in Virginia Esqr.,"* Introduction, pp. xl-lxxxvi. Bassett, the editor, notes only three agencies for Byrd, whereas official documents record four agencies in addition to the first mission.

had, "a fine house, . . . sowes yeerly a store of Hempe & Flax and causes it to be spun; he keeps Weavers, and hath a Tan-house, . . . hath eight Shoemakers, forty Negroe servants, yeerly sowes abundance of Wheat, Barley &c., kills store of Beeves, and sells them to victuall the ships when they come thither, hath abundance of Kine, a brave Dairy, Swine great store, and Pottery; he married the Daughter of Sir Tho. Hinton. . . ."[5] It should be recalled that he, the Ludwells, George Sandys, the Reverend Philip Mallory, Edward Bennett, and other early agents[6] were natives of England, had been reared in English homes, educated in English schools, and had mingled until their majority in English social life, and hence were personally well qualified to represent the colonies. It must be noted that Edward Bennett was a rich London merchant, engaged on a large scale in the Virginia trade, and an active member of the Virginia Company. He not only established the first large plantation in Virginia in Isle of Wight County, to which he imported many servants, but was the owner of a fleet of vessels trading to Virginia and Newfoundland. He came over to Virginia only in 1626, after the death of his brother Richard, who had been managing his estate, but his presence in the House of Burgesses may account for his choice in 1628 as one of the two agents dispatched to England that year. He was granted a letter of marque and commissioned to take enemy ships in 1627, probably in connection with the Duke of Buckingham's ill-fated expedition to relieve the Huguenots at La Rochelle when they were besieged by Richelieu, an appointment which stamped him as a man of consequence in England. His nephew, Richard Bennett, was distinguished as one of the parliamentary commissioners to reduce Virginia and Maryland after the colonial reactions to the Civil War in England. He rose from the lower house to membership in the council. A brief removal to Maryland with other nonconformists did not break his ties with Virginia, for he remained one of her most trusted citizens, a member of the council after his return from his agency until his death, and one of the three major generals of militia in 1666.[7]

[5] "A New Description of Virginia," Force, *Tracts*, II, no. 8, p. 15. He did not ever return to Virginia after his four years in the agency. See Cook, "Governor Samuel Mathews, Jr.," *William and Mary Quarterly*, ser. 2, XIV, 105-6.

[6] To this group belongs the elder Byrd though he, of course, never served as an agent.

[7] For Edward Bennett see *William and Mary Quarterly*, ser. 2, XIII, 119-27; for

The constant prominence of Francis Yonge did not arise from his several agencies, but his selection as agent arose from his prominence in South Carolina history for at least a quarter of a century. These agents often accumulated other offices. Yonge besides being on the council was appointed surveyor general of Carolina and of the Bahamas and told the Board of Trade that he had been chief justice in the colony but without salary. It is interesting that he resigned from the council in 1736, as he had decided not to return to South Carolina.

Thomas Harwood is another example of the prominent planter with large holdings of land who served at various times as burgess, speaker, and councillor in the Virginia assembly. Alexander Kellet had been not only a member of the Georgia council, but also provost marshal, when he consented to appear before the Board of Trade in 1756 as a special agent.[8] Here also must be classified the brother of the more famed Sir Edwin Sandys, George Sandys, who was himself one of the most cultivated men of his age. He arrived at Jamestown in the train of Governor Wyatt in 1621 to enter upon his duties as colonial treasurer, more particularly to collect the quitrents. Appointment to the council followed very shortly as a matter of course. Here also stands Colonel Francis Moryson, who after collapse of the royal cause of Charles I, in which he had held rank probably as major, became one of the fugitive cavaliers in Virginia. Within the space of a few years he was made speaker of the lower house of assembly, and even served as governor for something over a year upon the royal restoration. After acting in the interest of Virginia as one of the agents to secure repeal of the Culpeper grant, he served England in turn as a commissioner to suppress Bacon's Rebellion.

Instances of agents who had been selected from the lower house of assembly are not difficult to find. John Ash, the first embryo agent from South Carolina, was chosen probably for his prominence in the Commons House of Assembly because the very thing he was

Richard Bennett, Standard, "Abstracts of Virginia Land Patents," *Virginia Magazine of History and Biography*, III, 53-55.

[8] For Yonge in the post of surveyor general see C. O. 5/358, p. 78; for the chief-justiceship, *Journal of the Board of Trade*, 1734/5-1741, p. 21; for the resignation, C. O. 5/401, pp. 171-72; for Harwood, "Virginia in 1635," *Virginia Magazine of History and Biography*, VIII, 402, note; for Kellet, *Colonial Records of Georgia*, XXVI, 457.

sent to oppose was limiting membership in that body to Anglicans. He was the representative of Colleton County, settled largely by dissenters, and so the residents of that county were ready to send him, a leader among the dissenters, across seas to represent them before the proprietors.   Thomas Miller, who had gone home from the northern part of Carolina three decades earlier than Ash, was a member of the lower house.   Richard Beresford, a man of great landed property in South Carolina, is another instance of assembly-man turned agent.   Possibly the most interesting illustration of a man deliberately selected from the assembly occurred in South Carolina in 1722 when the dual agency was carefully balanced, Yonge of the council set off by John Lloyd of the House of Commons. To Governor Nicholson we owe the information that Lloyd was once secretary "to the late Mr. Craggs in the post office and likewise under him in the tower," which tells us that he was doubtless born in England.[9]

Several of the agents filled the honorable post of speaker of the lower house of assembly.   Cases in point are Kenelm Chesledyne, who returned from his special mission to England to become speaker; Edmund Gray, a Quaker, and a rather disreputable character despite his prominence as a large land-holder on the Saltina River in Georgia, who had been speaker before he was sent over by Georgia in 1752 to prevent the union of that province with her neighbor to the north;[10] and William Little, a ship's surgeon who had been brought over by Governor Reynolds as private secretary and general factotum, who was dispatched in 1757 on a special mission, possibly because he was at the very time presiding as speaker over the Georgia Commons House of Assembly.   He had filled a large array of minor posts, such as agent of Indian affairs, clerk of the assembly, justice of the peace, and aide-de-camp to the governor, before he rose to the speakership.[11]

[9] Stated in a letter to the Board of Trade, dated October 6, 1721.—C. O. 5/358, f. 110.

[10] Gray lived first in St. Paul's parish, and then moved to the neutral ground between the Altamaha and St. John's rivers south of Darien, a region sought by outlaws and criminals. Here he was visited by Governor Ellis, who thought he had remarkable ability but no common sense.—Smith, *The Story of Georgia and the Georgia People*, p. 39. The term was applied to a sort of no-man's land, neutralized by a treaty between the British and Spaniards in 1750.

[11] This statement is based on Governor Reynold's report to the Board of Trade, dated April 18, 1758.—C. O. 5/646, Bundle C, 31. See also *The Colonial Records of Georgia*,

Many other high posts in the colonial government were represented in the persons of various agents. Sir Thomas Lawrence, who after bitter attacks against him for insistence on collecting certain fees, as has been duly recounted, was strangely selected as agent for Maryland, not only filled the post of secretary but later the position of chief justice. Colonel Philip Ludwell has been noted as an outstanding member of the council of Virginia, but he also served his colony as speaker, deputy surveyor general, deputy auditor, and secretary of state. The proprietors even made him governor first of North Carolina and then of the entire province, with authority to appoint a deputy, a privilege of which he availed himself.[12] Thomas Ludwell, his brother, also held the post of secretary of the same province from 1660 to 1678, no less than eighteen years.[13] James Wright, a native son of South Carolina, served that colony for fifteen years as attorney general. The concurrence of the two houses in his appointment as agent gave great satisfaction after the disputes and competition of Charles Pinckney and Crockatt for the position. Wright's prominence is sufficiently indicated by his commission, first as lieutenant governor of Georgia during Governor Ellis' absence, and then appointment as governor upon that gentleman's resignation. As a further commentary on the personality of this agent, the last royal governor of Georgia, it might be added that he was

---

VII, 252-54; XIII, 152. Here occurred one of those instances of dissension between the council, which tried to remove Little from several of his posts, and the house, which seems to have been wholly dominated by the governor.

[12] Philip Ludwell came to Virginia about 1660. He seemed to have had the capacity of arousing the ire of the governors. Governor Howard removed him from the council in 1687 (C. O. 5/1305, p. 36), but he had a more serious difficulty with Governor Spotswood because of encroachment on a tract of 3,000 acres near Jamestown which had been set apart for the governor's use. Though the governor consented to mediation, the incident turned Ludwell against him. Spotswood brought charges against Ludwell and dismissed him from the office of deputy auditor in 1716.—C. O. 5/1317, pp. 437-44.

Ludwell could arouse the ire of others than the governors, as the following statement of Colonel John Gibbs, who claimed the governorship of Carolina, proves: "Publish & declare, That Phillip Ludwel is a Rascal, imposter, & Usurpr: all which shall be justified in England and if any of the boldest Heroe living in this or the next Country will undertake to Justify the said Ludwel's illegal, Irregular proceeding, let him call upon me wth his sword, and I will single out & go with him into any part of the King's Dominions, & there fight him in this Cause, as long as my Eyelidds shall wagg." This is dated June 2, 1690.—C. O. 5/1305, p. 113. For an account of his life, see Virginia Magazine of History and Biography, I, 174-78.

[13] Thomas Ludwell may have served in the wars of Charles I, as he is referred to as lieutenant.—William and Mary Quarterly, X, 172.

knighted by the British government in 1772.[14] William Smith conferred honor on the post by his acceptance, for he was a chief justice in the colony of North Carolina.

Sometimes men were asked to act as agents because of their general prominence and standing rather than because they were members of the council or house of assembly or holding government office. The Reverend James Blair, that stormy Scotchman, was, of course, a tower of moral strength through a long life, fifty-four years of which were spent in Virginia as commissary of the Bishop of London. His choice for the agency to secure the college charter resulted from his leadership among the clergy in presenting a petition for this purpose to the governor of Virginia. Logically, the assembly asked him to help draw up a petition to the king and queen; the next step followed as a matter of course—a request that he present it. His success in soliciting the charter brought fresh laurels—presidency of the new college and continued leadership in Virginia to the day of his death.[15] John Barnwell came of one of the distinguished families of South Carolina. A gentleman, Dublin-born of influential connections, who reached South Carolina in quest of adventure, he soon attained public office as deputy secretary, clerk of the council, and comptroller. Military service against the French and Spanish in Queen Anne's War and, more importantly, against the Tuscarora and Yemassee Indians brought dispatch as an agent to England and thus acquaintance with Governor Nicholson and then command of the Southern forces. Repeated membership in the Commons House of Assembly but added to his prominence so that selection to serve with Joseph Boone as co-agent after the revolution of 1719 was a natural step. Probably the best evidence of the impression of ability and force which he created is the fact that he was consulted by the British government as to the new form of government for the

[14] C. O. 5/375, K, 149; C. O. 5/376, L, 75; *Acts of the Privy Council, Colonial*, IV, 398, 482. Wright was the son of Chief Justice Robert Wright, who incurred the anger of the Commons of South Carolina for his defense of the Habeas Corpus Act during Johnson's administration.—Jones, *History of Georgia*, I, 541.

[15] *Journals of the House of Burgesses*, 1659/60-1693, pp. 343, 353, 491. For an account of Blair see *D. A. B.*, II, 335-37. The long and stormy career of Blair is too well known to call for extended treatment here. Born in Scotland, educated at the College of Edinburgh, he migrated to England and then to Virginia. Less well known is the fact that he was suspended in April, 1695, from the council for misconduct till further orders by Governor Andros, but the Privy Council on November 3, 1695, ordered Andros to restore him.—C. O. 5/1358, pp. 293-94, 302-3.

colony, and his advice was sought on the establishment of a frontier post. His reward took the form of a seat on the council.[16] William Knox was a large rice planter with other agricultural interests in Georgia, who had a warm, personal friendship with James Habersham. During his absence as agent in London he left the supervision of his interests to this friend. Knox made himself unpopular in his own colony by his advocacy of the Stamp Act, causing even a temporary breach in his friendship with Habersham, so that he was discontinued as agent for a time. His stature can be measured, however, by the fact that he became under secretary of state to the Earl of Hillsborough and to Dartmouth.[17]

It was logical and wise, when the agency attained a regularized position and thus became a fixed charge on the provincial treasury, for the thrifty colonials to seek their agents on the scene, as has been intimated. Here their choice might be said to lie between Americans who had returned to England to live, or Britishers who had enjoyed the advantage of a sufficiently long residence in some one of the colonies to be familiar with conditions here, or merchants trading to the colonies. A surprising number could qualify under each of the categories.

In one colony, however, the issue became clear-cut between a colonial sent over from America and some one resident in Britain. At the assembly session of 1724 the Commons House of Assembly of South Carolina voted to appoint one Kingsmill Eyre, apparently an Englishman, agent for that province. The upper house insisted on an appointee to be sent over from the colony. The governor held that Eyre would be a proper appointee provided that some person prepared to answer any objections to colonial actions be first sent over from the colony to give a true account of the situation. He urged Colonel Barnwell as qualified in every way, but as the house refused to depart from its choice, it soon became apparent that it was too late in the session for any action.[18]

A native American who knew the situation first hand, whose sympathies would be presumably with the colonials, and who was resid-

[16] "Barnwell of South Carolina," *South Carolina Historical and Genealogical Magazine*, II, 47-50; *Virginia Magazine of History and Biography*, V, 391-92; *D. A. B.*, I, 639-40.

[17] William Knox also secured the post of crown agent for East Florida.

[18] Journal of the Commons House of Assembly of South Carolina, V, 425, 426, 455, 444, 467.

ing permanently in England might be regarded as the ideal choice in this category. When John Carter, a barrister at law of the Middle Temple, was commended to the Board of Trade as "solicitor" for Virginia to succeed Blakiston upon his death, one of his qualifications was his being a native of Virginia. Again we see choice of a young man who had studied in London, the son of a member of the Virginia council who had in the words of the governor "the most considerable Estate of any man in the Coun[try]."[19]

Colonel John Fenwicke, who was designated in 1744 as a special aid to Fury to get a paper currency bill through, was certainly selected because of being a citizen of South Carolina, where he had sat for many years on the council, and hence was conversant with her problems.[20] Although he resigned from the council in December, 1746, as he had no intention of returning to Carolina, he kept his interest in the colony, recommending his son to succeed to his seat.[21]

William Middleton illustrates the colonial preference in agents at this time as completely as if he had not declined the appointment to the agency in 1756. Born in South Carolina, he was first elected to the Commons House of Assembly and then appointed to a seat in the council. When he inherited large estates in both Carolina and England, he resigned from the council in 1754 after twelve years' service in order to reside in Suffolk. That the colony had not misplaced its confidence in his loyalty is attested by the fact that he visited Carolina and the Northern colonies in 1772 and that in 1774 he supported the petition against the Boston Port Bill.[22]

Grey Elliott was an important planter of Georgia and, almost by the same token, a member of the council, who added the further provincial post of deputy auditor. He left Georgia shortly before

[19] *Journal of the Board of Trade,* 1718-1722, p. 379. For Governor Spotswood's comment about him see C. O. 5/1319, p. 78.

[20] He held the position of major-general of the South Carolina militia at times.— McCrady, *South Carolina under the Royal Government,* p. 229, note. The facts stated in the text are brought out by a representation to the Board of Trade.—*Journal of the Board of Trade,* 1741/2-1749, p. 162.

[21] Not to be confused, however, with Edward Fenwick, who with thirty other Americans resident in London at the time protested against the Boston Port Bill.

[22] *South Carolina Historical and Genealogical Magazine,* I, 233-34; XXXIII, 247, note. He died in England in 1785. It is thought that he was educated in England, and he certainly visited the homeland in 1739. He was a trustee for the Society for the Propagation of the Gospel in Foreign Parts.

January, 1772, to reside in England. To him, as a colonial resident in England, the Commons House turned when it was felt desirable to assure the colony an agent in case of Franklin's absence. Elliott was doubtless at first regarded as a councillor on leave.[23]

No more dramatic figures in this group are to be found than Thomas Barker and Alexander Elmsly, both of whom had long been members of the lower house of the North Carolina assembly, and both of whom were residing in England in 1774. To them jointly was intrusted the address to the crown from that province in 1774 in protest against the coercive acts of the British government. The former was born in Rhode Island in 1733, but came to North Carolina about 1735, where he became a lawyer of influence in the Albemarle section and even treasurer of the province until his removal about 1761 to England. The latter had wielded considerable influence in that same section. Their action in substituting their own version of an address and of the poor reception accorded that action by the colony has been told. There only remains to add that Barker after almost twenty years' absence remained true to the land of his birth, for he returned to North Carolina in 1778 by way of France, subscribing his oath of fealty to the state the day after his return.[24]

The supreme example of the American resident temporarily in England who was trusted by all the colonies and not merely by the colony of his nativity, was Benjamin Franklin. Sent over first by Pennsylvania and kept almost continuously in London from 1757 to 1775, he came to mean to all the colonies the outstanding American resident, truly a minister at the Court of St. James, a fact which explains his choice as agent by several of the colonies. But the story of his career has been too often told to require repetition here.

The type of Britisher who was acceptable to the colonials varied from time to time. Very early a London merchant might be chosen solely because of contact with colonial trade. Interesting illustration of the last principle stated was the selection of Peter Pagan by the Maryland assembly. The contact certainly seems to have been tenuous, for research reveals nothing but the office, held from

[23] *Colonial Records of Georgia*, XII, 188.
[24] Ashe, *History of North Carolina*, I, 434; *Colonial Records of North Carolina*, IX, 1208-9.

1689 to 1691, of collecting a tax of fourteen pence per ton on ships going to the province of Maryland to be paid to Lord Baltimore. It will be recalled that when Pagan found himself too pressed by his own business affairs to continue the agency, he turned it over to one Isaac Milner, likewise a London merchant, whose connection with Maryland must have been even more tenuous, for the writer was unable to unearth any contacts.[25] Peregrine Fury was another example of London merchant tendered and accepting an agency. Certain British merchants from their wealth and prominence in the business world became familiar to the American colonials by name and so were sought out. Thus one might say Micajah Perry, interested particularly in the tobacco trade of Maryland and Virginia, just escaped being an agent for Virginia, for he acted as intermediary to deliver the income from a certain bequest, which was to be spent in spreading Christianity among North American Indians, to the trustees of the College of William and Mary for the training of nine or ten young Indians. Perry served, it is well to recall, as agent for Pennsylvania. A letter by Governor Spotswood to Colonel Blakiston was sent in 1710 unsealed to Mr. Perry, together with a letter in which the latter gentleman was asked to negotiate the matter discussed—the dropping of William Byrd II, from the council—in the event of Blakiston being out of town. Certainly that is tantamount to a special, strictly limited agency. Although Perry is occasionally loosely referred to as "agent," the writer finds no documentary evidence that he was ever formally appointed agent by any of the Southern colonies.[26]

Then there was the native of the British Isles who had resided for some years in one of the American colonies and knew colonial conditions and sentiments first-hand. An early illustration was the merchant, Michael Marshall or Marshart who seems to have been in Virginia long enough to be elected a burgess in 1727 and selected with Wyatt and Bennett to negotiate the tobacco difficulty. Jeffrey

[25] See above, Chapter I.
[26] Bruce, *Institutional History of Virginia*, I, 396-97; Spotswood, *Official Letters*, I, 1-2. There were other occasions when he seemed to be representing a colony unofficially, if temporarily. On September 11, 1696, he appeared before the Board as spokesman for both Virginia and Maryland.—*Calendar of State Papers, Colonial*, 1696-1697, sec. 204. The records seem to refer to him as *agent* for Virginia and Maryland in at least one place.—*Ibid.*, sec. 1157. For Perry's agency for Pennsylvania see Wolff, *The Colonial Agency of Pennsylvania*, pp. 31-33, 38-39.

Jeffreys was in Virginia for at least a brief period as factor for his uncle, John Jeffreys, a grocer of London, to whose business he succeeded. The fact that the colony recognized an able man in making him agent is attested by his later career: he became an alderman in London, was knighted, and sat in parliament. South Carolina found several men with just that background to serve her interests. Samuel Wragg, who succeeded Francis Yonge as agent in 1727, was one of that number. With his brother Joseph, Samuel had migrated to that province some time before March, 1710/1. Like many a man of ability in a young community, he rose rapidly to prominence. In 1712 he was a member of the lower house; in 1717 he was a member of the council, a position in which he was maintained after the colony became a royal province until his death. After about a decade as merchants in Charleston, where the brothers greatly increased the capital they had brought thither, Mr. Samuel Wragg either returned to London or divided his time between the mother country and Carolina, continuing, however, his commercial relations with the colony. He was frequently summoned to the Board of Trade for testimony as to the Carolinas between the years 1723 and 1738. The records of July, 1738, to April 14, 1742, even present him appearing in the rôle of "agent" for the assembly of North Carolina. As early as January, 1723/4, the colony turned to this prominent merchant, asking his aid for their agent Francis Yonge in his search for a printer to be sent to the colony. Rice to the value of a thousand pounds was shipped to Wragg for the purpose. His failure in this particular enterprise did not discourage the colony from turning to him a few years later for a special piece of soliciting.[27] In classifying him it is difficult to decide between returned colonial and Britisher resident in the colony.

Stephen Godin was particularly interested in the making of tar in the Carolinas, in sugar, and in the tobacco trade during the decade of the twenties of the eighteenth century. He appeared before the

[27] *Journal of the Board of Trade*, 1728/9-1734, p. 257; *ibid.*, 1722/3-1728, pp. 141, 254; McCrady, *South Carolina under the Royal Government*, p. 145. His experience in 1718 illustrates the hazards of the time; as he was outward bound from Charleston to England, his vessel was taken by a pirate ship just off the bar, and he was redeemed only after many hardships and a large ransom of specie and drugs.—*South Carolina Historical and Genealogical Magazine*, XIX, 121; McCrady, *South Carolina under the Proprietary Government*, pp. 589-92. He was buried in South Carolina in 1750.—Smith, "The Baronies of South Carolina," *South Carolina Historical and Genealogical Magazine*, XI, 88.

Board of Trade on several occasions, furnished data concerning the making of tar, and clearly consulted his own interests as a merchant. He urged a bounty on tar and was concerned about an act for paper bills of credit. In January, 1724/5, he urged that all ships bound from the plantations to Africa, Europe, the Madeira or Western Islands should be obliged to touch at ports in Britain before their return to America. There are many evidences scattered through the Board of Trade Journals from 1716 to 1731 of recognition of his prominence as a merchant in the Carolina trade.[28]

For many years James Crockatt was one of the leading merchants of Charleston. Although he was not called upon to serve as agent until eight years after he had resigned his seat in the council of South Carolina, which he did shortly after his removal to London in 1739, where he immediately engaged in business, the legislators of the colony valued his experience as merchant and trader with the Indians. They obviously trusted him from the knowledge they had acquired of him in business and in the council to such a degree that they kept him as their agent for seven years.[29]

Henry Eustace McCulloh had his attention drawn early to North Carolina by the huge grants—over a million acres—granted his father and his associates in 1737 in western North Carolina by George II for a company, of which he was leading spirit.[30] The

[28] *Journal of the Board of Trade*, 1722/3-1728, pp. 37-38; 143; *ibid.*, p. 99; 1714/5-1718, pp. 158-59; 1718-1722, pp. 19, 220.

[29] *South Carolina Historical and Genealogical Magazine*, XXVIII, 144, note 1; *Journal of the Board of Trade*, 1734/5-1741, p. 385; C. O. 5/374; for the letter from William Bull, president of the South Carolina council, to the Board of Trade, May 22, 1741, telling of Crockatt's resignation from the Council, see C. O. 5/368, G, 52; Smith, *South Carolina as a Royal Province*, p. 165. He was evidently obnoxious to Governor Glen.

[30] Moore, *History of North Carolina*, I, 88. There is some evidence that the father acted as agent for the governor of that colony in 1727; and he is alluded to as agent for the province in February, 1736/7. The king issued an order for two patents of land to be granted to McCulloh senior, one for 72,000 acres on the northeast branch of the Cape Fear River, the second of 60,000 acres at the head of the Neuse River and upon the upper branch of the Cape Fear. These grants were largely for speculative purposes, and became involved in controversies with the Protestant settlers brought in because of conflicting claims with South Carolina. In 1767 Henry McCulloh, the father, and his associates surrendered their grants to the king and later were released from the accumulated quitrents. He still had valuable land, which he sold until the Revolution; this begot constant friction with the North Carolina government.—*Biographical History of North Carolina*, VIII, 323-28; Haywood, *Governor William Tryon and His Administration in the Province of North Carolina*, p. 54; Raper, *North Carolina, A Study in English Colonial Government*, pp. 118-19.

It was McCulloh senior who was agent for the Six Northern Counties in 1747 in the

son entered the American scene in 1761 and resided here continuously until 1767. He accumulated several public positions: appointment to the council, membership in the high court of chancery, and the post of collector of the port at Edenton (Roanoke), though the duties of the last office were soon delegated to a relative. It was immediately after his return to England that he sought and secured the agency of North Carolina. He was clearly a man of culture and of more than ordinary ability. His character has been sharply assailed, for he was accused of shrewd and unscrupulous practices.[31]

James Abercromby, bred to the law, was of the family of Abercromby of County Banff, Ireland, though our interest in him here is as a Britisher. His contacts with America were far-extended, ranging from commissioner of South Carolina to run the boundary line between that colony and North Carolina in 1734 to serving as judge advocate for General Sir James St. Clair in the expedition of 1746 to America, from attorney general of South Carolina to private agent of Governor Glen. A surprising period of service in the Southern colonies preceded his agencies, for he had served nearly thirteen years as attorney and advocate general in South Carolina prior to 1743, and aspired to the chief justiceship of that colony though without success. He seems to have long besieged the high ministers of state, Lord Cathcart and the Duke of Newcastle among others, for some government post. But certainly many years of residence in America lay behind him when he assumed the agency first of North Carolina, and then five years later that of Virginia, holding the agency of both provinces for some years.[32]

---

dispute before the Board of Trade over representation in the assembly. There is a good brief discussion of this election controversy in *Biographical History of North Carolina,* VIII, 328. During the years he spent in the colony, 1740-1747, he acted as inspector and controller general of revenues. He is not to be confused with another Henry McCulloch, secretary of the colony.—*Ibid.,* p. 329, note.

[31] McCulloh junior made a second visit to North Carolina from October, 1772, to June, 1773, to look after the property which his father had transferred to him. He was in England at the opening of the Revolution; though he tried to return in 1778, he was detained in New York. His large holdings in North Carolina were confiscated.—*Ibid.,* pp. 332-33. For statements as to his character, see Haywood, *op. cit.,* p. 55; McRee, *Life and Correspondence of James Iredell,* I, 9; *Colonial Records of North Carolina,* V, xxxii.

[32] See his petition for his pay for work on the boundary line, C. O. 5/365, pp. 212-13; for his post as attorney general, see C. O. 5/3621, p. 56; C. O. 5/388, p. 344. A note in the council records alludes to him as "Secretary of Virginia Affaires."—"Early Westward Movement of Virginia," *Virginia Magazine of History and Biography,* XII, 343.

The British barrister seemed to enjoy some popularity as agent. Though there are some striking early illustrations of barristers serving the Northern colonies, the first conspicuous case in the Southern colonies is Ferdinand Paris, serving Maryland from 1739 to 1746. His experience illustrates how a lawyer might very readily be drawn into the work of an agency. First he served the interests of individuals of Maryland. As early as November 18, 1730, he had signed a petition of one Jacob Henderson on behalf of the clergy of Maryland. The first entrance of Paris on the colonial stage for Maryland may be regarded as a success, for Lord Baltimore assented to the act in behalf of which the petition was presented. Paris proves also to have been the lawyer of the Penn family, a connection which inevitably meant contact with the affairs of Pennsylvania, and which was probably responsible for his post as agent for that province from 1731 to 1740. Still other contacts with the colonies preceded his agency for Maryland; namely, he attended the Board of Trade with a Captain Tomlinson, agent for New Hampshire, as solicitor for that colony in May, 1733; in April, 1734, he was again attending the Board of Trade in behalf of an individual interested in land holdings in New York; he appeared for Rhode Island in a boundary dispute with Massachusetts. His appearance before the Board as solicitor for Penn against Lord Baltimore in October, 1734, was probably no disqualification when the Maryland assembly was looking for some one to oppose their proprietor. His interest in America was probably still further stimulated in 1739 by his being asked by the solicitor of the Treasury to defend the crown's interest in the renewed Fairfax claim to a part of Virginia. It was now a short step to becoming agent for the colony of Maryland in 1739.[33] It is a conspicuous fact worth recording that if a British solicitor became involved in the work of one colony, he was likely to be drawn into service for others. Hence, let it be noted that in addition to the two agencies mentioned above and the services for individual colonials,

He secured some office from the Duke of Newcastle in 1762.—Add. MSS, 32936, p. 329. British Museum. See also Dinwiddie *Official Records*, I, 37-38, note.

[33] Calvert Papers, XXIII, 39, 41, 295 1/2; *Journal of the Board of Trade*, 1728/9-1734, pp. 343; 383; 413; 430. As evidence that the colonies were not the only agencies to keep people waiting for their pay, the complaint of Paris against the British government on that score might be recorded. On May 23, 1745, he complained that his services of 1739 in connection with the Fairfax claim were still unpaid.—Treasury Papers, T, I/335, No. 96.

Paris acted as solicitor for the lieutenant governor of Pennsylvania in 1755; as solicitor for the clergy of Virginia in 1759, complaining of a change relating to their salaries; as solicitor for the town of St. Iago de la Vega in Jamaica; and made numerous appearances for West Indian planters.

Maryland chose wisely in selecting Ferdinand John Paris. Versed in the precedents of the various offices with which he must deal, familiar with the procedure before the many boards and commissions having to do with provincial affairs, at home with the official red tape of the government, and well acquainted with the personnel of the different offices, he had been piling up experience with the Board of Trade for almost two decades so that by 1739 he enjoyed a reputation for being a shrewd and skilful barrister. He seems to have been indefatigable in his labors, and yet able to play the courtier in the drawing room when he wished to fall in "accidentally" with certain persons useful in his work.[34]

As further evidence that serving a colony as solicitor led sometimes directly to the agency, the experience of John Sharpe and of Arthur Lee might be cited. John Sharpe acted as solicitor for Massachusetts and had the opportunity to decline the agency of the Bay Colony in 1755 when Bollan resigned, while in the course of his long and active life he was agent for no less than five of the West Indian Islands.[35] Lee, a Virginian resident in London during the years preceding the Revolution—and during the Revolution too—had been retained as counsel by Franklin in support of a petition to the king from Massachusetts Bay in 1773; before long he was asked to act as agent to succeed Franklin for the lower house of that colony.[36] Other barristers serving as agents are Edward Montague and Hugh

[34] *Journal of the Board of Trade*, 1754-1758, pp. 120, 113-14; *ibid.*, 1759-1763, p. 46. For a brief sketch of Paris see Wolff, *The Colonial Agency of Pennsylvania*, pp. 39-41; Correspondence of Penn Family, p. 11.

[35] John Sharpe was agent for Barbados from 1735 to 1756; for Jamaica from 1733 to 1756; for Antigua, 1751-1756; for Nevis, 1751-1756; for St. Christopher, 1751-1757.— Penson, *The Colonial Agents of the British West Indies*, App. II; *Maryland Magazine of History*, VII, 121. In passing it might be noted that this scion of a distinguished family, brother of Governor Horatio Sharpe of Maryland, held various government offices at different times, sat in the House of Commons, and was held worthy to be one of the guardians of Frederick, sixth Lord Baltimore.

[36] The fact that Lee was employed as counsel to aid Franklin is noted in Lee, *Life of Arthur Lee*, II, 237. Lee had given up the practice of medicine in Virginia for the study of the law in London, where, however, he took up his pen, as *Junius Americanus*, in behalf of liberty.

Hammersley, who had already won a reputation as secretary to Lord Baltimore, which fact probably accounts for his selection as agent by the Maryland council. Montague, although he had early won some notice at the bar of the House of Commons in connection with an election case, had not, according to Abercromby—not, to be sure, a disinterested witness—been active at the Temple for some ten years prior to his appointment as agent, and it was thought that the stipend, even of £500 might not induce him to leave the country life which he had been leading.[37]

There was the period, rather early in the eighteenth century, when the colonies seemed desirous of engaging for agents the clerks employed about the various boards and government offices in London. John Sharpe, who, as noted above, was so popular as agent among the West Indian colonies, was solicitor to the treasury and had, through a lively correspondence, contact with the Duke of Newcastle and other prominent statesmen. Charles Delafaye, agent for Jamaica from 1728 to 1731, was a clerk in the office of the secretary of state for the Southern Department, rising in time to the post of under secretary of state. To spare the reader a long list of names with which we are not concerned in this study, suffice it to say that a list of at least ten colonial agents can be compiled who were at the same time filling government posts.[38] While this tendency did not become marked in the North American agencies, the fact that it was conspicuous in connection with the West Indian agencies should be noted, for it probably had its influence in the case of a few appointments. Six of the number cited above do concern the colonies of the American mainland. Henry Wilmot, who served

[37] For Hammersley, see Edgar, *A Colonial Governor in Maryland*, p. 213; *Archives of Maryland*, II, 352. For Montague see letter of Ludwell to Governor Dinwiddie, dated March 22, 1759, C. O. 5/1329, p. 369.

There are two other barristers who aided an agent, but they do not fit into this group as both seem to have lived in Virginia for a period at least: Edward Chilton, who was attorney general of Virginia sometime between the date of his arrival in Virginia, 1682, and 1696, when he became attorney general of the Court of Admiralty of Virginia; and Henry Hartwell, apparently a distinguished lawyer of Virginia, who was in England at the time of the Jeffreys agency in 1697 and consented to accompany Jeffreys to lay a petition before the Committee of Plantations.—*Virginia Magazine of History and Biography*, III, 12, note; *William and Mary Quarterly*, X, ser. 1, p. 33; Bruce, *Institutional History of Virginia*, I, 696.

[38] Penson, *The Colonial Agents of the British West Indies*, pp. 167-68. She includes Pownall, who had just left his post as secretary to the Board of Trade.

as agent for New Jersey from 1766 to 1769,[39] was connected with the office of secretary of state. Thomas Beake, whom we have barely named as an early agent of St. Christopher, was a clerk in the Privy Council office. Peter Leheup is the striking illustration of this tendency among the Southern colonies. He was acting as clerk of the Privy Council in 1723 when he was asked to take on the agency of Virginia. Many years later, while still agent for Virginia, he was brought to trial on April 19, 1755, for malfeasance as one of the receivers in a lottery and fined heavily. He seems also to have been in the Treasury Office as controller of exchequer bills where he declared that he had executed his duties without any perquisites beyond the salary for over forty years from the instituting of the office by his father-in-law. This office was taken from him abruptly presumably some time before 1757 at the time when the Duke of Newcastle fell from favor. It would appear that Peregrine Fury was employed in the paymaster's office of the Horse Guards in 1755.[40] William Blathwayt, a civil servant who rose to be secretary of state and secretary at war to William III, lives in American history for his knowledge of the affairs of the Board of Trade. In 1675 he entered the Plantation Office and served as secretary to the Lords of Trade from 1679 to 1696, holding also part of that time the appointment to the office of surveyor and auditor general of plantation revenues. Hence, Virginia in securing his good offices in 1692 was availing herself of the services of one who might indeed be termed an expert in plantation affairs. John Povey, cousin and brother-in-law of Balthwayt, succeeded his relative as presiding clerk in the Plantation Office from 1680 to 1696. His claims to consideration for the chief post when the Plantation Office was reorganized in 1696 were disregarded, but Blathwayt succeeded the next year in having Povey made a clerk in ordinary to the Privy Council. It was while holding one or the other of these posts that

[39] For Wilmot see *ibid.* He also served Antigua, Montserrat, Nevis, and St. Christopher as agent.

[40] *Ibid.*, p. 252. Beake also served as agent for Pennsylvania.—Wolff, *op. cit.*, p. 26. For Leheup, see Dinwiddie, *Official Records,* I, 1, 139 note, 140 note, 210, 211, 237. He also served as agent for Barbados, 1735-1736, with John Sharpe and George Tissier.— Penson, *op. cit.*, p. 250. For statement as to the trial, see *The London Magazine*, 1755, pp. 186, 250. On July 19, 1769, he begged the Duke of Newcastle to be reinstated in the Treasury Office.—Newcastle Papers, British Museum, Add. MSS, 32968, p. 100; *The Royal Kalendar* (1755, p. 70) shows him in the Treasury Office listed as one of four chief clerks. For Fury see Newcastle Papers, Add. MSS, 32851, f. 421.

he acted as agent for New York, Virginia, and Maryland(?), appointments which he probably owed to his cousin's efforts.[41]

It was not long before the possibility of pernicious effects of such relations between the colonies and employees in the government offices was perceived, at least by the Board of Trade. A certain Anthony Sanderson, a clerk at the Plantation Office, was serving Massachusetts as agent from 1722 to 1724. On April 30, 1724, the Board took peremptory steps to put an end to any such practice. The Board directed its secretary to dismiss any clerks so employed from their posts at the Plantation Office if they continued as agents. The next day came a petition from Sanderson, praying to be allowed to continue his agency until the conclusion of the dispute then pending in Massachusetts between the assembly and the governor. The terse reply of their Lordships was that they did not see cause to alter their decision.[42]

If colonials could cast covetous eyes on clerks and civil servants, they were not unaware of the possible advantage of having colonial agents sitting in parliament. Again, the impetus in this direction came from the West Indian colonies which secured several agents from among members of the Commons, or were able to retain their services after they had been elected to seats in parliament. Ten sitting members of parliament are recorded by Miss Penson as agents for the West Indies, covering the period from 1705 till long after the mainland colonies had severed their relation with Great Britain. Taking the North American colonies as a whole the proportion of agents who sat in the British parliament was far smaller: Sir Henry Ashurst, Micajah Perry, who sat in the House of Commons, the mighty Edmund Burke, who honored New York by ac-

[41] For a comprehensive treatment of Blathwayt see Jacobsen, *William Blathwayt: A Late Seventeenth Century Administrator, passim.* For Povey, see *ibid.,* 298-302, 319, note; for his agency of New York, *Calendar of State Paper, Colonial,* 1689-1692, p. 692; for Maryland, *Archives of Maryland,* XXV, 45; for Virginia, *Executive Journals of the Council,* I, 187, 255, 441, 383; II, 34, 138, 317. Despite Miss Jacobsen's assertion that Povey acted as agent for Maryland, the writer finds no proof in Maryland archives. The reference in this note only indicates that he may have written seeking the post.

[42] *Journal of the Board of Trade,* 1722/3-1728, p. 87. It is rather a puzzling fact that this prohibition against civil servants acting also as agents seems to have been lifted after the American Revolution. George Chalmers was appointed chief clerk to the Board of Trade after the reorganization of colonial business in 1782 and had the main responsibility for the administrative work till his death in 1825; yet he is listed as an agent for the Bahamas from 1792 to 1826 [*sic*].—Penson, *op. cit.,* pp. 167 and App. II.

cepting its agency, Richard Jackson, Barlow Trecothick, and Charles Garth. Of this meager number Charles Garth represented three Southern colonies and sat in parliament for Devizes borough, Wiltshire.

It is also striking that choice of an agent to act as spokesman in the House of Commons came for the Southern colonies only very late in their history. At first blush this might appear the wisest of all choices, for it meant not only a partisan to defend and oppose but to give timely notice also of unfortunate government moves before it should be too late. Garth affords a good example of this last-named advantage.[43] When Lord Barrington, secretary of war, brought in on March 13, 1769, a bill to continue the Mutiny Act in America, Garth immediately notified the other agents. Furthermore, a member would, of course, have a place on committees of parliament, sometimes as chairman, and thus a voice even before measures reached the floor of the Commons. Of course, the agent could not always enforce his views; when Garth brought to the committee a clause for granting to the colonials the same consideration as to time and deductions for prompt payment allowed by several acts to British merchants, his proposition lost out with the Treasury Bench, and he was left to find solace in the thought that payment of the duties in England before exportation would relieve the colonists of drain on their specie.[44] Furthermore, these men were in a position to give circumstantial information of the secret sessions to the colonies such as no one outside the membership of the Commons could give, which should have made the colonials see the British point of view if there had been any way of bridging the widening gap. Garth sent Maryland such a meticulous account of the debate and action of the Commons and in the House of Lords on the repeal of the Stamp Act covering almost eighteen pages of print, and a

[43] On January 31, 1767, Garth gave the Committee of Correspondence of South Carolina a hint of impending taxes despite repeal of the Stamp Act. "I cannot," he wrote, "conclude this Letter without informing you that upon the 28th Instant when in the Committee of Supply we were upon the Estimate of the charge of his Majesty's Land forces and Garrisons in the Plantations, administration was called upon to Show if any Steps or measures had been thought of or taken to relieve the people of Great Britain from a Burthen. . . ." The chancellor replied that he should bring in propositions which he hoped in time would ease the "people of England and yet not lie too heavy on colonials." "Garth Correspondence," loc. cit., XXIX, 132. See Return of the Names of Every Member of Parliament, 1696-1877, p. 144.

[44] "Garth Correspondence," loc. cit., XXXI, 55; XXVIII, 231.

twenty-three page letter on the same subject to South Carolina. A special sense of responsibility led Garth to almost constant attendance at parliament during the action on the repeal of the Stamp Act. He declared that he had never been absent a half-hour during the entire debate. The colonies probably accused him of being willing to compromise on the Mutiny Act because rather than lose the entire clause he accepted an amendment to his proposal to restrain the billeting of soldiers in colonies where a provincial law provided quarters.[45] Garth had already been serving South Carolina three years before he succeeded to his father's seat in the House of Commons. That colony, with an eye perhaps to the father's influence when selecting the son, was fully conscious that he was now in a new position of enhanced effectiveness.[46] Charles Garth was well descended, the grand nephew of a celebrated physician and poet. Of his sincerity in serving his colonial employers loyally and of extreme conscientiousness in the discharge of his duty there can be no question. To an unusual degree he understood and sympathized with the American position in their dispute with the mother country.[47]

[45] This long account to Maryland is found in the *Maryland Historical Magazine*, VI, 287-305; to South Carolina in *South Carolina Historical and Genealogical Magazine*, XXVI, 68-92. For his action on the Mutiny Bill, see *ibid.*, XXXI, 56.

[46] For comment in South Carolina when he entered parliament, see *South Carolina Gazette*, April 20, 1765.

[47] As illustrative of his sincerity, see the following excerpt from one of his letters to the assembly of Maryland, dated February 26, 1766: ". . . in opposing as I have done to the utmost of my Power this late Attack upon the general Liberty and Happiness of the subject in America, at the same Time that I was thereby discharging the general Duty of every subject under this excellent Constitution, I was pursuing the Dictates of my own Conscience, and putting in Practice Principles that I had early imbibed, without expecting any other Approbation, than that of a Heart conscious to itself of having done what it ought."—*Maryland Historical Magazine*, VI, 283.

A libel found inscribed on the wall of an apartment near the State House of Georgia seems to be aimed at Garth, judging by the date. Apparently it was written before December 10, 1762, as it seems to have accompanied a message from both houses of assembly to the governor, bearing that date.

> Carolina her Agent must Sorely bemoan,
> And each Votary of Hermes reecho the groan,
> Thy Fortune aspiring, He no more can Raise,
> His Sons shall no longer thy Eloquence Praise.
> Is it ambition Courts thee with Soft Soothing air
> Or Power or Riches that make thee Repair
> To Climate so Sultry!
>
> It is not ambition alone does invite,
> But Power and Riches both equal delight;
> For what makes all doctrines most Plainly appear,
> It cannot be less—than a thousand a year.

Hermes, it will be recalled, is the god of lawyers and thieves.

Only to a very limited extent is the religious consideration, which played an important part in the maintenance in office by Rhode Island of the Quaker, Richard Partridge, or in the appointment by Puritan Massachusetts of Jasper Mauduit, present in the Southern colonies and then only early in their history. Certainly John Ash was selected by the dissenters of South Carolina to present their grievances because he was an outstanding defender of those views; Joseph Boone, who was sent to replace Ash upon the latter's death, was likewise recognized as a leader among the dissenters, and one can scarcely escape the feeling that the religious issue prompted his selection when agents were sent in 1715 to protest against the extraordinary powers granted to Chief Justice Trott, as it is significant that even then the dissenter was balanced by a churchman, Richard Beresford. Their mission was primarily to adjust grievances with the proprietors or, in case of failure, to appeal to a higher power. It cannot be said that Boone reflected the highest ideals, for in his zeal to forward the cause of the dissenters, he was both inconsistent and insincere: he praised the Fundamental Constitutions to the proprietors and at the same time tried to invoke the hostility of the Board of Trade in order to overthrow the church. Evidently during the period that the colony was seeking the overthrow of proprietary rule, the South Carolina assembly remembered only his known zeal for the liberties of the country, his thorough knowledge of the conditions in South Carolina, and his valuable experience in England as an agent.

Whatever may be said about the preference of the colonies for British merchants or returned colonials, for lawyers or members of parliament, there is no doubt that they desired men of influence who could establish contacts with the leading statesmen of the government. So indirect were these contacts sometimes that acquaintanceship with the secretary at the Board of Trade was valued, or acquaintanceships which would merely open the way to some greater figure. Ex-Governor Blakiston, in seeking to press the appointment of one Ludwell (not the earlier agent) to the Virginia council, went to Blathwayt, former secretary to the Lords of Trade, in his behalf, accompanied by Micajah Perry. In this instance the agent felt that he should carry special weight because of a favor he had just done the auditor general, though, he adds, "I joyn with you he is hard to make any impression upon, but by ye method you mention"—a generous gratuity.[48] Blakiston, however, claimed to have some "interest" with most members of the Board of Trade. Governor Nicholson in recommending the Reverend Mr. Blair to the Board of Trade when he was dispatched on his second mission declared that he was well known to his late Grace of Canterbury and to the Bishops of London and Salisbury.[49]

One of the qualifications urged for Peregrine Fury by Governor Glen in proposing him to the South Carolina lower house was that "he had the Ear of such great Men & could at all Hours have ready & easy access to them" and declared later that the province ought to reappoint him, such action being proper acknowledgment to "his noble Patron, whofe power we all know is not lefsened by length of time and We are equally certain that his Interest in them is not diminifhed." By patron he doubtless referred to the Duke of Newcastle. Perhaps his highest commendation came from Governor Glen, who felt that there were few persons so proper to be agent, though he had "no Reason in the world to be partial to him." It would appear that Fury was a merchant, for Henry Laurens drew constantly on him.[50]

But woe betide the agent if it were suspected that he had lost favor with the men of influence! A comment by Governor Dinwiddie about Leheup tells a volume. To the Earle of Albemarle he wrote on June 18, 1754 (?), that Peter Leheup, "being under the Frowns of the Ministry, I believe is turned out of all his office[s]" and that he intended accordingly to recommend James Abercromby to succeed him.[51] Abercromby, for his part, was the

---

[48] Blakiston got the appointment for Ludwell, for he wrote the latter: "Mr. Blath: had conferred it upon you with a good grace and his man had order . . . to write your Commission, wch is to be sent to Mr. Perry this week."—*Virginia Magazine of History and Biography*, IV, 16.

The necessity of fees is so well illustrated here, even with high officials that the recommendation of the Governor to the House of Deputies of Maryland should be noted: he urged, since Blathwayt was the only person he or Colonel Blakiston could apply to for the ease of that province, the serious consideration of settling some annual salary on "Blathwayte" as the accounts must all pass through his hands as auditor general.—*Archives of Maryland*, XXVI, 80.

[49] The letter was dated May 5, 1697.—C. O. 5/1307, f. 221.

[50] For Newcastle's recommendation, see Journal of the Council of South Carolina, V, 112; for the governor's, see Journal of the Commons House of Assembly, XXIX, 744.

[51] Dinwiddie, *Official Records*, I, 210. This was, of course, because of the charge of malfeasance in connection with the lottery.

close friend of General Abercromby, and this friendship proved a matter of signal importance when toward the close of his general agency for Virginia the colonies were to share in the parliamentary grant, because that general had the allotting of the money.[52]   The chief qualification of Hugh Hammersley in the eyes of Governor Horatio Sharpe, and presumably of the Maryland council, when they were considering a separate agent in 1766, was the fact that he was Calvert's great friend and adviser.[53]   Finally, there can be no doubt that Georgia was deeply influenced in selecting Benjamin Franklin for her agency by the knowledge that he had entree to some of the most highly placed men in England.   Instances could be vastly multiplied if this study included all the several hundred agents of the thirteen colonies.   Arthur Lee, for instance, won by his writings the friendship of Burke to such a degree that he asked the great statesman to accompany him to present a petition to Dartmouth and won also the friendship of the great literary light, Samuel Johnson.

When the survey is turned to the special agents, one realizes that almost without exception one confronts the abler men of the respective colonies.   There is no need to comment on those men who have already fallen into other categories—James Blair, William Byrd, Francis Yonge, or on the men who belong to the genesis period.   Our number then shrinks to the small group of the Randolph family, who went over from Virginia, and to an outstanding South Carolinian, Charles Pinckney.   Sir John Randolph became through his own mental endowment and varied gifts the lawyer most distinguished in Virginia during the first half of the eighteenth century.   Benefiting by his excellent training he attained high office, though fate granted him only a short span of life: clerkship of the House of Burgesses, a remunerative and influential office; and after his return from his second agency, the post of speaker of the house, to which he added in the same session the treasurership of the colony.   His unique honor, that of being knighted by the king, was a recognition of his legal abilities and diplomatic skill.   Distinguished in

[52] The writer has been unable to establish any blood relationship, though the name suggests that possibility.
[53] Although Governor Sharpe made the statement in 1759 in a letter to his brother William, that relation between the two men probably remained true in 1766.—*Archives of Maryland*, IX, 352.

the front rank of sons of Virginia by any fair appraisal stands the son of Sir John, Peyton Randolph. Honors were heaped upon him: he, too, was speaker of the House of Burgesses, became attorney general, president of the revolutionary convention of Virginia, and finally president of the Continental Congress.[54] Perhaps it is sufficient to say of Isham and Edward Randolph that they were worthy scions of the distinguished family to which they belonged, for both were brothers of Sir John Randolph. The former was twice elected to the House of Burgesses and was appointed adjutant general. Edward, who, it will be recalled, found his appointment as agent withdrawn, chose a sea-faring life and traveled in his own ships between Virginia and England at least as late as 1756. His residence in England, for it is thought that he never had a home in Virginia, was probably responsible for his selection in 1740. Though not a native-born son, Charles Pinckney spent twenty-six years of his life in South Carolina, much of it "in his Majesty's service," as he himself put it, as member of the council and chief justice. Leave of absence from the last post, when he undertook the special agency in 1753, was granted on the score of health, a plea which seems justified by the fact of his death a few months after his return.[55]

There remains only to point out the plural agency holding. One is reminded, in watching the selection of the agents, of childrens' choosing games where the players seem able to think of only one person to "choose." In order to emphasize the degree to which plural holding of office prevailed, it seems desirable to touch on other colonies outside the Southern group where overlapping occurred for Southern agents—even in the West Indies. Jeffrey Jeffreys, the first instance of a London merchant to be agent, served not only Virginia in 1691, but acted for the Leeward Isles from 1692 to 1697. Nathaniel Blakiston, as should be abundantly clear by this time, served both Maryland and Virginia though there is not exact coincidence of dates. Thomas Beake undertook soliciting for Pennsylvania in 1720 and served St. Christopher from 1724 to

[54] For Sir John see *Virginia Magazine of History and Biography*, XXXII, 136-41; *D. A. B.*, XV, 361-62. For Peyton Randolph, *ibid.*, pp. 367-68.

[55] Pinckney was one of five members of the South Carolina council in England at the same time. The above facts were culled from his statement to the Board of Trade on May 29, 1754.—C. O. 5/374, K, 92. For a few facts see *D. A. B.*, XIV, 614.

1733. Samuel Wragg found it possible to attend to the agencies of both North and South Carolina though his agency for the latter came in the twenties and was a special agency for a brief period only. Abercromby looked after the agency matters of North Carolina as well as of Virginia though his duties for the former were terminated four years after he began those for the latter. Ferdinand Paris served Maryland and Pennsylvania, both of which provinces he served long and well. Garth served three of the five Southern colonies—South Carolina, Maryland, and Georgia, while Grey Elliott added the agency of the Bahamas in 1785 long after all connection with Georgia had terminated. The list could be vastly extended for the other colonies. Dennys De Berdt, agent for Massachusetts from 1765 to 1770, appears also as agent for Delaware; Richard Partridge, the Quaker who served Rhode Island so many years, found time to look after the agencies of Connecticut, New Jersey, and Pennsylvania. John Sharpe might almost have been accused of collecting agencies, for we know that he acted for five of the West Indian colonies and barely missed a sixth agency on the mainland; Henry Wilmot did as well, for he rendered service to four West Indian islands—or tried to, for he was dismissed by one for negligence—besides the North American province of New Jersey.[56] Kilby was agent for Nova Scotia as well as Massachusetts; Samuel Smith for St. John's as well as for the council of North Carolina. Benjamin Franklin, the prince of agents, served not alone his native state, but also New Jersey, Georgia, and the lower house of assembly of Massachusetts.

In justice it must be added that there was some opposition voiced to this plural office-holding. Dinwiddie tried to recommend Abercromby to South Carolina for that agency, but it was feared that the people would object since he was the agent for North Carolina— evidently there was no objection to his agency for the more remote colony of Virginia. Dinwiddie ventured to say that his candidate would resign from the North Carolina post if he had assurance of the South Carolina appointment.[57] In Georgia the council disagreed, on the ground of divided allegiance, to the ordinance appointing

[56] This has been compiled from Appendix II of Miss Penson's book and the Appendix to Burns, *The Colonial Agents of New England.*
[57] Dinwiddie, *Official Records,* I, 408.

Garth agent, insisting that the South Carolina agent could not be a proper appointment for Georgia, but they declared themselves ready to concur to any other "unexceptionable" person. The outcome of the dispute has already been described.[58]

[58] C. O. 5/647 (no page given); stated in a letter from Governor Wright to Secretary Shelburne, dated April 6, 1767. The case of William Knox, agent for Georgia, is not cited for two reasons: first, his Georgia agency had terminated before that of East Florida began; and, secondly, the agency for East Florida was a crown agency and continued after the colonial agency had ended.—C. O. 391/86, p. 9.

CHAPTER 9.

THE FINANCIAL BURDEN OF THE AGENCY

THE title which stands at the head of this chapter should be a misnomer, for the small salary paid the agents ought hardly to have been burdensome to the colonies. To the Englishman who took on the office it probably at first—but not for long—appealed as an easy way to add a stipend to his other earnings and hardly entered his calculations by the honorable name of salary. But to pioneers, wresting their living from the soil under the hard conditions of a new country, it appeared and was a burden. Occasionally, the agent professed indifference to the pay. Blakiston rendered Maryland a year's service gratis, though with a sharp proviso, it must be confessed, for future honoraria; McCulloh tried to appear indifferent to the monetary reward, but with little success. He wrote grandly to Colonel John Harvey of North Carolina on July 24, 1769: "With respect to the salary, if any is named, I wish it may be respectable,—both with relation to the former, [the colony] as well as myself,—But at the same time, I pledge my Honor, that I do not, will not, desire a single penny in payment, till the province shall be fully able and inclined to do it.—I am really and truly ambitious of the honor of being your agent, independent of every meaner motive, . . .[1] Again in 1770 he protests, "my chief view in applying for the Agency, was the Hope and Honor of serving the province. . . . I never sought the appointment from pecuniary motives, for I can truly say that the greatest part of the present allowance is not sufficient to answer any necessary extraordinary expenses of cloaths and Carriages,—but I would not wish the point to be agitated, . . ."[2]

The amount allowed the agent by the various colonies naturally

[1] *Colonial Records of North Carolina*, VIII, 59.
[2] *Ibid.*, p. 183.

engages first attention. For the genesis period payment was made, as to other officials, in the only medium of exchange, tobacco. John Pountis was to receive four pounds of tobacco from every "tithable" person in the colony as his compensation. The precise method by which the cost of his agency was to be defrayed has fortunately been preserved. The assembly decreed that so much of the "best merchantable" tobacco should be levied on the planters the next season as would amount to £200 in money with interest; it was to be brought in to James City by the last of October and to be turned over to Sir George Yeardley, Treasurer George Sandys, and two merchants, for which they were obligated to one John Harte, a London merchant, who had agreed to advance that sum to Pountis. Any surplus arising from the tobacco collected was to be invested in gunpowder after the cost of the freight on the tobacco was deducted.[3] Exactly the contingency for which the Virginians tried to provide, namely, the nullity of the act if "Pountis fhall nott Arrive in England," did arise immediately by his death. The council asked to be excused from paying the administrator of Pountis' estate the sum stipulated, "as no money was expended and our suite not pfecuted."[4] The charge of Sir George Yeardley's voyage in 1625 was met in similar fashion, with 5,000 weight in tobacco thought "fitting" for the "oversight of Sir George's affaires." The tobacco already collected for Pountis was ordered sent to England and charges for Sir John Harte for the bond of £200 were deducted, before the remainder was turned over to Sir George.[5] By 1628 the colony was ready to meet the charges of their agents, Wyatt, Bennett and Marshart, and it also promised "if by yor dilligence you fhall effect anything for the good of this Country, wee shall for that alfo give you fatisfaction to yor contents," by which they seemed to offer them a special honorarium to their complete satisfaction if success crowned their efforts.[6] Again in 1639 a tax in kind was imposed to "reward the care" and pay the expense of the agent "engaged in watching the colony's interests," by whom was meant Sandys, the levy this time

[3] The act provided that if Mr. John Pountis should not arrive in England, or if the money were not paid, then the act was to be "voide."—*Journals of the House of Burgesses, 1619-1658/9*, p. 41.

[4] *The Records of the Virginia Company of London*, IV, 559-60.

[5] Wyatt, "Documents of Sir Francis Wyatt," *William and Mary Quarterly*, ser. 2, VII, 130.

[6] *Journals of the House of Burgesses, 1619-1658/9*, p. 5.

amounting to 4,102 pounds of "regulated" tobacco.[7] A record in the statutes of 1654 indicates that sheriffs and collectors were assembling tobacco to cover the expenses of the agency of Colonel Samuel Mathews.[8] To Governor Berkeley, while serving as agent in 1661-1662, was allocated, as befitted his high station, 200,000 pounds of tobacco, which was then worth £2,000 sterling, almost the equivalent of a year's salary. To Philip Mallory, who went over about this same time in behalf of church affairs, the assembly voted 11,000 pounds of tobacco to be paid by the next levy.[9]

When we reach the agency of Moryson, Ludwell, and Smith, which was created in 1674 to contest the Culpeper grant, the individual tax to support the agency appears in the record: fifty pounds of tobacco on every "tithable" for two years in succession, an amount which was felt a great grievance when many citizens did not own a foot of ground. To this was added, as a means of creating a sufficient fund, a fine of thirty to fifty pounds of tobacco on every person who lost a suit in a county court, of fifty to seventy pounds if his case was brought in a general court, and, finally, there was appropriated a part of the revenue of the two shillings tax per hogshead of tobacco. Moryson and Smith were each to receive £150 that year and the same further payment the next year as the assembly deemed merited. Secretary Ludwell and Colonel Daniel Parke were authorized to receive the money resulting from the sale of the tobacco sent into England to pay the agents. If the agents found it necessary to borrow one or two thousand pounds, they were empowered to do so, the assembly guaranteeing repayment at six per

---

[7] Robinson's Transcripts, p. 232; Bruce, *Institutional History of Virginia*, II, 519. Virginia seemed to have difficulty with the incompetency of the sheriffs who collected this levy in the Charles River country. At the session of October, 1640, it was resolved that since by the neglect of an undersheriff the tobacco was so much "damnified" that a great part was altogether unmerchantable, the chief sheriff was ordered to satisfy Sandys with the full quantity of 4,102 pounds of "regulated tobacco being good and merchantable."—*Minutes of the Council and General Court of Colonial Virginia*, p. 472.

[8] The note at the session of 1653 of £250 to be sent the Virginia agent, Samuel Mathews, seems to be the result of accident. A Dunkirk ship, which had violated the navigation laws by clearing a Virginia port without paying fees, was held forfeit and appraised at £400 sterling. Apparently a portion of this went over in cash.—Hening, *Statutes*, I, 385, 382, 383 note. For the entry of 1654 see *Journals of the House of Burgesses*, 1619-1658/9, pp. 92, 93.

[9] The usual salary of the Virginia governor in castle dues, license fees, tobacco, corn, and customs was then equal to rather more than $12,000.—Campbell, *History of the Colony and Ancient Dominion of Virginia*, pp. 252-53. See also Hening, *Statutes*, II, 17, 34.

cent interest. The assembly also undertook to repay sums borrowed locally for the agency at the same interest, and the governor was to appoint persons in every precinct to deal with these sums of money. The last notice of an allowance of tobacco to care for an agency encountered by the writer was of an allotment of 8,260 pounds to Thomas Ludwell at the session beginning February 20, 1676/7.[10]

It is clear that by this time a fund for this purpose was deposited in London through bills of exchange which the colony claimed the right to create and dispense. But the British government challenged the right of Virginia to dispose of this considerable sum by issuing an order forbidding the agents to use any more of that money without a royal warrant. There was usually no interference with the activities of the early agents or with the use of agency funds, but this case of the Culpeper grant involved a matter of prime importance to the king.[11]

The only other Southern colony where agents received appropriations in the form of tobacco grants was Maryland where the financial arrangements for Peter Pagan bore a close resemblance to those for Virginia agents of the seventeenth century—those of a pioneer country. For a special service before his formal appointment as agent the Maryland assembly voted £20 sterling which was to be paid him in England, reimbursement being promised the financial agent in tobacco reckoned at the value of six shillings per hundred pounds f.o.b. in Anne Arundell County. Presumably the tobacco was to come from the general levy. In 1692 when Maryland was adjusting the cost of Coode's and Cheseldyne's mission to England to justify the revolution in that province, their expenses were to be met by a special assessment on the persons and estates of the inhabitants; 100,000 pounds of tobacco were to be paid to Cheseldyne in addition to another sum, the exact amount of which cannot be ascertained because of the mutilation of the records. A little later that same year it was voted to pay the rest of Cheseldyne's account in tobacco computed at the rate of seven shillings per hundred pounds.[12]

[10] Hening, *Statutes*, II, 313-14; Bruce, *Institutional History of Virginia*, II, 520; *Journals of the House of Burgesses*, 1659/60-1693, pp. 62, 81.

[11] Hening, *Statutes*, II, 430; Flippin, *The Royal Government in Virginia*, pp. 185-86.

[12] *Archives of Maryland*, XIII, 416, 467, 410; XXXVIII, 97. The record for 1692 is so badly torn that part of the entry is lost.

By 1680, when Virginia decided to establish a regular agency, she arranged a fixed salary of £100 a year in money which was paid until 1716 on the warrant of the governor on the receiver general[13] out of the tobacco revenue, a tax of two shillings per hogshead on tobacco. The exceptions were Ludwell's agency in 1688, that of the Reverend Mr. Blair in 1691, and Byrd's first agency, the expenses of which were met from money raised by the impost on liquors. In the year 1717 an additional stipend, charged to the quitrents, brought the salary to about £300 a year during Nathaniel Blakiston's agency. Leheup applied for a continuance of this additional salary on the quitrents, but was told that he had too much from the treasury office to expect more. However, he and former agents appear to have received extra payments for contingencies from the tobacco revenues besides gratuities granted from time to time by the assembly. In fact, his compensation was declared by Abercromby at a later date to have been more generous than the £200 paid the agent in the middle of the century without any other allowance whatever for contingencies.[14]

The increase in salary to £200 seems not to have been made until the late fall of 1754,[15] but was continued to Abercromby even after he became agent for the governor and council only, the last such entry appearing for the half year ending September 1, 1774. Evidently Abercromby had not shown due appreciation for the increase in his salary, for which Governor Dinwiddie claimed credit, for the executive rebuked him in a letter of June 6, 1755, in the following terms: "You sh'd also have wrote a Let'r of Thanks to the Council for the Augmentat'n of Y'r Salary. You know People

[13] The records show this salary of £100 being paid as follows: in 1696, *Executive Journals of the Council*, I, 348, II, 64; to John Povey in 1701, *ibid.*, pp. 138, 208; in 1702, *ibid.*, p. 276; in 1703, *ibid.*, II, 317; to John Thrale in 1704, *ibid.*, p. 365; to John Carter in 1723, *ibid.*, IV, 40; to Leheup in 1739, *ibid.*, p. 438.

An entry in the Burgesses' *Journal* for April 29, 1692, shows bills of exchange ordered lodged by the treasurer in Governor Corbin's hands for William Blathwayt to the amount of £200 sterling, but it does not appear for what length of time.—*Journals of the House of Burgesses*, 1659/60-1693, p. 407. It also appears that when Ludwell was sent over by the House of Burgesses in 1688, he was ordered paid £250 sterling out of the import tax on liquors.—*Ibid.*, pp. 351, 356, 362, 365, 366.

[14] This statement is based on an account by Abercromby (C. O. 5/1329, p. 357). See also *Executive Journals of the Council*, III, 438; C. O. 5/1342, p. 129.

[15] The semi-yearly payments can be traced from April 25, 1728. See C. O. 5/1321, p. 116; C. O. 5/1324, pp. 9, 45, 95, 101, 132, 152, 174, 185. For Leheup's plea for more pay, see C. O. 5/1739, 357; C. O. 5/1333, p. 257.

in y's Part of the World expect ret's for Favours, and a proper let'r is soon wrote."[16]

When the agent performed some special service for the House of Burgesses with the approval of the governor and council, he was compensated by the house out of the general funds. An instance of such service for the house is needed for clarity. Abercromby called attention in a letter to Governor Fauquier on December 28, 1758, to services on the supply bill of parliament and a salt bill and other business more immediately concerning the assembly, for which he declared that he had not received the smallest allowance from the lower house during his agency. Abercromby, it would appear, would have liked to have his salary derived from the quitrents and a yearly allowance of £50 additional for contingent expenses. But instead of gaining an increase from the quitrents, there was some talk in the spring of 1759 of dropping him altogether on the ground that one agent was sufficient.[17]

The salary was fixed by the House of Burgesses for its agent in 1759 at a far more generous figure than anything offered before, £500 per annum, but was designed as "full compensation for his trouble and expenses." In other words, the burgesses did not propose to have to deal with incidental expenses, of which we shall hear more directly.[18]

With the turn of the century there came in Maryland, too, an end of tobacco levies, or at least, of quotations of the agent's pay in terms of tobacco. Pounds sterling now became the order of the day. The first appropriation for Blakiston, that for salary due September 17, 1705, but not voted until April, 1706, was fixed at £120. On that same date, the House of Delegates deferred the salary which would be due September 17, 1706. His vicissitudes in holding the Maryland agency, as have been recounted, were many; likewise, he suffered vicissitudes in salary. It would appear that in

---

[16] C. O. 5/1333, p. 257; Dinwiddie, *Official Records*, II, 57.

[17] Leheup received large gratuities from time to time from the assembly.—C. O. 5/1329, p. 357; Abercromby Letter Book, pp. 120, 73; C. O. 5/1729, p. 377. Evidence that the House of Burgesses paid special sums is clear from a letter by Governor Dinwiddie to Abercromby of April 26, (1754): "The 15£ due from the Ho. of Burgesses, I believe was a Neglect, but (1) shall at a proper time remind them thereof."—Dinwiddie, *Official Records*, I, 138-39. See also a letter from Abercromby to Blair of the Virginia council, dated November 18, 1758, about the agent's "demands on the House of Burgesses."—Abercromby Letter Book, pp. 115, 120.   [18] Hening, *Statutes*, VII, 276-77.

1714, during his second period of service, his salary shrank to £100, though the only note on the subject is one of a council message to the lower house which states that out of a "generous Sense of the good Affection this province bears him," he had accepted a salary of £100, despite the arrangement of 1702. It requires no very lively imagination to conjecture that Maryland, smaller and younger, had been disturbed by the more modest salary paid by Virginia. Entries for 1716, 1718, 1719, and 1721 show the salary as £100. It is to be hoped that he was paid in the intervening years. It is pleasing to record that the members of the House of Delegates, niggardly though they showed themselves to Blakiston, agreed in 1721 after his dismissal to pay him *pro rata* on the next year's account until such time as he could reasonably receive notice of his discharge.[19] The salary at this time came from the public levy. The conception of a proper reward for this service had not expanded by 1739 in Maryland, and so Ferdinand Paris served his seven years at the old rate, though extra charges enter in 1741, as will be explained later. The significant difference, however, must be noted that his salary was paid by private subscription.[20] By 1766, when the House of Delegates was determined to have its own agent, by extralegal means if necessary, it fixed the salary for Charles Garth at £150 per year, as a nearer approach to the £200 paid at this time by Virginia to the agent of the governor and council.

The bitter quarrel between the council and the house over the long-standing issue of an agent, and the quarrel between the two houses over the salary of the clerk of the council, with consequent impossibility of passing an agency bill, necessitated some way of financing the agent other than by an appropriation when the two houses finally reached the agreement that each might have an agent to appeal to the king—but without allotment of public money. Hence, in addition to opening a subscription, which was an old story, they turned to a device which was indeed novel. They opened a lottery

[19] The reader is again reminded that Blakiston offered to serve one year without pay. For the action of 1706 and 1707, see *Archives of Maryland*, XXVI, 550, 610; XXVII, 49; for the statement of 1714 see *ibid.*, XXIX, 458; for the entries of 1716 and 1718, *ibid.*, XXX, 587, XXXIII, 190, 445; for 1721, *ibid.*, XXXIV, 256.

[20] *Ibid.*, XLIV, 332. This entry is for 1746. We are indebted to Governor Sharpe for a statement as to the method of payment.—*Ibid.*, p. 59. The necessity of paying an agent by subscription was not peculiar to Maryland, for Massachusetts was obliged to pay Wilks by this device on one occasion.—Burns, *Colonial Agents of New England*, p. 20

to raise £1,000 for Garth's salary and expenses with many of the most prominent men in Maryland, including several members of the house, acting as managers of the lottery.[21] The plan was published in the *Maryland Gazette*, the *Virginia Gazette*, and *Pennsylvania Journal*. The issue of December 11, 1766, of the *Maryland Gazette* announced that a list of prizes would be published, to be paid as soon as the drawing was finished, those not claimed within six months after the drawing to be held as generously donated to the cause. In large type the issue proclaimed, "Life without LIBERTY is worfe than DEATH." Prospective subscribers were advised that tickets were to be had from any of the managers and most of the delegates of the house. No less than 2,500 prizes, ranging from £500 to £2 and aggregating £1,000, constituted the bait; 5,000 tickets were to be sold at 30 shillings each; the house set out to raise £7,500. Two and a half per cent was to be deducted from the prizes to pay expenses. The drawing was to be held in the court house at Annapolis on the last Monday in May or sooner, if the tickets were all sold.[22]

The venture started off well. On February 26, 1767, the *Maryland Gazette* exulted that such a number of the tickets of the Liberty Lottery had been sold that the managers expected to draw before the date first named. And then it began to slump despite repeated advertisements.[23] On September 17, the Maryland paper announced that from the best estimate about 800 of the original 5,000 tickets were still for sale and that the drawing had been put off for the second time until the Monday after the first Tuesday of October, when it would occur even though some tickets remained unsold. By October 28 the managers had decided that, as the winter was

[21] The resolve of December 6, 1766, ordered, "That it is the duty of members of the Committee & all members of the House to receive from all persons who think fit to contribute, any sum or bill of exchange, for carrying out those Disputes, to be applied as the Committee thinks best & the Committee must render to the next Assembly account of their proceedings."—Journal of the Lower House, 1762-1768, p. 485.

[22] Among the directors were Charles Carroll of Carrollton, William Murdock, William Paca, Thomas Sprigg, Thomas Ringgold, Henry Hall, John Hall, Thomas Johnson, and Samuel Chase. All were named in the act.—*Ibid.* Some comments by Ringgold are found in his letters to Samuel Galloway in the Galloway Papers.

[23] The announcement appeared in the following issues of the *Maryland Gazette*: Dec. 18, 1766; Jan. 1, 1767; Jan. 8, 22, 29, Feb. 5, 12, Mar. 5 (in the Supplement), Apr. 9, 16, 23, May 7, 14, 21, 28, July 9, 23, 30, Aug. 6, 13, 27, Sept. 17, and May 12, 1768.

too advanced after the November courts, the drawing should not occur until late the next May—that is in 1768. Though members of the House of Delegates took the final 500 tickets on their private account, the drawing was again postponed till late July. The loudly heralded Liberty lottery could hardly be proclaimed a success.[24]

While the regular salary for the agent in South Carolina may be stated as £200 from as early as 1714,[25] there were many irregularities and extra compensation for special services. As the value of a pound in South Carolina currency was about one-seventh of the British pound sterling, the sum appropriated usually stood in the colonial statutes as £1,400 currency. The first arrangements for Kettleby in 1712 at what the writer considers the inception of the regular agency were rather unusual with the idea of a bonus for zealous—and successful—work. The agent was to receive £150 South Carolina currency (about £21 sterling) as an encouragement to undertake the agency, £150 more when parliament passed an act continuing the bounty to the importers of naval stores to England from South Carolina, and £500 when—the word might better be if—it passed an act allowing free exportation of rice from the province to Spain, Portugal, and all places in Africa and America, both the continent and islands, with a proportional sum for those places to which the agent could procure such direct exportation.[26]

The only record of pay to Boone and Beresford, when they were sent over in 1715, appears as £2,000 in the Journal of the Commons House of Assembly. To Colonel Barnwell £1,000 was transmitted in 1720, derived from the general levy on lands and Negroes.[27] The

[24] See ibid., for Dec. 11, 1766, Feb. 26, Sept. 17, Oct. 29, 1767. Rather caustically Governor Sharpe commented March 11, 1767: "You will see by the Scheme published in the inclosed Gazette what Arts they practize to draw peoples Money out of their Pocketts but I am told (it would have failed) if the Pennsylvanians had not bought whole Books."—Archives of Maryland, XIV, 384.

[25] This was the salary of Kettleby after 1714, of Yonge in 1725, and of Fury.—Journal of the Commons House of Assembly of South Carolina, X, 357; of Crockatt.—Ibid., XXX, 456, 489; of Wright in 1756.—C. O. 324/60, p. 264; of Garth in 1762.—Ibid., pp. 266-67. The one exception seems to be Samuel Wragg in 1733/4 when an entry of a payment of £33 6s. 3d. sterling for four months would seem to indicate a yearly salary of only £100.—Ibid., VIII, 49.

[26] Smith, "The Baronies of South Carolina," The South Carolina Historical and Genealogical Magazine, XV, no. 2, p. 151; McCrady, South Carolina under the Proprietary Government, p. 517; Statutes of South Carolina, II, 601-2; for the law fixing his salary at £200, see ibid., p. 621.

[27] Journal of the Commons House of Assembly, V, 87. Recorded for the session of April 27, 1716; Statutes of South Carolina, III, 251.

appropriation for Yonge and Lloyd when they were designated for the journey in 1721, shows the sizable sum of £3,100: £1,000 to Yonge and Lloyd each, £1,000 for the voyage, and £100 in joint stock.[28] When Yonge's agency went into the second year, the Commons House of Assembly voted to add £100 sterling to his reward if he got rice off the enumerated list. As the council had voted on December 7, 1722, to give him £200 in lieu of salary and perquisites, this brought his "encouragement" to £300 sterling.[29] By 1725 the assembly concluded that it was necessary for him to have a fixed salary and placed it at £200 sterling to be paid semi-annually, payable out of money received from Britain on account of Fort King George.[30] Another irregularity was the payment to Governor Johnson about 1731 of £500 sterling for his services in England in trying to put South Carolina under royal rule, but here as elsewhere the services of a governor seem to rate higher than those of the more lowly. Fury, Crockatt, and Wright received £200 as salary or its equivalent in colonial currency together with further sums for expenses.[31]

Twice in South Carolina history there is hint of payment in kind to support the agency. In 1721 the statute provided that the agents should take bills of exchange or the produce of the province along with them; and in 1724 the governor declared that he did not see how the agent could be given a choice in his pay, as there was no South Carolina money in England, but felt that the assembly should order the £1,800 payment out of the rice in the treasurer's hands to be shipped with a letter of credit to make up any deficiency.[32]

For the brief period of the fully accredited agency in North Carolina the salary seemed to differ between the time of Abercromby and that of Jouvencal and McCulloh, the former receiving apparently only £100 while the latter two were paid £200 sterling with McCulloh receiving £300 yearly for the late period of 1771

[28] Public Records of South Carolina, I, pt. 1, p. 91.

[29] Journal of the Commons House of Assembly of South Carolina, III, 165, 322.

[30] Statutes of South Carolina, III, 251. This did not cover the cost of Yonge's agency, as will be shown, even for the year September, 1723, to September, 1724.

[31] C. O. 5/388, p. 39. For Fury see Journal of the Commons House of Assembly of South Carolina, X, 357; for Crockatt, ibid., XXX, 456; for Wright, see C. O. 324/60, p. 264. The writer finds no evidence of appointment of Governor Johnson as agent.

[32] Statutes of South Carolina, III, 147; Journal of the Commons House of Assembly of South Carolina, VII, 17.

to 1773. As was often true, the irregular agency of Chief Justice William Smith from 1731 to 1733 was paid for only in February, 1734/5, in a lump sum of £1,000.[33] The agents were paid from the public treasury and not from a special fund.

The record of pay to Benjamin Martyn must be disregarded in this study as the generous salary of £350 was paid him out of the civil establishment of the crown for the colony of Georgia, and probably proved in the spending not so generous, for clerk hire and all other incidentals attending his office must come from this sum.

When Georgia attained a bona fide agent in the person of Knox, the stipend provided was only £100 and "reasonable" expenses, but when it is noted that this was his appointment in 1762 as assistant to Martyn, the salary seems not unwarrantably small. Franklin's salary, when in 1768 he added the Georgia agency to his several others, was set modestly at the same amount, £100 sterling, but reasonable charges and disbursements were allowed in addition. In 1773 the colony increased it by £50, but in 1773 when the colony designated Grey Elliott to act in Franklin's absence, the salary was fixed in the ordinance at the old figure of £100. When the Commons House of Assembly insisted in opposition to the council in appointing Garth as agent, it indicated £100 as the salary.[34]

Hence, surveying the entire colonial period, we see that the salaries for the agents of the five Southern colonies ranged from £50 to £500, the average standing at perhaps £200, with allowance sometimes for expenses.

Naturally, the special agencies were paid on a special basis, as travel expenses had to be provided. The sum which appealed to the colonials as reasonable to cover such expenses would appear to be around £250 for a short stay abroad. It is noticeable that that was

[33] The statements with regard to Abercromby's salary are confusing. An entry of October, 1748, states that for his trouble and expense in soliciting the affairs of North Carolina up to that time and to March 25 next he should be allowed £100 sterling; and also the further sum of £50 sterling yearly for two years after March 25.—*Collection of all the Public Acts of Assembly of the Province of North Carolina*, 1752, p. 278; for Jouvencal see *Colonial Records of North Carolina*, VI, 1214; for McCulloh's salary see C. O. 324/60, pp. 286, 287, 290-91 and also *Colonial Records of North Carolina*, XI, 237-38; for the pay to Chief Justice Smith, *ibid.*, IV, 151.

[34] For Knox's salary see *Colonial Records of Georgia*, XIII, 731; for Franklin's salary, C. O. 324/60, p. 330; for Grey Elliott's, *Colonial Records of Georgia*, XV, 602; for Garth's, *ibid.*, XVII, 366. Furthermore, as a young colony, Georgia demanded less work of her agents than did the older colonies.

the sum allotted Colonel Philip Ludwell when he was sent back to ask action against Effingham in 1688; a slightly smaller sum, £200 sterling, was put into the hands of the Reverend Mr. Blair in 1691 to enable him to solicit a charter for the college, though assembly-men rewarded his success later with the larger sum of £250 for his "great service."[35]   Strangely enough, almost the same sum[36] was held necessary when they turned to a Londoner, Jeffrey Jeffreys, in 1691; they were even ready to promise to refund any further sums he might have to spend.[37]   On the other hand, when they caught one of their own colonials abroad, it must have been a temptation to press him into the service for as little as might be.   The lower house of Virginia could not be charged with being mean, however, for in 1701 it promised young Byrd £300 to be used as occasion required. By 1718, when the lower house again took advantage of his presence in London, it insisted on paying him £300, as salary, a sum to which the council agreed only in May, 1722.   It might also be noted that the special agent for South Carolina received a remittance for the year September, 1723, to 1724 of £1,800, colonial currency which amounted probably to £300 or less at that time.[38]

When an agent was asked to solicit one particular matter, remuneration took the form of a flat sum which depended on the labor involved and the ability of the colony to pay.   Virginia sent Aber-cromby the sum of £100 for presenting an address of condolence to the king for the lower house in 1752; and Georgia remitted Garth £50 for presenting a petition against the Stamp Act in 1765. Maryland sent with her address and petition for the same occasion a bill of exchange for £150.

Two hundred pounds, however, was still thought adequate for the expenses of Isham Randolph in 1732 with no evidence of later reward, while South Carolina held £300 enough for Francis Yonge when he went over in 1735 to assist the regular agent in soliciting

[35] For Ludwell see *Journals of the House of Burgesses*, 1659/60-1693, p. lxiii, for Blair see *ibid.*, pp. 372, 491.

[36] Stated in a letter from the Board of Trade to Governor Nicholson, dated March 26, 1705.—C. O. 5/1361, p. 59.

[37] C. O. 5/1306, p. 124; *Journals of the House of Burgesses*, 1659/60-1693, p. 375; Bruce, *Institutional History of Virginia*, II, 520.

[38] The House voted him £300 for expenses.—*Journals of the House of Burgesses*, 1695/6-1702, pp. 317, 333; for the dispute between the two houses, *ibid.*, 1712-1726, p. 352; *Executive Journals of the Council*, II, 207.   For South Carolina see C. O. 5/359, p. 153.

a particular matter, and he was warned to expect no more. The striking example of generosity was the reward of £1,000 voted John Randolph without opposition to defray his expenses for the journey to England in 1728 and as a reward for his "faithful and Industrious Application there in the Service of this Colony" in gaining repeal of an act obnoxious to Virginia. His second agency in 1732 was rewarded with more than double his previous remuneration.[39]

One of the aspects connected with the financial side of the agency which must have been most annoying to the provincials here unaccustomed to the British system of incessant fees was the drain for incidental expenditures. These numerous fees were inescapable. Nowhere has the situation been put more clearly or tersely than by Abercromby; what he wrote in 1758 reflects statements made a half century earlier by Increase Mather and presents succinctly a situation which prevailed throughout the colonial period. He wrote to Mr. Blair, president of the Virginia council, on March 18, "as these Articles are actually standing Taxes upon the Agent, unlefs he carrys on the service as a Smuggler in office, more than as the Representative of your Government, he cannot forego such Expence." He classified these expenses into standing and capital expenses; first, coach and chair hire; secondly, gratuities, especially at Christmas to public officers and servants of the ministers of state. Coach hire, a tender point in the colonies, from the variety of business in the city, at the courts, and about town, amounted at least, according to Abercromby, to £40 a year; and the gratuities to servants ran on the average to twenty-five guineas a year. A fairer classification would seem, to the writer, to add at least two other categories; a third, the amount of which Abercromby does not specify, but which we know was high, was postage; and a fourth, the numerous, often heavy, fees. Incidental personal expenses, arising from the service, he mentions but leaves vague, so that it is a bit difficult for the modern student to distinguish them from personal expenses inseparable from any other service.[40]

[39] *Journals of the House of Burgesses*, 1727-1740, p. 64; *Legislative Journals of the Council*, II, 758. The exact sum voted to John Randolph in 1732 was £2,200. The speaker was ordered to let him know "how sensible the Houfe is of his perfonal Merit" and from the chair was to "return him the thanks of this Houfe."—*Ibid.*, p. 64. For the sum voted Isham Randolph see *Executive Journals of the Council*, IV, 272.

[40] Abercromby Letter Book, pp. 69, 72. He speaks only of gifts at Christmas, but they seem to have been constant.

The character of the gratuities and fees requires a little closer analysis. They included presents to clerks in the public offices, gifts, or, as we would say today, tips to doorkeepers, messengers, office tenders, tips at Christmas to the servants at the ministries, fees to the clerks of the Privy Council for references and orders in council, fees at the Board of Trade for representations to the Privy Council and for reports of progress, fees at the Council for reports, and charges for the security bond, when money grants were involved.

As these fees varied little for the various agents, they might be called fixed charges. Sometimes they were put so vaguely by the agents that the colony did not know what allowance should properly be made for incidental charges. That led necessarily to vagueness on the part of the colonies, but occasionally they showed a proper spirit in meeting such charges, as when Maryland informed Blakiston that he would be paid, "what extraordinary Charge he shall be at in solliciting his Affair over and above what is agreed on."[41] Likewise Virginia in 1705 readily ordered Byrd reimbursed to the amount of £6 17s. 6d. expended by him in the New York affair—referring to the demand for Virginia to send troops to New York.[42]

An account of sundry disbursements by Leheup amounting to £20 16s. 6d. was allowed; unexplained is the allowance of £79 3s. for obtaining pictures of the king and queen, presumably, however, pictures of the sovereigns which had been ordered by Virginia.[43] Sometimes, not too grudgingly, a sum was allowed primarily to keep the good will of the agent. Payment to Leheup by Virginia in 1727 is a case in point when the Council urged payment of £50 10s. 2d. that "he may not hereafter be difcouraged from negociating the publick affairs of his Government with equal Zeal and Succefs," or when the South Carolina council refused to deduct £94 from Yonge's salary as it would "cramp him and be of ill consequence to our affairs."[44]

The specific amounts disbursed for various purposes are not only illuminating, but interesting. The fees for postage for instance, would have dug a big hole in the agent's pocket, if he had been obliged to meet them. South Carolina allowed on one bill

[41] *Archives of Maryland*, XXIX, 326.
[42] *Journals of the House of Burgesses*, 1702/3-1712, p. 157.
[43] *Executive Journals of the Council*, IV, 214.
[44] *Legislative Journals of the Council*, II, 744; Journal of the Commons House of Assembly of South Carolina, VI, 160.

£19 16s. 2d. for this one item; Maryland paid £2 6d. in 1741; Garth claimed from South Carolina for this one purpose for the period August to September, 1766, £11 5s. 9d. Garth's bill for postage for his entire agency to South Carolina came to more than £25.[45]

Certain other items were necessarily heavy. Abercromby in 1758 had had to travel to Lord Loudoun's home, a journey which cost four days' horse hire £10 10s.; fees to the clerk of the Privy Council for references and orders of the Council he lists as amounting to £7 16s, and fees to the Board of Trade for representations to the king in council as £4 4s.; and fees to the Council in Mr. Camm's case, £13 13s. Garth in 1766 entered one item: "Attendance with the Address to the Secretary of State and presenting same to His Majesty" as entailing an expense of £4 4s.; a second item, for printing the address (of thanks from South Carolina for repeal of the Stamp Act) in the London Gazette, amounted to £4 1s.; a third, for sundry meetings with the agent of New York touching the constitution of judges in America, cost £2 2s.; and a fourth item, significant though modest, was 10s. to the new secretary's porter.[46] A few additional items shed light: for copying of a New York memorial sent to the Plantation Office, £2 2s.; for two fair copies for transmission to the South Carolina Committee of Correspondence, 10s.; for New Year's gifts to servants at the Plantation Office 42s., at the Treasury Office 42s., at the office of the secretary of state, 42s., and a like sum at the office of the Privy Council—a total of £8 8s.; and to clerks for copying extracts at the Plantation Office, £3 3s. Fees to a clerk at the Council office with fees for the petition read, orders of reference, and order for confirmation mounted to no less than £8 5s. An attendance with the merchants at their meeting to assure that a given act was explained to them in order to gain their support brought an item of £2 2s. A special trip to London from Garth's home in Devizes during August, 1769, cost South Carolina £8 8s.[47] When one issue dragged a long time, the extra expenses

---

[45] *Archives of Maryland*, XLIV, 332; for Garth's claim see "Garth Correspondence," *loc. cit.*, XXIX, 118.

[46] Abercromby Letter Book (no page given); *ibid.*, p. 81 for other of Abercromby's items; for Garth's see "Garth Correspondence," *loc. cit.*, XXIX, 117-19.

[47] *Ibid.*, XXX, 173-75, 228; XXXIII, 229; for a letter of Aug. 2, 1769, to show why he came to town, XXXI, 128.

could mount very high. Abercromby notes a solicitation for the protection of Virginia which began under Fox as secretary of state, continued under Sir Thomas Robinson, and was successfully concluded only under Pitt.

Agents were evidently tempted to estimate a flat sum to cover certain types of recurring expense in order to avoid keeping exact records. Abercromby, for instance, in the long-drawn-out affair alluded to above entered his expenses at £100, though he confessed that he had kept no account. A statement by Grey Elliott, as well as the loose records of Abercromby, is illuminating on this point. On July 12, 1779, the former wrote to the Georgia Commons House: "It is usual for the Agents to charge 10s. per Day, every time they attend at the Secretary's of State's Office, or any other public Business, but I have charged what I really disbursed."[48] It is difficult to interpret some of the entries in the expense accounts. It would appear, however, that the agents felt justified in a certain charge for their time in attendance at the various offices. When attendance at the Treasury is entered as costing over three pounds, one is forced to conclude that coach hire and fees are superadded to a charge for the agent's time beyond what he regarded as covered by the flat annual salary. The statement above by Elliott confirms that opinion.

One of the oddest expenses which this research has uncovered fell upon Crockatt in 1751. It will be recalled that Captain Charles McNaire had come to England for recompense for his activity in soliciting repayment for South Carolina expenditures in aiding Georgia. McNaire had not been many weeks in London before he was arrested for a debt of about £45. Crockatt immediately advanced the amount of the fees for the writ, £2 2s., as the captain was without friends or money; and, as he could carry on no application from within the jail, the agent felt obliged to pay his bail for three days, amounting in all to £63 12s. Crockatt knew that McNaire could not repay him and so he wrote the Committee of Correspondence that he "must naturally have recourse to the Assembly for relief." The house reimbursed the agent with a warning that it would pay no other allowances for McNaire.[49]

The mere cost of bills of exchange was far from a negligible item

---

[48] Abercromby Letter Book, p. 82; *Colonial Records of Georgia*, XV, 602.
[49] Journal of the Commons House of Assembly of South Carolina, XXVIII, 40.

for the colonies. South Carolina, for instance, in 1775 voted that the sum of £778 12s. 8d. should be paid Garth to make good the loss which had accrued in remitting the money in bills of exchange from 1769 to 1773.[50] The equivalent of this in sterling would be about £111 for this one item.

A few totals show the reader how impressive these incidentals could become when added to the salary. For purposes of comparison we might well choose the decade of the fifties as typical for the period of the well-established agency. During the year of March, 1752, to March, 1753, South Carolina paid Crockatt £1,357 16s. 2d., which added to the £48 9s. 6½d. paid the clerk of the Committee of Correspondence and the reimbursement for McNaire brought the cost of the agency for that year to £1,851 9s. 8½d.—South Carolina currency of course.[51] The charges on North Carolina were less onerous. Its Committee of Correspondence had remitted to Abercromby, on November 25, 1758, for the period of his agency, £1,474 5s.; the Committee on Accounts reckoned that the colony still owed him £332 9s. 7d., making in all £2,393 5s. 6d. His salary, as stated, was £616 13s. 4d. sterling for six years and to the end of the session, and his incidental charges came to £263 11s. for six years, a modest average for incidentals of about £44 a year. But this full amount the colony refused to allow him.[52] In Georgia, as would be expected, disbursements were not heavy. In addition to the salary of £100, the early agent, Knox, disbursed only £16 2s. 6d. in one year, while Benjamin Franklin seems to have rendered no bill for incidentals.[53]

In Virginia Abercromby estimated the contingent expenses at £50

[50] Ibid., XXXIX, 281.

[51] Ibid., XXVIII, 404. Fury's expenses from December 2, 1746, to November 18, 1748, were very much less—£200 for salary and only £187 2s. 6d. for incidentals.—Ibid., XXIV, 337. But it would amount to much the same when translated into colonial currency.

The cost of the agency for March, 1758-March, 1759, under Wright's direction was much the same (without the sum for McNair); namely £1,031 12s. 11d.—Ibid. XXXIII, 203, his incidentals coming only to £105 16s. 9d. This is apparently colonial currency.

[52] At an earlier period, November 1, 1747, to March 1, 1749, a period of close to a year and a half, incidentals came only to £18 18s. sterling.—Colonial Records of North Carolina, IV, 1021. For the full sum paid him, 1751-1758, see ibid., V, 970. The Committee on Accounts was willing to allow him only £190 18s. on his incidental expenses.

[53] Colonial Records of Georgia, XIX, pt. 1, pp. 119-20. The writer has found no incidental expense account for Franklin for Georgia.

a year sterling in 1758, and asked that that item be handled by an addition to his yearly salary, holding that it was "by no means beyond the nature of the Expence incident to the Service," but too great to be thrown upon him. The total cost of the agency for Virginia, including salary and gratuities, was computed in 1755 at about £2,000 a year or about £600 British currency. Of course, in the sixties, when the lower house was maintaining its own agent at £500 a year and the upper house its own agent at £200, the cost to this colony, probably reaching £2,500 colonial money, was far higher than anywhere else among the Southern colonies.[54]

The colonies were far from paying these extra expenses without demur. As must be expected in a new country where money was hard to get, all extra charges were scrutinized closely. The Commons House of South Carolina wrote their agent in 1723 that they would allow his item of £19 16s. 2d. for postage and an item of £14 7s. 4d., but that an article of £3 13s. was "well Paid out of the money Sent you by the Gentleman of the late Corporation" and that another article of £39 "ought not to be reimbursed you there being three Hundred Pounds as a premium given to the Person who Procurs the Enumeration of Rice to be taken off."[55] An entry in the same colony's Journal of March 28, 1734, is sufficiently illuminating: Governor Johnson urged justice to Samuel Wragg and accordingly the house voted to allow £147 disbursed by him as fees to the attorney and solicitor general of Great Britain. As late as the fifties the governor of Virginia was constantly admonishing Abercromby on this delicate subject. On April 26, 1754, Dinwiddie wrote him: "As to the Compl't of Gratuities on the Council's Affairs, it met with no great Opposit'n, but I think You sh'd have wrote me a Let'r of Y'r being satisfied with w't they gave You, that I c'd have shewn it to them." More pointed was the terse comment in a letter of February 18, 1755: "You must now be tender in Y'r extra Cha's, and no Coach hire, w'ch I promised to write You on y't subject."[56]

[54] Abercromby Letter Book, p. 74; Flippin, *Royal Government in Virginia*, p. 186. My estimate of £2,500 is based on the assumption that the incidental expenses for the agent of the upper house continued about as before, but with no incidentals for the agent of the burgesses. It is also possible that the assembly would not allow such generous charges to the agent of the governor and council.

[55] Journal of the Commons House of Assembly of South Carolina, V, 312-13.

[56] Dinwiddie, *Official Records*, I, 138-39, 506.

Again, a few months later we find Dinwiddie writing about Aber-cromby's account for incidentals: ". . . but I know the Council do not expect You should charge any Incidents, however, I shall at a proper Time push it." But the proper time seemed slow in com-ing, for by November 15 he had not thought proper to present the private bill of expense as "they [the members of the council] in private Conversation, say they expected no Bills of Charge after the Augmentat'n of the Salary. I therefore tho't proper to decline it at y's Time."[57]

Gradually the colonies came to realize that these charges for coach hire and tips were necessary for the proper and dignified dis-charge of the agent's duties, and so we find the newest colony making provision in 1761 for an additional £50 annually to the agent for defraying the expenses of coach hire "over and besides his reason-able charges and disbursements," but requiring that he lay an account of such disbursements before the Georgia house yearly.[58]

Occasionally an agent was considerate and sought to protect the colony against excessive charges. Witness Charles Garth, who told the South Carolina committee in 1769 that since he had had to pay over two hundred pounds in fees at both houses of parliament when the act for exporting rice freely to South America was first passed, he had resisted paying again when the act was to be merely renewed.[59]

The incidental charges became more pronounced when the agents were soliciting the parliamentary grants of 1757 and 1758. The charges for fees of all sorts and bills of exchange undoubtedly were legitimately heavy, but the agents insisted on a two per cent com-mission, as they regarded the heavy additional work as outside the province of their regular agency duties. Human nature being what it is, they scented extra cash for themselves when extra cash was coming to the colonies. Exact figures as to the fees are helpful. Abercromby, for instance, listed fees at the office of the Auditor of Exchange running up to £39 15s.; fees of £17 11s. at the Pell Office; of £20 at the Teller's Office, for the sign Manual; fees for a bond of security of £3 3s., insurance, presumably; and fees at the Ex-

[57] *Ibid.*, II, 115, 277. This may, of course, have been a fresh bill of expenses.
[58] *Colonial Records of Georgia*, XIII, 628-29.
[59] "Garth Correspondence," *loc. cit.*, XXXI, 128.

chequer Office. The total of such fees for Virginia's share of the £200,000 grant of 1758 totaled no less than £130 14s. 8d.[60] Abercromby's Letter Book reveals exactly the same items for incidentals entered against North Carolina as for Virginia but with different sums, except the amount for travel expenses to Lord Loudoun's home, with its four days' horse hire, from which one is perhaps justified in concluding that he divided his expenses between the two colonies, as a charge of rather more than ten pounds would not be excessive for a journey of that length.

The "usual" two per cent commission, as Abercromby terms it, charged by the agents for collecting the parliamentary grant provoked some difficulty, and not alone because it was a sizable sum, amounting for Abercromby on the two grants to Virginia to £1,320 7s. James Wright charged £248 11s. as his commission on the South Carolina portion of the £50,000 parliamentary grant. While the colonies seemed to accept the principle of a commission to the agents, the amount caused bickering. South Carolina disallowed a part of Wright's claim and objected because the money was not paid over promptly by the agent to the provincial treasurer, insisting on trying to recover it after Wright had become governor of Georgia. In North Carolina and Virginia the problem of a commission was complicated by the presence of two agents, one for each branch of the legislature. Though the North Carolina assembly had hastened to reappoint Abercromby as agent, when it saw that it was likely to lose its share of the grant because of lack of an agent, the council had appointed Samuel Smith as its agent. Abercromby insisted on the full commission, as his by "justice and equity," as he had negotiated the affair alone, even functioning between the time he was discharged in 1757 and his reappointment for the lower house in December, 1758. In Virginia the case was less clear. In the first place, she refused to allow more than one and one-half per cent commission, and the Committee of Correspondence directed the agent of the House of Burgesses, Montague, to oppose the passing of the accounts at the Treasury, if Abercromby refused to acquiesce in that adjustment. The account of the agent of the council was not settled until May, 1763, when the House of Burgesses instructed their agent,

---

[60] Abercromby Letter Book, (pagination missing in this part). The Pell Office was formerly a division in the Exchequer for entering accounts and disbursements on the rolls.

Montague, to settle with Abercromby by allowing him £140 commission on the money which he had received at the Exchequer.[61]

The agents might justifiably have felt aggrieved over the paucity of their recompense for laborious work, but their grievance was vastly aggravated by the difficulties in the way of collecting that meagre pay. The difficulties were attributable, not alone to poverty-stricken treasuries, but also to the quarrels between the branches of government in the colonies.

The salary due Colonel Blakiston on September 17, 1706, from Maryland had not been paid by April 11, 1707. The agent tried to bring pressure through his attorney on the House of Delegates to make proper provision for his past salary and the salary which would soon be due. In some way his salary for 1705-1706 was omitted with the result that the lower house referred the matter to the Committee of Accounts to search the journals and report the cause of the error. When on December 9, 1708, the house allowed Blakiston arrears, these were allowed only to the close of 1707. The council properly recognized that his dismissal from the agency the next day did not absolve the province of its financial obligation to him and tried to have his arrears of fifteen months' salary met, but the less conscientious house callously referred action even in November, 1710, to the next session. "Satisfaction" had not yet been fully given him by October, 1711.[62]

Kettleby likewise had difficulty in collecting from South Carolina the two hundred pounds due him when that colony terminated his agency. In June, 1717, Kettleby's financial agent appeared before the lower house, to which he had been referred by the treasurer, to plead his cause. The house ordered that as the treasury was nearly empty because of the Indian Wars, Kettleby could not be paid, but that he should be provided for as soon as money came into the treasury. It was not until May, 1726, that the assembly voted Francis Yonge £150 in part for his former agency, which had terminated March, 1724/5.[63] Leheup's first experience with Virginia in

[61] Journal of the Commons House of Assembly of South Carolina, XXXV, 44-45, 74; Abercromby Letter Book, entry for June 6, 1760; "Proceedings of the Committee of Correspondence," Virginia Magazine of History, XI, 22, 24, 122; Journals of the House of Burgesses, 1761-1765, pp. 34, 37, 193.
[62] Archives of Maryland, XXVII, 49, 113, 302, 305, 548; XXIX, 12-13.
[63] Journal of the Commons House of Assembly of South Carolina, V, 317; III, 322.

regard to finances in 1727 was no doubt a shock; ordered to secure the king's assent to a certain act of the Virginia legislature, he set a fee held so exorbitant that the House of Burgesses refused to allow it, despite the fact that Leheup had been successful.[64]   Even well into the century the colonies were sadly remiss in their payments to their agents.   In 1733 Joseph Wragg had to press the South Carolina assembly to pay the arrears of salary due his brother Samuel from four years of agency and to reimburse him for the sums he had advanced, along with a reasonable sum for his expenses.   As seemed frequently the case, the council recommended payment in this instance, but the house in niggardly fashion allowed only £36 11s. and £147 which the agent had paid out as fees to the attorney and solicitor general.   They were behind in their accounts with Fury in May, 1742, as much as £662 16s. 8d., which could easily have embarrassed the agent unless he were a man of large means.[65]

The agents expressed themselves often on this subject in no uncertain terms.   Abercromby told Governor Dobbs on March 4, 1758, that he expected remittances by bills of exchange or from the parliamentary grant to North Carolina.   "Justice and my service do entitle me to your Consideration."   He objected strenuously to members of the council being paid from the quitrent fund until the arrears were in some degree met or until there was a better prospect of the quitrents producing a sinking fund above the annual salary to officers already on the fund.   Grey Elliott asked Georgia to settle his account of disbursements and salary and reminded the house that he had never received any salary for the time he acted from 1773 to 1775 in Franklin's absences, and seemed to resent the fact that, though appointed to succeed Franklin, he did not succeed to his salary.[66]

[64] *Journals of the House of Burgesses*, 1727-1740, pp. xviii, 45, 46.
[65] Journal of the Commons House of Assembly of South Carolina, VIII, 67; *ibid.*, p. 63.
[66] Abercromby Letter Book, pp. 65-66, 77-78; *Colonial Records of Georgia*, XV, 602. Lest it be thought that the Southern colonies had a monopoly of treating their agents shabbily, it might be pointed out that by 1710 Britishers were wary of appointment by the colonies. Champante wrote to New Jersey on November 8, 1710, that he was so sensible of the debt of the province that he would not depend on an increase of salary, but "wtever it is I must insist on ye certainty of its paymt."—Rawlinson, MSS, A 272, f. 256, Bodleian Library.   De Berdt also had difficulty in collecting a grant to his father as agent of Massachusetts in 1772, though in this instance it was owing to interference by Lord Hillsborough.—Historical Manuscripts Commission, *Fourteenth Report*, App. X: *MSS. of the Earl of Dartmouth, American Papers*, II, 88.

At times the governors were themselves disturbed over the treatment of the agents. Governor Dobbs wrote Abercromby on December 28, 1757, that he had refused to write him until he knew whether the assembly would renew the appointment, as he feared that the agent would be ill paid for his past services for North Carolina. He had spoken to the speaker of the lower house about reappointment, but had found members so "crusty" in granting money for public services that he expected little from them. When they would not even allow the agent's extra expenses nor pay him what he had earned, Dobbs felt that he could not give him any "further trouble."[67]

The poor agents sometimes became the victims in the quarrels between the governors and lower houses of assembly and between the two houses. An early instance was the quarrel over the reward to Colonel Philip Ludwell despite the benefits he secured for Virginia. The burgesses ordered £250 sterling paid him out of the import tax on liquors. The council, however, had not joined in the address sent home by the house on its own responsibility—had in fact dissented from every item embraced in it—and bided its time. That time came when the house tried to express its gratitude in tangible form, for the upper body seized its opportunity to insert some items in the appropriation in return for the allowance to the agent. Meanwhile he was kept waiting for his pay while the houses bickered. A few decades later a similar controversy arose over a grant to Byrd in 1718, but this time the dissident element was the governor. The council readily agreed to the amount of £300, but the governor refused to accept that item because he was opposed to sending the address which the agent was to deliver and also opposed to the appointment of an agent as unnecessary. The council then supported the governor because of a technical point in "tacking" to the book of claims a thing of a different nature and because they knew of no service by Mr. Byrd worthy of such a reward. They felt that the sum was given merely as an encouragement to prosecute a charge against the lieutenant governor. The governor signed with the distinct proviso that this item was excepted. It was four years before the council assented to a resolution that the sum should be paid Byrd.[68]

[67] Colonial Records of North Carolina, V, 788-89.
[68] Journals of the House of Burgesses, 1712-1726, p. xl; for the governor's message

Friction over the pay to Boone and Beresford arose early in connection with the agency question in South Carolina. Naturally, Deputy Governor Daniel, an appointee of the proprietors, would not consent to an appropriation of £2,000 in 1716 to defray the expenses of agents sent to destroy the proprietors' charter. He held up the tax bill till that clause was struck out. As a matter of fact this dispute dragged on for several years after the province came under royal rule.[69]

Even sharper was the dispute between the House of Commons and the governor over the article of £1,500 in the estimate of 1722 for Boone's services as agent. Governor Nicholson in a special message in 1722 and again in 1723 objected to this item for services presumably performed for His Majesty's government without application to His Majesty, and declared that when he was in England he knew of no such services performed by Boone. The house naturally adhered to its position, pressing even in 1725 for the payment to Boone, but the quarrel had now become one between the lower house and the council, as the council rejected the bill for payment on the ground that Boone had tried to negotiate the sale of the province instead of permitting it to come under the control of the king. A similar order for payment in December, 1725, and a reminder in 1726 were ignored by the council, and there the matter seems to have been dropped so that Boone presumably never received his pay.[70]

The tactics to which the House of Burgesses resorted in 1754 to secure to Peyton Randolph payment for his services as special agent are typical of the indirect methods sometimes necessary to keep their promises to the agent. In 1752 when the burgesses proposed to send their attorney general over, they voted to pay him £2,500. Since the council had authorized the pistole fee, they objected to the

see pp. 237-38. The sum was granted May 23, 1722.—*Ibid.*, p. 335; *Legislative Journals of the Council*, II, 669.

[69] Journal of the Commons House of Assembly of South Carolina, V, 87; for the Governor's message see *ibid.*, p. 130; Smith, *South Carolina as a Royal Province*, pp. 160-61.

[70] *Ibid.*, pp. 289, 290-91; Journal of the Council of South Carolina, II, 25; III, 31-39, 248, 327; Journal of the Commons House of Assembly of South Carolina, VI, 20, 191, 195; VI, 458, 469; VII, 220, 240. A slight dispute over the salary for Crockatt in 1755 between the two houses was resolved by the governor expostulating with the council for their rejection of the bill.—C. O. 5/375, K, 116.

appointment, but the burgesses in 1754 tried to force the appropriation by attaching the item as a rider to the grant of £20,000 for defense. Despite the approaching French and Indian War, the governor and council refused to accept the bill with the rider. The lower house in turn rejected the overture of the governor to assent to a separate bill for Randolph's salary with a delaying clause until the royal pleasure should be made known. The house voted the supply bill at the next session without the rider. Randolph reported on his agency to the house on May 12, 1755, and received the fervid thanks of the house for his energies. But it appears likely that he never received anything more substantial. Despite the approaching French and Indian War, the governor and council refused to swallow the bitter dose, and the house scored no victory in the payment of their agent.[71]

Abercromby had his difficulties with North Carolina in collecting the sum due him when that colony terminated his agency. As of March 25, 1758, he computed the arrears at £586 19s. 1d. He besieged the governor for his good services with the assembly and insisted that the money could be had from the parliamentary grant if not from taxes. On December 20, 1758, at long last, the assembly resolved to pay him £332 9s. 7d. out of the parliamentary grant for his "expenses and faithful Services" during his agency—a sad reduction for the agent.[72]

Garth encountered difficulty in Georgia in collecting his salary. Elliott, a member of the council, entered a protest in March, 1767, against paying Garth because the service had not been agreed to by that body. When the question of his salary came formally before the upper house in February of the next year, it unanimously declared that Garth had never been regularly appointed agent and that no order could issue for the payment of the £100 which he sought.[73]

[71] The governor in a letter to the Board of Trade, dated May 10, 1754, denounced the action of the House of Burgesses and reported that the speaker, who was also treasurer of the colony, declared he would not issue his warrant for the money.—C. O. 5/1328, p. 211. See also his letter to Sec. Robinson of Sept. 25, 1754.—Dinwiddie, *Official Records*, I, 324. See also *Journals of the House of Burgesses*, 1752-1758, p. xx; Miller ("The Virginia Committee of Correspondence," *William and Mary Quarterly*, XXII, ser. 1, pp. 2-3) is in error in saying the rider passed. See Hening, *Statutes*, VI, 435-38.

[72] Abercromby Letter Book, p. 76; for a letter to Governor Dobbs of April 20, 1758, urging his aid with the assembly, *ibid.*, p. 97; for the decision to pay him, see *Colonial Records of North Carolina*, V, 1035-39.

[73] *Colonial Records of Georgia*, XVII, 364-65; X, 433.

The question of the transfer of money for the use of the agents in England constituted a problem of exchange. In the earlier agencies money was sometimes transmitted through a relative, as to Colonel Samuel Mathews, Sr. in 1654 through his son and to William Byrd II, through his father.[74] After 1680 the regular agents on some occasions obtained the necessary funds from some London merchant upon instructions of the receiver general by order of the council. It has already been noted that money was placed in the hands of one Gawin Corbin for the use of William Blathwayt, special agent for Virginia in 1692, and for the Reverend Mr. Blair. For Blakiston's use the Virginia council ordered in September, 1709, that the receiver general give directions to Micajah Perry to pay him whatever money he had expended and to advance from time to time what he needed for his negotiations, the London merchant to be reimbursed out of the two-shilling tax per hogshead on tobacco.[75] Maryland tried to arrange for the pay of Ferdinand Paris in 1745 by transferring money raised by a two pence per hogshead duty on tobacco exported out of its colony to London. The funds were to be lodged with a London merchant named James Buchanan to the credit of the Maryland House of Deputies and applied to pay the agent and defray his incidental expenses.[76] The financial broker for Montague, serving Virginia in 1769, was John Norton and Sons, a well-known London firm of the middle decades. On January 13, 1769, R. C. Nicholas, the treasurer of Virginia, wrote Norton that he was taking the liberty of drawing on him for the £1,000 sterling which the House of Burgesses would owe Montague by the succeeding March.[77]

[74] Cook, "Governor Samuel Mathews, Junior," *William and Mary Quarterly*, ser. 2, XIV, 106.

[75] *Executive Journals of the Council*, III, 222.

[76] *Archives of Maryland*, XLIV, 81, 109-10.

[77] One remark in Nicholas' letter remains unexplained: "I did not think it handsome to send Mr. Montague to Scotland for his Money, which is the Reason of my giving you this Trouble." One wonders if the colony had been dealing with a financial agent in Edinburgh.—Norton, *John Norton and Sons, Merchants of London and Virginia*, p. 83.

CHAPTER 10.

COÖPERATION AMONG THE AGENTS AND WITH THE MERCHANTS

"IN UNITY lies strength" is a precept which was early appreciated by the agents of the mainland and the islands—and acted upon. The first instance of an embryonic effort, at least, at securing unity of action among some of the agents came at a remarkably early date. In the commission issued in March, 1627/8, to Sir Francis Wyatt, Edward Bennett, and Mr. Marshart they were instructed in one article as follows: "That you enforme yor felues how the bufynes of the Contract ftandeth, at the Pfent & acquaint yor felues wth the Agent of the *Bermudas & St Christophers*, to the [end?] you may (if you can agree) proceed iontly togeather both for the bettr effecting of yor bufines, & p^{r}ceedings wth lefse chardge."[1] Since their mission was to protect the planters against the king's monopoly in tobacco, one wonders just how great would be the interest of those islands, but the note struck for economy is readily explicable. The writer finds no agents for the colonies named.

The next instance of united action by several agents does not appear until November, 1696, when the *Journal* of the Board of Trade reveals a petition from the proprietors and agents of several American provinces—which ones are not stated—desiring a copy of the representations made by that Board to the late Lords Justices about the settlement of attorneys general in the several plantations.[2]

A decade and a half[3] elapsed before we encounter the next recorded instance of coöperation on the part of any of the Southern

---

[1] *Journals of the House of Burgesses*, 1619-1658/9, p. 50.

[2] C. O. 391/9, p. 231.

[3] Osgood gives an account of coöperation between a Virginia representative and the agents of New England and New Jersey in 1697 for the uniting of New England and New York under one government. See *The North American Colonies in the Eighteenth Century*, I, 267-68. Pursuit of the investigation does not yield sufficiently clear or reliable data to justify inclusion here.

agents.   At the Board of Trade session of December 1, 1715, there were present Jeremiah Dummer, long-time agent of Connecticut and Massachusetts, Mr. Ludwell of Virginia—though Blakiston was then the regular agent—a Colonel Cleland, and Mr. Woodbridge of the Barbados.   The subject before the Board was Dummer's memorial about the seizure by the Spaniards of some New England ships which had been loading salt at Tortugas and the Bahamas.   Colonials were agreed that such captures were not only prejudicial to the governments of New England but to the sugar islands and, apparently, to the Virginians, as the planters could not provide food for the Negroes without salt fish.   Dummer had testified at an earlier session that the English had gathered salt on the island of Tortugas without interruption for forty-five years and did not doubt but that he could find old West Indians in England who would testify that the colonials of the North American mainland had gathered salt at that point before 1667.[4] There is also evidence that Colonel Philip Ludwell was in England with Robert Carter and Lightfoot—possibly John L. Lightfoot of the council—to work for removal of Governor Nicholson from his post in Virginia, but there is no evidence that he had a formal appointment as an agent.   These early examples of coöperation of representatives seem to have been informal, but they are significant as an early indication of the way in which colonial representatives would combine forces.   It might be called the genesis of coöperation.

There are what might be called four classic instances of general coöperation among the agents during the eighteenth century: the effort to prevent passage of the Molasses Act of 1733; to thwart a better administration of the Molasses Act in 1750-1751; to secure reimbursement for expenditures in the later intercolonial wars; and to oppose the taxation policy of the British government dating from 1763 to 1776.   The Southern agents participated in all of these efforts.   There are, however, a number of minor instances of coöperation with which we must deal before we come to these instances of effective, significant, combined action.

First, for a few cases of coöperative handling of specific problems by two or three agents.   To cite a few bits of evidence one might note that in 1758 Wright, then agent for South Carolina, approached

[4] *Journal of the Board of Trade,* 1708/9-1714, pp. 486, 474.

Abercromby for a joint application of his colony and of Virginia to parliament for the privilege of importing Bay salt into the Southern provinces, a privilege already allowed to the Northern provinces. Though this project was evidently widened to embrace other agents, in 1765 the agents of these same two colonies were still wrestling with that same old salt problem.[5] Again in 1762 the agent of South Carolina was coöperating with the agent of Georgia for a continuation of the bounty on plantation indigo which would soon expire. A few years later South Carolina directed its agent to assist the Northern colonies if they made an application against interference by the naval vessel on the Newfoundland station with the colonial fishery at that point. The agent of the Maryland upper house in 1767 declared that he would in concert with the Virginia agent use his utmost efforts to support the quarantine law, for repeal of which a contractor for the transportation of convicts was petitioning.[6] He hoped also for the support of South Carolina through its agent. One problem of 1766, which started with consultation between Garth and the agent of New York under instructions from the South Carolina Committee of Correspondence but was soon extended to the other agents, dealt with the method of appointing judges in America. Garth's bill of expenses shows "sundry" meetings with the New York agent on this subject.[7] In 1770 the agents of the Southern colonies— which meant in this instance all except Maryland—combined to prevent reduction of the bounties on naval stores imported into England from America. A few interested merchants of London had won the approbation of the Treasury for a statute to reduce the bounty on tar, pitch, and turpentine and had already secured the general approbation of the Board of Trade, to which it had in regular procedure been referred. At this juncture one of the agents "got wind" of it and drew up with the other two a petition to show that the reasons

[5] Abercromby Letter Book, p. 79. Abercromby had to secure authorization from Virginia to make the application to parliament that the cost, £200, would be divided.—*Ibid.*, p. 92. At the same time he seemed to be working with James Wright of South Carolina against a petition of Governor Morris of New Jersey for a salt monopoly.—*Ibid.*, pp. 83-84. For the action of 1765 see *Journal of the Board of Trade*, 1764-1767, p. 213.

[6] "Garth Correspondence," *loc. cit.*, XXVIII, 87; for the action on the quarantine law see letter of Hammersley to Governor Sharpe, dated August 24, 1767, *Archives of Maryland*, XIV, 419. He hoped for the aid also of Garth and the gentlemen in the trade.

[7] "Garth Correspondence," *loc. cit.*, XXIX, 44-45. He hoped to find the other agents disposed to join in the application.

which had first actuated the statute granting bounties continued in full force. Garth, McCulloh, and Montague in addition to their own joint petition got one sent in by merchants of Bristol and other "out-ports."[8]

It even happened that when the Commons House of Assembly of South Carolina became embroiled in a dispute with their governor over the election law in the famous Gadsden case, it issued instructions to its agent, since it felt confident that publicity could result in no disadvantage to its cause, to furnish the agents of all the colonies and islands with a printed copy of the case as sent by the house; the agents would see that the issue was not confined to South Carolina and would lend their aid.[9] It does not appear, however, that such aid was forthcoming.

There is an early record in 1732 of coöperation between agents in preparation for actual warfare which should not be omitted. As early as April, 1732, a letter from New York was read to the Virginia council, asking them to join in presenting to the king the encroachments of the French from Canada, symbolized by their building a fort at Crown Point on "Corlaers Lake" within three days' journey from Albany. The response of Virginia was voiced by an order to Leheup to aid the New York agent in his application for the removal of the French from Crown Point and for prevention of any future encroachment.[10] There is also some evidence in 1756 of united action by the agents to secure money for defense.

An instance in connection with Indian affairs dates from 1767. A letter from Alderman Trecothick, then agent for New Hampshire, was read to the Board of Trade on November 17, expressing the views of the merchant traders to North America and of several of the agents, who had met about two weeks before to discuss the management of Indian affairs and new governments in the interior of North America.[11]

[8] In their petition the agents stressed the fact that reduction of the bounties would hurt the planter, the British merchants, and public interests of the kingdom, besides being a violation of good faith, since the bounties had been continued until 1779. For the petition in full see C. O. 388/57. Montagu's story of his dealings with the other agents is printed in "Proceedings of the Virginia Committee of Correspondence," *loc. cit.*, XII, 166-67.

[9] *A Full State of the Dispute betwixt the Governor and the Commons House of Assembly of South Carolina*, p. 5.

[10] *Executive Journals of the Council*, IV, 265.

[11] *Journal of the Board of Trade*, 1764-1767, p. 429.

Activity by the agents relating to the persistent problem of plantation currency can be made intelligible only if certain economic facts are stressed. Owing to the unfavorable balance of trade the colonies of the North American continent were steadily drained of specie. Naturally, the legislatures of the various colonies resorted to the usual devices to create an adequate currency, the chief of which was paper money. This inflationary measure was detrimental to creditors, largely British merchants, who protested long and loudly. Through most of the eighteenth century the British government undertook to regulate provincial currency against strenuous colonial opposition. Parliament passed a bill regulating plantation currency in 1751 despite the arguments of the agents that the issuing of paper bills was necessary under the conditions; it instituted further regulation in 1764.

Possibly one of the hardest tasks which confronted any agent was to "reconcile" the merchants, as Abercromby put it, to an act for paper currency. Agent Fury was called on in 1734 to answer an argument by Samuel Wragg and William Wood, in behalf of some merchants of London and Bristol trading to South Carolina, in remonstrance against a paper currency act of 1731. The act would provide for an issue of about £104,000 paper currency and for continuing a duty on Negroes. It is an interesting fact that Wragg asked the Board of Trade to study a paper entitled, *A Further Humble Representation of the Council of the Province of South Carolina*, made to the king on December 19, 1728, on the subject of paper currency. It is interesting because Wragg had been agent for South Carolina in 1728 and probably knew of the existence of that paper solely by virtue of that fact. He now, six years later, speaking as a merchant, answered the remonstrance of the governor, council, and Commons House to the merchants' protest with perhaps an unfair advantage. It required fifty pages for Wragg and the other merchants to unburden their hearts on the position of South Carolina on the currency question, but Agent Fury seemed able to condense his reply, submitted to the Board on December 3, 1734, into eight pages.[12] The Board in due time, January, 1733/4, repealed the act as violating the king's instructions to the governor.

The same question came up in the history of Virginia. Aber-

[12] C. O. 5/363, f. 120.

cromby made an effort around 1757 to save a currency bill making paper a legal tender in that colony, calling frequently upon the London merchants who shipped to Virginia to prevent an application for repeal. To the credit of the merchants, it may be said, that they frankly informed him of their intention to work for repeal of the act. He wrote to Governor Dinwiddie in some perturbation of mind on November 3, 1757, because he had received no instructions on the law and failed to find it at the Plantation Office. He gloomily added that "it will require very strong arguments to support it" if it is contrary to the legal-tender clause. The merchants feared loss from payment of debts in paper or a twenty-five per cent depreciation if payment in sterling had been stipulated, but were not unanimous in their view of the operation of paper money. In 1763 there arose the question of the redemption of paper money in Virginia. The agent was instructed that a part of the agitation over paper currency was owing to those who had speculated; having taken advantage of high war prices, they wanted to reap even more profit by having paper money no longer legal tender and thus getting lower exchange. There was probably some truth in this argument, but no doubt the colonial laws did cause some injustice to British merchants.[13]

Although the currency question led to coöperation among some of the New England agents as early as 1740 and although the Southern colonies suffered disallowance of many currency bills, it was only late in the provincial period that there is evidence of coöperation on the part of the Southern agents to cope with this problem. A letter of Governor Bernard to the secretary of state in London of August 25, 1767, affords some proof that several of the agents, at least, were soliciting jointly for permission to create paper currency. The Massachusetts governor was concerned over publication in the London papers that De Berdt, agent of the Bay colony, had joined the other agents although that colony was greatly opposed to paper money. Likewise, Garth's accounts attest to such coöperation, for he charged up for April, 1766, attendance at a meeting with these agents on the paper currency issue.[14]

[13] *Virginia Magazine of History and Biography*, XI, 345-48 and note; see also Miller, "The Virginia Committee of Correspondence," *William and Mary Quarterly*, ser. 1, XXII, 7-8.

[14] "Garth Correspondence," *loc. cit.*, XXIX, 118.

Not the least interesting aspect of coöperation between agents was the help extended in personal matters. One agent would help out another by presenting a petition for him or by attending at the Board of Trade in case of his necessary absence. Charles Garth, for instance, on one occasion in 1768 asked his friend, Montague, to wait upon the secretary of state with a petition to the king from the lower house of assembly of Maryland, as he could not attend to the matter at that time.[15]

Now we come to the conspicuous cases of concerted action between all or most of the agents. The first, in 1731, related to the complaint of the sugar islands against the illicit trade between the Northern colonies and the French and Dutch plantations to the prejudice of the British islands of the West Indies. The fact that an extensive commerce, both illicit as well as legitimate, existed between the West Indian Islands and the North American colonies of the mainland was well recognized; likewise, the fact that this commerce was closely bound up with the triangular trade between the continental colonies, the West Indies, and Africa, involving the three basic commodities, rum, molasses, and slaves. The legal interchange between the mainland and the British West Indies was considerable, but the forbidden trade with the French, Dutch, and Spanish islands flourished until it was an offense to the British sugar planters and a stench to the British government. It must be recognized that as the plantations on the American continent increased in size and economic strength, the British West Indies proved unable to offer a sufficient market for the products of the mainland, and were likewise unable to supply the ever-growing demand for their tropical products on the part of those Northern colonies. Hence, as Andrews points out,[16] these latter colonies were forced to look for other markets for their products and other sources of sugar and molasses, and the flourishing commerce which sprang up with the foreign islands in the Caribbean area was in response to the economic law of supply and demand.

Given the attitude of the government and the planters of the sugar islands, controversy was inevitable and the activity on the part of the agents was just as inevitable. The planters of these islands

---

[15] "Correspondence of Governor Sharpe," *Maryland Historical Magazine*, XII, 381-82.
[16] For a comprehensive statement see Andrews, "Anglo-French Commercial Rivalry, 1700-1750: The Western Phase," *American Historical Review*, XX, 539-56, 761-80.

had in the second quarter of the eighteenth century, when the West India interest was at its height, a well-organized lobby in London, endowed with abundant funds and directed by colonial agents[17] and, to a greater degree, by absentee planters residing in London. It became so effective that it actually controlled at one time no less than forty seats in parliament.[18] These agents had previously exerted every effort to further their interests to the detriment of the continental colonies with the result that the agents of the mainland, far less influential, began to pool their strength. Under the Navigation Acts the islands had control of the legitimate English and North American markets; they now set themselves to gain suppression of the illegal trade carried on by the North American merchants, a trade which threatened their monopoly. This they achieved by the Molasses Act of 1733.

During the three years that that bill was being discussed before its passage, the North American agents exerted every effort for its defeat. At the first session of the Board of Trade at which this question of remedial legislation came up, that of December 10, 1731, no official agent of the Southern colonies was present. Francis Wilks, agent for Massachusetts and Connecticut, John Sharpe, apparently a solicitor on this occasion though he had been an agent for Barbados a few years earlier, and the Charleston merchant, Samuel Wragg, were informed of the complaint and asked to consult the merchants trading to the colonies of the North American continent as to their views on the proposed legislation. They were to present to the Board their written objections. On the next occasion, ten days later, in addition to Wilks and Sharpe, Partridge of Rhode Island, Belcher of Massachusetts, Fury of South Carolina, and Paris as solicitor, though he was also agent for Pennsylvania at this time, appeared along with several merchants interested in the trade of the Northern colonies to present the answers of the North Americans to the complaints of the islands of Barbados, St. Christopher, and Antigua.[19] In April, Partridge petitioned the House of Lords on

[17] Miss Penson concludes that the West Indian agents did not play a very great part in the activity of 1731-1733. As Barbados and Jamaica had no official agents just then, the solicitation was done by men of less regularized position.—*Colonial Agents of the British West Indies*, p. 122.

[18] *Gentleman's Magazine*, XXXVI, 229. The members of parliament were either West India planters, descendants of planters, or those who had interests there.

[19] *Journal of the Board of Trade*, 1728/9-1734, pp. 256-57 for December 10; for

the subject; the following March Partridge once more protested when the bill came up again, at the same time presenting a petition to the Commons, which this body refused even to receive.[20]

The act, proposing prohibitory duties on molasses, sugar and rum imported into the continental colonies from the West Indian colonies of other powers than England, was intended to revive the declining trade of the British West India planters. For two years the Northern agents were able to fend off its enactment, but they were finally defeated despite endless petitions and presentations of the case. It is interesting that three of the agents bore the expense of defending their cause. The Molasses Act was finally passed and went into effect in 1733.[21]

Much more significant was the coöperation in 1750-1751 when it was proposed to put an end to all trade between the Northern colonies and all foreign settlements. It is well known, of course, that the Molasses Act of 1733 was freely violated and that little effort was made to enforce it, for it would have crippled the commerce of the Northern colonies.[22] The illicit trade with the foreign islands continued until 1750. Since this trade averaged about £500,000 a year in American exports, the reader can readily understand the constant pressure of the West India planters to secure a monopoly of the trade on the one hand and the persistence and vigilance, on the other, of the North American agents when it was threatened. The Southern colonies were little involved in the conflict between the two groups of interests, which continued steadily until 1753. The War of the Austrian Succession from 1740 to 1748 brought a renewal of the dispute and brought representation and counter representation before the Board of Trade for three years. The Board of Trade sought in a thorough-going survey to gain evidence of the illicit trade

December 20, p. 259. For a discussion of this trade see Greene, *Provincial America*, 1690-1740, pp. 179, 288-90. Wragg may have been representing South Carolina unofficially as his agency had ended several months earlier and Fury had only been appointed on August 20. Probably the latter had received notice of his appointment between December 10 and 20, as he appeared on the latter date.

[20] *Journal of the House of Commons*, XXII, 79.

[21] Kimball, *Correspondence of the Rhode Island Governors*, I, 19-20; *Statutes at Large*, 6 George II, chapter 13.

[22] The customs officers by giving fraudulent clearances acted in collusion with the colonial importers in evading the law. For a statement as to the effect of enforcement, see Howard, *Preliminaries of the Revolution*, pp. 106-9.

carried on by the North American colonies with the foreign islands. The Northern agents retained a solicitor and counsel to oppose the West Indies petition, asking time to acquaint their respective colonies with the complaints against them. Three times a week for the several months between October 13, 1750, and January 10, 1751, the Board discussed this question. The Northern agents—to drop into the language of the Board in designating the colonies of the mainland—were put to work, gathering data as to the price of rum, molasses, syrups, sugar, and paneles (a coarse brown sugar from the Spanish islands) in each colony. When Ferdinand Paris insisted on November 13 on a reasonable time being allowed to secure answers from the colonies, he was strongly supported by the other Northern agents. On November 22 the Board room must have been overflowing with the agents, merchants, planters of the sugar islands, and their respective solicitors only to find the meeting postponed by the Board for lack of certain information. The Board called for data as to the value of the goods exported from England to each of the Northern colonies from 1720 to 1730 and from 1738 to 1748, the amount of duty paid in those colonies on the tropical imports from 1733 to 1750, and also the amount of duty paid in those colonies on rum, sugar, and syrups from any foreign settlements between those same years. Crockatt of South Carolina made a strong point of the fact that impediments placed in the way of the French islands getting lumber from North America would in the end be detrimental to the British sugar islands. Nearly all the agents had some plea to make—Bollan for Massachusetts, Abercromby for North Carolina, and Robert Charles for New York. The last two joined in a plea which was a forerunner of later arguments: that the proposed remedy was a monopoly prejudicial to Great Britain and destructive of the birthright of the people of North America. The Board had to allow the question to be postponed until the following November in order to allow the North American agents opportunity to consult their home governments. A concession, limited prohibition, offered by the sugar planters was as distasteful to the Northern agents as the original proposal.[23] Among the many memorials

[23] *Journal of the Board of Trade*, 1749/50-1753, pp. 119, 125, 127, 131, 134, 138, 149, 229, 364, 391; C. O. 5/38, pp. 120, 125, 128. For a copy of a notice from John Sharpe on James Crockatt of renewal of application for the prohibiting act see Journal of the Commons House of Assembly of South Carolina, XXVII, 106.

presented by the Northern agents and the interested merchants was one which sums up the tenor of all the arguments offered to the House of Commons, a group in which were several at the same time merchant and agent.

The petitioners firmly believed that such a law would "immediately defeat the Growth and Increaſe of all our Northern Colonies, and in ſhort Time will deſtroy their Trade and Navigation, their Ship-building, their cod, Whale, and other Fisheries, their Fur and Peltry Trades, their Rice, Indico, and Tobacco Trades, their Pitch, Tar, and Turpentine Trades, and all their other Trades and Buſineſs, to the great Hurt and Damage of at leaſt Two Millions of his Majeſty's moſt uſeful and good Subjects, Inhabitants of the Britiſh Northern Colonies in America, whoſe whole Time, Subſtance, Labour, and Induſtry, are employed, both by Sea and Land, to furniſh this Kingdom with Naval Stores, and other Neceſſaries, for our own uſe and alſo for ſupplying the Markets of Germany, Holland; the Produce of all which, together with the Freight of their Ships, and generally the Ships themſelves, is all returned to, and centers here, and is laid out in the Woollen, Iron, and other Manufactures of this Kingdom; and thereby adds greatly to the Riches and Strength of the Kingdom, by thus bringing in ſo great an Increaſe annually to the national Stock, and conſequently is an Advantage to all Degrees of Men amongſt us, to the Landholder, the Merchant, the Tradeſman, the Artificer, and the Labourer; ſo that this great Hurt and Damage will not be confined to his Majesty's uſeful and good Subjects, the Inhabitants of the Northern Colonies, but, in its Conſequences, might extend to the great Hurt and Damage of the Trade, Navigation, Wealth, and Strength of this Kingdom, and of every Individual in it, and will finally diſtreſs our own Sugar Colonies."[24]

This time the activity of the group of continental agents supported by irrefutable arguments staved off the adverse legislation until 1764, when the Sugar Act finally passed despite the efforts of the agents to convince the merchants and members of parliament that the colonial trade could not bear the Sugar Act. On April 5 it received the royal approval and may be regarded as actually inaugurating the opening of the Revolutionary struggle, as it involved far

[24] *Journal of the House of Commons,* XXVI, 183-84.

more than raising the duty on sugar. The preamble declared that the duties levied were granted to the king because the raising of a revenue in the American colonies in order to defray the cost of defending them was just. It confirmed and extended the act of 1733; it raised the duty on sugar but lowered it on molasses; it levied heavy duties on various foreign products; it diminished the drawbacks on reëxportation from England; and it forbade absolutely importation of rum or spirits by the colonies from foreign plantations or trade with the French islands of St. Pierre and Miquelon. It prescribed new and rigorous rules for enforcement of the acts of trade. It doubtless added to the irritation caused by the Stamp Act the next year.[25]

In the effort to secure for their respective colonies reimbursement for their expenditures in the intercolonial wars, the agents took their third major concerted action. The word that parliament was about to make grants for such reimbursement spread no doubt like wild fire among the agents and brought them flocking wherever it was to be discussed. The Board of Trade devoted its session on January 16, 1756, to the letter of the secretary of state which indicated that a sum of money was to be asked of parliament for the assistance of the king's subjects in America. As one scans the roll of the agents present—for New York, New Hampshire, New Jersey, Virginia, North Carolina, Massachusetts Bay, Connecticut, Rhode Island, Maryland, and Pennsylvania, it is conspicuous that no one attended for South Carolina, or Georgia. It was on this occasion that Cecilius Calvert, secretary to Lord Baltimore, attended for Maryland. Little knowledge of psychology is necessary to vizualize the numerous meetings of the agents, collectively or in groups, sometimes perhaps stormy, before the respective shares were adjusted. We may be certain that James Wright and James Abercromby met repeatedly, the latter in behalf of both Virginia and North Carolina, during 1758 and 1759, for a flat sum of £50,000 had been allocated as the portion for Virginia, North Carolina, and South Carolina. Probably there was little danger of dissension when it was a question of increasing the amount of the claim. Abercromby, for instance, says that he prevailed on the South Carolina agent to enter £6,000 for the forts and

[25] On this occasion the same arguments were brought forth but did not avail.—Stiles, *Extracts from the Itineraries and Other Miscellanies of Ezra Stiles*, pp. 220-21.

arms which had been voted by North Carolina in 1754 and an additional £4,700 which he estimated by information from former residents of North Carolina had been granted in 1758; South Carolina could also increase the sum already indicated.[26]   In connection with the second grant Abercromby informs us that as the parliamentary session of 1759 drew toward its close, the agents drew up a joint application in order to escape being "tied," as he called it, to dancing constant attendance at the next session of parliament.   The Treasury asked the agents to agree on their respective portions.   Evidently the agents of the Southern colonies escaped the bickering which might easily have resulted from such a situation, and did result for the New England agents; this was owing, partly at least, to the fact that in the South only three colonies were concerned, and only two agents, and to the further fact recorded by Abercromby of "perfect good Understanding" subsisting between the two men.   But Abercromby did not escape all unpleasantness, for he tells us about a month later that after all the American agents had been heard "much squabbling arose thereupon," some of them, particularly New York, arguing that they should have credit for what had been given by them to Virginia.[27]

Far more frequent and covering a longer period of time, cooperation in connection with the Stamp Act controversy came at a time when the seriousness of the issue at stake must have weighed heavily on the shoulders of the various agents.   The story of the marked change in Britain's colonial policy after the close of the Seven Years' War with its recognition of Britain as the predominant power on the North American continent has been told often and well.   Suffice it here to say that after a century of comparative neglect, during which the colonies had steadily developed their own local institutions, political customs, and, what was more significant, their own economic systems, the colonials were utterly unwilling to bend to a new policy of imperial control which involved reassertion of dormant powers and even an extension of the realm of imperial

[26] The wording of a note among the Treasury Papers is sufficiently explicit: "Apportionment of the £50,000 granted by Parliament anno 1757 to the Provinces of Virginia, North, and South Carolina adjusted and agreed to by the Agents concerned in this Case for three Provinces."—T. I/376, E, 201.   For Abercromby's estimates for the forts and arms see Abercromby Letter Book, pp. 139-41.

[27] See entries of May 19, 1759, in the Abercromby Letter Book, p. 137; of May 20, p. 151; of June 25, p. 161.   Note that Maryland and Georgia did not share in the grant.

supremacy. Here was a matter of equal concern to all the colonies, in which success could be secured by the agents only by unity of purpose, strategy, and action. Some degree of coöperation began early and was sustained throughout the years of conflict. As early as 1763 the House of Burgesses urged the agents of Virginia to get the agents of the other colonies to coöperate in pressing objections against the proposed Stamp Act; but though the agents seem to have tried to obey their instructions, neither parliament nor the British public could grasp the seriousness with which their action was viewed in the colonies. Today, it is difficult to realize that the measure which did more than anything else to alienate the American colonies passed through a half empty House of Commons.[28]

Meanwhile the same factors in Virginia which were developing to break down the separatism so characteristic of the American colonies were operating in the North. Massachusetts and other colonies were instructing their agents to join with the other agents in action against what appeared to them British aggression on colonial "rights." Massachusetts in 1765 instructed Jasper Mauduit, one of its agents, to join the other agents in furthering the purposes of its memorial. Leaders in New England, especially Thomas Cushing of Massachusetts Bay, were grasping the necessity of joint action.[29] Naturally, the agents were active individually. They secured many personal interviews with various government officials, seeking to modify their views by argument and cogent data; they offered numerous petitions individually as well as collectively; they lobbied in parliament; they presented their case through such members of parliament as were agents and such others as they could win over. They bombarded the public through the press. But, above all, they learned to coöperate, developing a highly effective organization.

As the threat of the distasteful tax legislation to secure revenue from the colonies became acute, several joint sessions of the agents as a group were arranged with George Grenville, at which the latter frankly portrayed the financial plight of the realm with a debt doubled by the recent war. The stamp tax was thought the most equitable and easiest way for America to contribute her share toward

[28] Andrews, *Virginia, the Old Dominion*, p. 243.
[29] For a fuller discussion of the coöperation of the New England agents see Burns, *Colonial Agents of New England*, pp. 129-36.

the burden. In an effort to delay or prevent the pending law, Franklin, Garth, Ingersoll and Jackson, the last two representing Connecticut, were delegated by their fellow-agents to attend on Mr. Grenville. At the interview held in February, 1765, that minister carefully explained his attitude; Agent Jackson declared that this program would "subvert" the colonial legislatures by securing the independence of the governors and other royal officials regarding salaries; the cabinet minister denied this as a possibility and terminated the interview by saying that the House of Commons would give due consideration to the objections which had just been voiced. A later conference showed Grenville unchanged. On this occasion Israel Mauduit, a British merchant and brother of the Massachusetts agent, who sometimes represented his brother, asked Grenville for the main heads of the act under consideration but received a refusal.[30]

This crisis greatly increased the development of joint activity by the several agents, a fact attested by the correspondence of Garth, as well as Ingersoll, Mauduit, and others. In the years immediately following the enactment of the Stamp Act the definite organization of the North American agents for united action took shape in an effort to secure its repeal. It should be emphasized that they never became a formal group, but regular meetings were held, memorials were drawn up jointly, special tasks assigned to certain agents, and the colonial opposition to the parliamentary action thus made far more effective than it would have been by individual action—even though unsuccessful. The British officials found it convenient to recognize the common organization, for Lord Hillsborough asked them in 1769 to attend together in order to save him the trouble of explaining the matter repeatedly.[31] The Garth correspondence abounds with references to meetings, consultation, and joint action, as do the letters of other agents—Mauduit, Johnson, and De Berdt. The agents collectively waited on the government officials, especially Lord Hillsborough, who was secretary of state for the American colonies after 1768 but whose imperialistic point of view was only irritated by the firm opposition of the agents, who exerted their ut-

[30] See *Letters to Jasper Mauduit*, in Massachusetts Historical Society *Collections*, LXXIV, 74, 147 note; "Ingersoll Papers," *New Haven Historical Society Papers*, IX, 314, 331-32; Griffith, *Historical Notes of the American Colonies and Revolution*, p. 19.
[31] *Trumbull Papers*, in Massachusetts Historical Society *Collections*, ser. 5, IX, 304-6.

most endeavors to alter his views on colonial policy. They were told plainly in a long conference that the plan of parliament was to repeal many of the duties. The secretary constantly denounced the plantations for their refusal to acknowledge the right of the British government to levy these and any taxes on the colonies.[32] Joint action was probably at its height during the years when these duties were being argued and repeal agitated. Judging by Garth's correspondence, one would think that few steps were contemplated except in coöperation with the other agents.

Balked in their efforts to prevent the passage of the taxation measures the agents were generally directed to join with the other agents to obtain a repeal of the acts which had imposed duties and to prevent the billeting of soldiers in America. South Carolina's directions to Garth in April, 1768, are so suggestive of the spirit of the times that they merit quotation: "And We are further directed to desire you will always, without waiting for Particular Instructions, join the Agents of the other Colonies in all matters where the general Interest of North America is concerned."[33] Speaker Randolph wrote for the Virginia lower house to the houses of assembly of North Carolina and New Jersey on May 9, 1768, that their Mr. Montague was enjoined to consult the agents of the other colonies and to coöperate with them in every measure that was thought necessary on the delicate question then before America.[34] By November South Carolina followed up her general instruction of April with specific instructions to Garth to join the agents of the other colonies for repeal. By December even Georgia had joined the procession by requesting its recently appointed agent, Franklin, to "concur" with the other agents for repeal of the hated acts and for restoration of the harmony which they earnestly desired to exist betwen the colonies and the mother country.[35] McCulloh promised the Committee of

[32] *Ibid.*, pp. 304-6.

[33] "Garth Correspondence," *loc. cit.*, XXX, 180.

[34] *Colonial Records of North Carolina*, VII, 749 for the letter to that state; for the identical letter to New Jersey, see C. O. 5/989, pp. 72-73.

[35] C. O. 5/391, pp. 156-57. For Georgia see Stevens, *History of Georgia*, II, 68; and for the letter of the speaker to Franklin, *Colonial Records of Georgia*, XV, 25. Georgia's caution and delay in joining the rest of the colonies is well illustrated by a letter of April 15, 1765, from the Committee of Correspondence to Agent Knox: "In regard to your joining the Northern Agents in any Matter, they may have in charge from their Constituents, we are only directed to acquaint you, that, so far, as you suppose we are interested in their applications, you will Cooperate with them, . . . and in respect to the

Correspondence of North Carolina his faithful, enthusiastic coöperation with the other agents, convinced that a spirited and vigorous coöperation of the several agents was a "probable and efficacious means" for success.[36]

Garth, for his part, had been coöperating also on other matters. Already before the instructions of April, 1768, had been dispatched, immediately after the introduction into parliament of a bill for new vice-admiralty courts in America, he had asked Dr. Franklin, Mr. Charles, and Montague for a conference on the subject. At the consultation they were joined by Mr. Johnson, agent of Connecticut, and a Mr. Delaney of New York. In this case it became clear that the act contemplated no new extension of power, and so the agents felt that opposition was unnecessary and unwise. Garth's alarms had not been justified.[37]

Meanwhile by November, 1768, the agents had been meeting weekly in order, according to Garth, "to consult together, and to Act as Exigencies offer." At these meetings they considered whether it was practicable to procure repeal of the act for duties without raising the issue of the right of parliament to levy the taxes. They urged that Dr. Franklin prepare the draft of a petition as much in accord with American sentiments as possible, but unexceptionable to the British government. When it was considered at a later meeting, Garth, though he did not approve of the Franklin draft in all respects, did finally subscribe to it, and it was signed by all except the agents of New Hampshire and North Carolina.[38] Meanwhile feeling became so strong against the American agents that they were excluded from the galleries during debates on colonial affairs, though William Johnson evaded the rule at least once. The agents pressed steadily for repeal of the Townshend duties. Evidently through 1770 and 1771 they were together at the various government offices.

Stamp duty, which as far as appears to us, may be as equal as any that could be generally imposed upon the Colonys, yet, we must own, the manner of imposing it greatly alarms us, as we know not, where the precedent may end, and however it may be with any or all of the Northern provinces," Georgia is in no state to bear "new Burthens."—Habersham, *Letters,* p. 32.

[36] *Colonial Records of North Carolina,* VIII, 57.

[37] Letter to the Committee of Correspondence of South Carolina, dated February 29, 1768, "Garth Correspondence," *loc. cit.,* XXX, 216.

[38] *Ibid.,* XXX, 232; XXXI, 52-53. Franklin's petition was against certain duties payable in silver and to be used for the cost of justice and government.

A final flood of petitions to parliament could not prevent passage of the coercive acts of 1774 despite the activity of Franklin, Arthur Lee, and others. This concerted action was undoubtedly largely responsible for the repeal of the Townshend duties except on tea in 1770.

That as late as July, 1775, some of the agents were still serving, is proved by the fact that the Continental Congress at its second session transmitted a memorial to the king and another address to the people of Great Britain to Richard Penn, William - Bollan, Arthur Lee, Edmund Burke, Thomas Life, and Charles Garth. Penn and Lee delivered the original to the king through the secretary for the colonies and received in return the statement that "no answer would be given." With that act the colonial agency for the North American provinces as an institution may be regarded as terminated.[39]

Probably the most delicate task demanded of the agents was coöperation between two agents of the same colony. Even that was attained. While the situation of having two agents in Massachusetts seems strange, even with the tradition of independence there, it is remarkable that the struggle over the agency question should have produced two agents each in three of the Southern colonies—Virginia, Maryland, and North Carolina. Of course repeatedly three, and once four, agents were dispatched on a given mission, but that was during the early period while the agency was being developed; repeatedly during the eighteenth century a special agent was sent over, as has been noted, to aid the regular agent or for a particular task; but the situation which made the question of coöperation delicate was when each house of the legislature had its own agent. Abercromby was naturally greatly concerned when the House of Burgesses insisted on appointing its own agent in 1759. Immediately arose the question of allocation of duties, which Abercromby took up with Montague, as has been related in Chapter II.

[39] There appears frequently in Garth's bills of expenses: "To several Attendances & Meetings with the agents—£10-10/."—*Ibid.*, XXXIII, 229. Another item gives £6 6s. For the account of the petition of the second session of the Continental Congress see Lee, *Life of Arthur Lee*, I, 46.

Franklin, Lee, and Bollan had offered another petition to the House of Commons in January, 1775, and asked to be heard at the bar of that body, which request was refused. Franklin appeared, doubtless, as agent of Pennsylvania and Massachusetts rather than as agent for Georgia.

When Abercromby spoke on July 20, 1759, of his relations with Samuel Smith, who was selected by the North Carolina council in March, 1759, to look after the interests of that province in the next parliamentary grant, he quite frankly declared: "I am obliged much against my Inclination to go on smoothly with Smith, in order that no advantage may be taken of our not Concurring together, in getting the Money from the Treasury. . . ."[40]

When it came to the critical issue of the British policy of taxation, the rivalry between the two houses was submerged and the Virginia council, which had objected so strenuously to the appointment of a separate agent for the lower house, directed Abercromby to join Montague, "the Agent for this Colony"—by which words they made a great concession—in applying for redress of grievances.[41] Abercromby and Montague pulled together valiantly during the Stamp Act agitation.

Finally, the attitude of the Board of Trade in dealing with double agents had to be defined. It found a *modus operandi*, notification of both agents simultaneously, if notification was necessary.

The reader has already been made aware of the influence and power of the British merchants.[42] There now remains a closer examination of the coöperation which the agents sought from the merchants and often found. It was through the agents that the merchants ascertained the wishes of the colonists as to goods and settling of accounts. Even in Cromwell's time one of the agents of Virginia, Samuel Mathews, joined his signature to that of divers merchants, traders, and planters in the colony of Barbados and in Virginia, together with thousands of mariners and handicraftsmen, to a petition to the Lord Protector and his Council of State. It may perhaps not be a false assumption that it was Mathews' activity which secured the names of the merchants and traders.[43] Such power as the British merchants wielded must, of course, be reckoned with by the colonies and their agents. Colonel Edmund Jennings, Micajah Perry, and other merchants trading to Virginia represented

[40] Abercromby Letter Book, p. 185.

[41] For the division of their respective duties see above, Chapter II.

[42] For a discussion of the importance of the British merchants see Burns, *op. cit.*, pp. 136-40; in connection with the West Indies, see Penson, *op. cit.*, pp. 196-201.

[43] *Calendar of State Papers, Colonial*, 1574-1660, p. 417; *Virginia Magazine of History and Biography*, XVIII, 45-46.

successfully to the Commissioners of Customs and the Lord High Treasurer in March, 1704/5, their reasons why certain ports and places mentioned should be selected rather than others for the discharge and loading of ships. Boone and Beresford won the cooperation of the merchants trading to South Carolina in 1716 for their petition for soldiers to be sent to protect the province; the merchants had been sympathetic to a "distressed" province because of the value of naval stores produced by that colony. And in 1734, one of the several occasions when Francis Yonge was serving as a special agent, he and Fury, along with Oglethorpe for Georgia, rounded up a number of merchants to attend the Board of Trade on August 7 in behalf of a measure they were defending.[44]

Garth seems to have been particularly busy in enlisting the aid of the merchants. His correspondence shows a petition which he drew up for the remission of part of the high duty on rice signed by twenty merchants, and another to continue the bounty on indigo signed by seventeen merchants. Help from the merchants of London and Bristol was available for free importation of iron and revival of the bounty on hemp, and for leave to import salt directly from foreign parts into the Southern colonies.[45]

While the merchants never meant to the mainland colonies just what they meant to the British West Indies, partly because there

[44] *Ibid.*, XIX, 17; Entry Book of the Board of Trade, C. O. 5/1293, pp. 71-74; *Journal of the Board of Trade, 1728/9-1734*, p. 405.

[45] "Garth Correspondence," *loc. cit.*, XXXI, 142-44. See also his letter to the Committee of Correspondence of February 5, 1770, *ibid.*, p. 141.

Of course, the agents did not always secure the aid of the merchants; in fact, their influence was sometimes exerted adversely to the desires of the colonials. One instance is the lighthouse at Cape Henry. Virginia had passed an act in 1752 for erecting one, the utility of which to the trade and shipping of both Virginia and Maryland was admitted, but the agents representing the two colonies, Abercromby and Calvert, were directed on December 19, 1758, when the act was before the Board of Trade, to consult with the principal English merchants trading to those provinces and report their sentiments to the Board. On January 16 following, Abercromby reported that the merchants objected to any tax upon ships to support the lighthouse. Though the Board of Trade had been inclined to have the measure taken up as a government act on the ground of its being a general utility, in which case the two colonies would still be expected to contribute to the expense, the Privy Council disallowed the act, influenced possibly by the reluctance of the merchants to pay any sort of toll.—*Journal of the Board of Trade, 1754-1758*, pp. 436-37; *ibid.*, 1759-1763, p. 1. For report of Abercromby on the attitude of the Board, see Abercromby Letter Book, pp. 119-20; and for Abercromby's report to Secretary Pownall, dated July 9, 1759, after consulting the merchants, see C. O. 5/1329, p. 203. It should be added that the Board felt that the Virginia law carried its operation beyond its territorial jurisdiction into Maryland and could not recommend assent on that ground also.

were not large numbers of absentee planters as from the West Indian islands to influence issues by personal contact, the opinions and good will of the men trading to the North American provinces was of the utmost importance. The agents tried to capitalize the selfish interests of those traders and shippers. In view of the early settlement and development of the West Indies, it is astonishing to find the statement made by one James Knight of Jamaica, writing from London to a correspondent in the island in March, 1725/6, emphasizing the disadvantages under which the affairs of his island suffered compared with those of Virginia. Of all the British colonies, he declared, Virginia had worked out the best means of managing her interests in London. She had, he states, two agents,[46] who twice each month regularly held meetings with the planters and merchants concerned in the colony, "and consult with them what is proper to be done for the Service of the Country." To defray the expense of these meetings funds were raised on all goods imported from Virginia, a treasurer being appointed to receive the contribution of six pence on every hogshead imported. Knight reported that the two agents "go hand in hand without any clashing or jeolousie." This policy, he felt, was not very practicable for Jamaicans, for the Jamaica assembly had alienated the English merchants so that when planters and merchants met in London there was constant friction.[47] While the Jamaica planter saw the Virginia merchants' organization from the outside and was therefore unaware of possible friction, his comment affords illuminating and valuable information.

The research also reveals a reference in the *Universal Spectator and Weekly Journal* of August 10, 1734, to frequent "Meetings or Clubs of particular Merchants, either fix'd or occasional, as of the Turkey and Italian Merchants, the Spanish, the Portuguese, the French, the Flandercan, the German, the Danish, the Swedish, the Muscovite, the Dutch, the Irish, the West India, the Virginia, the

---

[46] The two agents were at this date the regular agent, Leheup, and perhaps Byrd, the latter serving for the entire assembly. That body was again taking advantage of his visit to England on his own concerns. See above, Chapter III.

[47] Add. MSS, 22677, ff. 1-2, British Museum. The letter is dated March 18, 1725/6. The writer is not satisfied that the contribution of six pence per hogshead on goods imported from Virginia was a separate assessment for these meetings in London. Knight may have heard vaguely of the two-shilling levy on tobacco as the source of funds to support the agent.

Carolina, New York, and New England merchants."[48]   Though possibly a margin of exaggeration must be allowed the writer of the article in claiming frequent meetings, it is clear that such meetings did occur, as for example, of the Portugal merchants in January, 1739/40,[49] and in all likelihood in a more permanent organization of the Society of London Merchants, trading to Virginia and Maryland.[50]   Reference to this society exists in 1757 though there is no evidence to connect it with the fortnightly sessions of Virginia merchants and planters described above.   It is not certain that there existed a permanent society of North American merchants in general, though the meetings of the merchants interested in the North American trade from 1765 to the outbreak of the American Revolution were both numerous and important.

The importance and the explanation of the attitude of the merchants become obvious with the presentation of two facts: first, many of the agents were themselves merchants; and, secondly, the merchants had a large stake in the prosperity and good will of the colonies. Mercantile interests always thrive under peaceful conditions and vice versa, suffer under disturbed conditions, even under economic warfare. Concretely stated, the colonials were in debt to British business houses to the extent of several millions of pounds, debts which would be gravely jeopardized by a governmental policy which created friction between the colonies and the mother country.   So important was another consideration that it is difficult to separate one from the other as primary or secondary: the danger of threatening the extensive market of British manufacturers and shippers in the colonies by the new policies of Grenville and Townshend.   The American colonials had instinctively known how to put pressure on the English traders by the boycott; no sooner was the boycott in operation, than the mercantile classes and manufacturing towns in England began to buzz with activity somehow to conciliate and appease the colonies.   The Stamp Act sent out waves of commotion in ever-widening circles which were felt in the merchants' associa-

[48] The article appeared in an abbreviated form in the *Gentleman's Magazine*, IV (August, 1734), 431-32 under the title, "Proposal for a Merchants' Club."

[49] Such a meeting is noted in the *London Daily Post and General Advertiser*, January 17, 1739/40.

[50] Reference to this society is to be found in Chatham Papers, Bundle 95.   See also Hotblack, *Chatham's Colonial Policy*, p. 49.

tions, in the taverns, coffee houses,[51] and parliament. Committees were set up to deal with the agents, to arrange joint meetings with them, and to attend hearings of parliamentary committees. The interest of the merchants and manufacturers was inspired solely by considerations of business and so was not cloaked under arguments of constitutional and philosophical right. As a matter of fact, the merchants did not share the convictions of the colonials as to inherent rights or sympathize with their challenge to parliament. They were ready to coöperate to correct conditions which hurt trade and no further. In fact, there are on record differences between the agents and the merchants on the philosophical aspects of the question. With the theory of mercantilism the British merchant had no quarrel as he thereby secured to a large degree a monopoly in imperial trade. Indifferent to the arguments of the agents when they pointed out that the Sugar Act would lower the cash surplus of the North Americans and thus reduce purchases in England, the merchants went into action when the colonials began to countermand orders unless the Stamp Act were repealed.[52]

Delegates from the merchants appeared with the agents at sessions arranged with members of the ministry; often agents and merchants consulted together to concert measures of opposition.[53] Then followed circular letters from the merchants' association to the manufacturing centers insisting on their support of an application to parliament against the obnoxious law and on their bringing pressure to bear on their representatives in parliament to repeal it. These manufacturing towns responded so that parliament was deluged with petitions hostile to the bill.[54] The merchants often met the agents at the Kings Arms Tavern and other inns to canvass the situation and exhaust every means of pressure to repeal the act.[55] At a crowded

[51] The coffee houses in London connected with the North American colonies are well known, as the Maryland Coffee House and the Pennsylvania Coffee House.

[52] *Letters to Jasper Mauduit*, pp. 171-79.

[53] "Ingersoll Papers," *loc. cit.*, pp. 331-32.

[54] Add. MSS, 330/333, p. 88 ff. The merchants of Bristol transmitted to their representatives in parliament an account of conditional orders from North America amounting to £200,000. The Londoners then computed the amount of their conditional orders. —"Proceedings of the Virginia Committee of Correspondence," *loc. cit.*, XII, 164.

[55] A score and more of petitions poured in from every considerable manufacturing town.—*Journal of the House of Commons*, XXX, 499; Hinkhouse, *Preliminaries of the American Revolution*, p. 64. London, Bristol, Liverpool, Halifax, Lancaster, Manchester, Leicester, and Glasgow among other places sent in petitions.

hearing of parliament the committee of merchants trading to America through their chairman, Barlow Trecothick, made a deeper impression during his three and a half hour examination before the House of Commons than the agents had done by his parading statistics to show the effects of the boycott on British prosperity and the financial stake of Englishmen.[56] Under such a barrage it is no wonder that the law was repealed though with a Declaratory Act. The merchants were thought to have spent in meetings, messages to the manufacturing towns, and on entertainment to members of parliament nearly £1,500.[57]

Coöperation of agents with merchants appears in still one other instance. The mutiny bill, according to Lord Shelburne's own admission, was modified by their action; namely, by omission of a clause which would have quartered British soldiers on private citizens in America. Interesting light is shed on the practices of the time by a statement in one of the British papers that a committee of merchants entertained at Kings Arms Tavern in Cornhill for Charles Garth and Richard Glover for their zealous "endeavours and ready assistance" at the last session to prevent the billeting of soldiers on private homes in America.[58] The agents sought and secured the coöperation of the merchants though with less enthusiasm than earlier against the Townshend Acts; there followed the old round of propaganda, pressure, and joint meetings. Franklin urged an intensive boycott by the colonists; again the merchants became vocal at a drop of £700,000 in trade. The retention of the duty on tea made the repealing of the Townshend measures a very limited success.

[56] *Cambridge History of the British Empire*, I, 600, note. This is the famous occasion when Trecothick was asked if the Americans would accept a mitigation of the act and replied that no modification would reconcile them—nothing less than repeal.

[57] Franklin, *Works*, VII, 341.

[58] *Lloyd's Evening Post and British Chronicle*, August 16, 1765.

CHAPTER II.

ANNOYANCES AND REWARDS OF THE OFFICE

THE AGENT faced other annoyances besides those connected with the difficulty of collecting his salary. The difficulties of reimbursement for the agent were so integrally connected with the difficulties of securing funds to meet the expense of the agency that no division of the financial aspect of the subject seemed possible. Here, however, the other annoyances connected with the office of agent arise properly for discussion.

First in the list of annoyances come the frequent and long delays in dealing with the various government offices. For three months in 1757 after the resignation of Lord Halifax from the presidency of the Board of Trade, no material business was transacted until finally, after complaints of stoppage of business Halifax, at the request of Secretary Pitt, reassumed his office shortly after October 20.[1] Delays by no means began in 1757, for as early as 1708 Blakiston was writing to the governor and council of Virginia that he had been at the Plantation Office to lay before the Board of Trade a matter concerning the patenting of land, but "there was noe Board." He had been told, however, that their Lordships would be in town "in a week or ten days," and he assured the council that he would not "faile to attend them as soon as they meet."[2] Leheup complained of the Commissioners of Customs in 1730. He had had no opportunity to be heard until he protested; then he was given one day's notice that the Virginia act in which he was interested would be considered December 17; he attended only to be informed, that, as the commissioners did not have leisure for the matter that day,

[1] This is based upon a statement of Abercromby to Colonel Young, written October 20, 1757. Halifax was to return to town for work the next week.—Abercromby Letter Book, p. 32. He resigned again definitely in 1761.

[2] "Miscellaneous Colonial Documents," *Virginia Magazine of History and Biography*, XIX, 19-20.

he should have a copy of their decision before it was sent to the Board of Trade; their secretary held the copy of the communication to the Board two days, December 29-31, expecting his attendance, and then sent it forward. Leheup not unnaturally protested to the Board of Trade that he had not been heard on the subject and certainly an opportunity restricted to two days was hardly ample.[3] Ultimately the Commissioners of the Customs were punished for their delays, for they had to present to the Board of Trade a reply to the agent's objections.

The agent most vociferous on the subject of official delays was Abercromby, who may from the tenor of his communications be described not unjustly as irascible. In November, 1758, he is found complaining of the Lords of the Treasury, who, despite "his repeated and preſsing applications" had not made time for a hearing of the tobacco revenue case: ". . . none but them who had experienced the Delays at the Treasury can judge of the Difficultys attending Negociations there: the chief Point now urged is a Reference to the Auditor Gen[l]. was this got over, I shall so far have the Field before me."[4] While the same agent was negotiating one of the parliamentary grants, he found the delays so irksome that he actually undertook the journey to Lord Loudoun's home in Scotland to adjust Virginia's claims, and this although before his Lordship left town he had had several conferences with him.[5] Almost a year later, he reported to Governor Fauquier on that subject: "Of all the Solicitations I ever was engaged in, this has proved the most tedious and troublesome, owing generally to the Difficultys and Delay given us by a certain Noble Lord, whose Approbation to our Claim became Neceſsary."[6] Undoubtedly it was such delays that inspired Garth's four-day journey to assure access to one of the secretaries of state.

The agents experienced difficulty in securing access to important papers. The red tape and routine of the various boards must have been trying, to say the least. As early as 1689 Ludwell wrote to the Board of Trade that "yo[r] Pet[r] waited divers tyms at M[r] Blaithwayts office for a copy or Sight of ye Lord Howards Answer, but

---

[3] Letter of Carkasse, secretary of the Commissioners of the Customs, to the Board of Trade, dated Mar. 11, 1730.—C. O. 5/1322, f. 110.

[4] Entries of Nov. 17 and 18, 1758, Abercromby Letter Book, pp. 104, 115.

[5] *Ibid.*, pp. 171-72.

[6] Entry of May 10, 1760, Abercromby Letter Book (no page given).

could not obtaine ye favor of either one minute before the tyme of hearing, although yo Pet[r] Aſured M[r] Blathwaite he did not Intend to reply in wrighting to it, nor had yo[r] Pet[r] any Design in it, but ye hopes of being Informed by it, what thoſe Crymes were for w[ch] thoſe great Severities were inflicted, of w[ch] his L[fe] had till then kept us in Ignorance, . . ."[7] His patience won its due reward, for the above application to the Lords of Trade for a copy of Lord Howard's answer was indorsed on the back, "granted." There are other instances, however, when the agents were denied all access to certain papers. Byrd, for instance, in 1704 sought to get a copy of a paper affecting the interests of Virginia, at the instigation of Richard Beverley, but it was denied. Francis Yonge in 1722 was sent for by West, counsel of the Board of Trade, to be informed that exception had been taken to an act of South Carolina dealing with trade with the Indians, but the secretary refused to state the objections or to tell by whom they were made, though it later appeared that they had been made by the Virginia agent. In this case it also becomes clear how the frailties of human nature on the part of secretaries and clerks could annoy the agents. West promised to send for Yonge when he had spoken to a Mr. Bamfield, but presumably forgot all about the matter, and reported to the Board that he had informed the South Carolina agent of the objections of the Virginia agent. Yonge, for his part, supposing that he was to answer objections to the law, and not to offer arguments for passing the law, awaited the summons which never came.[8]

The formality and care with which the papers were guarded is perhaps best illustrated by the experience of a Northern agent, Robert Charles, who acted for New York. The Board had become even more jealous as to its records than in 1747. On December 23, 1757, he asked permission to search all the public transactions of New York from 1664 to 1719 and of New Jersey for the same period relative to the boundary between those two colonies. He was told on January 21, 1758, that the Board had ordered a search made by one of their own officers in order to have laid before the Board a list of all papers relating to that question; the Board then would be

[7] C. O. 5/1305, f. 66, dated Nov. 20, 1689.
[8] For Beverley see C. O. 5/1314, Bundle 63; C. O. 5/371, Bundle H, 56. The only Bamfield or Bampfield encountered in the Board of Trade Journals is a George Bampfield, agent for New York and Barbados.

able to decide what attitude to take with regard to copies or extracts from the papers. After a month's interval, the agent was told that after another delay to permit the clerk's search of the papers, their Lordships would deliberate on his request and decide on an answer![9]

Equally irritating would be the situation when the agent had gone to the Plantation Office to secure a copy of a certain paper of the utmost importance to the matter then in hand only to find that the paper had been referred to some other official. Abercromby, working on the Two-penny case, was formally notified that the Reverend Mr. Camm had through his solicitor exhibited a remonstrance to the Board of Trade against the above-mentioned act. Such notice was tantamount to an order to prepare his side of the case for future hearing. When he asked for a copy of the act and Camm's remonstrance against it, he was told that the act had been laid before the Bishop of London.[10]

Unquestionably one agent would be jealous of secret sources of information open to another. A case in point concerned all the agents, and the leak was the French ambassador. In January, 1776, Governor William Franklin, son of Agent Benjamin Franklin, reported to Lord Dartmouth a rumor that through the French embassy action taken in the Privy Council percolated to some of the agents.[11]

Interminable delays in securing instructions from the colonies were, no doubt, difficult for the agents to contend with, but more explicable than the delays interposed by the home offices. There existed then no way to shorten the broad stretch of the Atlantic, but agents doubtless yearned for shears to cut the red tape of officialdom. When several months had to intervene between the time an agent dispatched a letter of inquiry and receipt of the answer—not to mention the times when the letter or its reply was lost by its capture by an enemy or pirates—the agent must have often felt quite out of touch with the Committee of Correspondence. Sometimes the committees were grossly at fault. Abercromby wrote to the committee of North Carolina on December 15, 1757: "It is now above nine months since I had the honour of hearing from you, my several letters of the 26th of last May and of the 12th July have all

[9] C. O. 5/1295, pp. 239-40.   [10] Abercromby Letter Book, p. 147.
[11] Historical Manuscripts Commission, *Fourteenth Report*, App. X: *MSS of the Earl of Dartmouth, American Papers*, II, 411.

been acknowledged. . . ." But to provoke a reply apparently, he sent copies of these letters by a sloop of war by courtesy of the Lords of the Admiralty.[12] Of course, when letters miscarried, as they not infrequently did, the agent was left as much at sea as by neglect to write him. It is easy to picture Abercromby running to the "plantation office," as he called the Board of Trade in June, 1760, to inquire about the last packet. There he learned that the acts which had been recommended to his attention had miscarried, as well as the letter bearing his instructions from the Virginia council. He thought it probable that the letter to Montague from the Committee of Correspondence of the burgesses had been lost in the same packet.[13] Garth, as a member of the British House of Commons, knew well the desirability of being forehanded in any dealings which concerned parliament, and so in June, 1766, he suggested to the South Carolina Committee of Correspondence that it place in his hands by the following November any commands or instructions it intended to give him relating to activities for the next year, as the ministry and men in high office had little time for propositions submitted after parliament opened. Experience of the past year had taught him the necessity of the warning.[14]

The most embarrassing of all the delays was failure to notify the agent promptly of dismissal or reappointment. He was often left in doubt whether to cease his solicitation or to "carry on." The remarkable thing is the degree to which he did "carry on" when in doubt as to his status. It would appear that Abercromby, for one, was actuated by a genuine desire not to let the affairs of the colony suffer. That sincerity can best be conveyed to the reader through his own words as expressed in his letter of March 13, 1758, to Governor Dobbs of North Carolina: "I must hereupon repeat to you, that I think myself in Duty bound to attend to your Provincial affairs notwithstanding the expiration of the Law, til such time as I am inform[ed?] discharged from this Trust, and let me assure you, that Duty to the Province more than any other motive, leads me still to interest myself that their Interest may not suffer so far as I can prevent." He concluded from the silence of the Committee

[12] Abercromby Letter Book, p. 58.
[13] Entry of June 1, 1760, Abercromby Letter Book (no page), Abercromby to Governor Fauquier.
[14] "Garth Correspondence," loc. cit., XXVIII, 233-34.

of Correspondence that they were not authorized to write him, but he justifiably wanted an explicit statement of the action taken by the colony. Hence, he continued to work with Agent Wright, acting for South Carolina, against a salt monopoly.[15] He took a similar attitude toward Virginia when he was displaced as colonial agent and became representative only for the council. It would appear that he had first heard unofficially that the House of Burgesses had assumed the right to set up its agent so that he was in doubt whether he should continue in any capacity. He felt in honor bound to continue handling the many matters under-way after the adjournment of parliament until the adjournment of the Board of Trade.[16] While he felt himself hampered in his negotiations, he continued his efforts for the parliamentary grant by special request of the assembly and assured the Committee of Correspondence that he would do his best, in accordance with their instructions, to see that the money did not come under the disposal of certain persons there or abroad, to whom they apparently objected. He reminded them that this matter had given him "infinite Trouble, more so of late, since the Controversy about the Agency stands in the way of my Service."[17] He would not allow his resentment at the far more generous salary voted by the assembly to Montague as especial representative of the burgesses to interfere with the continuance of his duty.[18]

The statement that every agent was subjected to criticism, frequent and often bitter, is not very far from the truth. Criticism came from the colonies and from the home government; from the lower house of assembly, from the council, and from the governor; for not following instructions and again for not exercising his own judgment. Exceeding instructions, often only another way of exercising discretion, brought some agents into trouble with the colony. Furthermore, the unhappy experience of one agent in this respect was not lost on another. Abercromby, to cite an example, took note of the unhappy situation of the agent of Massachusetts, who about 1757

[15] Abercromby Letter Book, pp. 83-84.

[16] "I must neverthelefs continue in the Service, for there are so many things brought on the Anvil since the Breaking up of Parliament which I could not give Motion to sooner, I cannot withdraw my Service now they are under Consideration, before the long Adjournmente of the Board."—*Ibid.*, p. 157.

[17] *Ibid.*, p. 192.

[18] "However disagreeable to me to act on so depreciated an Establishment from that of my succefsor to be I must nevertheless continue in the Service, . . ."—*Ibid.*, p. 157.

had interposed a petition in some matters then before parliament, and because he had no particular instructions for such a case, escaped "committment" only through the intervention of friends.[19]

The colonial records are filled with expressions of dissatisfaction on the part of the assembly with the agents.[20] Even the early agents, selected obviously for their sympathy with the view of the majority of the colony and for a particular object, did not escape criticism. The assembly once probably saved the feelings of Ludwell by offering the following defense: ". . . it being taken notice of that some ill-disposed persons have endeavoured to aspearse his honour in the said trust and negotiation." It was therefore ordered that Mr. Secretary Ludwell "be publiquely justified as haveing well performed, and duely rendred account of his said trust and negotiation, and that he have all due redresse against those persons soe aspersing and villifyeing of him." Even a purchasing agent, such as Peter Pagan primarily was, could be told that the arms he had purchased for Maryland were "very bad," that the arms which he might send in the future must be "sanguined" to prevent rust, and that he must send flints to make up a deficiency in the consignment of the previous year.[21] That Joseph Boone could not escape the strictures of the governor for his "poor services," was natural, as the executive was fighting for continuance of the status quo and his position.

The sharp criticism of Fury by the Council in opposing his reappointment in 1737 was matched by the defense of the Commons House of Assembly.[22] Criticism of Fury first became serious in 1742-1743 when a faction tried to suspend him, but only succeeded in creating a Committee of the Commons House to inquire into his reasons for not printing and publishing the report of the committee on the causes of the failure of the expedition against St. Augustine, and further to inquire into his conduct in the dispute between South Carolina and Georgia over the right of navigation of the Savannah

[19] *Ibid.*, p. 93. Presumably commitment meant to prison.
[20] The bluntly stated dissatisfaction with Benjamin Martyn was rather discontent with the type of agency he represented than with the man himself and so need not detain us.
[21] Hening, *Statutes*, II, 422-23: *Archives of Maryland*, XXIII, 130.
[22] Journal of the Council of South Carolina, 1737-1741, VII, 21; Journal of the Commons House of Assembly of South Carolina, January 16, 1738-June 7, 1739, XII, 90. It is likely that these respective resolutions do not relate to the same action on the part of the agent, but the attitude of each house is accurately reflected.

River. At this stage the council did not regard a committee necessary on the first point and saw no misconduct in his handling of the
Georgia affair; hence no inquiry appeared proper to that body. The
resolution of the lower house revealed the real grounds of the complaint; a group—even the Committee of Inquiry—was convinced
that he was so attached to the service of Oglethorpe, owing to his
post as agent for the regiment of foot in Georgia, that in any dispute between South Carolina and the General, Fury would not act
against the interest of the General. Rather grudgingly the committee declared that Fury's past conduct in his agency did not appear
"blamable." In 1744 a committee reported on Fury's failure to
print a report on the St. Augustine expedition. The Committee of
Inquiry found that while he was not blamable for not printing the
report, he was open to censure for not giving his reasons to the Committee of Correspondence, for appealing to Governor Glen, and for
referring the Committee to a letter written by him to Colonel Pinckney of the South Carolina council. A letter by Governor Glen revealed that he and several others in England had feared harmful
results from printing the report. The lower house, however, taking
action on May 17, 1744, held the agent blamable for not printing
the St. Augustine report, as he was wholly without discretion.[23]
Finally, a third committee to inquire into his conduct was created in
the session of 1745-1746. Persistent criticism won out finally in
June, 1746, when the house struck out the item of £1,400 for his
salary.[24]

It seems strange indeed to find a colonial governor attacking an
agent for lack of zeal in the matter of paper money, and yet that is
exactly what Governor Glen attacked in Crockatt. The governor
expressed fear that parliament would disallow a South Carolina law
for an issue of paper money unless it were fully informed. While
he felt that Crockatt might possibly "prefer the good of Carolina

[23] The fear of General Oglethorpe seemed to lie at the root of all this attack on Fury.
The committee feared that he had private reasons for not publishing printed papers with
the least imputation of blame on Oglethorpe. Furthermore, in 1742 South Carolina
intended to beg the king to send three companies of soldiers, which might clash with the
commission of Oglethorpe. For the report of 1742 see Journal of the Commons House of
Assembly of South Carolina, January 28, 1741/2-July 30, 1742, XVII, 445; for the
report of 1744, ibid., XIX, 406-9; for the action of the Commons House, ibid., pp. 446-48.
[24] This committee was created on March 20, 1745/6.—Ibid., XXI, 420; the salary
item was struck from the estimate June 13.—Ibid., p. 568.

to his own private Interest yet we can never flatter ourselves that he who, I am informed, has been hitherto a constant Enemy to paper Money can become all at once an Advocate for it, so sudden a Transition is what we have no reason to Expect."[25]

In North Carolina in 1774 McCulloh had to encounter the hostility of Samuel Johnston, who wrote to Alexander Elmsley: "What our agent wrote concerning the increasing the jurisdiction of the Inferior Court has had a very bad effect. . . . I never, as you know, approved of him, and at last joined in crying down the necessity of an agent unless on particular occasions and for special purposes; when the House resolved on remonstrating against the Instruction regarding attachments, M[r] Barker and you were named by the Southern Gentleman and I have no doubt but that should it ever be thought necessary to have a standing agent it may be easily procured for one or both of you, tho' the Cape Fear people can hardly find it in their hearts to forgive you for [not?] fixing the Governor's House at Cape Fear."[26]

Criticisms of the agent by individual citizens were not wanting. Alexander Elmsley in 1774 wrote scathingly of Henry E. McCulloh because during his absence on a visit to America he had intrusted to his father the negotiation of a certain court bill which was not approved, though he added that the "old man is the best agent of the two." The failure to get the bill approved, however, undoubtedly increased the general dissatisfaction with McCulloh as agent and led to the assembly's allowing the agency bill to expire.[27]

Abercromby could scarcely hope to escape criticism, and the research student cannot fail to learn of it from the vociferous expostulations recorded in his Letter Book. On May 3, 1759, he wrote Blair, president of the Virginia council: "I doubt not by the next opportunity to be able to remove the severe Censure thrown upon me by the Gentlemen of the Council of Neglect of Duty in the Case of the Merchants petition against Paper Money Acts." No agent gave greater offense than Knox by his defense of parliament in the Stamp Act action. Habersham in a letter to the agent, October 28, 1765, wrote: "Your letter intitled, the Claims of the Colonies ex-

[25] Ibid., p. 365, entry for Dec. 13, 1749.
[26] Colonial Records of North Carolina, IX, 1071.
[27] Ibid., pp. 999-1000.

amined has given the greatest Umbrage, and I am affraid has not left you a single person, who will open their mouths for you in the Assembly, and I think not one of your friends up Stairs can justify your making that publication, tho' some of them have endeavored to offer the best reasons, that presented, to soften your taking this Measure—I am sure your particular friend here does not approve of it, and very heartily wishes it had never appeared"—referring presumably to himself.[28] Garth suffered a sharp rebuke from South Carolina for joining in a petition without reserving the "Right of the Inhabitants of the Colonies to be Taxed only by their own Representatives." The members of the house were "extremely concerned to find, you should have thought yourself 'Warranted under the general Recommendation transmitted to you, to give your Assent and Approbation to that Petition.' "[29]

But no agent was castigated as was E. M.—undoubtedly Edward Montague—by Junius Americanus in the *Maryland Gazette:* "A man who fells his Country, is to them a Monfter; a character almoft beyond their Conception. You are an Agent; they fuppofe you an Advocate for that Province; they have no other Reprefentatives at the Court of Great Britain; they have relied on you with Confidence, and rewarded your profeffed (I wish I could say real) Services, with Liberality; By infinite Art, you have for many Years fucceeded in impofing on their unfufpecting Temper; Accident has difcovered your Principles and Connections, or they might much longer have cherifhed a Serpent to fting them. How infinite muft be their Aftonifhment, when they find of a Truth, that you are in clofe Union with their Enemies, their unrelenting Perfecutors." He then charged that Montague and Robert Charles, agent for New York, and some other agents acquiesced in 1764 in the Stamp Act under the conditions that they might name the provincial stamp officers, and that Montague be made an officer in Company——— by a "professed Enemy to American Freedom,"[30] by whom Junius was probably

[28] Abercromby Letter Book, 146. Habersham did not agree with Knox, but opposed the claims of parliament, and did not approve of the refusal to take steps for securing repeal.—Habersham, *Letters,* p. 44.

[29] The letter from the Committee of Correspondence of November 19, 1768, had been written hastily and the members did not expect that Garth would consent to any petition wherein the right of taxation was not expressly asserted.—"Garth Correspondence," *loc. cit.,* XXXI, 59-60.

[30] In the issue of January 25, 1770; copied in C. O. 5/1283, p. 49. Jared Ingersoll

referring to Grenville. The writer, it must be added, has been unable to verify all these charges, though the fact that Jared Ingersoll accepted the post of stamp officer in Connecticut lends color to the charge.

Agents might have to contend with treachery on the part of their constituents. Francis Yonge found that most of his letters to the governor, which that official communicated to the assembly, were sent back to England, a situation which the executive stigmatized as "villanous" and the authors of which he hoped to run down and make "publick examples."[31] The situation could be exactly reversed, and the agent betrayed to the governor by some one in England. Such a case occurred in 1774, when a petition of Garth was sent back to Governor Bull in South Carolina by Lord Dartmouth.[32] And, finally, the correspondence of the agents was occasionally copied by the governor and returned to a high ranking minister in the home government. One of the notorious instances is, of course, Governor Hutchinson's tampering with the letters of Lee and Franklin to the lower house of Massachusetts.[33]

The agents were bombarded not only by the colonials, but by the members of the British government on the eve of the revolt. Dartmouth commented on the correspondence between persons in England and leaders of the faction in America, the very letters just noted, in a communication to General Gage of June, 1774. Proofs of this "dangerous and unwarrantable" correspondence had been betrayed to the government through copies of two letters, one from Dr. Franklin, dated July 7, 1773, the other from Arthur Lee, dated December 25, 1773. Both letters were expressed in such terms as made it "very much to be wished that such Evidence could be obtained of the Authenticity of them as might be the grounds of a proper Proceed-

---

was agent for Connecticut from October, 1764, to July, 1765, sent over to help secure rejection of the Stamp Act.

[31] Journal of the Council of South Carolina, 1722-1724, II, 263-64.

[32] Stated in a letter by Dartmouth to M. (?) dated Jan. 8, 1774.—C. O. 5/396, p. 2.

[33] Hutchinson inclosed in a letter to the Earl of Dartmouth, March 30, 1774, a copy of a letter from Mr. Lee to the house (probably the letter of Dec. 25, 1773). The governor wrote: "The Speaker to whom it was directed having lent it to a gentleman, he copied it, and the same person who furnished me with a copy of the letter which I transmitted in October procured this, being in a publick station and thinking himself bound in duty to the King to promote His Majesty's service."—Historical Manuscripts Commission, *Eleventh Report*, App. 1, Part V: *MSS of the Earl of Dartmouth*, p. 350.

ing thereupon." Gage was, therefore, urged with "secrecy and caution" to procure the originals or some regularly attested copies to transmit to Darmouth.[34] One gets a sense of the dangerous path which Franklin was treading from such thoughts in the minds of the British ministers and from excerpts of letters to the provincial newspapers. "I have been with Doctor Franklin," wrote one correspondent. "I find the ſtorm againſt him much abated; though I believe he has not in the least remitted his attention to the intereſts of his much injured country. . . ." Franklin's courage had not been broken, for it is to this very person that he used his famous expression about the taxation policy of Britain: ". . . it was determined not only to rivet the chains, but make the colonies pay for the iron to do it."[35]

The agent might even be accused of tampering with government letters. De Berdt, Massachusetts agent, found himself charged in an intercepted letter from Governor William Franklin to the Earl of Dartmouth with procuring by unfair means copies of letters to Dartmouth and transmitting them to America; in this, it was charged, lay his *merit*; he had thus abused the confidence of Dartmouth, who was cautioned against him. De Berdt promptly quoted the letter to the earl, denouncing the accusation as false and refuting the charge.[36]

The penalties which fell on the agent for thus incurring the displeasure of the home government or of the colonial authorities was heavy. The reader will recall that Byrd narrowly lost his seat at the board of the Virginia council, and Peyton Randolph saved his post as attorney general by eating humble pie, as is sufficiently attested in Governor Dinwiddie's letter to the Board of Trade of February 10, 1755: "Your Letter—recommending Mr Randolph to be reinstated in his office, & the Reaſons you are pleased to aſsign for that are so just & good, that I beg leave to acquaint you he has strongly acknowledged his Errors in leaving his office without his Majesty's Leave; & has aſsured me by his Letter that he will for the Future be very diligent in his office for His Majesty's Service, & behave with all due Respect & Regard to me, . . ."[37]

[34] C. O. 5/765, p. 327.
[35] *Pennsylvania Gazette*, Sept. 28, 1774, quoting a letter of Franklin's of July 23, 1774; C. O. 5/1285, p. 149.
[36] Historical Manuscripts Commission, *Fourteenth Report*, App. X: *MSS of the Earl of Dartmouth, American Papers*, II, 420.   [37] C. O. 5/1328, f. 320.

The council of South Carolina took bitter offense in 1774 at one of Garth's petitions to the king, prepared in obedience to the directions of the lower house of assembly, in which he brought a charge against the president of the upper house as delinquent in his duty. The council denounced the petition as "abfurd, unparliamentary, and unconstitutional and is a fcandalous Libel upon the Upper Houfe of Affembly of this Province, tending to deftroy the ancient Conftitution of this Government." The council could often go beyond verbal strictures, and in this instance threatened to refuse concurrence to a provision for the agent's salary and expenses when these items came before them in a tax bill. [38]

Again and again one agent or another found his position jeopardized. Sometimes he weathered the storm; sometimes he was summarily dismissed. Knox was assailed in the council of Georgia in March, 1764, but his friend Habersham was present to defend him. Indeed, the latter boldy seized an opportunity to mention having heard that Knox's agency was considered by some a "job," evidently meaning that he had been selected by some underhand political arrangement. Every person present, acording to Habersham's report to Knox, declared that the agent had acquitted himself properly and more than deserved his salary, disclaiming that they had ever considered his appointment a "job." [39]

Occasionally the agent was not even allowed to resign from an irksome office. Crockatt, for example, signified such a desire in a letter read in the South Carolina council on February 7, 1754, as stated in Chapter II. He declared that for some time the post had been incompatible with his plan of life at that time; that he had never been accustomed to attending constantly at the offices to so little purpose; that he had frequently wished that he had never accepted the honor; and that he would long since have asked the assembly to dismiss him if he could have found a proper person to recommend. But even after such a blunt statement the assembly

[38] A full account of the controversy between the two houses, into which it is not necessary to enter here, is given in the *South Carolina and American General Gazette*, Mar. 11-18, 1774. Governor Bull commented on the council's attitude toward Garth in a letter to Dartmouth, dated Mar. 24, 1774.—C. O. 5/396, p. 28.

[39] Habersham concludes significantly, "I suppose you intended, I should make some such use of what you wrote me."—Habersham, *Letters*, p. 17.

directed the Committee of Correspondence to write him to reconsider. [40]

Sometimes the attacks on the agent's position were owing to
petty politics. This seems to have been true of Abercromby in
North Carolina, who had somehow incurred the hostility of Governor Dobbs. The agent expressed in a letter to Samuel Swann his
appreciation for the latter's support in the lower house and for the
support of that gentleman's brother in the council, but knew that
they could not defeat the opposition of the governor's party. Rather
maliciously he expresses the wish that he could remove Dobbs but
"favor attends all governors."[41]

Outright dismissals from the agency were far from rare. Early
instances were Blakiston by Maryland, and Kettleby by South Carolina. South Carolina finally dismissed Peregrine Fury in 1749,
as we have seen, after several futile gestures. The reason alleged
was their conviction of his neglect of provincial business of great
importance on several occasions arising from having too many irons
in the fire. Fury on his part seemed determined to end all relations
with the colony, for he absolutely refused to join two men who had
been vested with power to solicit South Carolina affairs for the
time being. He seemed especially to resent the reduction of his
salary by one half. Virginia dismissed Leheup, and at a later date
the burgesses would not have Abercromby for what they regarded
as the colonial agent—a virtual dismissal. Mr. Nelson of the upper
house cherished ill will toward Abercromby because he felt that the
latter had neglected his duty in connection with a paper money act.

When Abercromby began to get rumors of a new agent for Virginia, he declared that he would have "taken it unkind in my friends
to have dealt so abruptly by me without a notice of such Event likely
to take place. . . ." In 1758 he had seen a copy of the bill which
proposed appointing Paris as the agent of the Virginia burgesses.
Abercromby, fighting for his post, in characteristic strain presented
his arguments to Governor Fauquier: "Upon the face of this Bill
it carries with it its own Condemnation, for whatever Person should

[40] Journal of the Commons House of Assembly of South Carolina, Jan. 8, 1754-Oct.,
1754, XXIX, 122. One should also recall the outbursts on the subject by the New England agent, Ashurst.

[41] Abercromby Letter Book, p. 144. For thanks to Swann of June 1, 1759, see *ibid.*

act under the Authority of such a Bill must necefsarily become An Agent for Faction in Place of Agent for Government, nor will the Liberality of the House of Burgefses by the Salary proposed for their Agent, establish the Rectitude of the arbitrary Principles of the Committees Authority over such Agent." He held on tenaciously since the council had rejected Ferdinand Paris, and declared that he took it for granted that he was at liberty to correspond with the governor without incurring the censure of the assembly.[42] Within little more than three months he was relegated to an agency for the upper house and governor only. Within another year, however, he was writing, because of a prospect of soon being in parliament, "the Disappointment of your Agency sits very light on me: 'tis the Manner more than the Matter that I have Grounds to resent"; but if the governor and council did him justice, he declared he would part on good terms with the public. For some time there was grave danger that all his salary from Virginia would be cut off because, in the words of President Blair of the council, "Some of them do threaten a motion to lay aside Mr Abercromby, as thinking one Enough, so that Nothing is done here towards Geting him an augmentation from the Quit-rents as he & I expected."[43] His prospects of a seat in parliament must have waned abruptly, for within a few weeks he was found arguing hard for the necessity of an agent for the governor and council, for the whole business of the colony was really done under the direction of those officials. ". . . it is extremely prudent in you to consider the Impropriety of corresponding in matters of Government with an Agent under the Direction of a Committee of Assembly."[44]

Knox was dismissed by Georgia because he had the audacity to advise the people to submit to the stamp tax. The assembly on October 28, 1765, ordered the Committee of Correspondence to lay his correspondence before them. Though they found nothing objectionable in the correspondence, they believed that he could not act independently for them, when he was at the same time acting as

[42] *Ibid.*, pp. 120-21.

[43] *Ibid.*, pp. 77; 160; 169; C. O. 5/1329, p. 377. For a long legalistic argument by Abercromby on the subject, see *ibid.*, p. 344. They opposed Abercromby because of his proceedings in the pistole fee case.—Abercromby Letter Book, p. 169.

[44] *Ibid.*, p. 174.

crown agent for East Florida, and they definitely took exception to his pamphlet defending the course of parliament, for they interpreted his action in obtruding himself into the controversy as a bid for favor with the ministry. If so, he had his reward, for he was promoted to be an undersecretary of state in Great Britain. Such an attitude by Knox, who had resided in Savannah and had held high office in Georgia, and who was thought to be devoted to the interests of America, was regarded with amazement and indignation.[45] The law for reappointment of Garth was postponed and set aside by the council of Georgia in 1768. Jouvencal's agency for North Carolina was suspended by the Board of Trade.

The annoyances and difficulties which beset the path of the agent can perhaps be no better summed up than in the words of Abercromby, even though they related then to a particular issue —negotiations for a parliamentary grant: ". . . judge then from this state of the case, with what dexterity I must steer my course for the honour and for the Interest of Government in Virginia, and what difficultys are to be met with, in this negotiation, when Public & Privat interest interfere; difficultys I expect, of such a nature, might be increas'd rather than obviated, by the interposition of the Virginia Merchants."[46]

The rewards of the office, in comparison with the irritations, seem meagre indeed. First in the list comes approbation. Sometimes the expression of approval and the thanks were undoubtedly motivated by genuine gratitude; but sometimes it would seem that agents were being put off with fair words. Indeed, when one considers the paucity of the salary, it might appear strange that the colonial assemblies did not more frequently eke out the salary with kindly words. When the agencies were young, and especially if a situation developed for passing judgment on the agent before there had been time for any serious blunder, words of appreciation may be found, more often forthcoming, it might be added, from the council than from the house. The council of South Carolina after only two

---

[45] John Campbell, crown agent for Georgia, also published a tract of over a hundred pages on the subject, which occasioned no surprise because of his position.—Stevens, *Short History of Georgia*, II, 42-43. See also Johnson, *Georgia as Colony and State*, p. 127.

[46] Abercromby to President Fairfax of the council, September 5, 1755. "Miscellaneous Colonial Documents," *loc. cit.*, XVII, 386.

years of Kettleby's agency, expressed themselves in the following generous terms: "The Commiſsioners [appointed to correspond with the agent] have laid before us his letter, . . . wherein we cannot but take notice of the great zeal and diligence of that gentleman for the good of this Province, which we think deserves a publick acknowledgment."[47] The Commons House likewise, but in more restrained fashion, voted him thanks a few days later with, what may have been more welcome, assurance of pay the next session. The warmth of relations between Blakiston and Maryland may perhaps be measured by the degree of verbal appreciation. In 1715 the assembly was "firmly persaded of the strict Hon^r and Justice as well as great Affection of the said Nathaniel Blakiston Esqr. towards this Province and also of his indefatigable Endeavours for the true Interest of both Lord [Baltimore] & People." In 1716 they were even obsequious: "Wee think our selves under more obligations for your frequent good services than your Generosity would allow us to Compensate.

"Wee must never the less yet desire a Continuance of your favourable Sollicitations and nothing in us shall be wanting, to demonstrate the grateful sense wee have of your good offices. . . ."[48] But the gratitude of the lower house faded as they measured intangible results from the agency against tangible pounds. South Carolina found words of approbation for Francis Yonge's work in 1734: he had "taken a great deal of pains" and had made "very juſt remarks." His defense of the Appropriation Law was held so good that the Committee of Correspondence recommended that it be read in the house.[49]   Maryland "approved" the conduct of Ferdinand Paris in 1741 in representing the zeal of Maryland for His Majesty's service by providing for five hundred men for military service.[50] There is the ring of genuine and merited gratitude to Montague in the words of the Committee of Correspondence in 1760: "And we were no less pleased with your immediate Resolution to give up your Claim to any Advantage arising from the Rec't of that Money, as soon as you thought any Delay in the remitting it might possibly be a Prejudice to this Colony. From this step, we are persuaded that

[47] Journal of the Commons House of Assembly of South Carolina, IV, 269.
[48] For 1715 see Archives of Maryland, XXXIII, 60; for 1716, XXX, 541.
[49] Journal of the Commons House of Assembly of South Carolina, IX, 84-85.
[50] Archives of Maryland, XLII, 199.

you will on every occasion prefer the Good of the People you represent to any private views."[51]

The warm words used by Maryland in June, 1768, to express their "high opinion" of Garth and his regard for the rights of America, and the thanks of Georgia to that same agent for his part in the repeal of the Stamp Act were not perfunctory; undoubtedly the thanks of Georgia to Knox in 1766, and of North Carolina to McCulloh in 1771 were honest recognition of services faithfully performed, though the assurance to Knox of "entire satisfaction" with his conduct was soon to be reversed.[52]

The rewards sometimes took a more material form. The reader has been made cognizant, as the records of the various agents have been followed, of agents returning from England with pleasant government appointments tucked in their pockets.[53]

Agents were in a position to profit in other tangible ways from their posts. William Knox, while he was in England as agent, petitioned and received a grant of five thousand acres of land in Georgia for purposes of a settlement.[54] It certainly was no disadvantage to the group of four men who were applying in 1770 to the Treasury for a purchase of land near Fort Stanwix, recently acquired by the king from the Indians, that one of their number was the well-known agent, Dr. Franklin.[55] To Arthur Lee Massachusetts presented a tract of land of considerable value as a compensation for his services as agent and as a mark of gratitude. Georgia's gratitude to Franklin took a less material but a permanent form; when the colony became a state, it recorded his name permanently on its map by bestowing

[51] Dated November 5, 1760, "Proceedings of the Virginia Committee of Correspondence," loc. cit., XI, 12.

[52] "Correspondence of Governor Sharpe," loc. cit., XII, 377, Colonial Records of Georgia, XIV, 366; ibid., XVII, 269; Colonial Records of North Carolina, IX, 206.

[53] Note has been made of Philip Ludwell returning a member of the council; Blair was admitted to the council a few years after his first mission to England; Edward Chilton was named advocate of Virginia; John Porter was named a deputy for one of the proprietors of Carolina; Barnwell returned a member of the council and also with a commission putting him in charge of the erection of forts on the Altamaha River.—C. O. 5/1312, pt. 2, f. 494; C. O. 5/1359, p. 206; C. O. 5/1307, f. 68; Virginia Magazine of History and Biography, V, 392.

[54] Colonial Records of Georgia, IX, 493-94. As a non-resident he could not apply to the governor for a grant of land.

[55] The Ohio Company later joined with this group, withdrawing their petition in order not to interfere with or delay Franklin's purchase.—C. O. 5/1332, pp. 315-16, 383.

it on a county and on its first educational institution, Franklin Academy.[56]

Probably the strangest aspect of the agency was the fact that a position to which were attached so many annoyances and so few genuine rewards should be so assiduously sought. But as always where there is a salaried post, there were aspirants for the position. Candidates had eyes only for the emoluments; they seemed blind to the difficulties and unpleasantnesses until experience had made them wiser.

The reader will recall that Nathaniel Blakiston sought the agency of Maryland so eagerly that he offered to prove the worth of his services. In 1723, when the appointment of John Carter as secretary of Virginia left the position of agent vacant, no less than three men, as has been earlier related, were seeking the post—Byrd, Leheup, and a Mr. Langley. The person last named had been recommended by Governor Orkney in 1721 when the post fell vacant by the death of Blakiston; but now, embarrassed by three candidates, the governor left the choice to the council. They found their way out of the embarrassment of rejecting their fellow countryman Byrd by declaring that inasmuch as Leheup had already been employed to solicit one aspect of the work, in the event of the absence of Carter, they felt obligated to continue him as agent to succeed Carter.[57]

Candidates besought men of eminent position for their influence. An application for the agency of South Carolina, dated 1746, from an obscure Francis Hutchenson to Andrew Stone, evidently secretary to the Duke of Newcastle, turns up in the papers of the latter. After waiting on Peregrine Fury to verify the report of his resignation, Hutchenson "paid his Duty to his Grace," who referred him with a favorable answer to Stone. One paper which has been preserved is the request of the applicant to the secretary begging the latter to prepare a recommendation for Newcastle to sign "in such Terms as

[56] Lee, *Life of Arthur Lee*, I, 35 note; Coulter, *Short History of Georgia*, p. 104.
[57] *Executive Journals of the Council*, IV, 29-30.

It should be noted in passing that annoyances connected with the office were equally great in the Northern agencies, and that the post was equally sought. A single illustration might be drawn in John Champante, who anxiously watched the agency of New York. The phrase he used to Governor Hunter on November 10, 1710, tells the whole story: ". . . if my friends carry ye Agency for me."—Rawlinson, MSS, A. 272, f. 259.

may best answer the Ends of my troublesome Application." The eagerness with which the post was sought is suggested in a letter from one of the South Carolina council to Hutchenson urging him to apply to the Duke, since it was the latter who had first recommended Fury to the Carolina assembly; "there is great Reason," he urged, "for giving the utmost dispatch least another should be appointed before his Graces letter reaches them."[58] A letter accordingly went forward to Governor Bull but Newcastle carefully directed that the letter be delivered to the assembly only when the post was actually vacant, as he did not wish to do anything to the prejudice of Fury, a justifiable precaution, for Fury did not give up the post until some three years later.[59] His caution is hard to explain when we find an entry in the Journal of the Commons House of Assembly which shows that the Duke's letter recommending Hutchenson to the assembly, as well as Stone's letter to the governor, was read to the assembly on June 11, 1747, though Fury resigned only in May, 1749. As soon as Fury was definitely out of the agency, two persons began to bring pressure on friends in the colony.[60]

Among all those who sought the Southern agencies none seemed more eager or persistent than Abercromby and McCulloh. Indeed, so eager was the former for the Virginia agency that he paid the retiring agent, Leheup, £100, a considerable sum of money, evidently for his influence with the Virginia council. This aroused Governor Dinwiddie's ire, for he held it "monstrous" that Abercromby agreed to give "that man any Money," for he had "no Int't here to recommend any Person, and Y'r giving him Money for a Place he c'd have no Pretentions to name to, and under his present Disgrace [of dismissal], is surely very inconsiderately done." Evidently Abercromby had already approached Lord Albemarle, a step of which Dinwiddie also disapproved until he was appointed

[58] Newcastle Papers, Add. MSS, 32709, p. 123, British Museum. A phrase in the letter of Hammerton (the member of the council who was obviously in London at the time) suggests that there might be other applications sent from England for the position. He says that the appointment might be made soon, "as there are two Ships just agoing to that Province."—*Ibid.*, p. 125.

[59] Stone's letter to Governor Bull is dated November 29, 1746, a full month after Hutchenson's letter of October 29, requesting the recommendation.—C. O. 5/388, p. 427.

[60] Journal of the Commons House of Assembly of South Carolina, XXII, 730; Newcastle Papers, Add. MSS, 32709, f. 125.

by the council, when his concurrence as governor of the province would have been sought. From the tenor of the correspondence it is obvious that Abercromby was Dinwiddie's candidate, but he assures the former frankly that the burgesses were so jealous of the council, that he need not think that they could be prevailed on to have the same agent.[61] Within about seven months Dinwiddie informed the agent that there were two other persons being presented for the agency, but he thought Abercromby could rest easy during his governorship for he was persuaded that "none can be appointed with^t my Approbat'n," a boast which was supported by his procuring an increase of salary for his candidate.[62]

It even appears that Abercromby had an eye on the agency of South Carolina in 1755, for he was thanking Governor Dinwiddie for his overtures to Wragg and Colleton.[63] But he frankly recognized that he had strong competition for the post in Pinckney and Crockatt, and had no desire to serve under Governor Glen, for whom he had acted as English agent with unhappy experience.[64]

McCulloh's first solicitation for the agency of North Carolina seems to have been from Soho, London, dated September 13, 1767, addressed to John Harvey, a personal friend. Suggesting that special agents would be needed to secure repeal of the restrictive acts, he offered his services gratis, craving only "the honor of the Service" and conceiving himself "amply recompensed," if he could merit approbation. He would not have any mention made of a pecuniary acknowledgment, but adds, "I would choose to have that matter left to their future discretion entirely," showing that he was not wholly disinterested. From his knowledge of North Carolina and his connections through his father with almost every dis-

---

[61] Dinwiddie, *Official Records*, I, 211, 237. Dinwiddie reproached Abercromby for not consulting him.—*Ibid.*, p.506.   [62] *Ibid.*, p. 507.

[63] The writer cannot be certain of the spelling of this name from Abercromby's execrable penmanship but has adopted the conventional spelling.

[64] The author cannot satisfactorily explain the exact relation in which he stood to Governor Glen, and so will merely quote the allusion in Abercromby's words: ". . . while Mr. Glen heads that Province, I should not expect pleasure in the service, and as little Justice, deserted by everybody he threw himself into my hands, for taking charge of his Public Letters, he proposed for my trouble £50 per an. three years without any manner of acknowledgment, at length I drew upon him by good luck I got my money & then discharged myself from all correspondence with him."—Abercromby Letter Book, Entry of Jan. 6, 1755 (no pagination here). The letter seems from the context to be to Governor Dinwiddie.

tinguished "Character of Business in the Kingdom" he had reason to think that his offer would not be viewed as improper, but he begged that if he could not be named in an "honorable" manner, no effort be made in his behalf.[65] In the following May, he was still seeking the appointment, although the council had refused assent, a "negative" which he stigmatized as "arbitrary and injudicious." He believed that the "absolute necessity of an appointment will be apparent at your next meeting, and that if the Council continue their obstinacy, I think it may very well be done by vote of your House." He was desirous that his friends should exert themselves for the appointment of himself or his father.[66] Persistence won its reward, for by July 24, 1769, we find him expressing his thanks to Colonel Harvey, to whom he felt he chiefly owed the appointment;[67] in July, 1771, he was reminding the Committee of Correspondence of the approaching expiration of his term and soliciting a reappointment.[68] Alexander Elmsley clearly wanted the North Carolina agency in May, 1774, recognizing that the "grand difficulty" for him lay with the council, but confident that if ways could be devised to interest the governor, that board would vote as he directed. He concluded his application to Samuel Johnston, a friend, by an offer to have Thomas Barker write to the chief justice and other important persons in his behalf. The interesting point is that the appointment had already been made, and that it was jointly to Elmsley and Barker.[69] The last instance of applying for the post of agent comes as late as 1780, when Grey Elliott wrote the Georgia Commons House of Assembly that while he had not presumed in his last letter relating to arrears to offer his services as agent for fear this might appear improper, he now saw fit to do so.[70]

Undoubtedly there were many instances similar to that of John Norton, who presumably sounded out some one in London or in the colony as to the possibility of appointment, but who without encouragement did not pursue the matter. Because they were not

---

[65] For his entire letter see *Colonial Records of North Carolina*, VII, 517-18.

[66] He was so bent on the agency that he wrote to two friends in North Carolina, Col. Fanning and Col. Harvey, on the same day, May 20, 1768.—*Ibid.*, pp. 753, 755.

[67] For his acceptance, addressed to the Committee of Correspondence, dated July 14, 1769, see *ibid.*, VIII, 55; for the letter to Harvey, see p. 58.

[68] *Ibid.*, IX, 12.   [69] *Ibid.*, IX, 999-1000.

[70] *Colonial Records of Georgia*, XV, 599.

pressed, most of these cases have probably never come to light. This London merchant, of the famous firm of John Norton and Sons, had obviously written to Robert C. Nicholas in Williamsburg, Virginia, in 1771 as to his chances for appointment to the Virginia agency. Rather oddly, the situation appeared to that individual to indicate that that colony would "employ a standing Agent no longer," though it might occasionally have some one solicit a particular matter. Then there follows the illuminating statement, "I don't know any Person in London whom I could repose so implicit a Confidence in as yourself. As an individual you know it is not in my Power to determine any Thing of this Sort, & therefore can at present only express my Wishes."[71]

Sometimes, it would appear, unsuccessful candidates sought to injure the person whom they held responsible for their defeat. As early as 1723 we encounter evidence that a Mr. Shelton so earnestly desired the agency of Virginia that failure to secure it led him to hostility against the governor. At least Governor Nicholson interpreted his remarks villifying him as "malicious" and attributed them to the fact that he would not make him agent for the colony. Further, a Mr. Child boasted, according to Governor Dobbs, that he had appeared against a certain petition of the council of North Carolina because that body refused to make him the provincial agent; otherwise he would have procured the approval of the petition.[72]

In the light of these revelations one is inclined to close this chapter with the query: Why was the post sought—sought zealously, as has been shown in this study? For the colonial sent to England the question is perhaps explicable; he probably felt his selection from among his fellows an honor, anticipated with pleasure the contact with important British officials, and had pleasure in a visit to the homeland, which out of his own resources he could probably not afford.[73] The colonials who were making a trip to England on their

---

[71] [Norton], *John Norton & Sons, Merchants of London and Virginia*, p. 150.

[72] Nicholson to the Board of Trade, October 14, 1722: "As for Mr. ſhelton's reflections upon me I hope in God I shall make it Appear to your Lordships that they are Malicious & the principal reason I suppose is that I would not make him Agent for this his Majesties Province, but I hope likewiſe to make it Appear to your Lordships that I had some Reasons that it ſhould not be done. . . ."—C. O. 5/359.

[73] Some cases might be cited where New Englanders accepted what they knew would prove a difficult mission with extreme reluctance. Such a case was presented by William Stoughton and Peter Bulkley in 1676 to defend the claim of Massachusetts against the claim of Mason and Gorges.

own personal affairs accepted the charge possibly as a civic duty or
for the momentary prominence it gave them. The explanation for
the Britisher or the British merchant returned to England after a
period of residence in a colony probably lay in the age-old problem
of bread and butter. A man must earn his living, and he seeks his
means in what appears the best way available. From the outside
the agency appeared a dignified, respectable post—in a word, a
gentleman's position. Compared with the positions available before
the era of colonial settlement, here was a new type of post opening
up, and new fields always appear attractive. Again to the uninitiated
solicitor, it must have seemed an easy way to add a stipend to his
never too large income. It was only after he was in the toils of the
new duties that he realized from the inside how the work of the
agency consumed time needed for his personal affairs. When too
disillusioned, he occasionally abandoned the post in disgust, as we
have seen was the case with Peter Pagan and James Crockatt. Sometimes, like Abercromby, despite all the annoyances, he held on to the
post with a death grip.

CHAPTER 12.

SUCCESSES AND FAILURES

SINCE this study centers primarily about the regular agents, it will be sufficient at this point to state briefly the results of the special agencies, in which category in this phase of the study will be lumped for convenience the early agents of the genesis period as well as the special emissaries of the eighteenth century. A careful checking of the results actually achieved has led to the surprising conclusion that as a whole the successes are less striking than the failures. Only Sir Francis Wyatt, Colonel Philip Ludwell in his mission against Effingham, and James Blair may be regarded as achieving successes for Virginia in the seventeenth century. It is therefore easy to understand the statement of Sir Henry Chicheley, when as colonial agent in 1673 he reluctantly admitted that the agents who from time to time had been employed by the Virginia assembly had failed to rise to the public expectation, either through unskilful management or through the slight influence possessed by the persons they had employed to aid them.[1] Where striking victories were won, it was sometimes less the result of the agent's activity than of the force of circumstances. John Porter in 1707 carried home an order for the removal of Governor Carey largely because he had won the powerful aid of Archdale, a co-religionist and one of the Carolina proprietors; Joseph Boone's success in 1709 in overthrowing the religious qualification act must be attributed to the coöperation of the British merchants and the liberality of the church dignitaries; the success of Boone and Barnwell in 1720, following the complete failure of Francis Yonge the preceding year with the proprietors, arose from fortunate circumstances, for they pleaded their cause before a government predisposed to a sympathetic hearing of grievances as a means of overthrowing proprietary rule; and Georgia would have received equal rights with other crown colonies with or

[1] *Calendar of State Papers*, 1669-1674, sec. 1118; C. O. 1/30, no. 51.

without Edmund Gray's efforts.[2] John Randolph scored a victory in 1728 when by wise handling he won a repeal of the law forbidding importation of stripped tobacco, but went down to defeat four years later because the English people were utterly opposed to an excise law. Isham Randolph attempted the impossible when he opposed the organized weight of the sugar lobby, and Peyton Randolph's mission can claim to have won only a partial success. The failures among these special agents were fully as numerous as the successes.

Of far more significance in evaluating the worth of the agency is the work of the regular agent. Here the acid test is probably his success in winning confirmation of colonial legislation or in preventing parliamentary action which might prove hostile to the colonies. Certainly, measured by this test, the failures of the agents were numerous. The sharp rebuke administered to Byrd enunciates the fundamental principle by which provincial laws were to be measured: "We are surprised to find that any objection would be made to an Instruction of this Nature, since it can never be supposed that the Plantations had or could have the Power of making any Laws which might be prejudicial to the Trade & Navigation of this Kingdom, for whose Benefit & Advantage the Plantations were first settled and still are maintained."[3]

It must be admitted that acts covering every phase of the life and government of a colony were disallowed by the British officials from time to time, but it is possible to distinguish those on which the Southern agents failed most frequently: those relating to trade, revenues, finance, debts, and paper currency. British merchants were clearly the cause of disallowance of laws dealing with trade which were not conducive to their interests. Furthermore, any acts which even slightly contravened the prerogatives of the British government were promptly annulled. Even where Virginia sought assent for emergency acts to run less than two years and acts repealing legislation which had not had royal approval, it was jealously denied as unwise.

Failures in this field must be recorded against each of the important Southern agents. To cite only a few, in order not to weary the reader, we might note a Virginia act of 1728 for levying a duty

[2] Gray may have expedited the civil government for Georgia as stated in Chapter II.
[3] C. O. 5/1365, p. 190.

on imported slaves which was disallowed despite Leheup's earnest efforts;[4] Fury failed for South Carolina on a quitrent act of 1731, as did Abercromby with a similar act for North Carolina;[5] Francis Yonge in 1733 carried to the Duke of Newcastle with a favoring letter from the governor an Act to Prevent Suits to Judges and Magistrates on Account of the Habeas Corpus Act, but he was unsuccessful in preventing repeal.[6] In 1753 the Board of Trade denied the petition of the Virginia assembly to be allowed to repeal or alter laws once confirmed without a suspending clause, and, as if to emphasize its dissent from colonial claims, it immediately recommended disapproval of eight laws except in one small particular of local import. In the group was one which was approved—directed against construction of wooden chimneys![7] Abercromby in support of the famous Two-penny Law could not succeed against the Reverend Mr. Camm, for the Board of Trade reported for disallowance, not only on the ground of unfairness to the clergy, but also of violation of the royal instruction concerning the suspending clause.[8] Jouvencal failed in an effort to alter the quorum in the assembly; Garth records in his correspondence several failures.[9]

The legislation with which above all the agents might expect difficulty and probable disallowance was that for issuing paper bills of credit. The two agents for Virginia were unable in 1763 to satisfy the British merchants or the government of the soundness of the

[4] C. O. 5/1322, p. 27.

[5] C. O. 5/364, p. 146. The South Carolina act required all lands received by patent from the proprietors or their governors to be registered in eighteen months or to be declared vacant. The act brought a sharp struggle between the two houses and the chief justice of South Carolina.

[6] *Collections of the Historical Society of South Carolina*, II, 184, 262. Yonge had also failed to win confirmation of an act for the government of Charleston in 1723.— C. O. 5/381, p. 30.

[7] C. O. 5/1367, pp. 15-19. The Privy Council decreed accordingly.—*Ibid.*, pp. 29-30. In the group disallowed was one permitting the killing of hogs which were running about loose. Such extravagance was not to be allowed with British approval!

[8] Osgood, *The American Colonies in the Eighteenth Century*, III, p. 478. It should be noted that the Reverend Mr. Camm lost the point of retribution. See also "Proceedings of the Virginia Committee of Correspondence," *loc. cit.*, X, 347-53.

[9] *Colonial Records of North Carolina*, VI, 1006; "Garth Correspondence," *loc. cit.*, XXX, 229, 170; C. O. 5/408, pp. 64-65; C. O. 5/380, pp. 178-79. Garth's failures were in part as follows: an Act for Establishing Circuit Courts, and to obtain repeal of the Additional Instruction of the 14th of April, 1770, which imposed restrictions with regard to the issue of public money. Both of these bills were from South Carolina. The house also claimed the sole right to dispose of public money, an attitude which brought a dispute with Governor Bull.

paper currency of that province, so that what really resulted was a mandate from the Board of Trade to remedy this legislation under threat of parliamentary action to abolish bills of credit. The Act for Relief of Insolvent Debtors was declared inadequate for giving security to the merchants; and the legislature was held wanting not only in proper respect to the crown, but also in justice to the merchants in refusing to comply with the recommendation in the king's instruction of July 3, 1759. Garth was no more successful than other agents when it came to the South Carolina act of August, 1769, for issuing bills of credit to the value of £106,500. He reported to the Committee of Correspondence that it was "reported for repeal."[10]

Failures were, of course, recorded in other matters. To secure grants of money from the home government was difficult. Crockatt, for instance, found his application to the Treasury for a grant of money for South Carolina for gifts to the Indians thwarted by the Board of Trade, which advised the king that "that colony appeared in a more flourishing and improving State than it had ever been before," and hence it saw no reason for complying with the request. Garth met discouragement in an effort to remove two officials from the South Carolina government, action evidently desired by the colonial officials, who complained of plural office-holding; he also found the effort to void a land grant made by the governor of Georgia too uphill a fight to hope for success.[11]

To record the successes of the agents is a more grateful task than to record the failures. Certain types of duties were, in their very nature, more likely than others to meet with success. The appeal for arms and ammunition to defend a frontier colony against the natives, and, later against the encroachments of the Spanish and French, especially when the mother country was engaged in a war with these countries, was bound to receive sympathetic consideration. It was to the interest of Britain to help the colonies defend themselves, and it is to be noted that in times of peril the colonies were expected to make a valiant effort for their own defense. Nathaniel Blakiston chalked up such victories of grants of arms and munitions with Maryland. Equally simple, it would appear, was his task to

[10] "Garth Correspondence," *loc. cit.*, XXXIII, 118; C. O. 5/394, p. 89.
[11] C. O. 5/672, p. 54; "Garth Correspondence," *loc. cit.*, XXIX, 216; XXX, 170.

secure a "commissary-general of Stores of Arms and Ammunition," whom we would today call more simply an inspector.[12]   Agents could also score successes in securing troops and forts for their respective colonies, as when Alexander Vander Dusen, with two other agents, petitioned for troops for South Carolina.   Though the red tape in the British official system delayed serious consideration for three years, the time came when it was finally decided to send over three companies under command of this very Vander Dusen now commissioned lieutenant colonel.[13]   The South Carolina *Gazette* of January 25, 1746, announced the arrival of Vander Dusen with Captain Pascal Nelson and Robert Hudson on the transport *Pelican* together with sixty recruits and noncommissioned officers.   This was certainly a modest force to hold the French, and the assembly was held to its promises of additional pay to the British soldiers and of barracks for their accommodation.[14]   Francis Yonge seems to have secured reimbursement from England for the charges South Carolina had incurred in building the fortification at the Altamaha River shortly before 1722.   Confidence in assistance from the mother country could, however, easily be misplaced, as was demonstrated when the South Carolina assembly voted an advance of £1,000 in 1756 to build a fort in the Cherokee country, not doubting it would be repaid by the king's order.   The new governor arrived with directions to apply to the assembly for a free gift for that purpose.[15]

[12] This official was to ride through the provinces and inspect the arms and ammunition in every county to see that they were kept fit (according to an entry of July 8, 1708).— *Archives of Maryland*, XXV, 242.   Blakiston secured arms and ammunition in June, 1708.— C. O. 5/727, p. 88.

[13] Smith, *South Carolina as a Royal Province*, p. 194.

[14] Evidence to this effect is found in a letter from Governor Glen to the secretary of state, dated February 11, 1745/6.   After commenting on the arrival of Vander Dusen and the privates, he says: ". . . upon which I sent a message to the Assembly, desiring that they would fulfil their Engagements and Promises, with regard to these Troops.   They immediately came to an unanimous Resolution to make a Provision for the additional pay to the officers and Soldiers, and likewise for building Barracks for their Reception."— C. O. 5/388, p. 407.

[15] Evidence is not at hand that the money promised Yonge was actually paid, but when England assured a colony of reimbursement, there is every presumption that it was paid.   See Journal of the Commons House of Assembly of South Carolina, 1722-1727, VI, 72.

Sometimes the colony was put off with such slight military assistance that it was utterly valueless, as when the plea of Agent Wright set forth that the South Carolina legislature had spent in the year 1757, £70,000 sterling on new forts and on repairs to old forts.   He begged not reimbursement but a company of gunners and "matrosses" (soldiers in an artillery train to assist gunners).   The Privy Council feebly directed the commander in

Outside of Georgia, where a crown policy prevailed, the agents met with some slight success in getting grants for presents for the Indians. Crockatt won a grant of £3,000 for this purpose in 1748, and again in 1749 to be invested in suitable goods "properly sorted" under that gentleman's personal supervision; he petitioned for a like sum in 1752; and in June, 1748, won a recommendation from the Board of Trade to the Treasury for a grant of £2,000 to be sent to the Indians bordering on South Carolina.[16]

Bounties on indigo and naval stores constituted another field in which the agents could score successes. Garth with satisfaction reported to South Carolina on March 23, 1770, that the Board of Trade had reported favorably on his memorial for a continuation of the bounty on indigo for seven years, but at the same time he did not encourage expectation of any changes in the bounties on naval stores. It is interesting to note the claims made at the same time by McCulloh for credit from North Carolina that the bounty on tar had not been reduced.[17] Wresting from parliament concessions in exporting rice to foreign countries is a matter of historical record, though the credit due to agents in this liberalization of policy is usually lost sight of. In 1734 Governor Johnson called the attention of the lower house of South Carolina to the "unwearied Pains" of Agent Wragg, "especially in his Application and Attendance in obtaining the Rice Act so beneficial to this Province," which extended free export of rice from South Carolina to the foreign West Indies and to the mainland.[18] Garth claimed credit, partly no doubt as a member of the British House of Commons, for having conducted through that body the bill for free importation of rice for another year in 1768; and he secured in 1772 a later date for limitation of free importation

---

chief to send a small detachment if they could be spared to instruct the people of that colony in the use of the guns and mortars.—C. O. 5/376, p. 78.

[16] The writer found no evidence that the sum petitioned for in 1752 was granted; it probably was, as there is a note of his petitioning for the same sum in 1753 when the gifts were to be made to the Indians bordering on Georgia as well as those near the Carolina border.—C. O. 5/373; C. O. 5/403, pp. 245-47.

[17] "Garth Correspondence," loc. cit., XXXI, 240; Colonial Records of North Carolina, VIII, 181. McCulloh wrote March 20, 1770: "I have exerted myself to the uttermost, & have pretty well overset the Gent[n] who were for reducing the bounty on Tar."

[18] As Governor Johnson was in London during almost the whole of Wragg's agency, he would be in a good position to judge that agent's activity.—Journal of the Commons House of Assembly of South Carolina, VIII, 67.

of that commodity than had been proposed by the ministry: namely, until May 1, 1780.[19]

Some successes are to be noted for the agents in getting approval of the colonial laws. Leheup's success in getting the king's consent to a Virginia act of the session of 1726/7, laying a duty on liquors, has already been mentioned, as this was the occasion when the burgesses repudiated his fees as exorbitant. At the same time he obtained a royal order for settling the boundaries between Virginia and North Carolina. This agent seems to have been rather fortunate in the type of legislation he had to solicit, for he secured the royal approbation to several later acts of 1736 of minor importance.[20]

It is conspicuous that for laws like those last noted, affecting only the colony, the agent could usually secure the royal assent. It will be recalled that the quarantine act to protect Virginia against gaol fever was allowed to stand; a law granting salaries to the attorney general and to the clerk of the court of pleas was allowed with the logical recommendation that the salaries should be "fixed" to the office rather than granted to the individual; and cautiously the Board of Trade proposed, in considering one law of narrow scope, that the king permit the governor to assent to acts for five counties where there had been a failure of the tobacco crop to pay the clergy in money, provided the clergy consent to the change.[21]

[19] "Garth Correspondence," loc. cit., XXX, 235. On May 6, 1772, he was felicitating South Carolina on having secured extension of the date from December, 1772, to May 1, 1773; and then on December 19, 1772, he reported a bill having passed the House of Commons the day before, granting free entry until May 1, 1780.—Ibid., XXXIII, 236, 238, 270.

[20] An amendment to an Act for Settling Titles and Bounds of Land; for Preventing Unlawful Shooting and Ranging; for the Better Support of William and Mary College; for Confirming Titles of Certain Lands in the Northern Neck; and for Allowing increased Pay to the Council.—Executive Journals of the Council, IV, 214, 217. The writer has found only the report of the Board of Trade to the Privy Council, approving the increase of salary to members of the council under date of February 13, 1753, but as that body held it reasonable and as it covered only expenses of attendance at the General Court, there is reason to think that it would be allowed by the Privy Council.—C. O. 5/1367, p. 12. However, it is not to be found in Hening.

[21] C. O. 5/1368, pp. 367-68; C. O. 5/391, pp. 103-4; C. O. 5/1368, pp. 182-83. If the provincial legislation were a matter of small concern to Britain but of concern to some prominent individual, the home authorities might seek evasion. Such an instance arose when Lord Baltimore was seeking repeal of the Maryland Law of Bounds, while Agent Blakiston declared that repeal would be prejudicial to the colony. To appease the proprietor the Board of Trade decided that it was too important to Maryland to be totally repealed; hence, both parties were directed to consult and prepare some clauses which might be mutually satisfactory to lay before the Board.—C. O. 5/391, 15, pp. 387-88, 402.

On the credit side of the ledger, however, there remain for consideration certain positive, if intangible, factors concerning which conclusions should somehow be drawn.

Approaching the question negatively first, it seems quite clear that the existence of the agency must have prevented in some instances much more severe measures on the part of the home government and must in others have postponed such action. A striking case in point is the Sugar Act of 1764, which in all likelihood, except for the agents, would have been enacted in 1751. Again, the concerted action of the agents in forcing the repeal of the Stamp Act may have delayed the Revolution about a decade. One advantage in having an agent came out in negative fashion in connection with the first parliamentary grant. North Carolina was convinced that she had lost out sadly compared with her sister colonies because she had had no official agent to watch over her interests, as the Board of Trade refused to recognize Jouvencal, since he was the appointee of the house only. The authorities of that colony were vividly conscious that they had spent about £66,000 in order to aid in the war, more than one half expended for services outside the province, yet were to receive only about one-eighth that amount.

The agent might exercise some influence on the choice of the governor. Agent Blakiston, for instance, wrote the governor and council of Virginia in February, 1709, that Lord Orkney, the governor of Virginia, "was pleased to bring Coll: Spotwood and me together, who is ye Gentleman upon whom ye Goverm't is I hope Happily Devolved. . . ." He definitely threw his influence for Spotswood.[22] He could also endeavor to predispose the inhabitants of the colony in favor of a governor. He remarked to the council in October, 1708, of Colonel Hunter, who had been captured by the French on his way to assume the direction of his colony, that if the new executive were as well known in Virginia as he was in England, the Virginians would lament their misfortune in his capture.[23]

The agent very definitely affected the political currents in the colony. Sometimes this influence was no more important than trying to assure good will between the governor and some prominent colonial. The night before Colonel Spotswood left London for

[22] "Miscellaneous Colonial Documents," *loc. cit.*, XIX, 21-22.
[23] *Ibid.*, p. 20.

Virginia to assume office, he called to take leave of Blakiston; the latter placed some letters in his hands, among others one to Colonel Ludwell, which hinted that an invitation to the governor to visit Green Spring, Ludwell's home, might be to that colonial's advantage.[24] The same agent tried to smooth away the resentment of a certain Barkley, when Spotswood refused to swear him into the council though he had queen's leave for the appointment.[25]

Richard Bennett, as Virginia agent in London, was undoubtedly able to explain his action as one of the parliamentary commissioners in Maryland to the satisfaction of Cromwell and the Council of State and thus smooth the course of colonial affairs between those two colonies during the troubled Commonwealth period.[26]

When feeling was tense in the decade before the American revolt, the communications of any agent could not but carry weight. The following sane statement as to the state of affairs in Britain by Arthur Lee, probably to a leader of the rebels in Boston, is worth quoting, though not from the pen of a Southern agent: "In no sense of policy is it our interest to quarrel with this country, if we are not compelled to it. If they are obliged to retract from the exercise of their assumed power now, when will they be able to renew it? . . . they will be glad to maintain their supremacy without attempting to bind us in all cases whatsoever, and it is surely better for us to submit silently to that degree of subordination, till the gentle course of nature shall bring us to maturity and independence, than by a premature, doubtful, and dangerous struggle to hazard the ruin of the whole British Empire."[27] British subjects urged Franklin as late as 1775 to use all his influence to compromise the dispute between the colonies and the mother country.[28]

The agent must indubitably have been listened to when in the

[24] "Some Colonial Letters," *Virginia Magazine of History and Biography*, IV, 17. The revelation of the possibilities of affecting personal relations through the agent is just as great as if this particular letter had not fallen behind the table and so failed to go into the packet handed Spotswood.

[25] Blakiston wrote Ludwell on July 18, 1714, that he had persuaded Lord Orkney to write Spotswood to "accomodate this matter soe that this triviall resentmt may be laid in Oblivion." He also wrote the governor frankly giving his views.—*Ibid.*, p. 23.

[26] Shown in a letter by Governor Digges to Cromwell, dated June 29, 1655.—Rawlinson MSS, A, 27, f. 783, Bodleian Library.

[27] Historical Manuscript Commission, *Eleventh Report*, App. I, Pt. V; *MSS of the Earl of Dartmouth*, pp. 344-45.

[28] See a letter from Will Strahan to Franklin, of July 5, 1775, *ibid.*, p. 381.

early days he strove to guide and advise the colony as to the proper approach to the home authorities and as to what the government would accept. In 1711 Blakiston assured Ludwell that parliament could never be prevailed ón to allow naval stores to be paid for even in part by the tobacco customs, as they were all appropriated, and as for a proposal of building ironworks, "you cannot conceive what an ill Relish any thing has here that may but have ye least aspect to interfere wth ye planting of tob°."[29] Occasionally, the frank recognition by an agent of the importance of the colony to the mother country must have been music to the ears of the frontiersmen, usually made to feel the provincial inferior, and therefore made him amenable to the suggestions of the agent. Blakiston wrote in 1711: "I am under some concerne to see our Grandees as some are so Regardless of ye Interest of Virginia as to be Constantly seeking that Country of ye [mutilated] that was always appropriated to Defray ye Contingent Charges of ye Gover^{mt} your hive of Virginia brings a great deal of Hony to this Nation and costs them nothing. . . ."[30] Franklin was undoubtedly right in December, 1774, when he disregarded the preference of the Americans for having their petition presented to the king as many Americans and merchants attending as could be assembled, and followed the simple procedure of delivering it to the Earl of Dartmouth.[31]

Sometimes that advice to the colony took a material form. As we have had occasion to note, Crockatt, as a good business man, saw an opportunity for a new industry in South Carolina in the encouragement given by parliament about 1751 by removing the duty on potash made in America, especially since the price on that article had lately almost doubled. He promptly wrote the Committee of Correspondence, urging the planters in that colony "to turn their Thoughts and Hands that Way as he was convinced were they once able to make say tolerably good the Profit attending the same would soon induce them to continue making it."[32]

[29] "Some Colonial Letters," *loc. cit.*, IV, 19-20.

[30] *Ibid.*, p. 20.

[31] Though the petition came addressed to Franklin, it was consigned to five agents—Burke, Garth, Lee, and Wentworth, in addition to the recipient. Wentworth declined to act, as the petition asserted their claims in a "high tone and with offensive expressions." Historical Manuscripts Commission, *Eleventh Report*, App. I, Pt. V: *MSS of the Earl of Dartmouth*, p. 372. This was Paul Wentworth, agent for New Hampshire.

[32] Journal of the Commons House of Assembly of South Carolina, XXVII, 69.

The agent could chide and rebuke and advise when he thought it advisable. The reader is reminded of several such instances which have appeared in these pages: Blakiston's rebuke about the size of the tobacco gauge when reporting his defense of Virginia against the claim for loss in freight charges on tobacco by the shipowners comes readily to mind.[33] Abercromby in 1758 chided North Carolina for not having made acknowledgment to the king's ministers for the grant of money of that year as had Virginia.[34] That same agent suggested delicately that it might be prudent for the council to "turn their Thoughts" to the parliamentary grant as the final expedient for replacing the deficiencies of the tobacco revenue in case the application to the treasury for a part of the quitrents were rejected.[35] Garth advised South Carolina that petitions from the assemblies signed by the speaker carried more weight than one introduced into the Commons House merely under an agent's name.[36]

An alert agent could scarcely fail to have constructive suggestions for the British officials. Boone and Barnwell, fresh from Carolina in 1720, where the presence of the Spanish at St. Augustine was felt only too keenly, made several practical suggestions: no ammunition or other military stores should be exported to the Spanish at Florida by British subjects; and custom house officers should not be concerned in foreign trade.[37] The information furnished the Duke of Newcastle by Abercromby, then attorney general of South Carolina, one of three agents sent to aid Fury in November, 1742, must have impressed that high official. It revealed the strength of the Spanish attack against Georgia as greater than the Carolinians had imagined

[33] In a letter to the governor and council of Mar. 10, 1707/8, *Virginia Magazine of History and Biography*, XIX, 16-17.

[34] Abercromby Letter Book, p. 78.   [35] *Ibid.*, pp. 117-18.

[36] "Garth Correspondence," *loc. cit.*, XXIX, 41.

[37] The suggestion above was made to the Board of Trade.—C. O. 5/358, p. 52. One of the most important suggestions came from two Northern agents, but they are so significant for American history that they merit citation here. Chidley Brooke and William Nicoll, agents for New York in 1696, offered suggestions for the proper defense of New York against the encroachments of the French. First, taking Canada; if that were not feasible, the appropriation yearly of £1,000 for presents to the Five Nations; a garrison of 1,000 men on the frontiers of New York for the period of the war (King William's War); a stone fort at Albany and several other places; recruits and military stores sent yearly for the period of the war; the sending of five or six young men to reside among the Indians to learn their language; and the sending of some clergy among the Indians to convert them. There was much food for thought here for the Board of Trade.—C. O. 391/9, pp. 100-1. The abstract in the *Calendar of State Papers, Colonial*, (1696-1697, p. 103), is too brief to be helpful.

possible, while the weakness of the British colonials was indicated by
the fact that scarcely a thousand men could be assembled from the
country in ten days to reinforce Charleston. Bluntly he revealed
that Charleston or Port Royal would have been laid in ashes if the
foe had come into either of these harbors and the whole country
along the Pou (Pee Dee) River abandoned.[38] Similarly the French
and Indian War produced from the special agent, Charles Pinckney,
a "scheme" for the defense of South Carolina against the French
presented to the Board of Trade on December 2, 1756.[39] In a very
different field the Georgia agent offered to the Board in 1768,
as we have seen, some carefully thought out suggestions about the
silk culture of that province.[40] Henry McCulloh, agent for the
Six Counties, was responsible, as is well known, for the first suggestion of a stamp tax. He made such an impression with his plan
for an American stamp law in 1763 that a conference was arranged
between him and the Board of Stamps, preliminary to its consideration by the Lords of the Treasury. McCulloh declared that he
never intended that any of the money raised by the scheme should
be sent to England, but meant to raise a fund in the colonies to
obtain a credit for issuing exchequer bills to enable the colonies to
support the militia and provide cash for Indian presents. He even
thought of it as a move to raise bounties to encourage settlements
in the colonies. He felt convinced that in time additional duties
could be raised so as to relieve the mother country, but knew that
any such attempt then would meet with the fullest opposition.[41]

Probably the richest contribution made by the agents was as a
medium of communication with the British people This work must
be pronounced definitely successful. This possibility of the office

[38] Newcastle Papers, Add. MSS, 32699, f. 541.

[39] C. O. 5/375, K, 147.

[40] C. O. 5/650, f. 152. See above, Chapter V.

[41] The reader is aware that Henry McCulloh was not a regular agent, but his suggestion is indicative of how important the opinions of an agent of any sort might become.—Hardwicke Papers, Add. MSS, 36226, ff. 357-60. "A State of the several Articles
proposed by Mr. McCulloh to be stamped and the duties thereon, with Miscellaneous
Representations Relative to our Concerns in America, likewise a state of all the different
articles which are now stamped in Great Britain, in order to fix reportable articles
which are to be inserted in the law intended for imposing stamp duties in America
and the West Indies," repays careful study on this subject.—Add. MSS. 35910, ff.
136-205. This is doubtless the plan which brought against McCulloh the charge of
first suggesting the Stamp Act, but the reader will note what he says as to the uses to be
made of the money raised.

was early recognized. Illustrations such as Leonard Strong's appeal to the British public in his *Babylon's Fall* and others recorded in this study will readily occur to the reader. By the time we reach the period of the controversy over British policies of taxation in the latter half of the eighteenth century, the colonials were thoroughly conscious of the power of public opinion. When Virginia sent several addresses to the agent with instructions for presenting them, she provided for the contingency of the House of Commons' refusal to receive the petition addressed to it. In that event he was directed to have the substance printed and distributed over the nation in order to make the British people cognizant of the liberties which the Americans claimed as fellow subjects.[42] A printer might have refused to print such a remonstrance sent by mail; a persistent agent could surely assure its being printed. In at least one striking instance the value of having an agent on the scene was illustrated: news of the Battle of Lexington and Concord reached the Massachusetts agent eleven days before General Gage's account. The Provincial Congress took depositions as to the events of April 22, which they dispatched to their agent with a covering letter, "To the Inhabitants of Great Britain," through a Captain Derby of Salem, who reached London on May 29. Arthur Lee had the letter published with its account of the battle, announcing that the original affidavits were open for inspection at the Mansion House.[43]

If the agents were alert they could be of great value to the colony by securing and transmitting information of coming events. A case in point was the advance notice sent by Garth of the concerted action of some merchants to have the bounty on tar and turpentine removed. The session of parliament was too advanced to secure action that year, but Garth's warning and the copy of the minutes of the Board of Trade on the measure forewarned the interested colonies so that they were prepared to cope with the matter at the next session.[44]

Several of the agents took prompt measures to anticipate and prevent actions which appeared to them unfavorable for the colonies. They applied the principle of the ounce of prevention. It is illumi-

[42] *Virginia Magazine of History and Biography*, IX, 354-55.
[43] Hart, *Commonwealth History of Massachusetts*, III, 6.
[44] "Garth Correspondence," *loc. cit.*, XXXI, 124-27.

nating as to the attitude of the agent to recall that early in the
history of the agency Blakiston was concerned about the proceeds of
a certain tax being diverted into the British treasury lest they never
be recovered.[45]   Garth profited by the experience of Benjamin
Franklin, who found upon arrival at the Board of Trade to support
certain acts passed by the Georgia assembly that the acts, arriving
by an earlier boat than his letter, had been immediately considered,
as if to anticipate any defense by the agent.   Garth, therefore, did
not rest content in asking to be informed of all acts as soon as possible, but left an order for a copy of a given act to be made for him
on its arrival.[46] Montague, equally alert in regard to the proposed
Vandalia Company, sought by a caveat at the Board of Trade, to
which it was certain to be referred, to prevent the carving up of
Virginia. He then planned, when the affair came before the Board,
to ask time to secure from the colony its approbation or objections.[47]
On another occasion Garth proved equally alive to the interests of
South Carolina when he found that the proper officer at the Treasury
had instructions to prepare a bill upon a certain proposition to be
presented to Parliament. He promptly lodged a memorial by way
of caveat to stop further proceedings until the matter had been fully
considered by the Board of Trade. Again by close attention to the
South Carolina *Gazette* he forestalled the possibility of a new assembly being summoned to meet at Beaufort instead of at Charleston,
as has been told. It is indicative of the fact that the protests of
agents did count that Dartmouth wrote Garth immediately after
the arrival of the next mail from America that the assembly would
sit at Charleston.[48] These services were negative—in the nature of
prevention—but none the less successful services.

First and last the agents were ambassadors of good will, even
though they enjoyed no such prestige or honor as did a minister of

[45] "Miscellaneous Colonial Documents," *loc. cit.*, XIX, 14-15.

[46] "Garth Correspondence," *loc. cit.*, XXX, 222. See above, p. 209.

[47] His petition to the Board of Trade was well stated: "That your Pet^r conceiving his
constituents totally ignorant of such Application to the Lords of Treasury & that their
Lordships are uninformed of the Circumstances above stated, humbly submits it to your
Lordships Wisdom & Justice whether before any further Proceedings is had on the Subject refer'd to your Lordships the Colony of Virginia sh'd not have Notice & Time given
to offer such Objections as may occur agst the Completion of such Grant."—"Proceedings
of the Virginia Committee of Correspondence," *loc. cit.*, XII, 159-61, 163. See also
Journal of the Board of Trade, 1768-1775, p. 166.

[48] "Garth Correspondence," *loc. cit.*, XXXIII, 266, 270-71. See above, pp. 208-9.

a foreign country. When one of the colonial agents rose to great prominence, as did Franklin, such distinction was the result of his own rare ability and engaging personality rather than of the office he held. Aptly termed ambassadors, they were also clerks and sometimes almost lackeys, more or less cuffed around by the colonial and home governments. The degree to which they succeeded in promoting good will on both sides of the Atlantic is again one of the intangibles which it is impossible to evaluate. The harm to the cause when one of the agents gave offense to the British government is obvious. If that resentment grew too grave, the agent became, of course, valueless to the colony. The case of Peter Leheup has been commented on. Abercromby also gave great offense by a protest presented in support of the council of Virginia. It was directed against the action of the Privy Council in ordering that £1,000 of the money raised in that colony by the tobacco duty be sent to South Carolina. Naturally, the action was held by the provincial council and by the agent as illegal and impolitic.[49]

The agents must never forget for one minute that they were liaison officers. Garth's hesitancy at certain times proved his knowledge of the views of his friends in South Carolina.[50] He must receive credit for trying to be absolutely impartial in his presentation of matters on which there was a difference of view between the colonies and the mother country.[51]

Discretion on the part of an agent could bring rich returns or do a province decided harm. Occasionally lack of discretion could be of grave import, as when Agents Barker and Elmsley by securing the exemption of North Carolina from the bill restraining the trade of the colonies to England and the British West Indies in 1775 might have ranged that province on the wrong side of the controversy. The two agents in suppressing the petition sent them and in drawing up another in "more decent terms," although themselves differing on the subject, were conscious that their initiative might give bitter offense.[52] On the other hand, Garth's initiative and even

---

[49] "Virginia Legislative Papers," *Virginia Magazine of History and Biography*, XVII, 383-84, note.

[50] See his letter of Mar. 12, 1769, "Garth Correspondence," *loc. cit.*, XXXI, 53.

[51] *Ibid.*, XXIX, 229; XXX, 235.

[52] Letter of Elmsley to Samuel Johnson, Apr. 7, 1775, *Colonial Records of North Carolina*, IX, 1208-9.

violation of instructions in 1766 redounded to the benefit of South
Carolina. The diffidence with which he reported his independence
of action in 1766 indicates, however, a wholesome fear of the assembly: ". . . relying upon the knowledge you have of my Zeal & Wishes
to the Welfare and Liberty of America for your forgiveness in not
literally carrying your Commands into Execution forthwith upon
the Rece'pt thereof; it is upon this Account I have been so particular
in this Detail that my Conduct and Action may speak for themselves,
which indeed as you will have seen in the Course of this Epistle
waited not for instruction to steer by."[53]

In general it can be safely asserted that the agents were loyal
to the colonies down to the eve of the revolt. The acid test was
the attitude taken by the agent toward the American claims between
1765 and 1775. Here, on the whole, the British-born agents were
strikingly sympathetic toward the colonial point of view. The loyalty
of Franklin, Knox, Lee, and the other Americans we may take
for granted, but Barlow Trecothick, Richard Jackson, and, above all,
Edmund Burke and Charles Garth were towers of strength to the
American cause. Only Edward Montague among the Southern
agents proved utterly unsympathetic—even hostile. The change
in his attitude came after 1770, for in that year, speaking apparently
without mental reservation, he is found saying: ". . . if by unwarrantable Measures was meant Combinations & Mutual Agreements to
be content without Manufactures of the Mother Country the Censure
was improper and too severe, because nothing deserved to be deem'd
highly unwarrantable, but what is illegal." And then he added in his
own words: "I imagine the first subject of Deliberation will be
America & you may depend on our utmost Efforts to obtain Relief
for it in the most Extensive Degree."[54] Note, however, the changed
view by October, 1775: "I read all your Prints from Charles Town
to Boston, and find Truth in none and no other meaning but continuing the Delusion of the poor Ignorant People, who must be sacri-
fised by Thousands to gratify the Pride and ambition of that damn'd
Rascal John Adams. If your Designs are Completed, and you should
become a separate State I hope he will turn out another Cromwell.

[53] "Garth Correspondence," *loc. cit.*, XXVI, 88.
[54] Letter of Montague to the Committee of Correspondence, Jan. 10, 1770, "Proceedings of the Virginia Committee of Correspondence," *loc. cit.*, XII, 158.

. . . Such a Peal of Thunder is preparing for you that will shake even the Apalatian Mountains."[55]   Loyalty to the cause for which the agent was working, another intangible, certainly was important in tipping the scales for success. It seems self evident that Garth could not with the other agents have scored the victory he did in the repeal of the obnoxious Stamp Act if his heart had not been in the cause he was espousing.

In truth the agency was not a highly successful institution. It was impossible for any agent to satisfy the assembly and the people of the colony. The task demanded was impossible. He must tread a wary path between the insistent demands of the colonials on the one hand and the strong convictions of the supremacy and prerogative of government on the other. The members of the colonial assemblies were too prejudiced, partly because of ignorance of imperial problems, too partisan temperamentally, too selfish, and too unjust to make it possible for an agent long to afford satisfaction in the Southern colonies. Whether the ill feeling had been aroused against governor, proprietor, or against the agent himself, the provincials— probably because they were provincials—could not be content with simple justice.

Nevertheless, as one studies the records, the conviction crystalizes that the colonies were justified in maintaining the agencies largely because of these intangibles. They were in very truth ambassadors, interpreting the provincials to the British government and people, and in turn striving to bring the British attitude to the comprehension of the colonials. In a singularly difficult position, susceptible of criticism from both sides, most of the agents, whether American or British-born, maintained their loyalty to both and kept the balance of their judgment level. They were able officially to recognize a difference of interest between the English merchants and the colonials and hence were able to remove much confusion and even to define the issue. The rise of agents for the lower house of assembly and the growing control of the agents by the lower house, when there was no separate agent, shows the determination of the colonists that the old way of conducting business by governor and council must be supplemented by a new mode, one established and controlled by

[55] "Historical and Genealogical Notes and Queries," *Virginia Magazine of History and Biography*, XIX, p. 416.

the delegates of the people. There is a clear recognition of the difference of interests between Britain and her colonies. The issue once defined was bound to lead to a rupture unless Great Britain could have the wisdom to recognize the divergence of interests and develop a flexibility of government in time to save to the Empire her North American colonies. The liaison officer might see the issue and fear for the Empire, but no such officer could force clarity of vision on the type of men who were then directing British destinies.

APPENDICES

APPENDIX I

LIST OF THE AGENTS OF THE SOUTHERN COLONIES
Dates show actual Period of Service—not dates of appointment
or Dismissal[1]

I. Virginia

John Pountis................ 1624
Sir George Yeardley.......... 1625
Sir Francis Wyatt............ 1626
Sir Francis Wyatt...........⎫
Edward Bennett............⎬ 1628
Michael Marshart..........⎭
Captain Francis West........⎫
William Claiborne (?).......⎬ 1629-1631
Thomas Harwood...........⎫
Dr. Francis Pott............⎬ 1635-1636
George Sandys 1640
Colonel Samuel Mathews...... 1652-1657
Richard Bennett............. 1655-1657
Edward Digges.............. 1657
Governor William Berkeley.... 1661-1662
Phillip Mallory.............. 1661 (Special religious mission)
Colonel Francis Moryson...... 1663-1670
Sir Henry Chicheley.......... 1673 (Special to present petition to the king)
General Robert Smith........ 1673-1676
Francis Moryson............. 1674-1676
Thomas Ludwell 1674-1676
Phillip Ludwell.............. 1688-1690 (Special for House of Burgesses)

[1] Too many factors are involved to make it practicable to give references.

Regular Agents

Jeffrey Jeffreys. 1691-1693
William Byrd, Jr. 1698-1699
John Povey. 1699-1703
John Thrale. 1703-1704
Nathaniel Blakiston. 1705-1721
John Carter 1722-1723
Peter Leheup 1723-1754
James Abercromby. 1754-1761
                          1761-1774 (For the council and gover-
                                    nor)
Edward Montague. . . . . 1761-1772 (Virginia agent, but more
                                    especially representing the
                                    house)

Special Agents

William Blathwayt. 1692
Reverend James Blair. 1691-1693
Reverend James Blair. . . . . 1697 (Joined with regular agent)
William Byrd, Jr. 1697
John Povey. 1699-1703
William Byrd, Jr. 1702-1703
William Byrd, Jr. 1718-1720
William Byrd, Jr. . . . . 1721-1725 (At intervals)
Reverend James Blair 1726-1727
John Randolph. 1728-1729
Isham Randolph. . . . . 1732 (To aid Leheup on the sugar
                                    bill)
John Randolph. 1732-1733
Peyton Randolph 1754-1755
James Abercromby. . . . . 1752 (For a special address to the king)

II. Maryland

Leonard Strong. 1655
John Coode. . . . . }
Kenelm Chesldyne . . . . } 1690-1691
Peter Pagan 1692-1694
                          1697-1698 (Purchasing agent)
Isaac Milner. . . . . 1698-1699 (Purchasing agent)
Sir Thomas Lawrence. . . . . 1695-?   (February-November)
                          1698-1699

Nathaniel Blakiston 1702-1708,
                                     1712-1721
Ferdinand Paris . . . . 1739-1746 (For lower house only)
Charles Garth . . . . 1766 (Special to present resolutions of
                                      Stamp Act Congress for
                                      Maryland)
Charles Garth . . . . 1767-1775 (For the lower house only)
Hugh Hammersley . . . . 1767- ? (For the council only)

III. North Carolina

Thomas Miller 1676-1677
Thomas Eastchurch . . . . 1676-1677 (Not clear he is an agent)
John Culpeper . . . .⎫
George Durant . . . .⎬1679
Edmund Porter . . . . 1703-1705(?)
John Porter . . . . 1706-1707(?)
Arthur Goffe . . . .⎫
Edmund Porter . . . .⎬1725-1726(?)
Nathaniel Duckenfield . . . .⎭
William Smith . . . . 1731-1733 (Against Gov. Burrington)
Samuel Wragg . . . . 1738-1742 (For the assembly)
Henry McCulloh . . . . 1747-1751 (For the six Northern
                                      Counties)
James Abercromby 1749-1758
James Abercromby . . . . 1759- ? (Continued by the lower
                                      house)
Samuel Smith . . . . 1759-1764 (For the council only)
Couchet Jouvencal 1761-1763
                                      1763-1765 (For the lower house only)
Henry E. McCulloh 1770-1773
Alexander Elmsley . . . .⎫
Thomas Barker . . . .⎬1774-1775 (Special)

IV. South Carolina

John Ash . . . . 1703-1705(?)
Joseph Boone . . . . 1705-1706 (May have been longer)
Landgrave Abel Kettleby 1713-1716
Joseph Boone 1715-1720
Richard Beresford 1715-1717
Joseph Boone . . . . 1720-1721 (In England)
Colonel John Barnwell 1720-1721

Francis Yonge .... 1722-1728 (With lapses in 1724, 1726)
John Lloyd................. 1722-1723
Francis Yonge 1726
Samuel Wragg .... 1726 (Associated with Yonge)
Samuel Wragg .... 1727-1731 (Special)
Stephen Godin .... 1728-1730 (For the council only)
Peregrine Fury............. 1731-1749
Francis Yonge .... 1733-1736 (To aid Fury on special task)
                       1737   (To aid Fury on a money bill)
Colonel John Fenwick........ 1746 (Joint agent with Fury)
Colonel John Fenwick........ 1747 (Special to coöperate with Fury for a money bill)

James Abercromby .... ⎫
Capt. William Linvingston.... ⎬ 1742-1745 (All three to aid Fury. Special)
Alexander Vander Dusen..... ⎭

Alexander Vander Dusen...... 1748 (Special to aid Fury)
                       1754 (Special to aid Crockatt)
James Crockatt............. 1749-1756
Charles Pinckney .... 1753-1756 (Special)
James Wright.............. 1757-1760
Charles Garth............. 1762-1775(?)

V. Georgia

Thomas Stephens, Jr.......... 1742
Edmund Gray 1752
Benjamin Martyn........... 1753-1763 (Part Crown Agent)
William Knox.............. 1762-1763 (To aid Martyn)
William Knox.............. 1763-1765 (Sole agent)
Charles Garth.............. 1766 (Early to present petition against the Stamp Act for lower house. Special)
Benjamin Franklin........... 1768-1774
                       1774-1775 (Acknowledged by the Lower House and possibly functioning until his departure for America)

Grey Elliott . . . . 1773-1775 (To act in Franklin's absence. May have served until 1779)

Alexander Kellet. . . . . 1756 (Special)

William Little. . . . . 1757 (Special to present an Address)

APPENDIX II

Entries of Attendance at the Board of Trade by Abercromby

March 21, 1749/50. The order of the Lords' Committee of the Council referring the case to the Board of Trade was read. Abercromby was present and moved that a day be appointed for a hearing.

March 26, 1750. Both Abercromby and McCulloh were present, and April 24 appointed for the hearing.

April 3, 1750. Mr. Lamb reported on the acts passed in North Carolina between November, 1746 and October, 1748. The Board ordered that the Act for Regulating the Assembly, etc., and the Act for fixing the Seat of Government, etc. should be referred to the attorney and solicitor general with the petition and papers relating to them, and that the hearing of the parties fixed for April 24 be canceled. Abercromby and McCulloh were informed of the decision on the following day; Abercromby prayed for a speedy hearing.

December 11, 1750. The attorney and solicitor general's report on the act was read.

January 11, 1750/51. Abercromby laid his petition before the Board.

February 6, 1750/51. His memorial asking that the Board consider the Act for Regulating the Assembly etc. was read.

February 8, 1750/51. Abercromby and his counsel, Sharpe, were present at the Board session; the next Thursday appointed for hearing the petition of the Six Northern Counties against the act.

February 14, 1750/51. Agents McCulloh for the Six Northern Counties, and Abercromby, for North Carolina, attend with their solicitors. The petition is heard.

February 23, 1750/51. Abercromby present with his solicitor and counsel; McCulloh present with his solicitor. Abercromby's counsel refuses to plead the case unless counsel for the other party is appointed.

March 13, 1750/51. Abercromby's petition, asking to be heard against the attorney and solicitor general's report was read.

March 15, 1750/51. McCulloh's memorial relating to his complaints against the governor, Mr. Johnston, was read, and further papers relating to the subject laid before the Board.

March 20, 1750/51. Abercromby and McCulloh with solicitors and counsel were present, and the following papers were read: the Order in Council of January 15, 1747, regarding the petition; the petition itself; report of the attorney and solicitor general on the two acts; and Abercromby's petition, praying to be heard against the report of the attorney and solicitor general.

Abercromby's counsel made a long defense of the action of the governor in allowing an assembly of such small numbers to pass the act, stating that those absent had deliberately stayed away, thinking no business could be done, and proving that no act had been invalidated in England because a majority of the House was absent. To prove his facts he read a great many papers: i.e., acts, minutes of assembly, reports from Mr. Lamb and the Board of Trade, memorials, etc.

March 29, 1751. The parties again attended, and the counsel for the petitioners made a long speech, saying that the petitioners' insistence that a majority was necessary to form a quorum was authorized by the governor's proclamation, as he had often adjourned the assembly when it lacked a quorum. He read many papers to prove his opinion and to prove his points.

June 19, 1751. The memorial of McCulloh, complaining of the conduct of the governor of North Carolina was read.

June 27, 1751. McCulloh's complaints and charges against the governor were again considered and further consideration postponed.

APPENDIX III

DOCUMENTS SENT BY MARYLAND TO THE AGENT, FERDINAND PARIS

A paper marked A, copy of the conditions of the plantation of Maryland in 1636, Lord Baltimore's letter and intentions to Leonard Calvert in regard to the lawn and fields of St. Mary's, Baltimore's several commissions and declaration in 1658.

A paper marked B, consisting of several acts of 1638, together with commissions to the secretary of the colony, the clerk and their bonds.

A paper marked C, a statement of the Case of Maryland and her Trade in relation to the Act of 1661 (repealed by 1741) and an Act for Port Duties.

A paper marked D, a statement of the Cast with regard to the Duty of Twelve Pence per Hogshead on Tobacco.

A paper marked 5, A Statement of a Case and Opinion in regard to it.

A paper marked E, a Message regarding the Three Pence per Hogshead on Tobacco for Arms (Part of an act of 1704).

A paper marked G, which consisted of a commission, a copy of the House Journal for May, 1739; extracts of the Journals for 1707, 1715, and 1716; Address to the King; Votes and Proceedings of the House of Delegates of 1732; and Laws of 1732.

A paper marked Q, extracts from the Journal of the House of Delegates for April, 1737, regarding receiving gold through the agent of the proprietary.

Paper marked C, copies of eighteen acts.

BIBLIOGRAPHY

I. GUIDES AND BIBLIOGRAPHIES

Andrews, Charles M., and Davenport, Frances G. *Guide to the Manuscript Materials for the History of the United States to 1783, in the British Museum, in minor London Archives, and in the Libraries of Oxford and Cambridge.* Washington, 1908.

————. *Guide to the Materials for American History to 1783, in the Public Record Office of Great Britain.* 2 vols. (Vol. I, State Papers; Vol. II, Departmental and Miscellaneous Papers.) Washington, 1912-1914.

Calendar of Virginia State Papers and Other Manuscripts. Edited by W. P. Palmer and others. 11 vols. Richmond, 1875-1893.

Channing, Edward, and Hart, Albert Bushnell. *Guide to the Study of American History.* Boston, 1896.

Evans, Charles. *American Bibliography. A Chronological Dictionary of all Books, Pamphlets, and Periodical Publications printed in the United States of America from the Genesis of Printing in 1639 down to and including the year 1820.* Vols. I-VIII. Chicago, 1903-1914.

Griffin, A. P. C. *Bibliography of American Historical Societies. Annual Report of the American Historical Association for the year 1905.* Vol. II.

Hasse, Adelaide R. *Materials for a Bibliography of the Public Archives of the Thirteen Original States. Annual Report of the American Historical Association for the year 1906*, II, 239-572.

Jameson, J. F. "Guide to the Items relating to American History in the Report of the English Historical Manuscripts Commission," *Third Annual Report of the Historical Manuscripts Commission*, App. III. *Annual Report of the American Historical Association for the year 1898*, pp. 611-708.

Sainsbury, W. Noel. "The British Public Record Office and the Materials in it for Early American History," *Proceedings of the American Antiquarian Society*, New Series, VIII, 376-89. Worcester, 1893.

Swem, E. G. *Virginia Historical Index.* 2 vols. Roanoke, 1934-1936. An index to the statutes and historical magazines of Virginia.

Whitney, Eden. *Bibliography of the Colonial History of South Carolina. Annual Report of the American Historical Association for the year 1894,* pp. 563-86.

Winsor, Justin. *Narrative and Critical History of America.* 8 vols. Boston and New York, 1884-1889.

II. PRIMARY SOURCES: MANUSCRIPTS

A. IN ENGLAND

The Archives of the Home Government provide a mass of important material relating especially to the work of the agent in England. As stated in the text, this official came into contact with almost every branch of the government; dispersed, therefore among the records of these bodies are to be found numerous references to the activities of the colonial representative.

Some discrimination as to the relative importance within this large body of material is desirable and possible. Naturally, the most valuable of sources under this head are the papers of the successive committees, councils, and commissions into whose hands the business of the American colonies passed. Fortunately, the papers of the Committee of the Privy Council of 1675 to 1696 and of its successor, the Board of Trade of 1696 to 1782, cover the entire period of the regular agency and are extant. Parliamentary and Privy Council records, while important, vary definitely in value from time to time, as plantation affairs obtruded themselves on parliament only in times of crisis and can be followed with greater ease in their progress through the Plantation Office than through the Privy Council because they were constantly referred to the Board of Trade by the Council. Great value must be attached to the private collections of manuscripts of the ministers of state because of the constant unofficial intercourse between the agents and members of the administration or of parliament, for accounts of which we must depend upon the written records of one or another of the parties concerned.

1. Public Record Office

Of first importance are the records of the Privy Council, which have been calendared; of the Committees of the Privy Council, 1675 to 1696; of the several Councils for Foreign Plantations, 1660 to 1674; and of the Board of Trade. The Minutes for the years 1675 to 1696 are found in C. O. 391/1-8; correspondence and other papers in the miscellaneous

series C. O. 1, to the year 1689 and thereafter in two series for each
colony, classified as "Original Correspondence" and "Entry Books." For
the early Restoration period, 1660 to 1664, minutes are in the miscellaneous series, C. O. 1 with correspondence distributed under a date classification. Correspondence for the years 1670 to 1674 continue to be
found in series C. O. 1, while heads of proceedings are in C. O 5/1.
After organization of the Board of Trade in 1696 the minutes are in
C. O. 391/9-89, while correspondence and other papers are placed in two
series for each colony. The early volumes for the years 1696 to 1704
have been calendared, as will be shown, and the data since 1704 printed
as *Journals of the Commissioners for Trade and Plantations.*

Second only in importance to the official records of the councils and
committees are the papers of the several secretaries of state. In addition
to the official sources in the several series of "Original Correspondence"
and "Entry Books" are unofficial sources such as the following which
have been used with profit:

The Chatham Papers, Correspondence of the Elder and the Younger
Pitt.

Papers of the Earl of Dartmouth, Secretary of State in the American
Department. (These are more conveniently used through the Historical
Manuscripts Commission *Reports.*)

In addition to the regular series of official records for each colony,
there are miscellaneous series labeled C. O. 5, C. O. 318, and C. O. 323,
in which much valuable data has been found.

In addition material of value was culled from the Admiralty Papers,
the Treasury Board Papers, and the Minutes of the Privy Council,
C. O. 5/1305.

2. British Museum

Correspondence of the Duke of Newcastle, Secretary of State for
the Southern Department, classified as Add. MSS 32686-32992, 33028-
33030.

Letter Book of Thomas Povey, 1655-1660, and collection of papers
belonging to Povey. These are classified as B.M. Add. MS 11411, and
B. M. Egerton MS 2395. These manuscripts are especially helpful as
they cover the period of Thomas Povey's early connection with the
agency.

Letters of James Knight, unofficial agent for Jamaica, 1725, classified as B. M. Add. MS 22677.

3. Bodleian Library, Oxford University

Rawlinson Manuscripts, classified as Rawlinson MSS, Bodleian.

B. IN AMERICA

1. Maryland State Archives, Annapolis

Black Books, Proprietary Papers. Eleven volumes of manuscripts, part of the Rainbow Series.

Miscellaneous Papers.

Votes and Proceedings of the House of Delegates, 1757-1774. The great bulk of material for the acts and proceedings of the Maryland Assembly has been printed in the *Archives of Maryland*, but the data for the period after 1763 must be sought from the manuscript volumes at Annapolis.

2. Maryland Historical Society, Baltimore

Calvert Papers.

3. State Archives of South Carolina, Columbia

Journals of the Commons House of Assembly, 1721-1776. Thirty-nine volumes. The journals of the House of Commons have been printed up to 1707; the journals of the Council only for August 25, 1671-June 24, 1680, and April 11, 1692-September 26, 1692.

Journals of the Council of South Carolina. Thirty-eight volumes of manuscripts.

Public Records of South Carolina. Thirty-six volumes of manuscripts. Three volumes have been printed covering the years 1663-1697.

Public Records of South Carolina—Extra Manuscripts. Four volumes. Copies from British Manuscripts to fill gaps.

4. Virginia State Library, Richmond

Abercromby Letter Book. A single volume of manuscripts bound in vellum, containing letters covering the period of his agency for Virginia and North Carolina. Most of it is in his own handwriting (execrable), and where it is by a copyist, it is interlarded with his corrections. Toward the close of the volume it becomes brief entries covering only a few lines. The last entry is for February 25 and March 1, 1773, though there appears before that an entry for April 9, 1773. At the back of the book in reverse order are about one hundred pages, extending from October 7, 1750, to February 13, 1756, where appear letters to Governors Johnston, Glen, Dinwiddie and some to the council.

Randolph Manuscripts. Three volumes of manuscripts.

5. *New York Public Library*

In the small collection of Maryland Manuscripts, the Galloway Papers, are to be found a few items referring to the Liberty Lottery.

6. *Pennsylvania Historical Society, Philadelphia*

Correspondence of the Penn Family.

III. PRINTED PRIMARY SOURCES

A. BRITISH OFFICIAL DOCUMENTS

Acts of the Privy Council of England, Colonial Series. Edited by W. L. Grant and James Munro. Hereford, 6 vols. 1908-1912. A calendar of the Privy Council Register in the Public Record Office and at the Privy Council office covering the years 1613-1783.

Annual Register, 1758-1941. 184 vols. London, 1758-1941.

Calendar of State Papers, Colonial Series, America and the West Indies (1574-1701). Edited by Cecil Headlam, J. W. Fortescue, and E. Noel Sainsbury. 14 vols. London, 1860-1911.

Calendar of Treasury Papers (1556/7-1734). Edited by Joseph Redington. 7 vols. London, 1868-1897.

Debates of the House of Commons (1768-1774). Edited by Sir Henry Cavendish. 3 vols. London, 1839-1843.

Historical Manuscripts Commission. *Eleventh Report*, App. I; *Fourteenth Report*, App. X: *The Manuscripts of the Earl of Dartmouth, American Papers*, Vol. II.

Journal of the Commissioners for Trade and Plantations (1704-1782). 14 vols. London, 1920-1938.

    This is referred to briefly as the *Journal of the Board of Trade*. The set used was not numbered but was labeled by years.

Journals of the House of Commons for the years 1733-1775. (Great Britain).

Journals of the House of Lords.

Records in the British Public Record Office relating to South Carolina, 1663-1697. 3 vols. Atlanta, Ga., 1928-1930.

Reports from the Committees of the House of Commons. Vol. I, 1733. Miscellaneous Subjects, 1715-1735. London, 1803.

    Printed by order of the House and not inserted in the Journals.

Return of the Names of every Member returned to serve in each Parliament. Parts i-ii, 2 vols. London, 1878.

The Royal Kalendar. 1744-1770. [n.p.], [n.d.]

The Statutes at Large from Magna Carta to the twenty-fifth Year of the Reign of King George the Third. Edited by Owen Ruffhead. Revised, corrected, and continued by Charles Runnington. London, 1786.

Statutes of the Realm to the End of the Reign of Queen Anne. Edited by T. E. Tomlins and others. 12 vols. London, 1810-1828.

Thurloe, John. *A Collection of the State Papers of John Thurloe, Esq.* 7 vols. London, 1742.

B. COLONIAL AND STATE DOCUMENTS

Acts passed by the General Assembly of the Colony of Georgia, 1755-1774. Wormsloe [printed at Philadelphia], 1881.

Archives of Maryland. Edited by William Hand Browne, Bernard Steiner, and J. Hall Pleasants. 58 vols. Baltimore, 1887-1941.

A Collection of all the Public Acts of Assembly of the Province of North Carolina. Edited by Samuel Swann. New Bern, 1752.

The Colonial Records of North Carolina. Edited by William L. Saunders. 10 vols. Raleigh, 1886-1890.

The Colonial Records of the State of Georgia. Compiled and published under Authority of the Legislature by Allen D. Chandler. 26 vols. Atlanta, 1904-1916.

A Digest of the Laws of the State of Georgia from its first Establishment as a British Province down to the year 1798 inclusive, and the Principle Acts of 1799. Edited by Robert and George Watkins. Philadelphia, 1800.

Documents relating to the Colonial History of the State of New Jersey. New Jersey Archives, ser. 1, Vols. I-X. Edited by William E. Whitehead and others. Newark, 1880-1906.

Documents relative to the Colonial History of the State of New York, procured in Holland, England, and France. Edited by E. B. O'Callaghan and others. 14 vols. Albany, 1856-1883.

Executive Journals of the Council of Colonial Virginia. Edited by H. R. McIlwaine. 4 vols. Richmond, 1925-1930.

Hening, W. W. *The Statutes at Large: Being a Collection of all the Laws of Virginia.* 13 vols. Richmond, 1809-1823.

Journals of the House of Burgesses of Virginia. Edited by H. R. McIlwaine. 13 vols. Richmond, 1905-1915.

Laws of Maryland at Large. Edited by Thomas Bacon. Annapolis, 1765.

Laws of the State of North Carolina (1715-1790). Edited by James Iredell. Edenton, North Carolina, 1791.

Legislative Journals of the Council of Colonial Virginia. Edited by H. R. McIlwaine. 3 vols. Richmond, 1918-1919.

Minutes of the Council and General Court of Colonial Virginia, 1622-1632, 1670-1676. Edited by H. R. McIlwaine. Richmond, 1924. The material for the years 1726-1753 is published in the *Virginia Historical and Genealogical Magazine,* Vols. XXXII-XXXIX.

Poore, Ben Perley. *The Federal and State Constitutions, Colonial Charters, and Other Organic Laws of the United States.* 2 vols. Washington, 1878.

The Public Laws of the State of South Carolina from its first Establishment as a British Province down to the Year 1790. Edited by John F. Grimké. Philadelphia, 1790.

The Records of the Virginia Company of London. Edited by Susan Myra Kingsbury. 4 vols. Washington, 1906-1935.

The Statutes at Large of South Carolina. Edited by Thomas Cooper and David McCord. 10 vols. Columbia, 1836-1841.

C. DIARIES, LETTERS, MEMOIRS, ETC.

Byrd, William. *The Writings of "Colonel William Byrd of Westover in Virginia Esq*^{r}*."* Edited by John Spencer Bassett. New York, 1901.

[Dinwiddie, Robert]. *The Official Records of Robert Dinwiddie, Lieutenant-Governor of the Colony of Virginia, 1751-1758.* Virginia Historical Society *Collections,* New Series, Vols. III-IV. Edited by R. A. Brock.

Franklin, Benjamin. *The Works of Benjamin Franklin.* Edited by Jared Sparks. 10 vols. Boston, 1836-1840. (With notes and a life of the author.)

[Habersham, James]. *The Letters of Hon. James Habersham, 1756-1775.* Georgia Historical Society *Collections,* Vol. VI. Savannah, 1904.

[Ingersoll, Jared]. *A Selection from the Correspondence and Miscellaneous Papers of Jared Ingersoll.* New Haven Historical Society *Papers,* Vol. IX. New Haven, 1918.

Keppel, George Thomas (Sixth Earl of Albemarle). *Memoirs of the Marquis of Rockingham and his Contemporaries.* 2 vols. London, 1852.

Kimball, Gertrude Selwyn. *The Correspondence of the Colonial Governors of Rhode Island, 1723-1775.* 2 vols. Boston and New York, 1902-1903.

Lee, Richard Henry. *Life of Arthur Lee . . . with his political and literary Correspondence. . . .* Boston, 1829.

McRee, Griffith J. *Life and Correspondence of James Iredell.* 2 vols. New York, 1857-1858.

[Mauduit, Jasper.] *Jasper Mauduit, Agent in London for the Province of the Massachusetts-Bay, 1762-1765.* The Charles Grenfill Washburn Collection of Letters and Papers. Massachusetts Historical Society *Collections,* Vol. LXXIV, Boston, 1918.

Moultrie, William, *Memoirs of the American Revolution so far as it related to the States of North and South Carolina, and Georgia.* New York, 1802.

Neill, Edward D. *Virginia Vetusta during the Reign of James the First. Containing Letters and Documents never before Printed.* Albany, 1885.

[Norton, John]. *John Norton & Sons, Merchants of London and Virginia: Being their Papers from their Counting House for the years 1750 to 1795.* Edited by Frances N. Mason. Richmond, 1937.

[Spotswood, Alexander]. *The Official Letters of Alexander Spotswood, Lieutenant-Governor of the Colony of Virginia, 1710-1722.* Virginia Historical Society *Collections,* New Series, Vols. I-II. Edited by R. A. Brock. Richmond, 1883-1884.

[Stiles, Ezra]. *Extracts from the Itineraries and other Miscellanies of Ezra Stiles, D.D., LL.D., 1755-1794, with a Selection from his Correspondence.* Edited by Franklin B. Dexter. New Haven, 1916.

Trumbull Papers. Massachusetts Historical Society *Collections,* Fifth Series, Vol. IX. Boston, 1885.

D. Contemporary Accounts and Pamphlets

Archdale, John. *A New Description of that Fertile and Pleasant Province of Carolina: with a brief Account of its Discovery and Settling, and the Government thereof to this Time.* London, 1707. Reprinted in Carroll, *Collections,* II, 85-120.

Beverley, Robert. *The History of Virginia.* Reprinted from the author's second revised edition published in London, 1722. Richmond, 1855.

Bradford, William. *History of Plymouth Plantation.* Published for the Massachusetts Historical Society. Boston, 1912.

Burke, Edmund. *An Account of the European Settlements in America.* 2 vols. London, 1757.

Chalmers, George. *Political Annals of the Present United Colonies from their Settlement to the peace of 1763:* Compiled chiefly from Records and authorized often by the Insertion of State Papers. London, 1780.

Force, Peter. *Tracts and other Papers relating principally to the Origin, Settlement, and Progress of the Colonies in North America from the Discovery of the Country to the Year 1776.* 4 vols. Washington, 1836-1846.

A Full State of the Dispute betwixt the Governor and the Commons House of Assembly of his Majesty's Province of South Carolina in America. With the proper Vouchers and Reasons in Support of the Proceedings of the House of Assembly, as transmitted to their Agent in Great Britain. [n.p.], 1763.

Hall, Clayton Colman (Editor). *Narratives of Early Maryland, 1633-1684.* New York, 1910.

Hammond, John. *Leah and Rachel, or the Two Fruitful Sisters, Virginia and Maryand.* London, 1656.
    Reprinted in Force, *Tracts,* Vol. III, no. 14.

Hartwell, Henry, Blair, James, and Chilton, Edward. *The Present State of Virginia and the College.* London, 1727.
    Originally written in 1697 at the desire of Mr. Locke.

Hewatt, Alexander. *An Historical Account of the Rise and Progress of the Colonies of South Carolina and Georgia.* 2 vols. London, 1779.
    Reprinted in Carroll, *Collections,* Vol. I.

Jones, Hugh. *The Present State of Virginia.* London, 1724.

Langford, John. *Refutation of Babylon's Fall.* 1655. Reprinted in Hall, *Narratives of Early Maryland,* pp. 247-74.

Oldmixon, John. *The British Empire in America, containing the History of the Discovery, Settlement, Progress and State of the British Colonies on the Continent and Islands of America.* 2 vols. Second edition, London, 1741.

————. *The History of Carolina: Being an Account of that Colony, originally published in the History of the British Empire in America.* London, 1708. Reprinted in Carroll, *Collections,* II, 391-461.

Stith, William. *The History of the First Discovery and Settlement of Virginia.* New York, 1865. Originally published at Williamsburg, 1747.

Stokes, Anthony. *A View of the Constitution of the British Colonies in North America and the West Indies, at the Time the Civil War broke out on the Continent of America.* London, 1783.

Strong, Leonard. *Babylon's Fall.* London, 1655.
    Reprinted in Hall, *Narratives of Early Maryland,* pp. 231-46.

Yonge, Francis. *A Narrative of the Proceedings of the People of South Carolina in 1709.* London, 1726. Reprinted in Force, *Tracts,* Vol. II, No. 10.

E. Newspapers and Articles in Periodicals

1. Newspapers and Magazines

Lloyd's Evening Post and British Chronicle, August 16, 1765.
London Daily Post and General Advertiser, January 17, 1739/40.
The London Magazine, Vol. XXIV (1755).
The Maryland Gazette for the years 1765-1768.
> The most complete file of this paper is found in the Maryland State Library at Annapolis.

New England Historical and Genealogical Register, Vol. LIX (1895).
Pennsylvania Gazette, September 28, 1774.
South Carolina and American General Gazette, March 1-18, 1774.
South Carolina Gazette for June, 1739, April, 1765, January, 1767, May, 1770, and July, 1770.

2. Magazine Articles

[Barnwell, John]. "Journal of John Barnwell," *Virginia Magazine of History and Biography*, VI, 42-55.

[Garth, Charles]. "Garth Correspondence," *South Carolina Historical and Genealogical Magazine*. Vols. XXVI and XXVIII-XXXIII, *passim*.

[Harvey, Sir John]. "Declaration of Sir John Harvey," *Virginia Magazines of History and Biography*, I, 425-30.

Kemper, Charles E., editor. "The Early Westward Movement of Virginia," *Virginia Magazine of History and Biography*, Vols. XII-XIII, *passim*.

"Miscellaneous Colonial Documents," *Virginia Magazine of History and Biography*, Vols. XVIII-XIX, *passim*.

"Proceedings of the Virginia Committee of Correspondence," *Virginia Magazine of History and Biography*, Vols. X-XII, *passim*.

"Proposals for a Merchants' Club," *Gentleman's Magazine*, IV, 431-32.

[Sharpe, Horatio]. "Correspondence of Governor Sharpe," *Maryland Historical Magazine*, XII, 370-83.

"A Short Sketch of the Transactions that led to the New Regulations of Commerce that have lately been neglected in Favour of the Colonies," *Gentleman's Magazine*, XXXVI, 228-31.

"Some Colonial Letters," *Virginia Magazine of History and Biography*, III, 349-59; IV, 15-23.

"Stamp Act Papers," *Maryland Historical Magazine*, VI, 282-305.

Stanard, W. G. "Abstracts of Virginia Land Patents," *Virginia Magazine of History and Biography*, Vol. III, *passim*.

"The Tilghman Family," *Maryland Historical Magazine*, I, *passim*.

"Virginia Colonial Records (Miscellaneous Records, 1621-1623)," *Virginia Magazine of History and Biography*, XV, 26-43.

"Virginia in 1635" (Abstracts by W. N. Sainsbury), *Virginia Magazine of History and Biography*, VIII, 299-306; 398-407.

"Virginia in 1656-1658," *Virginia Magazine of History and Biography*, XVIII, 151-58.

"Virginia Legislative Papers," *Virginia Magazine of History and Biography*, Vol. XVII, *passim*.

Withington, Lothrop, and Waters, H. F. "Virginia Gleanings in England," *Virginia Magazine of History and Biography*, Vol. XI, *passim*.

[Wyatt, Sir Francis]. "Documents of Sir Francis Wyatt," *William and Mary College Quarterly Historical Magazine*, ser. 2, Vols. VII-VIII, *passim*.

F. Non-official Compilations and Collections Embracing Some Primary Material

Biographical History of North Carolina from Colonial Times to the Present. Edited by Samuel Ashe, S. B. Weeks, and Charles L. Van Noppen. 8 vols. Greensboro, North Carolina, 1905-1917.

Carroll, B. R. *Historical Collections of South Carolina embracing many rare and valuable Pamphlets and other Documents*. 2 vols. New York, 1836.

Collections of the South Carolina Historical Society. 5 vols. Charleston, 1857-1897.

Hathaway, J. R. B. *North Carolina Historical and Genealogical Register*. 3 vols. Edenton, North Carolina, 1900-1903.

Hazard, Ebenezer. *Historical Collections consisting of State Papers and other Authentic Documents; intended as Materials for an History of the United States of America*. 2 vols. Philadelphia, 1792-1794.

Howe, Henry. *Historical Collections of Virginia: containing a Collection of the most interesting Facts, Traditions, Biographical Sketches, Anecdotes, etc. relating to its History and Antiquities, together with geographical and statistical Descriptions, to which is appended an historical and descriptive Sketch of the District of Columbia*. Charleston, 1846.

Salley, A. S., Jr., ed. *Narratives of Early Carolina, 1650-1708*. New York, 1911.

White, Rev. George. *Historical Collections of Georgia: containing the most interesting Facts, Traditions, Biographical Sketches, Anecdotes, etc., relating to its History and Antiquities, from its first Settlement to the present Time.* New York, 1854.

IV. SECONDARY WORKS

A. GENERAL HISTORICAL AND BIOGRAPHICAL WORKS

Beer, G. L. *The Origins of the British Colonial System, 1578-1660.* New York, 1908.

Bourne, H. R. F. *English Merchants: Memoirs in Illustration of the Progress of British Commerce.* 2 vols. London, 1866.

The Cambridge History of the British Empire. Edited by J. H. Rose, and others. 8 vols. New York and Cambridge, 1929-1936.

Cross, Arthur Lyon. *A History of England and Greater Britain.* New York, 1919.

Dictionary of American Biography. Ed. by Allen Johnson and Dumas Malone. 20 vols. New York, 1926-1937.

Doyle, John A. *English Colonies in America.* 5 vols. New York, 1882-1907.

————. "The Quarrel with Great Britain, 1761-1776." In *Cambridge Modern History*, VII, 144-74. Cambridge, 1903.

Greene, Evarts B. *The Foundation of American Nationality.* New York, 1922.

————. *Provincial America, 1690-1740.* The American Nation Series, Vol. VI. New York, 1905.

Griffith, Wm. *Historical Notes of the American Colonies and Revolution from 1754 to 1775.* Burlington, New Jersey, 1843.

Hinkhouse, Fred Junkin. *The Preliminaries of the American Revolution as seen in the English Press, 1763-1775.* New York, 1926.

Hotblack, Kate. *Chatham's Colonial Policy: A Study in the Fiscal and Economic Implications of the Colonial Policy of the Elder Pitt.* London, 1917.

Howard, George Elliott. *Preliminaries of the Revolution, 1763-1775.* The American Nation Series, Vol. VIII. New York, 1905.

Jacobsen, Gertrude Ann. *William Blathwayt, a Late Seventeenth Century English Administrator.* New Haven, 1932.

Lee, Richard Henry. *Life of Arthur Lee. With his Correspondence and his Papers on diplomatic and political Subjects and the Affairs of the United States during the same Period.* Boston, 1829.

Osgood, Herbert L. *The American Colonies in the Eighteenth Century.* 4 volumes. London, 1924.

———. *The American Colonies in the Seventeenth Century.* 3 vols. London, 1904-1907.

Perry, William Stevens. *The History of the American Episcopal Church, 1587-1883.* 2 vols. Boston, 1885.

Sharpless, Isaac. *A Quaker Experiment in Government: A History of Quaker Government in Pennsylvania, 1682-1783.* 2 vols. in one. Philadelphia, 1902.

B. Colonial and State Histories and Specialized Works

Andrews, Charles M. *British Committees, Commissions and Councils of Trade and Plantations, 1622-1675.* Johns Hopkins University Studies in Historical and Political Science. Baltimore, 1908.

Andrews, Matthew Page. *The Founding of Maryland.* Baltimore, 1933.

———. *History of Maryland: Province and State.* New York, 1929.

———. *Tercentenary History of Maryland.* 4 vols. Chicago and Baltimore, 1925.

———. *Virginia, the Old Dominion.* New York, 1937.

Arnett, Alexander Mathews, and Jackson, Walter C. *The Story of North Carolina.* Chapel Hill, 1933.

Arthur, T. S., and Carpenter, W. H. *The History of Virginia from its Earliest Settlement to the Present Time.* Philadelphia, 1852.

Ashe, Samuel A. *History of North Carolina.* 2 vols. Greensboro, North Carolina, 1908-1925.

Barker, Charles Albro. *The Background of the Revolution in Maryland.* New Haven, 1940.

Bibbins, Ruthella Bernard. *The Beginnings of Maryland in England and America.* Baltimore, 1934.

Bozman, John L. *The History of Maryland from its First Settlement in 1633 to the Restoration in 1660.* 2 vols. Baltimore, 1837.

Brock, Robert A. "Virginia 1606-1689." In Justin Winsor, *Narrative and Critical History of America,* Vol. III, Chapter 5. Boston, 1885.

Brown, Alexander. *English Politics in Early Virginia History.* Boston and New York, 1901.

———. *The First Republic in America: An Account of the Origin of this Nation.* Boston and New York, 1898.

Browne, William Hand. *Maryland: The History of a Palatinate.* Boston, 1884.

Bruce, Philip Alexander, and others. *History of Virginia.* 6 vols. Chicago and New York, 1924.

————. *Institutional History of Virginia in the Sevententh Century.* 2 vols. New York, 1910.

Burk, John Daly. *The History of Virginia, from its First Settlement to the Present Day.* 4 vols. Petersburg, Virginia, 1804-1816.

Burns, James Joseph. *The Colonial Agents of New England.* Washington, 1935.

Campbell, Charles. *History of the Colony and Ancient Dominion of Virginia.* Philadelphia, 1860.

Chandler, J. A. C., and Thames, T. B. *Colonial Virginia.* Richmond, 1907.

Claiborne, John Herbert. *William Claiborne of Virginia.* New York, 1917.

Cooke, John Esten. *Virginia: A History of the People.* American Commonwealth Series. Boston, 1896.

Coulter, E. Merton. *A Short History of Georgia.* Chapel Hill, 1933.

Crane, Verner W. *Benjamin Franklin, Englishman and American.* Baltimore, 1936.

Dodson, Leonidas. *Alexander Spotswood, Governor of Colonial Virginia, 1710-1722.* Philadelphia, 1932.

Edgar, Matilda Ridout. *A Colonial Governor in Maryland: Horatio Sharpe and his Times, 1753-1773.* London and New York, 1912.

Fiske, John. *Old Virginia and Her Neighbors.* 2 vols. Boston and New York, 1897.

Flippin, Percy Scott. *The Royal Government in Virginia, 1624-1775.* Columbia University Studies in History, Economics, and Public Law. New York, 1919.

Hart, Albert Bushnell, editor. *Commonwealth History of Massachusetts, Colony, Province, and State.* 5 vols. New York, 1927-1930.

Garland, Hugh A. *Life of John Randolph of Roanoke.* New York, 1856.

Hawks, Francis L. *History of North Carolina: with Maps and Illustrations.* 2 vols. Fayetteville, North Carolina, 1857-1858.

Haywood, Marshall De Lancy. *Governor George Burrington, with an Account of his Official Administration in the Colony of North Carolina, 1724-1725, 1731-1734.* Raleigh, 1896.

————. *Governor William Tryon and his Administration in the Province of North Carolina, 1765-1771.* Raleigh, 1903.

Howison, Robert R. *A History of Virginia from its Discovery and Settlement by Europeans to the Present Time.* 2 vols. Philadelphia and Richmond, 1846-1848.

Johnson, Amanda. *Georgia as Colony and State*. Atlanta, 1938.

Jones, Charles C., Jr. *The History of Georgia*. 2 vols. Boston, 1883.

Knott, A. Leo. *A History of Maryland, its agricultural products, commerce, manufactures, and statistics*. Baltimore(?), 19-(?).
Also in *Encyclopedia Americana*.

Leake, James Miller. *The Virginia Committee System and the American Revolution*. Johns Hopkins University Studies in Historical and Political Science. Baltimore, 1917.

Lingley, Charles R. *The Transition in Virginia from Colony to Commonwealth*. Columbia University Studies in History, Economics, and Public Law. New York, 1910.

McCrady, Edward. *The History of South Carolina under the Proprietary Government, 1670-1719*. New York and London, 1897.

————. *The History of South Carolina under the Royal Government, 1719-1776*. New York and London, 1899.

McMahon, John V. L. *An Historical View of the Government of Maryland from its Colonization to the Present Day*. Baltimore, 1831.

McRee, Griffith John. *Life and Correspondence of James Iredell*. 2 vols. New York, 1857-1858.

McSherry, James. *History of Maryland from its First Settlement in 1634 to the Year 1848*. Edited and continued by Bartlett B. James. Baltimore, 1904.

Mereness, Newton D. *Maryland as a Proprietary Province*. New York, 1901.

Moore, John Wheeler. *History of North Carolina from the Earliest Discoveries to the Present Time*. 2 vols. Raleigh, 1880.

Motley, Daniel Esten. *Life of Commissary James Blair, Founder of William and Mary College*. Johns Hopkins University Studies in Historical and Political Science. Baltimore, 1901.

Murdock, Kenneth B. *Increase Mather, the Foremost American Puritan*. Cambridge, Mass., 1925.

Neill, Edward D. *History of the Virginia Company of London with Letters to and from the First Colony never before Printed*. Albany, 1869.

————. *Virginia Carolorum: The Colony under the Rule of Charles the First and Second. A.D. 1625-A.D. 1685*. Albany, 1886.

————. *Virginia Vetusta, during the Reign of James the First containing Letters and Documents never before Printed*. Albany, 1885.

Penson, Lillian M. *The Colonial Agents of the British West Indies*. London, 1924.

Ramsay, David. *The History of South Carolina from its First Settlement in 1670 to the Year 1808.* 2 vols. Charleston, 1808.

Raper, Charles Lee. *North Carolina: A Study in English Colonial Government.* New York, 1904.

Rivers, William James. *A Chapter in the Early History of South Carolina.* Charleston, 1874. The appendix, constituting about one half of the book, consists of primary material.

————. *A Sketch of the History of South Carolina to the Close of the Proprietary Government by the Revolution of 1719.* Charleston, 1856. With an appendix with much primary material from the Board of Trade Papers.

Scharf, John Thomas. *History of Western Maryland: Being a History of Frederick, Montgomery, Carroll, Washington, Allegany, and Garrett Counties.* Philadelphia, 1882.

Schlesinger, Arthur. *The Colonial Merchants and the American Revolution, 1763-1776.* New York, 1917.

Skaggs, Marvin Lucian. *North Carolina Boundary Disputes involving her Southern Line.* Chapel Hill, 1941.

Smith, George Gilman. *The Story of Georgia and the Georgia People, 1732-1860.* Macon, Georgia, 1900.

Smith, William Roy. *South Carolina as a Royal Province, 1719-1776.* New York, 1903.

Snowden, Yates. *History of South Carolina.* 4 vols. Chicago and New York, 1920.

Squires, W. H. T. *Through Centuries Three: A Short History of the People of Virginia.* Portsmouth, Virginia, 1929.

Stanard, Mary Newton. *The Story of Virginia's First Century.* Philadelphia, 1928.

Steiner, Bernard C. *Maryland under the Commonwealth: A Chronicle of the years 1649-1658.* Johns Hopkins University Studies in Historical and Political Science. Baltimore, 1911.

Stevens, William Bacon. *A History of Georgia from its First Discovery by Europeans to the Adoption of the Present Constitution in MDCCXVIII.* New York, 1847.

Surtees, Robert. *The History and Antiquities of the County Palatine of Durham,* 3 vols., London, 1816-1823.

Tilghman, Oswald. *Talbot County, Maryland, 1661-1861.* Baltimore, 1915.

Wallace, David Duncan. *Constitutional History of South Carolina from 1725 to 1775.* Abbeville, South Carolina, 1899.

Wertenbaker, Thomas J. *Virginia under the Stuarts, 1607-1688.* Princeton, 1914.

Wheeler, John H. *Historical Sketches of North Carolina from 1584 to 1851.* 2 vols. Philadelphia, 1851.

Williams, T. J. C. *History of Frederick County, Maryland.* 2 vols. Hagerstown, Maryland, 1910.

Williamson, Hugh. *The History of North Carolina.* 2 vols. Philadelphia, 1812.

Wirt, William. *Sketches of the Life and Character of Patrick Henry.* Philadelphia, 1851.

Wolff, Mabel Pauline. *The Colonial Agency of Pennsylvania, 1712-1757.* Philadelphia, 1933.

Wright, Robert. *A Memoir of General James Oglethorpe.* London, 1867.

C. ARTICLES IN MAGAZINES AND PAMPHLETS

Andrews, Charles M. "Anglo-French Commercial Rivalry, 1700-1750: The Western Phase," *American Historical Review,* XX, 539-56; 761-80.

"Barnwell of South Carolina," *South Carolina Historical and Genealogical Magazine,* II, 47-88.

Bond, Beverly W. "The Colonial Agent as a Popular Representative," *Political Science Quarterly,* XXXV, 372-92.

"Colonial Attorney-Generals of Virginia," *William and Mary College Quarterly Historical Magazine,* ser. 1, X, 31-35.

Cook, Minnie G. "Governor Samuel Mathews, Junior," *William and Mary College Quarterly Historical Magazine,* ser. 2, XIV, 105-13.

Delaplaine, Edward S. "The Life of Thomas Johnson," *Maryland Historical Magazine,* Vols. XIV-XXI, *passim.*

Ervin, Samuel J. "The Provincial Agents of North Carolina," *James Sprunt Historical Publications,* XVI, no. 2 (Chapel Hill, 1919), 63-77.

Flippin, Percy Scott. "The Royal Government in Georgia," *Georgia Historical Quarterly,* Vols. VIII-XIII, *passim.*

Herrink, L. S. "George Wythe," *The John P. Branch Historical Papers of Randolph-Macon College,* Vol. III, no. 4 (June, 1912), pp. 283-313.

Jervey, Theodore D. "Barlow Trecothick," *South Carolina Historical and Genealogical Magazine,* XXXII, 157-69.

Kellog, Louise P. "The American Colonial Charter," *Annual Report of the American Historical Association for the Year 1903,* I, 186-341.

"Lord Chatham's Statue," *Magazine of American History*, VIII, 215-20.

Miller, E. I. "The Virginia Committee of Correspondence," *William and Mary College Quarterly Historical Magazine*, ser. 1, XXII, 1-19.

Schlesinger, A. M. "Maryland's Share in the Last Intercolonial War," *Maryland Historical Magazine*, VII, 119-49.

Sioussat, St. George L. "Virginia and the English Commercial System, 1730-1733," *Annual Report of the American Historical Association for the Year 1905*, pp. 71-97.

"Sketches of the Secretaries of the Colony of Virginia," *William and Mary College Quarterly Historical Magazine*, ser. 1, X, 168-75.

Smith, Henry A. M. "The Baronies of South Carolina," *The South Carolina Historical and Genealogical Magazine*, Vols. XI-XV, *passim*.

————. "Wragg of South Carolina," *South Carolina Historical and Genealogical Magazine*, XIX, 121-23.

Tanner, Edmund P. "Colonial Agencies in England during the Eighteenth Century," *Political Science Quarterly*, XVI, 24-49.

The Wiltshire Archaeological and Natural History Magazine, Vol. II (1855).

Index

INDEX

Abercromby, Gen., in connection with parliamentary grant, 228, 296

Abercromby, James, special agent for S. C., 133-34; secures exemption of S. C., from British law, 154 n; laments wasted effort against salt monopoly, 209-10; objects to Sugar Act, 221; frequency of attendance at Board of Trade, 219; bad penmanship of, 204 n, 227; complains of delays by colonies, 353-54; devotion to duty after dismissal, 354-55 and n; annoyances of office, 365; considers S. C. agency, 370; failures in legislation, 376; mentioned, 62, 147, 148, 187, 188, 239, 242, 311, 315, 319, 343, 344

— As agent of Va., 61; division of duties with Montague, 64-66 and nn; opinion of, concerning Montague, 65 n; special agent, 130; long service, 149; relates European politics, 157; supports council against governor, 160; to adjust quarantine act, 167; seeks grant for Ohio Indians, 182; recommends Corbin for council, 190; shows importance of proper warrants for grant, 194; share of in grant to Va., 195; deals with Bishop of London for clergy, 204; concerned about credentials, 215; sends news of grant to Va. in triplicate, 227-28; inclosed copies of important letters in dispatch, 228; research in Two-penny case, 231; receives copy of law from clerk of Board of Trade, 232 n; petitions Treasury for aid to tobacco revenue, 238 and n; interview with auditor general, 245; seeks attorney general's opinion on Va. agency law, 245; before committee of House of Commons, 246; personal career, 286; friend of Gen. Abercromby, 296; agent of two colonies, 298; rebuked for ingratitude, 304; desires salary from quitrents, 305; on incidental expenses, 312, 316-17; warned by Dinwiddie against incidentals, 317-18; divides cost of trip to Scotland

between Va. and N. C., 319; friction over amount of commission for grant, 319-20; coöperates about salt, 328; tries to save paper money act, 331; to act with Montague against British taxation, 344; complains of delays at Treasury Board, 351; journey of, to Lord Loudoun, 351; profits by experience of Mass. agent, 355-56; criticized by council, 358; fights to retain agency, 363-64; pays Leheup for agency, 369; gives offense to Privy Council, 388

— As agent of N. C., 78-80 and n; notifies Board of Trade of dismissal, 149; serves governor, 159; to aid McNaire, 200-1; refuses to be involved in N. C. quarrels, 206-7; chides N. C. for failure in courtesy, 207-9; solicits Admiralty Board, 241; salary of, from N. C., 309; total payable to from N. C., 316 and n; objects to arrears in pay, 321; problem in collecting salary, 324; coöperates with Agent Charles against Sugar Act, 335; relationship to agent for council, 344; chides N. C. for not acknowledging grant, 384; gives Newcastle data about weakness of Carolina, 384-85

Admiralty Board, solicitation of, by early agents for ships, 240-41

Agency, Va. act for, of 1759, 63-64, 64 n; lapse of in S. C., 72 and n; agency bill in Md., dispute between two houses over, 1739, 93-95; rider in Md. act of 1745 brings dispute, 95-96; rider in act of 1746, 97 and n; dispute in Md. to 1766, 99-104; discord over, between house and governor, 101; agent proposed for each house, 101-2; issue involved in salary dispute of clerk of council, 102-3; cost of, 214 n, 312, 313-14, 315-16, 317 n, 317-18, 319-20; post generally sought, 368-72; unsuccessful candidates, 372; reasons for seeking post, 372-73; reasons for lack of success in, 390